Advances in Experimental Political Philosophy

Advances in Experimental Philosophy

Series Editor:
Justin Sytsma, Associate Professor in Philosophy,
Victoria University of Wellington, New Zealand

Editorial Board:
Joshua Alexander (Siena College, USA)
James Andow (University of East Anglia, UK)
Florian Cova (University of Geneva, Switzerland)
Joshua Knobe (Yale University, USA)
Edouard Machery (University of Pittsburgh, USA)
Thomas Nadelhoffer (College of Charleston, USA)
Jennifer Nado (University of Hong Kong, Hong Kong)
Eddy Nahmias (Georgia State University, USA)
Noel Struchiner (Pontifical Catholic University of Rio de Janeiro, Brazil)
Pascale Willemsen (University of Zurich, Switzerland)
Jennifer Cole Wright (College of Charleston, USA)

Empirical and experimental philosophy is generating tremendous excitement, producing unexpected results that are challenging traditional philosophical methods. *Advances in Experimental Philosophy* responds to this trend, bringing together some of the most exciting voices in the field to understand the approach and measure its impact in contemporary philosophy. The result is a series that captures past and present developments and anticipates future research directions.

To provide in-depth examinations, each volume links experimental philosophy to a key philosophical area. They provide historical overviews alongside case studies, reviews of current problems and discussions of new directions. For upper-level undergraduates, postgraduates and professionals actively pursuing research in experimental philosophy these are essential resources.

Titles in the Series Include:
Advances in Experimental Epistemology, edited by James R. Beebe
Advances in Experimental Moral Psychology,
edited by Hagop Sarkissian and Jennifer Cole Wright
Advances in Experimental Philosophy and Philosophical Methodology,
edited by Jennifer Nado
Advances in Experimental Philosophy of Aesthetics,
edited by Florian Cova and Sébastien Réhault
Advances in Experimental Philosophy of Language,
edited by Jussi Haukioja
Advances in Experimental Philosophy of Logic and Mathematics,
edited by Andrew Aberdein and Matthew Inglis
Advances in Experimental Philosophy of Mind, edited by Justin Sytsma
Advances in Religion, Cognitive Science, and Experimental Philosophy,
edited by Helen De Cruz and Ryan Nichols
Experimental Metaphysics, edited by David Rose
Methodological Advances in Experimental Philosophy,
edited by Eugen Fischer and Mark Curtis
Advances in Experimental Philosophy of Free Will and Responsibility,
edited by Thomas Nadelhoffer and Andrew Monroe
Advances in Experimental Philosophy of Causation,
edited by Alex Wiegmann and Pascale Willemsen
Experimental Philosophy of Identity and the Self,
edited by Kevin Tobia
Advances in Experimental Philosophy of Action,
edited by Paul Henne and Samuel Murray
Advances in Experimental Philosophy of Law,
edited by Stefan Magen and Karolina Prochownik
Advances in Experimental Political Philosophy, edited by Matthew Lindauer
Advances in Experimental Philosophy of Medicine,
edited by Kristien Hens and Andreas De Block

Advances in Experimental Political Philosophy

Edited by
Matthew Lindauer

BLOOMSBURY ACADEMIC
LONDON • NEW YORK • OXFORD • NEW DELHI • SYDNEY

BLOOMSBURY ACADEMIC
Bloomsbury Publishing Plc
50 Bedford Square, London, WC1B 3DP, UK
1385 Broadway, New York, NY 10018, USA
29 Earlsfort Terrace, Dublin 2, Ireland

BLOOMSBURY, BLOOMSBURY ACADEMIC and the Diana logo
are trademarks of Bloomsbury Publishing Plc

First published in Great Britain 2023
This paperback edition published in 2025

Copyright © Matthew Lindauer and Contributors, 2023

Matthew Lindauer has asserted his right under the Copyright, Designs and Patents Act, 1988, to be identified as Editor of this work.

Series design by Catherine Wood
Cover image © Dieter Leistner / Gallerystock

All rights reserved. No part of this publication may be reproduced or transmitted in any form or by any means, electronic or mechanical, including photocopying, recording, or any information storage or retrieval system, without prior permission in writing from the publishers.

Bloomsbury Publishing Plc does not have any control over, or responsibility for, any third-party websites referred to or in this book. All internet addresses given in this book were correct at the time of going to press. The author and publisher regret any inconvenience caused if addresses have changed or sites have ceased to exist, but can accept no responsibility for any such changes.

A catalogue record for this book is available from the British Library.

Library of Congress Cataloging-in-Publication Data

Names: Lindauer, Matthew, editor.
Title: Advances in experimental political philosophy / edited by Matthew Lindauer.
Description: London ; New York : Bloomsbury Academic, 2023. | Series: Advances in experimental philosophy | Includes bibliographical references and index. | Summary: "Brings together cutting-edge research on the use of empirical scientific methods to illuminate traditional and contemporary issues in political philosophy"– Provided by publisher.
Identifiers: LCCN 2023026297 (print) | LCCN 2023026298 (ebook) | ISBN 9781350254251 (hardback) | ISBN 9781350254299 (paperback) | ISBN 9781350254268 (ebook) | ISBN 9781350254275 (epub)
Subjects: LCSH: Political science–Philosophy. | Political science–Methodology. | Political science–Research.
Classification: LCC JA71 .A387 2023 (print) | LCC JA71 (ebook) | DDC 320.01–dc23/eng/20230609
LC record available at https://lccn.loc.gov/2023026297
LC ebook record available at https://lccn.loc.gov/2023026298

ISBN:	HB:	978-1-3502-5425-1
	PB:	978-1-3502-5429-9
	ePDF:	978-1-3502-5426-8
	eBook:	978-1-3502-5427-5

Series: Advances in Experimental Philosophy

Typeset by Integra Software Services Pvt. Ltd.

To find out more about our authors and books visit www.bloomsbury.com and sign up for our newsletters.

Contents

List of Figures		viii
List of Tables		xi
Introduction *Matthew Lindauer*		1

Part 1 Traditional Issues in Political Philosophy with an Empirical Approach

1	Corruption, Shared Expectations, and Social Dilemmas *Cristina Bicchieri, Raj Patel, and Leena Koni Hoffmann*	25
2	Rules, Risk, and Agreement *Justin P. Bruner*	49
3	Does Equality Matter for Its Own Sake?: An Experimental Examination of the Leveling-Down Objection *Christopher Freiman and Adam Lerner*	63
4	What Does Labor Mixing Get You? *Shaun Nichols and John Thrasher*	75
5	Segregation and the Portfolio Theory of Identity *Ryan Muldoon*	87
6	Empirical Philosophy: How Engaging with Empirical Evidence Is Important for Theory as Well as Practice *Nicole Hassoun*	105
7	How Do People Balance Death against Lesser Burdens? *Veronika Luptakova and Alex Voorhoeve*	123

Part 2 New Directions

8	Automated Psycholinguistic Analysis of the Anglophone Manosphere *Mark Alfano, Joanne Byrne, and Joshua Roose*	161
9	Experimental Immigration Ethics *Mollie Gerver, Patrick Lown, and Dominik Duell*	187
10	Love vs. Money: Understanding Unique Challenges in Care Workers' Labor Organizing *Grace Flores-Robles and Ana P. Gantman*	215
11	Experimental Political Philosophy: A Manifesto *John Thrasher*	237

Notes on Contributors	258
Index	262

List of Figures

2.1	Expected utility and fairness rules. © Justin P. Bruner	54
2.2	Expected utility and fairness procedures for various correlation levels (six items). © Justin P. Bruner	55
2.3	Two preference profiles and corresponding Kendall coefficient score. © Justin P. Bruner	55
2.4	Distribution of individual payoff for MNW (white) and descending demand (light gray). For $g = 6$, $L = 21$ and 1,000 fair division problems. © Justin P. Bruner	57
4.1	Average ownership scores in Study 1, with error bars reflecting the standard error of the mean. Scale from 1 (Definitely Mary [the original owner of the material]) to 6 (Definitely Sarah [the person who contributed labor to produce the artwork]). © Shaun Nichols and John Thrasher	79
4.2	Average ownership scores in Study 2, with error bars reflecting the standard error of the mean. Scale from 1 (Definitely John [the person who picked up the rock]) to 6 (Definitely Mark [the person who contributed labor to produce the drawing]). © Shaun Nichols and John Thrasher	81
4.3	Percentage response in each category in Study 3. © Shaun Nichols and John Thrasher	83
5.1	On the priority model, adding even one agent attribute dramatically reduces segregation. © Ryan Muldoon	96
5.2	On the priority model, even with high similarity thresholds, more attributes sharply reduce segregation. © Ryan Muldoon	97
5.3	On the match model, segregation is much lower, but as similarity judgments require more attributes to match, this becomes too demanding such that the model cannot equilibrate. © Ryan Muldoon	98
5.4	On the Manhattan model, we again see lower levels of segregation than the base model. On this model, more restrictive social distance and higher threshold requirements both result in higher rates of segregation. © Ryan Muldoon	98
7.1	Matrix of responses to prioritization decisions. © Veronika Luptakova and Alex Voorhoeve	138
7.2	Experimental findings—the impact of status quo. © Veronika Luptakova and Alex Voorhoeve	139

List of Figures ix

8.1	Word cloud representing the six corpora under study. Word size represents prevalence. Word color represents document. © Mark Alfano, Joanne Byrne, and Joshua Roose	169
8.2	Dendrogram of the corpora under study. Greater vertical distance represents greater dissimilarity. © Mark Alfano, Joanne Byrne, and Joshua Roose	170
9.1	Marginal mean of how reasonable it is to deny a given migrant entry to the country by the reason for which entry was denied. We show 95 percent confidence bounds computed from standard errors clustered at the respondent-level. © Mollie Gerver, Dominik Duell, and Patrick Lown	195
9.2	Marginal mean of how reasonable it is to deny a given migrant entry based on whether they are a threat and whether they were forced to migrate. We show 95 percent confidence bounds computed from standard errors clustered at the respondent-level. © Mollie Gerver, Dominik Duell, and Patrick Lown	196
9.3	Marginal mean of how reasonable it is to deny a given migrant entry to the country by whether they would not be harmed as a consequence of returning home or whether harm they could be exposed to is known or unknown. We show estimates for threatening migrants only. We show 95 percent confidence bounds computed from standard errors clustered at the respondent-level. © Mollie Gerver, Dominik Duell, and Patrick Lown	197
A.1	Screenshot of one realization of the factorial vignette as shown to respondents in the UK sample. © Mollie Gerver, Dominik Duell, and Patrick Lown	205
A.2	Screenshot of one realization of the factorial vignette as shown to respondents in the US sample. © Mollie Gerver, Dominik Duell, and Patrick Lown	206
A.3	Marginal mean of how reasonable it is to deny a given migrant entry to the country by immigration case attribute and the between-respondent probability of harm treatment. We show 95 percent confidence bounds computed from standard errors clustered at the respondent-level. The figure omits the country of origin attribute for ease of display but categorizes the country of origin into a region of origin indicator. © Mollie Gerver, Dominik Duell, and Patrick Lown	207
10.1	Scatter plot and fitted regression lines depicting increases in fears of commodification and taboo trade-offs are negatively associated with strike attitudes (top panel) and support for labor organizing (bottom panel). © Grace Flores-Robles and Ana P. Gantman	227

10.2	Scatter plot and fitted regression lines depicting increases in fears of commodification and taboo trade-offs are positively associated with desire for moral cleansing. © Grace Flores-Robles and Ana P. Gantman	228
11.1	Taxonomy of Traditional Experimental Philosophy. © John Thrasher	242
11.2	Directed Acyclical Graph (DAG) of a Simple Instrumental Variable. © John Thrasher	248

List of Tables

1.1	Bribery as an Assurance Game	30
1.2	Bribery as a Prisoner's Dilemma	31
1.3	Personal Normative Beliefs	37
1.4	Reasons for Personal Normative Beliefs	38
1.5	Personal Normative Beliefs and Social Expectations	39
1.6	Vignettes with Varying Social Expectations	40
1.7	Mean Probability of Bribery Given Varying Social Expectations	41
2.1	Fair Division Problem Involving Six Items and Two Individuals (Aiko and Bing)	50
7.1	Results of Regression Analyses	144
8.1	Summary Word Counts for Six Corpora	166
8.2	Normalized Scores (Ranging from 0 to 100) for the Categories of Analytic, Clout, Authentic, and Tone	170
8.3	Frequency and Ratio of First-Person Singular and First-Person Plural by Corpus	171
8.4	Frequency of Positive Emotion, Negative Emotion, and Cognitive Process Words	173
8.5	Frequency of Anxiety, Anger, and Sadness	174
8.6	Frequency of Family, Friend, Female, and Male References, along with Female:Male Ratio	175
8.7	Frequency of Body, Health, Sexuality, and Eating Words	176
8.8	Frequency of Drives to Affiliation, Achievement, Power, Reward, and Risk, along with the Product of Affiliation and Power	177
8.9	Moral Foundations Profiles of All Corpora	178
8.10	Frequency of Dominant Masculinity, Subsidiary Masculinity, Misogyny, and Xenophobia	179
A.1	OLS Regression of the Outcome Measure on the Fully Factorized Attribute Reason for Which Entry Was Denied (Taking Either Unemployed or Immigration Quotas as Reference Category)	208

A.2 OLS Regression of the Outcome Measure on the Variable *Forced* Run on Observations of Migrants Who are Posing a Threat (Those on a Terrorist Watch List, with a Criminal Record, or Who had Contracted Covid-19)   209

A.3 OLS Regression of the Outcome Measure on the Variable *Forced* Run on Observations of Migrants Who are Posing a Threat (Those on a Terrorist Watch List, with a Criminal Record, or Who had Contracted Covid-19)   209

Introduction

Matthew Lindauer
Brooklyn College and CUNY Graduate Center

Political philosophy asks many important questions that matter to our lives as individuals and members of political communities. What is justice? What does the state owe to its citizens? Under what conditions are different forms of government likely to be stable and well-functioning? What does justice look like between members of different societies?

Philosophers working on these and other traditional questions have regularly appealed to empirical evidence, and sometimes sought it out themselves, in supporting their claims. This practice is found at least as early as Aristotle's investigations of the political variety of Greek city states in the *Politics* (350 BC/1998), where he notably also criticizes Plato for making unrealistic claims about human nature. According to the biographer Diogenes Laërtius (2006), Aristotle engaged in a comparative study of 158 constitutions, and this work informed his political theorizing. In recent work, John Rawls (1971; 1993; 2001) and political philosophers working in the current manifestation of the field that his contributions gave rise to have often taken factors like "publicity" and "stability" of theories and conceptions of justice into account, approvingly citing Rousseau's dictum that our theories are best when "taking men as they are and laws as they might be" (Rousseau 1762, 2).

It is therefore somewhat baffling that while other areas of philosophy have been well-represented in recent methodological discussions of the relevance of empirical research to philosophical inquiry, political philosophy has been largely absent from them. Indeed, there is as yet no Stanford Encyclopedia of Philosophy article on experimental political philosophy, while there is one for experimental moral philosophy (Alfano, Loeb, and Plakias 2018), and the general lack of explicit discussion of experimental political philosophy is acknowledged by other authors (see, e.g., Hassoun (2016) and John Thrasher's solo-authored chapter in this volume).

The point of this volume is to draw attention to advances in experimental political philosophy, a burgeoning and active area of inquiry. Sustained reflection on this field is

---

This research was made possible in part with funding from The Tow Foundation (Tow Faculty Research and Creativity Grant, Brooklyn College, CUNY).

well overdue. Indeed, many leading figures in political philosophy have been receptive to the use of empirical methods in psychology and economics to study political questions. Rawls spends considerable time developing a theory of moral psychology to ground his magnum opus *A Theory of Justice* on, which had a major influence on one of the most significant figures in twentieth-century psychology, Lawrence Kohlberg (1973). It is odd that political philosophy as it currently stands is both so heavily indebted to Rawls' work and has thus far largely avoided, and sometimes even been hostile to, empirical research methods of the kind that other fields and disciplines have taken on board.

However, there are signs that this resistance is waning, as it has throughout philosophy. Work by the researchers in this volume and the work that they cite are testaments to this fact. And further, there has always been a significant part of the field of political philosophy that was congenial to and sometimes involved in conducting empirical research, as shown in the important work of philosophers like Elizabeth Anderson, Kwame Anthony Appiah, Cristina Bicchieri, Gerald Gaus, David Miller, John Rawls, Amartya Sen, and Margaret Urban Walker.

This book brings together a diverse group of scholars from philosophy, psychology, political science, sociology, and economics, both to present their recent empirical research on contemporary and enduring political issues and to give their reflections on what it means for political philosophy to be empirically informed. Their work is sure to ignite further discussions and debates, pushing advances in political philosophy that challenge political thinkers to develop their work in conversation with, and sometimes as part of, the body of our best scientific research.

I will now give an opiniated overview, driven by my own reflections on historical and contemporary work, of some reasons why empirical research is not merely of side interest to political philosophers but part of political philosophy.[1] I show how existing empirical work fits into a number of the categories where I take empirical research to be philosophically important and also note areas that I take to be ripe for further empirical work where little (that I have been able to find at least) seems to have been done. I close by noting how the contributions to this volume fit into, and expand beyond, these categories.

1. Why Experimental *Political Philosophy*?

Before jumping into the existing literature in what I'm calling "experimental political philosophy," it may be helpful to think about the many reasons why empirical research would be relevant to, and indeed a part of, political philosophy in the first place. This may be a useful metaphilosophical exercise, to consider the aims of political philosophy and why some of these aims require empirical research. It also may help to see where prior research has focused its attention with respect to these aims, and to determine if there are any gaps that further research may fill. My treatment of these issues will by no means be exhaustive, but I hope to set out some of the main trends along which empirical research can be incorporated into political philosophy, leaving room for other approaches to develop, including some of those in the "New Trends" section of this volume.

One way into thinking about this topic is to hold that political theories and concepts, like "justice" and "equality," are needed for us to carefully examine the actual world and existing political institutions and practices that we and other human beings live and participate in: real world governments, states, legal systems, voting systems, and so on. This is similar to one view that Nicole Hassoun suggests in her piece on experimental political philosophy (Hassoun 2016, 234–5). While I agree with Hassoun that there is an important connection between the need for political philosophy to say something about actual institutions and empirical research when we are thinking about what concepts like "justice" and "equality" require, this level of description is very general, and she adds the idea of action guidance to spell it out (to be discussed). We'll need to dive deeper into the specific ways that political philosophy should be informed by empirical research. Imagine a philosopher who holds the view that, whenever we think about how actual institutions should be, the only way we will know anything of *philosophical* interest is by thinking about ideal justice from a purely conceptual point of view. For them, it is important for political theories and concepts to help us think about actual institutions. But the focus on actual institutions does not, on their view, require us to engage with empirical research as philosophers—in fact, it seems to recommend against it. So we will need to say something more substantive about how the focus on the actual implies that empirical research per se is important to political philosophy.

A slightly different starting point involves thinking about the specific ways that political philosophers themselves have viewed their work as responsive to and engaged with actual, as opposed to purely ideal, political institutions. One prominent such way is through two related but distinct requirements mentioned above that are prominent in both historical and contemporary philosophy: the "publicity" requirement and the "stability" requirement. Each of these has an important empirical component and demonstrates how quite a lot of empirical research that political philosophers have conducted and taken on board is philosophically important. I will take these two requirements in turn in Section 1.1 and 1.2. A further requirement that Hassoun mentions, as noted, that political theories should be action-guiding (2016, 235), is the third that I will discuss (Section 1.3). I will then turn to further questions involving motivation (Section 1.4) and also the relationship between political philosophy and recent work on conceptual engineering (Section 1.5). After taking stock (Section 2), I will then turn to brief descriptions of the contributions to this volume (Section 3) and how they relate to these and other topics where empirical research can be philosophically important.

1.1 Publicity

The publicity requirement is spelled out variously in the work of different philosophers,[2] but one natural interpretation holds that political theories, for example, theories of justice or legitimate government, must be justifiable to the public with whom these theories are implemented. Publicity arguably comes into Anglophone political theory in the social contract tradition, where the idea of agreement that all participants could or should accept is taken to be a mark of a good or legitimate theory of government. Rawls notably writes that the task of political philosophy is "to articulate a public conception of justice that all can live with who regard their person and their relation to society in a certain way" (Rawls 1980, 519), going on to make the even stronger claim that while "doing this may involve settling theoretical difficulties, the practical social task is primary." He takes himself to be in the social contract tradition of Locke, Rousseau, and Kant, who also focused on the idea of a compact that all participants could agree to as the charter of a just society.

Of course, there may be a large gulf between what people could or should agree to, on the one hand, and what they in fact will agree to, given their various preoccupations, biases, epistemic limitations, and so on. But in the absence of proof that the latter are negatively affecting their judgments, itself an empirical conjecture that researchers have often attempted to explore and control for (see, e.g., Inoue, Zenkyo, and Sakamoto (2021)), research looking at what kinds of principles people will accept bears on the publicity requirement.

Indeed, early research in the field (Sołtan 1982; Frohlich, Oppenheimer, and Eavey 1987b; 1987a; Frohlich and Oppenheimer 1993) looking at what principles actual people in experimental conditions, often meant to approximate Rawls' original position, tend to accept has been taken up by many political philosophers and bears precisely on the question of publicity. Frohlich et al.'s well-known results suggest that rather than maximizing the worst off position, which would be in line with Rawls' difference principle, people tend to accept "restricted utilitarianism" in their original position with a "thick" veil of ignorance setup. Restricted utilitarianism involves a minimum floor of income that all persons must satisfy and maximizing average utility as long as this floor is achieved. This is the "principle of restricted utility" that Rawls takes as the main competitor to his difference principle in *Justice as Fairness: A Restatement*, where he attempts to defend the difference principle on grounds outside of the choice within the original position, including publicity, reciprocity, stability, indeterminacy, and strains of commitment (Rawls 2001, 120–30). Notably, the latter grounds depend heavily on what will be acceptable and workable for actual persons, not parties to the original position, in a liberal democratic society of the kind familiar in the actual world.

David Miller and Gillian Brock have made contrasting claims about what further should be taken from Frohlich et al.'s results. Miller (2003) argues that these results and others (Lamm and Schwinger 1980) strongly suggest that people care about individuals' satisfaction of their needs, and inequality beyond this point should be taken into account, recommending the use of a measure that incorporates these desiderata. Brock (2009) instead considers the relevance of these results to global justice and takes them to show that parties to a global original position would select a sufficientarian principle of global distributive justice, whereby all individuals in the world are owed that their basic needs would be met.

Nicole Hassoun has conducted empirical research on this topic and argues that the results of a further study support a different view than Miller's (and Brock's) regarding which principles of justice are likely to be publicly accepted (Hassoun 2009). These results suggest that, contra Miller, people seem to accept a prioritarian principle, according to which we should focus on helping the least well-off, even if this means that overall need satisfaction is decreased.

As suggested, the literature on these issues has expanded considerably since Frohlich et al.'s path-breaking work on the topic. A cluster of issues have been explored in recent work surrounding whether a *unique* set of principles of justice will be selected from a given impartiality frame, like Rawls' original position, as well as whether any particular impartiality frame is uniquely publicly justifiable.

To the first of these issues, Frohlich et al. took their results to show that restricted utilitarianism would generally be chosen in the original position behind Rawls' "thick" veil of ignorance, that is, the veil that prevents participants from knowing who they are in the bargain in terms of race, gender, income, and other factors. Their results have been replicated in further research (Lissowski, Tyszka, and Okrasa 1991; Bruner 2018). Others have argued that we cannot expect a unique set of principles to be chosen under a single impartiality frame (Sugden 1990; Thrasher 2014; Skyrms 2014; 2016; Muldoon et al. 2014).

Moving away from the Rawlsian impartiality frame of the original position and veil of ignorance, other philosophers and social scientists have examined decision-making using an "impartial spectator" frame of the kind suggested by Adam Smith and David Hume. A number of these scholars have taken their results to show that convergence will occur under such a frame (Mitchell et al. 1993; Faravelli 2007; Herne and Mard 2008; Konow 2008; 2009). However, Michelbach et al. (2003) provide evidence that there can be dissensus in impartial spectator frames.

Notably, we have so far only been discussing the debate regarding uniqueness within a given impartiality frame. But even if one could establish that a certain way of specifying, for instance, the original position would lead to uniquely chosen principles of justice, there is still the remaining issue whether that impartiality frame itself is regarded as uniquely choiceworthy (Bruner and Lindauer 2020). This question is just as important given the aims that many social contract theorists have hoped their theories of justice would be able to satisfy, such as serving as a public conception of justice for a liberal democratic society. If there are parallel impartiality frames from which one can arrive at unique principles of justice but there is dissensus regarding which impartiality frame is better, we have merely shifted the problem to another arguably more fundamental level.

Bruner and Lindauer (2020) note that prior research on the original position suggests that restricted utilitarianism will be selected under this frame, while egalitarian principles like the difference principle tend to be chosen in impartial spectator frames, and explore the choice of impartiality frames themselves. They find that while the Rawlsian original position and impartial spectator frames received significantly greater support than a Scanlonian contractualist frame focusing on reasonable rejectability, the original position and impartial spectator frames did not perform significantly differently than one another. Given that these two frames did not receive significantly greater support than one another, this suggests that neither frame is uniquely justifiable to a democratic public.

Further, the results of another study in Bruner and Lindauer (2020, 471–73) suggest that the preference people have for one of these two impartiality frames and their preferences for either restricted utilitarianism or the difference principle do not predict one another. There seems to be little if any relationship between the impartiality frame that one finds most choiceworthy and the principles of distributive justice that one regards similarly. Notably, a majority of participants selected the combination of the impartial spectator and restricted utilitarianism, although again the relationship between these two components was not significant.

Bruner and Lindauer argue that their studies support the view that if social contract theory is to be saved, it must abandon its aspiration to find a unique publicly justified impartiality frame as well as a unique publicly justified set of principles of justices. This conclusion supports the views argued for by Gerald Gaus (2010) and Michael Moehler (2018). Gaus rejects uniqueness at both of these levels and moves away from the need to invoke an impartiality frame or collective decision procedure, instead holding that social evolution will result in a publicly justified contract. Moehler also rejects the idea of a unique social contract, but emphasizes that different social contracts may be settled upon in different societal circumstances.

Inoue, Zenkyo, and Sakamoto (2021) replicate Bruner and Lindauer's finding that uniqueness is not supported. They add additional controls for participants' competence and attention, and vary whether participants know or do not know the probabilities of the income distributions they might wind up in, the former associated with Harsanyi (1975) and the latter with Rawls. Notably, and contrary to Rawls' prediction, participants were more likely to go for restricted utilitarianism than the difference principle when they did not know these probabilities, and this was particularly true among the more careful participants. Choice of the difference principle decreased with the encouragement of self-examination, and no correlation was found between Rawls' original position and the difference principle.

1.2 Stability

A further and related reason why we might care about how actual people will respond to political concepts and theories is that the *stability* of implementations of these concepts and theories matters in our assessments of them. A society that is just for a short period of time but devolves quickly into a far worse, unjust society, one might think, is importantly deficient compared to one that remains stable and equally just, and perhaps even one that is slightly less just by some measure (e.g., that has a tax code that departs ever so slightly from what justice requires but that is still reasonably fair and good). Rawls (1993) articulates a notion of stability "for the right reasons" for liberal democratic theories of justice. On this line of reasoning, a theory of justice should not secure stable allegiance by giving government officials permission to scare the people into submission—such a form of stability would be both morally wrong and inconsistent with the spirit of liberal democratic theory, including its core commitments to freedom and equality. So determining what people will agree to on a stable basis through empirical research, much of which will overlap with work that bears on the publicity requirement, is another important empirical question for political philosophers to examine.

It is worth noting that quite a lot of the empirical research in the social contract tradition only looks at judgments at a particular point in time. Given this, it may be that such research tells us more about the publicity requirement than stability. After all, it *could* be that a given principle of distributive justice, let's say, would be accepted by all persons upon being asked to evaluate it once, but would not secure ongoing agreement, whereas another principle would secure initial agreement from slightly fewer (say 90 percent) of people, but those people would continue to endorse this principle, and perhaps eventually be able to persuade the others who did not initially endorse it. For this reason, it could be that longitudinal research or other data, such as judgments of confidence in agreement responses, would be valuable for looking at stability, beyond the contribution that initial public justifiability makes to it.

1.3 Action-Guidingness

A further way empirical research is relevant to political philosophy is through the desideratum that theories and concepts be "action-guiding" (Hassoun 2016; Lindauer 2020). In ethics, it's worth noting that a common objection to virtue ethics is that in focusing on what the virtuous person should do, as opposed to rules of action, theories of virtue may not be action-guiding in the way that consequentialist and deontological theories can be. Of course, some philosophers view action-guidingness as irrelevant to our theorizing about political concepts like "justice" (Cohen 2008; Estlund 2020). But others have thought that, for at least some of our purposes in doing political philosophy, action-guidingness should be taken into account as a factor in evaluating theories and concepts.

One way into establishing the requirement that theories and concepts should be action-guiding is through the idea that political philosophy, insofar as it bears on what ought to be done, must take feasibility considerations into account (Goodin and Pettit 1995; Southwood 2016; 2018). Southwood (2016) argues that feasibility bears on the "deliberative ought"—the ought of practical deliberation that we are supposed to consider when determining how to act. It would be inappropriate for an individual or a collective to aim to bring about goods that aren't feasible for them to bring about, at least in most circumstances. Further, part of why we should care about feasibility constraints is because we need moral and political philosophy to issue us guidance about what to do regarding real-world moral problems. This focus on problem-solving is sometimes thought to distinguish non-ideal theory from ideal theory (Mills 2005; Valentini 2012).

Other philosophers, such as John Rawls and Philip Pettit, have also sometimes argued that their views provide better guidance than the alternatives and that this is a mark in their favor. In addition to the theoretical grounds for his principles, largely originating from the choice situation of the original position, Rawls notes that his theory will provide clearer guidance than more sophisticated forms of utilitarianism like restricted utilitarianism, against which the choice in the original position of justice as fairness is less clear (Rawls 2001). Pettit argues that his republican conception of freedom can serve as a "moral compass" and regulative ideal for assessing and reforming societal policies and institutions (Pettit 2014). From a purely theoretical perspective, he holds, it is less obvious that we should choose his conception of justice over the alternatives, the libertarian and liberal conceptions of freedom. But accounting for the greater action-guidingness of his theory, the choice of republican freedom is supposed to be much clearer.

Notably, whether a theory provides helpful guidance to actual human agents is an empirical matter. We should also perhaps distinguish between different levels at which a theory could be action-guiding.[3] On the one hand, a theory may be action-guiding because it says there is a clear answer to the question what to do—as in the case of classic act utilitarianism; for instance, it is the act with the best consequences that should be performed. But in terms of how to concretely achieve the end set by the theory, act utilitarianism may provide less clear guidance. Similarly, Rawls' theory of justice may provide greater clarity on what policies will yield results that maximize the position of the worst-off, let's say, than restricted utilitarianism will in helping us to determine where the relevant income floor should be set. But Rawls notably says next to nothing about the question of transition to a just state or implementation of his theory. Action-guidingness, ideally, would include not only telling us where we ought to go but also how best to get there and what kinds of constraints we should observe, if any, along the way.

Relatedly, work on racial inequality and also work on measures of welfare have sometimes emphasized action guidance as a desideratum. For instance, a common criticism of colorblind policies is that they do not help us think about what to do about racial prejudice and inequality in societies that have historical and ongoing instances of these phenomena (Boxill 1992; Bonilla-Silva 2003; Anderson 2010; Mills 2011). In the literature on welfare, it is sometimes noted that subjective measures of welfare won't guide us in improving the welfare of the worst-off because their subjective reports are often influenced by adaptive preferences (Khader 2011).

In other work, I have discussed some of the research methods that could be used to examine the action-guidingness of theories (Lindauer 2020, 2139–40). Looking at the above cases, one can think of a variety of studies that could be but have yet to be conducted.

1.4 Motivation

A further issue that brings empirical research into contact with political theories and concepts concerns what kinds of actions these theories and concepts motivate when internalized. For many important thinkers in the history of political philosophy, the question of what kinds of motivations a given theory or form of government would produce in individuals is taken as philosophically relevant. Consider Hobbes' (1668) thought that an absolute sovereign would help to solve the problems of competition, diffidence, and vainglory left unchecked by the state of nature. People under his preferred form of government, the argument goes, would be motivated to adhere to the rules imposed by the sovereign and not destroy the civil peace that they have achieved. In Marx, we also see a focus on motivation in a kind of situationist belief that the motivations and attitudes needed to sustain communism would emerge once the means of production were transferred to the proletariat and a new ethos was produced in human beings in line with their "species-being," the true nature of humanity that capitalism alienates us from (Marx 1844). In *A Theory of Justice* (1971), Rawls pairs his conception of justice ("justice as fairness") with a theory of moral psychology that is supposed to explain why his principles of justice, and in particular the difference principle, are likely to produce the motivation to adhere to these principles and uphold just institutions, with an emphasis on the reciprocity built into the structure of the theory.

More recently, one key debate where political philosophy has engaged closely with the question of motivation concerns what citizens of affluent countries owe to the global poor. Two key approaches to this debate are often contrasted, one which focuses on the idea that we have positive duties to help the global poor, associated with Peter Singer (1972), and the other which focuses on the idea that we have negative duties to stop harming the global poor, associated with Thomas Pogge (2002).[4] Singer's well-known "shallow pond" argument draws an analogy between a situation in which we would presumably be morally required to sacrifice a great deal to save a single child at risk of drowning in front of us and our typical failure to donate money to charities that can save the lives of many children and adults with similar or lesser sacrifices. It is worth noting that this argument seems to have been quite important in the founding of the global Effective Altruism movement, a movement of people concerned to maximize the effects of their charitable giving and give significant portions of their money to help the global poor and work toward solving other important moral problems.[5]

By contrast, the negative duty approach holds that we are doing far more than failing to help the global poor. As citizens of rich democratic countries that help shape the rules of global trade, and that in many cases have a history of violent colonialism and that have participated in imperialism or its contemporary forms, we are causally relevant to the harm suffered by the global poor. That is, on Pogge's account at least, we are doing harm to the global poor. Charitable donation then is justified not merely on the grounds that we could be helping the global poor, like the drowning child that we could help out of the pond, but further that we are harming them. By analogy, if we've pushed the child into the pond, we bear additional responsibility for turning the child's precarious situation around.

Judith Lichtenberg (2010) argues that the moral psychology of these contrasting approaches to the problem of global poverty produces a kind of paradox of positive and negative duties. On the one hand, as Pogge has claimed (2002) negative duty arguments may be more motivating once accepted because they point to actions rather than omissions, and given that an act-omission bias seems to be well-supported empirically, people tend to view harmful acts as giving rise to stronger moral duties than omissions that result in harm (although this won't be true in all cases, such as perhaps Rachels' bathtub case (1975), or for all people). On the other hand, positive duty arguments may be easier to accept in the first place because they don't give rise to the same guilt produced by claiming that ordinary people are actively harming distant others, and so the reactance that guilt often generates will not be present. Holly Lawford-Smith (2012) also focuses on the "motivation question" and argues that negative duty arguments may be more motivating. It may be added that the causal link between the actions of ordinary voters in the United States, let's say, and the harm done by rules set by the World Trade Organization is not anywhere near as direct as in ordinary cases where people harm one another, and so getting people on board with the idea that such a causal relationship exists may be difficult. Barry and Øverland (2012; 2016) have developed the idea that this causal relation may be better cast as one of "enabling harm" and have also conducted some work in moral psychology exploring this relationship (Barry, Lindauer, and Øverland 2014).

A set of recent studies has sought to evaluate these claims about the motivational force of arguments concerning global poverty. Lindauer et al. (2020) finds that a shallow pond argument paired with an evolutionary debunking explanation of in-group bias, which could tend to make us see distant children as worthy of less concern than nearby children, can perform just as well in motivating charitable giving as an image of a child living in severe poverty of the kind used in prominent studies by Small, Loewenstein, and Slovic (2007), the "Rokia" studies. In each condition, participants on Prolific were told that they were entered in a lottery where they had a chance of winning $100 dollars. They were randomly assigned to the rational argument condition, the emotional appeal condition involving the single child, or a combined-appeal conditions (rational-emotional ordered, emotional-rational ordered). As noted, the rational argument performed similarly to the emotional appeal, where both generated greater charitable giving than a control condition. The combined rational-emotional ordered condition generated the greatest amount of giving, although not significantly greater than the other appeal conditions.

Buckland et al. (2022) explore the issue of comparing the effects of positive and negative duty arguments regarding global poverty. A first study found that only exposure to the positive duty argument made people significantly more likely to judge that people have a moral duty to donate to charities that combat severe poverty and to judge that it is morally wrong not to donate to such charities. However, the positive duty argument's effect on these judgments differed only from that of the non-moral control argument in this study, not the negative duty argument. The study also found that these arguments had a larger impact on the judgments of Spanish participants than those of American participants. A second study employed a lottery incentive to test the effects of these arguments on charitable giving behavior, but here the incentive was winning $20 and the chances of winning were concrete, 1 in 30. This study found that, with MTurk participants based in the United States, both the positive and negative duty argument were viewed as similarly convincing and produced similar effects on charitable giving. A third study with a similar setup to Study 2, with a larger sample size and a non-moral control condition of the kind used in Study 1, found that there was no significant difference in the convincingness or effects on charitable giving of the two arguments, although here only the negative duty argument produced significantly higher donations than the non-moral control argument.

These results bear on the motivation debate in the global poverty literature. To Lichtenberg's claim that positive duty arguments may be more readily accepted, it appears that both arguments are viewed as persuasive in general across these studies. One caveat, however, is that the positive duty argument is the only argument that produced significantly stronger attitudes regarding duties to the global poor in the first study reported by Buckland et al. On the second claim about the motivatingness of negative duty arguments (Pogge 2002; Lichtenberg 2010; Lawford-Smith 2012), there is also mixed evidence. On the one hand, the positive duty argument produced similar effects on charitable giving as an emotional appeal in Lindauer et al. (2020). And further, there was no significant difference in the effects of the positive and negative duty arguments in the second and third studies of Buckland et al. (2022). However, the negative duty argument was the one that gave rise to significantly greater giving than the non-moral control argument in the third study. It seems overly quick to conclude based on this finding that the negative duty argument will be more motivating in general, but it seems plausible that, in some circumstances, both arguments can motivate charitable giving.

Another approach that some authors have taken is to examine what moral principles are potentially motivating the charitable giving of people who are already donating. Nicole Hassoun, Emir Malikov, and Nathan Lubchenco (2016) take up this non-interventionist approach in a paper studying how patterns of giving on the micro-loan platform Kiva can be made sense of by different moral principles. They find that people tend to support giving more priority to those in greater need below a threshold, which suggests that both threshold and prioritarian principles motivate their attitudes and behaviors related to aid distribution. This work also aims to uncover the moral mechanisms that motivate charitable giving in relation to the problem of global poverty, and so is part of the literature on the motivational force of moral principles.

1.5 Conceptual Engineering

A further promising but underexplored line of research can be seen in the relationship between empirical research and issues in conceptual engineering. The focus on "ameliorative inquiry" ushered in by Sally Haslanger's work on gender and race (Haslanger 2000; 2012), exploring not merely what our current concepts do but what they might do in the sense of how they might better serve our political goals and moral values, immediately raises empirical questions about the real-world effects of our concepts. This shift away from merely analyzing received concepts to thinking about concept revision and implementation influenced and overlaps with other trends in the conceptual engineering literature, which also draws heavily on Rudolf Carnap's work on the explication of concepts (1950; 1955).

While thus far little empirical work has been done to test whether concepts that we use are the ones best suited to serve our political goals and moral values, it is in my view clearly an empirical question whether a given concept can play this kind of practical role (Lindauer 2020). Speculation alone won't do, and there are many examples of a priori theorizing about social consequences and effects of conceptual interventions not working out as anticipated (Marques 2020). Some starts have been made at uniting conceptual engineering and experimental philosophy (Machery 2017, Chapter 7), and there is much remaining room for research in this area at present.

2. Taking Stock

In this brief overview, I have detailed several of the most important ways empirical research can be brought to bear on topics in political philosophy. I focused on the publicity requirement, the stability requirement, action-guidingness, motivational questions, and the relationship between conceptual engineering and political goals. Much more could be said about each of these topics, and what I have provided is also not meant to be an exhaustive taxonomy of possible avenues for experimental political philosophy. But I do hope to have set out some of the topics that have helped to establish the field, motivated the field's importance for newcomers, and provided material for further reflection on the relationship between political philosophy and empirical research.

I will briefly introduce the chapters in this volume in the next section, and describe how many of them touch on these extant questions in the literature and raise new ones. Before doing so, I want to also discuss one of the key reasons why people might think that we don't need to conduct empirical research on ordinary people's judgments (which is notably only one type of empirical research) in order to make progress on questions in political philosophy. This is often referred to as the "expertise defense" which, under various guises, takes the intuitions and judgments of philosophers qua philosophical experts, rather than ordinary people, to be the ones that are solely relevant to the study of philosophical issues.

The expertise defense has come in for strong criticism over the years, with many papers calling into question whether philosophers' intuitions are more reliable than those of nonphilosophers (Weinberg 2009; Weinberg et al. 2010; Schwitzgebel and Cushman 2012; Tobia, Buckwalter, and Stich 2013; Horvath and Wiegmann 2022), and recently, in work by Daniel Kilov and Caroline Hendy, whether we can verify that philosophers are experts in modal reasoning of the kind often thought to be distinctive of philosophy (Kilov and Hendy 2022). While important, these are not the lines of criticism that I especially want to push here.

Rather, I instead want to note that some of the aspirations of political philosophy pull against the expertise defense in ways that may not be true of other areas of philosophy. When we seek to understand whether a theory of justice can be publicly justified, or stable over time for the right reasons, or whether it can serve as a useful guide to individual and collective action, or what kinds of motivation it will tend to produce, it seems especially implausible that we can appropriately explore these questions without thinking about the judgments and other psychological features of members of society beyond just the philosophers (Bruner and Lindauer 2020). This is not to deny that philosophers have some forms of expertise, for instance, in offering and assessing arguments regarding political questions. I have even argued that empirical research on many important political questions will benefit from the involvement of philosophers (Lindauer 2020), particularly if these questions are supposed to bear on the kinds of questions that we philosophers are interested in. Rather, I have emphasized that many of the core questions in political philosophy are distinctively ripe for empirical engagement and exploration, and further, in my view, would be very odd to approach without, at the very least, acknowledging that there is room for empirical investigation. A slightly different way of putting the point is that insofar as our tradition in political philosophy is supposed to be attuned to democratic societies and institutions, it must aim to understand and engage with the understanding of the *demos*, the people who are supposed to be not only the recipients of but also joint implementers of political ideas. There may then be another way in which the relationship between political philosophy and empirical research is distinctive or, at the very least, deeply interconnected.

Before diving into the contributions it is also important to note that there are other strong reasons to pay attention to the empirical effects of political ideas and principles that I haven't been able to give sustained attention to here. To mention perhaps the most important one, skepticism about the real-world impact of intellectual pursuits, if it is ever justified, seems especially unwarranted in the political case. It is sometimes noted that the Scottish historian and thinker Thomas Carlyle once responded to the criticism that he spoke too much of "ideas, nothing but ideas!" that "There once was a man called Rousseau who wrote a book containing nothing but ideas. The second edition was bound in the skins of those who laughed at the first" (see, e.g., MacIntyre 1998, 138). Whatever our views about the French Revolution and its aftermath, there is surely a point in Carlyle's reminder that many of the most impactful works of philosophy have been works of political philosophy. This should encourage a great deal of both care with and interest in their relations to the empirical realities that they respond to.

3. Descriptions of the Chapters in This Volume

Some of the chapters in this volume bear on these themes in political philosophy, while other chapters expand beyond them. Each of these tasks is important—showing how empirical research can inform work in political philosophy and how empirical research can sometimes guide us beyond the bounds of where traditional or current debates end. While the boundaries between these tasks are porous and there is often interplay between them in exciting new research, the first seven chapters are grouped under the heading "Traditional Issues in Political Philosophy with an Empirical Approach" and the last four are grouped under the heading "New Directions," which roughly correspond to these two ways of approaching experimental political philosophy.

The first chapter, by Cristina Bicchieri, Raj Patel, and Leena Koni Hoffmann, "Corruption, Shared Expectations, and Social Dilemmas," examines the nature of systemic corruption and the epistemic and normative attitudes that help to sustain it. Corruption is generally understood as a problem for good governance and productive political relations, giving rise to a familiar justification for the separation of powers, but addressing systemic corruption is a collective action problem beset by distinctive challenges. In a study involving surveys of 5,000 households across urban and rural areas in six of Nigeria's federal states, the authors find a strong disparity between participants' own normative beliefs about the acceptability of bribery for pass-marks on exams and their sense of other people's normative beliefs, which they take to be much more accepting of the practice, a phenomenon known as "pluralistic ignorance." Pluralistic ignorance can be demoralizing, leading to a sense of futility and fatalism about suboptimal practices. They use empirical research methods and Bicchieri's "social norms framework" to examine this problem and suggest interventions for addressing it, informing issues of "Publicity" and "Action-Guidance."

The second chapter, by Justin Bruner, "Rules, Risk and Agreement," uses computer simulation, a largely novel method in contemporary political philosophy, to shed light on traditional questions of what it means to divide resources fairly, which have dominated much of recent political thought. Bruner examines support for an often overlooked fairness rule in political philosophy, Maximum Nash Welfare, which selects the allocation of resources with the greatest product of agents' utilities (Nash welfare) where agents have disclosed their cardinal utility functions. He argues that the results of computer simulations suggest that Maximum Nash Welfare receives strong support under a contractarian decision procedure, and hence is a promising principle of distributive justice. Further, this support is stable across variations in people's attitudes toward risk and beliefs about the extent to which they have overlapping interests. These two factors correspond best to "Publicity" and "Stability."

The third chapter, by Christopher Freiman and Adam Lerner, "Does Equality Matter for Its Own Sake? An Experimental Examination of the Leveling-Down Objection," aims to undercut the Publicity or intuitive acceptability of telic egalitarianism, the view that equality is intrinsically valuable. Freiman and Lerner explore the motivation behind responses to the "leveling-down objection" to egalitarianism, which holds that since equality can be improved by bringing the better off down to the level of the worse off, and this implication is intuitively unacceptable, egalitarianism of this sort should be rejected. The move telic egalitarians typically make is to embrace the intuition that this result is not welcome by holding that equality has intrinsic value but this value is outweighed by other values, such as overall welfare or efficiency, in leveling down cases. Freiman and Lerner use the results of new empirical studies to argue that the tendency to regard leveled down worlds as better than nonleveled worlds in some respect is wholly explained by the general belief that the situation of the worst-off is improved in some way by leveling down the better off. When this confound is experimentally controlled for, they find that people do not regard leveled down worlds as intrinsically better in any respect, and hence maintain that this response to the leveling-down objection fails as a defense of telic egalitarianism.

The fourth chapter, by Shaun Nichols and John Thrasher, "What Does Labor Mixing Get You?," explores the extent of intuitive support for one of the leading theories of property acquisition in political philosophy, the "labor-mixing" theory. On this Lockean view one typically acquires a right to property by working on or exchanging some currency that is traceable to work for that property, "mixing" one's labor with it. In *Anarchy, State, and Utopia* (1974) Nozick raised a problem for the view by asking why mixing one's labor in these ways gives one a property right to the entire object, e.g., the clay and statue, rather than just the added value in that object that one's labor has produced, e.g., the statue alone. Nichols and Thrasher find that participants distinguish between these two kinds of ownership claims and that there is a genuine tension between them that does not seem resolvable for the labor-mixing theorist. This contribution also bears on the Publicity requirement, in this case for labor-mixing views of property.

The fifth chapter, by Ryan Muldoon, "Segregation and the Portfolio Theory of Identity," explores a problem of segregation first identified by the economist Thomas Schelling (1971). Schelling showed that people having weak preferences against being too much of a minority can lead to strong societal segregation, and that this can occur even when the same people prefer to live in diverse societies. Muldoon uses computer simulations to show that, while segregation can be very harmful to democratic processes by polarizing groups, a varied enough sorting based on identity can help to overcome it. On a "portfolio theory of identity," people have many traits that they can build their identity out of, rather than one identity that has to dominate their self-conception. Insofar as this is right, citizens can wind up being in different in-groups and out-groups at any given point in time, and thus the effect of a preference not to be in too small of a minority group can be blunted in giving rise to societal segregation. Greater diversity of identities, then, and salience of the variety of identifying characteristics that individuals can attribute to themselves, can help to solve the problem of segregation. In this sense, the paper both examines a problem and provides Action-Guidance on a possible solution to it.

The sixth chapter, by Nicole Hassoun, "Empirical Philosophy: How Engaging with Empirical Evidence Is Important for Theory as Well as Practice," gives an original and compelling account of the ways that empirical research can inform political philosophy. This chapter significantly extends prior work of hers on the topic, which as mentioned above, was some of the first to directly discuss the role of empirical research in political theorizing. Hassoun uses the theory of wellbeing and global health justice literatures as case studies that inform and support her general account, with important lessons for how empirical research not only helps examine current philosophical issues but may also open up new ones. In addition, she provides examples of the role of philosophy in research ethics and the ways that philosophical work can inform scientific research.

The seventh chapter, by Veronika Luptakova and Alex Voorhoeve, "How Do People Balance Death against Lesser Burdens?," uses empirical research methods to explore questions in healthcare justice. They examine the issue of trade-offs of large numbers of small burdens (e.g., toenail fungus) for a small number of large burdens (e.g., death), and the trade-off of large burdens against very bad but not as severe burdens (e.g., paraplegia). Many theorists have sought to limit aggregation such that a large number of the middle burdens can outweigh one large burden, but no number of small burdens can do so. In a UK population, they find that people do not always accept this kind of severity-based prioritization and examine the rationales that people give for their views. Some participants, however, did find limited aggregation more appealing than full aggregation across the spectrum of burdens. These results are not explained by status quo bias and seem to reflect genuine differences in the judgments of people in their sample population, which may reflect broader differences in thinking about healthcare justice. Further, some of the views they encounter are underrepresented in the philosophical literature but not necessarily without compelling rationales. Hence, the paper not only explores questions of Publicity for views of healthcare priorities but also brings to light new potential views that are worth examining the theoretical support for.

In Part II, "New Directions," four chapters address topics not previously given a prominent place in the literature and promise to spark much discussion. The eighth chapter, by Mark Alfano, Joanne Byrne, and Joshua Roose, "Automated Psycholinguistic Analysis of the Anglophone Manosphere," addresses the rise of online far-right communities that link men from around the world who share misogynistic and racist worldviews. These groups have been causally implicated in a number of terrorist attacks and other troubling events and trends, but this kind of political phenomenon has not been addressed in any sustained way in political philosophy thus far. Alfano, Byrne, and Roose take on this topic using corpus analysis of their texts and manifestos, revealing the distinct strands of commitments that each of these groups do and do not share, undoubtedly an important new step in addressing the challenges they pose to gender and racial egalitarianism and political liberalism. In conversation with José Medina's work on hermeneutical injustice, they show that some of the same techniques that may in other contexts be used to address such injustice can actually be coopted to reinforce it, empowering "Men's Rights" groups with linguistic and conceptual resources to entrench their distorted beliefs that they are ultimately victims. These results and reflections provide Action Guidance on how to better approach this important real-world problem, one that political philosophy aimed at promoting and protecting democracy should reckon with.

The ninth chapter, by Mollie Gerver, Dominik Duell, and Patrick Lown, "Experimental Immigration Ethics," uses empirical research methods to examine the ethics of immigration and immigration enforcement, prominent topics in contemporary political philosophy not yet subject to sustained empirical treatment. The authors specifically explore the issue of whether migrants' liability to harm impacts people's judgments about immigration enforcement policies. They find support in representative samples of the UK and US public for a principle of liability according to which it is less justified to impose immigration enforcement on migrants who pose no threat. Further, participants who were sensitive to this principle generally did not display bias in applying it. This research both explores the Publicity of potential principles of immigration justice and provides Action Guidance on the kinds of considerations to emphasize in public discourse if we want to have more just and humane policies toward vulnerable people seeking to enter our states' borders.

The tenth chapter, by Grace Flores-Robles and Ana Gantman, "Love vs. Money: Understanding Unique Challenges in Care Workers' Labor Organizing," addresses the dilemma that care workers often face in political organizing because care is perceived by the public to be inherently tied to love rather than self-interest. While labor organizing has received surprisingly little attention in recent Anglophone political philosophy, care work and care ethics have also generally not been at the center of the field, although this may be changing as the field finally becomes more open to feminist ethics and political philosophy. Using the "Sacred Values Protection Model" as a lens, the authors use empirical research to highlight the reasons why a sacred value like love and a secular value like money may be perceived to be traded off one another in this case, where such trade-offs are treated by many as taboo. They also draw out Action Guidance lessons about how we can increase public support for care work and labor organizing in this area.

Lastly, the eleventh chapter, by John Thrasher, "Experimental Political Philosophy: A Manifesto," offers an important and compelling methodological position that emphasizes the distinctiveness of experimental political philosophy. While approving of much work done in the field that uses the tools of experimental psychology, Thrasher also highlights research that draws on the techniques of behavioral and experimental economics, including the use of incentivized economic lab experiments and simulations. As noted in this introduction, it is worthwhile to have a great deal more self-conscious reflection on the role that empirical research should play in political philosophy. Thrasher's chapter is a valuable, original, and nuanced contribution to that discussion.

I am grateful to these contributors for their parts in creating this volume, the first of its kind focusing on the burgeoning field of experimental political philosophy. I would also like to thank Serene Khader, R.J. Leland, Ryan Muldoon, and John Thrasher for helpful feedback on particular chapters in the volume.

Notes

1 Some of this discussion will draw on the account that I developed in Lindauer (2020), though in more neutral terms and with somewhat different aims than I had in that article.
2 For a helpful overview of competing interpretations of the publicity requirement, see Gosseries and Parr (2022). For the purposes of this chapter, I largely steer clear of debates over how to interpret publicity and offer what I take to be the most compelling interpretation of the requirement, which has the benefit of being empirically evaluable. I discuss these competing interpretations in Lindauer (unpublished ms.), which this introduction draws some material from.
3 I am grateful to Joshua Knobe for helpful discussion on this topic.
4 See also Jaggar (2001; 2005) on negative duties and harming the global poor.
5 Different effective altruists focus on different moral issues, including global poverty, animal welfare, artificial intelligence alignment, and others. See https://www.effectivealtruism.org/ for further information.

References

Alfano, Mark, Don Loeb, and Alexandra Plakias. 2018. "Experimental Moral Philosophy." In *The Stanford Encyclopedia of Philosophy (Winter 2018 Edition)*, edited by Edward N. Zalta. https://plato.stanford.edu/archives/win2018/entries/experimental-moral/.

Anderson, Elizabeth. 2010. *The Imperative of Integration*. Princeton, NJ: Princeton University Press.

Aristotle. 1998. *Politics*. Translated by C. D. C. Reeve. Indianapolis, Ind: Hackett Pub.

Barry, Christian, and Gerhard Øverland. 2012. "The Feasible Alternatives Thesis: Kicking Away the Livelihoods of the Global Poor." *Politics, Philosophy & Economics* 11, no. 1: 97–119. https://doi.org/10.1177/1470594X10387273.

Barry, Christian, and Gerhard Øverland. 2016. *Responding to Global Poverty: Harm, Responsibility, and Agency*. New York: Cambridge University Press.

Barry, Christian, Matthew Lindauer, and Gerhard Øverland. 2014. "Doing, Allowing, and Enabling Harm: An Empirical Investigation." In *Oxford Studies in Experimental Philosophy*, edited by Joshua Knobe, Tania Lombrozo, and Shaun Nichols, 62–90. Oxford: Oxford University Press. https://doi.org/10.1093/acprof:oso/9780198718765.003.0004.

Bonilla-Silva, Eduardo. 2003. *Racism Without Racists: Color-Blind Racism and the Persistence of Racial Inequality in America*. Lanham, MA: Rowman & Littlefield.

Boxill, Bernard R. 1992. *Blacks and Social Justice*. Rev. edition. Lanham, Md: Rowman & Littlefield.

Brock, Gillian. 2009. *Global Justice: A Cosmopolitan Account*. Oxford: Oxford University Press. https://doi.org/10.1093/acprof:oso/9780199230938.001.0001.

Bruner, Justin P. 2018. "Decisions Behind the Veil: An Experimental Approach." In *Oxford Studies in Experimental Philosophy*. Vol. 2, edited by Tania Lombrozo, Joshua Knobe, and Shaun Nichols. Oxford: Oxford University Press.

Bruner, Justin P., and Matthew Lindauer. 2020. "The Varieties of Impartiality, or, Would an Egalitarian Endorse the Veil?" *Philosophical Studies* 177, no. 2: 459–77. https://doi.org/10.1007/s11098-018-1190-8.

Buckland, Luke, Matthew Lindauer, David Rodríguez-Arias, and Carissa Véliz. 2022. "Testing the Motivational Strength of Positive and Negative Duty Arguments Regarding Global Poverty." *Review of Philosophy and Psychology* 13, no.3: 699–717. https://doi.org/10.1007/s13164-021-00555-4.

Carnap, Rudolf. 1950. *Logical Foundations of Probability*. 2nd edition. Chicago: University of Chicago Press.

Carnap, Rudolf. 1955. "Meaning and Synonymy in Natural Languages." *Philosophical Studies* 6, no. 3: 33–47. https://doi.org/10.1007/BF02330951.

Cohen, G. A. 2008. *Rescuing Justice and Equality*. Cambridge, MA: Harvard University Press.

"Effective Altruism Website." n.d. Accessed August 4, 2022. https://www.effectivealtruism.org/.

Estlund, David M. 2020. *Utopophobia: On the Limits (If Any) of Political Philosophy*. Princeton, New Jersey: Princeton University Press.

Faravelli, Marco. 2007. "How Context Matters: A Survey Based Experiment on Distributive Justice." *Journal of Public Economics* 91, nos. 7–8: 1399–422. https://doi.org/10.1016/j.jpubeco.2007.01.004.

Frohlich, Norman, and Joe A. Oppenheimer. 1993. *Choosing Justice: An Experimental Approach to Ethical Theory*. 1. paperback printing. California Series on Social Choice and Political Economy 22. Berkeley: University of California Press.

Frohlich, Norman, Joe A. Oppenheimer, and Cheryl L. Eavey. 1987a. "Laboratory Results on Rawls's Distributive Justice." *British Journal of Political Science* 17, no. 1: 1. https://doi.org/10.1017/S0007123400004580.

Frohlich, Norman, Joe A. Oppenheimer, and Cheryl L. Eavey. 1987b. "Choices of Principles of Distributive Justice in Experimental Groups." *American Journal of Political Science* 31, no. 3: 606. https://doi.org/10.2307/2111285.

Gaus, Gerald. 2010. *The Order of Public Reason: A Theory of Freedom and Morality in a Diverse and Bounded World*. 1st edition. Cambridge: Cambridge University Press. https://doi.org/10.1017/CBO9780511780844.

Goodin, Robert, and Philip Pettit. 1995. "Introduction." In *A Companion to Contemporary Political Philosophy*. Oxford: Blackwell.

Gosseries, Alex, and Tom Parr. 2022. "Publicity." In *The Stanford Encyclopedia of Philosophy (Summer 2022 Edition)*, edited by Edward N. Zalta. https://plato.stanford.edu/archives/sum2022/entries/publicity/.

Harsanyi, John C. 1975. "Can the Maximin Principle Serve as a Basis for Morality? A Critique of John Rawls's Theory." *American Political Science Review* 69, no. 2: 594–606. https://doi.org/10.2307/1959090.

Haslanger, Sally. 2000. "Gender and Race: (What) Are They? (What) Do We Want Them To Be?" *Nous* 34 (1): 31–55. https://doi.org/10.1111/0029-4624.00201.

Haslanger, Sally. 2012. *Resisting Reality: Social Construction and Social Critique*. New York: Oxford University Press.

Hassoun, Nicole. 2009. "Meeting Need." *Utilitas* 21, no. 3: 250–75. https://doi.org/10.1017/S0953820809990045.

Hassoun, Nicole. 2016. "Experimental or Empirical Political Philosophy." In *A Companion to Experimental Philosophy*, edited by Justin Sytsma and Wesley Buckwalter, 234–46. Chichester, UK: John Wiley & Sons, Ltd. https://doi.org/10.1002/9781118661666.ch16.

Hassoun, Nicole, Emir Malikov, and Nathan Lubchenco. 2016. "How People Think About Distributing Aid." *Philosophical Psychology* 29, no. 7: 1029–44. https://doi.org/10.1080/09515089.2016.1211259.

Herne, Kaisa, and Tarja Mard. 2008. "Three Versions of Impartiality: An Experimental Investigation." *Homo Oeconomicus* 25: 27–53.

Hobbes, Thomas. 1668. *Leviathan: With Selected Variants from the Latin Edition of 1668*. Edited by E. M. Curley. Indianapolis: Hackett Publishing Company, Inc.

Horvath, Joachim, and Alex Wiegmann. 2022. "Intuitive Expertise in Moral Judgments." *Australasian Journal of Philosophy* 100, no. 2: 342–59. https://doi.org/10.1080/00048402.2021.1890162.

Inoue, Akira, Masahiro Zenkyo, and Haruya Sakamoto. 2021. "Making the Veil of Ignorance Work: Evidence from Survey Experiments." In *Oxford Studies in Experimental Philosophy Volume 4*, edited by Akira Inoue, Masahiro Zenkyo, and Haruya Sakamoto, 53–80. Oxford: Oxford University Press. https://doi.org/10.1093/oso/9780192856890.003.0004.

Jaggar, Alison M. 2001. "Is Globalization Good for Women?" *Comparative Literature* 53, no. 4: 298. https://doi.org/10.2307/3593521.

Jaggar, Alison M. 2005. "'Saving Amina': Global Justice for Women and Intercultural Dialogue." *Ethics & International Affairs* 19, no. 03: 55–75. https://doi.org/10.1111/j.1747-7093.2005.tb00554.x.

Khader, Serene J. 2011. *Adaptive Preferences and Women's Empowerment*. Studies in Feminist Philosophy. Oxford; New York: Oxford University Press.

Kilov, Daniel, and Caroline Hendy. 2022. "Pundits and Possibilities: Philosophers Are Not Modal Experts." *Australasian Journal of Philosophy* 75 (1): 1–20. https://doi.org/10.1080/00048402.2022.2058034.

Kohlberg, Lawrence. 1973. "The Claim to Moral Adequacy of a Highest Stage of Moral Judgment." *The Journal of Philosophy* 70, no. 18: 630. https://doi.org/10.2307/2025030.

Konow, James. 2008. "The Moral High-Ground: An Experimental Study of Spectator Impartiality." *MPRA Paper No. 18558*.

Konow, James. 2009. "Is Fairness in the Eye of the Beholder? An Impartial Spectator Analysis of Justice." *Social Choice and Welfare* 33, no. 1: 101–27. https://doi.org/10.1007/s00355-008-0348-2.

Laërtius, Diogenes. 2006. *Lives of Eminent Philosophers. Volume 1, Books 1–5*. Translated by R. D. Hicks. Reprint. The Loeb Classical Library 184. Cambridge, MA: Harvard University Press.

Lamm, Helmut, and Thomas Schwinger. 1980. "Norms Concerning Distributive Justice: Are Needs Taken into Consideration in Allocation Decisions?" *Social Psychology Quarterly* 43, no. 4: 425. https://doi.org/10.2307/3033962.

Lawford-Smith, Holly. 2012. "The Motivation Question: Arguments from Justice and from Humanity." *British Journal of Political Science* 42, no. 3: 661–78. https://doi.org/10.1017/S0007123412000063.

Lichtenberg, Judith. 2010. "Negative Duties, Positive Duties, and the 'New Harms.'" *Ethics* 120, no. 3: 557–78. https://doi.org/10.1086/652294.

Lindauer, Matthew. *The Fruitfulness of Normative Concepts*. Unpublished ms.

Lindauer, Matthew. 2020. "Experimental Philosophy and the Fruitfulness of Normative Concepts." *Philosophical Studies* 177, no. 8: 2129–52. https://doi.org/10.1007/s11098-019-01302-3.

Lindauer, Matthew, Marcus Mayorga, Joshua Greene, Paul Slovic, Daniel Västfjäll, and Peter Singer. 2020. "Comparing the Effect of Rational and Emotional Appeals on Donation Behavior." *Judgment and Decision Making* 15, no. 3: 413–20.

Lissowski, Grzegorz, Tadeusz Tyszka, and Wlodzimierz Okrasa. 1991. "Principles of Distributive Justice: Experiments in Poland and America." *Journal of Conflict Resolution* 35, no. 1: 98–119. https://doi.org/10.1177/0022002791035001006.

Machery, Edouard. 2017. *Philosophy Within Its Proper Bounds*. Oxford: Oxford University Press. https://doi.org/10.1093/oso/9780198807520.001.0001.

MacIntyre, Alasdair C. 1998. *A Short History of Ethics: A History of Moral Philosophy from the Homeric Age to the 20th Century*. 2nd edition. London: Routledge.

Marques, Teresa. 2020. "Amelioration vs Perversion." In *Shifting Concepts*, edited by Teresa Marques and Åsa Wikforss, 260–84. Oxford: Oxford University Press. https://doi.org/10.1093/oso/9780198803331.003.0014.

Marx, Karl. 1844. *Economic and Philosophic Manuscripts of 1844*. Edited by Martin Milligan. Great Books in Philosophy Series. Amherst, NY: Prometheus Books.

Michelbach, Philip A., John T. Scott, Richard E. Matland, and Brian H. Bornstein. 2003. "Doing Rawls Justice: An Experimental Study of Income Distribution Norms." *American Journal of Political Science* 47, no. 3: 523–39. https://doi.org/10.1111/1540-5907.00037.

Miller, David. 2003. *Principles of Social Justice*. 1. paperback, ed.3. print. Cambridge, MA: Harvard University Press.

Mills, Charles W. 2005. "'Ideal Theory' as Ideology." *Hypatia* 20, no. 3: 165–83. https://doi.org/10.1111/j.1527-2001.2005.tb00493.x.

Mills, Charles W. 2011. *The Racial Contract*. Ithaca, NY: Cornell University Press.

Mitchell, Gregory, Philip E. Tetlock, Barbara A. Mellers, and Lisa D. Ordóñez. 1993. "Judgments of Social Justice: Compromises Between Equality and Efficiency." *Journal of Personality and Social Psychology* 65, no. 4: 629–39. https://doi.org/10.1037/0022-3514.65.4.629.

Moehler, Michael. 2018. *Minimal Morality: A Multilevel Social Contract Theory*. Vol. 1. Oxford: Oxford University Press. https://doi.org/10.1093/oso/9780198785927.001.0001.

Muldoon, Ryan, Chiara Lisciandra, Mark Colyvan, Carlo Martini, Giacomo Sillari, and Jan Sprenger. 2014. "Disagreement Behind the Veil of Ignorance." *Philosophical Studies* 170, no. 3: 377–94. https://doi.org/10.1007/s11098-013-0225-4.

Nozick, Robert. 1974. *Anarchy, State, and Utopia*. New York: Basic Books, a member of the Perseus Books Group.

Pettit, Philip. 2014. *Just Freedom: A Moral Compass for a Complex World*. 1st edition. The Norton Global Ethics Series. New York: W.W. Norton & Company.

Pogge, Thomas W. 2002. *World Poverty and Human Rights*. Cambridge: Polity Press.

Rachels, James. 1975. "Active and Passive Euthanasia." *New England Journal of Medicine* 292, no. 2: 78–80. https://doi.org/10.1056/NEJM197501092920206.

Rawls, John. 1971. *A Theory of Justice*. Rev. 1999. Cambridge, Mass: Belknap Press of Harvard University Press.

Rawls, John. 1993. *Political Liberalism*. New York: Columbia University Press.

Rawls, John. 2001. *Justice as Fairness: A Restatement*. Cambridge, Mass: Harvard University Press.

Rousseau, Jean-Jacques. 1762. *On the Social Contract*. Translated by Donald A. Cress. 2nd edition. Indianapolis: Hackett Publishing Company, Inc.

Schelling, Thomas. 1971. "Dynamic Models of Segregation." *Journal of Mathematical Sociology* 1, no. 2: 143–86.

Schwitzgebel, Eric, and Fiery Cushman. 2012. "Expertise in Moral Reasoning? Order Effects on Moral Judgment in Professional Philosophers and Non-philosophers." *Mind & Language* 27, no. 2: 135–53. https://doi.org/10.1111/j.1468-0017.2012.01438.x.

Singer, Peter. 1972. "Famine, Affluence, and Morality." *Philosophy and Public Affairs* 1, no. 3: 229–43.

Skyrms, Brian. 2014. *Evolution of the Social Contract*. 2nd edition. Cambridge: Cambridge University Press. https://doi.org/10.1017/CBO9781139924825.

Skyrms, Brian. 2016. "Evolution, Norms and the Social Contract." *Arizona State Law Journal* 48: 1087–100.

Small, Deborah A., George Loewenstein, and Paul Slovic. 2007. "Sympathy and Callousness: The Impact of Deliberative Thought on Donations to Identifiable and Statistical Victims." *Organizational Behavior and Human Decision Processes* 102, no. 2: 143–53. https://doi.org/10.1016/j.obhdp.2006.01.005.

Sołtan, Karol Edward. 1982. "Empirical Studies of Distributive Justice." *Ethics* 92, no. 4: 673–91. https://doi.org/10.1086/292384.

Southwood, Nicholas. 2016. "Does 'Ought' Imply 'Feasible'?" *Philosophy & Public Affairs* 44, no. 1: 7–45. https://doi.org/10.1111/papa.12067.

Southwood, Nicholas. 2018. "The Feasibility Issue." *Philosophy Compass* 13, no. 8. https://doi.org/10.1111/phc3.12509.

Sugden, Robert. 1990. "Contractarianism and Norms." *Ethics* 100, no. 4: 768–86. https://doi.org/10.1086/293233.

Thrasher, John. 2014. "Uniqueness and Symmetry in Bargaining Theories of Justice." *Philosophical Studies* 167, no. 3: 683–99. https://doi.org/10.1007/s11098-013-0121-y.

Tobia, Kevin, Wesley Buckwalter, and Stephen Stich. 2013. "Moral Intuitions: Are Philosophers Experts?" *Philosophical Psychology* 26, no. 5: 629–38. https://doi.org/10.1080/09515089.2012.696327.

Valentini, Laura. 2012. "Ideal vs. Non-Ideal Theory: A Conceptual Map: Ideal vs Non-Ideal Theory." *Philosophy Compass* 7, no. 9: 654–64. https://doi.org/10.1111/j.1747-9991.2012.00500.x.

Weinberg, Jonathan M. 2009. "On Doing Better, Experimental-Style." *Philosophical Studies* 145, no. 3: 455–64. https://doi.org/10.1007/s11098-009-9405-7.

Weinberg, Jonathan M., Chad Gonnerman, Cameron Buckner, and Joshua Alexander. 2010. "Are Philosophers Expert Intuiters?" *Philosophical Psychology* 23, no. 3: 331–55. https://doi.org/10.1080/09515089.2010.490944.

Part One

Traditional Issues in Political Philosophy with an Empirical Approach

1

Corruption, Shared Expectations, and Social Dilemmas

Cristina Bicchieri, Raj Patel, and Leena Koni Hoffmann

1. Introduction

Much of the world's population today live in societies that are plagued by systemic corruption.[1] The consequences are dire. Widespread corruption erodes trust in political and economic institutions, leads to public and private underinvestment, and undermines the very conditions necessary for productive economic activity to take place. Societies in which endemic corruption is the norm are consequently some of the most politically unstable and poorest places in the world, and they consistently score the lowest on a wide range of human development measures. Solving the problem of corruption is thus a central task, if not *the* central task, of development policy.

Despite the centrality of this task, corruption scholars note that international anti-corruption policy has generally been a failure (Persson, Rothstein, and Teorrell 2013; Heywood 2017). It is a remarkable fact that after at least two decades of research and billions of dollars spent, we still do not have a satisfactory answer as to how to control corruption. Anti-corruption success stories are few and far between, and in many cases, states that have received billions of dollars from the international community for anti-corruption political reforms have higher levels of corruption than before they pursued those reforms.

This failure has led to a renewed interest in some of the most foundational questions of the field among corruption scholars and practitioners, provoking debates ranging from abstract questions about the basic nature of corruption as a social phenomenon to more empirical concerns surrounding operationalization and measurement (Rothstein 2011b; Persson, Rothstein and Teorell 2013; Marquette and Peiffer 2015; Heywood 2017; Marquette and Peiffer 2018; Persson, Rothstein and Teorell 2019; Marquette and Peiffer 2019). Some have urged for a "return to the causal explanations for the emergence of corruption" (Kubbe and Engelbert 2017, 1), while others—echoing similar but stronger sentiments—have called for a complete revision of the theoretical foundations of anti-corruption policy (Persson, Rothstein, and Teorell 2013). The stakes of this debate are particularly high given that an accurate

CB, RP, & LKH contributed equally to this chapter.

theoretical understanding of the problem and a precise grasp on the underlying causal structures that produce it are essential for designing effective and context-sensitive anti-corruption policies.

In response to such calls, a growing and influential literature that calls attention to the influence of informal norms on corrupt behavior has emerged over the past two decades (Bicchieri and Rovelli 1995; Bicchieri and Duffy 1997; Bicchieri and Fukui 1999; Bicchieri and Xiao 2009; Rothstein 2011a; 2011b; Persson, Rothstein and Teorell 2013; Kobis; Van Prooijen and Righetti 2015; Hoffmann and Patel 2017; Kubbe and Engelbert 2017; Persson, Rothstein and Teorell 2019; Hoffman and Patel 2021a; Hoffmann and Patel 2021b; Hoffmann and Patel 2022). A central insight of this work highlights the powerful influence of social expectations on behaviors related to corruption. The willingness to engage in or refrain from corruption is often deeply influenced by our beliefs about others' behavior (empirical expectations) and/or our beliefs about their personal normative beliefs (normative expectations). Variation in these social expectations has profound implications for the ways in which corruption manifests in those communities. Thus understanding the causal relationships in question is critical to both understanding systemic corruption as a phenomenon and devising policy to curb it. As we will show, under certain conditions, when people believe that others around them will cheat, they are also motivated to cheat, and so when the belief is widespread within a community, it thus becomes self-fulfilling in that they *all* cheat, and the society becomes trapped in the social dilemma of corruption.

Solving the collective action problem generated by systemic corruption requires a precise understanding of the constraints individuals face when abandoning old behaviors and adopting new ones. We should expect variation in these constraints from one practice to the next given the diversity of corrupt practices and the variety of reasons individuals may have for participating in them. Drivers may offer bribes at a traffic checkpoint because they have high empirical expectations—they expect that the majority of other drivers in their community would also offer a bribe. Police officers may solicit bribes at a traffic checkpoint because they have both high empirical and normative expectations—they expect other police officers to solicit bribes, and they believe that other police officers expect them to as well (Hoffmann and Patel 2017, vi). Interventions aimed at disrupting the former (offering a bribe) may be substantially different from those aimed at disrupting the latter (soliciting a bribe) because of the variation in the underlying social expectations that motivate the behavior. Careful empirical investigation into the underlying beliefs and expectations that support corrupt practices is thus essential to designing effective anti-corruption policy.

Our social norms methodology aims to render visible the invisible rules that govern systemic corruption. Through a long-standing partnership between the Penn Center for Social Norms and Behavioral Dynamics (PCSNBD) and Chatham House Africa Programme, we have carried out over 10,000 specialized social norms surveys and conducted hundreds of interviews across Nigeria since 2016. Applying Bicchieri's (2006; 2016) theory of social norms, the surveys and interview protocols were designed to uncover the underlying beliefs and expectations surrounding a diverse range of corrupt practices, such as traffic law enforcement corruption, healthcare corruption, gender and corruption, electricity sector corruption, examination malpractice, electoral corruption, and embezzlement for religious reasons.

In this chapter, we introduce our theoretical framework and present some key empirical findings from our work. In Section 2, we outline Bicchieri's definition of social norms as applied to corruption and explore the diverse roles that social expectations play with respect to specific behaviors related to corruption, as well as how they fit into our more general theoretical understanding of the social dilemma of corruption. We use examples and share insights gleaned from our empirical research in Nigeria throughout. In Section 3, we introduce our social norms methodology. In Section 4, we present tentative empirical findings from a study on pass-mark bribery in Nigeria, and in Section 5 we discuss policy implications. In Section 6, we conclude.

2. Corruption, Collective Action, and Shared Expectations

a. Social Norms: Some Definitions

In many cases, corrupt practices are supported by shared beliefs within a given community.

For example, if a police officer believes that (a) a majority of other police officers in the department solicit bribes at road checkpoints and (b) a majority of other police officers in the department expect other police officers to solicit bribes at road checkpoints, then we would expect to see widespread solicitation of bribes among that particular traffic law enforcement community. These two kinds of belief are, respectively, *empirical expectations* and *normative expectations*. While empirical expectations are beliefs about others' behavior, normative expectations are beliefs about others' personal normative beliefs. Personal normative beliefs are beliefs that express an individual's positive or negative evaluation of a particular practice.

> *Empirical expectations:* First-order beliefs about others' behavior.
> Example: "I believe that 90% of police officers solicit bribes at road checkpoints."
>
> *Normative expectations*: Second-order beliefs about others' personal normative beliefs.
> Example: "I believe that 90% of police officers believe that one should solicit bribes at road checkpoints."

Empirical expectations and normative expectations are *social expectations*. When social expectations have a causal impact on behaviors, we say that the behaviors are interdependent. Interdependence means that the preferences for adopting specific behaviors are *conditional* on social expectations: individuals choose a particular course of action because of what other people do (empirical expectation) or think (normative expectation). *Descriptive norms* are behaviors that are conditional on empirical expectations only. *Social norms* are behaviors that are conditional on both empirical and normative expectations. Descriptive norms and social norms are examples of interdependent behaviors.

Interdependent behaviors:

Descriptive norm. A descriptive norm is a pattern of behavior such that individuals prefer to conform to it on condition that they believe that most people in their reference network conform to it (empirical expectation).
Example: Coordinating with other drivers on which side of the road to drive.

Social norm. A social norm is a rule of behavior such that individuals prefer to conform to it on condition that they believe (a) most people in their reference network conform to it (empirical expectation), and (b) that most people in their reference network believe they ought to conform to it (normative expectation).
Example: Tipping at restaurants in the United States.

Many behaviors, however, are not conditional on social expectations. When this is the case, we say that the behavior is independent. Sometimes individuals choose a particular course of action because they believe it to be a moral obligation, as when a Muslim refuses to eat pork because they consider it haram. *Moral norms* are collective practices that are driven by shared moral rules. At other times, individuals choose a particular course of action because they believe it satisfies an immediate practical need, as when an individual uses an umbrella in order to remain dry in wet weather. *Social customs* are collective practices that are driven by shared prudential concerns.

Independent behaviors:

Moral norm. A collective practice that is driven by a shared moral rule. Moral rules are typically unconditional on others' behavior or beliefs.
Example: Eating halal if Muslim.

Social custom. A collective practice that is driven by shared prudential concerns.
Example: Using umbrellas when it rains.

Corrupt practices may be descriptive norms, social norms, moral norms, or social customs. A specific corrupt transaction may involve different kinds of collective practices, as when the solicitation of a bribe is driven by a social norm and the payment of that bribe is driven by a social custom. Diagnosing the precise characteristics of a particular corrupt practice is essential to designing an effective anti-corruption policy. Different collective practices call for different solutions, and a policy designed to disrupt one kind of behavior will likely be ineffective at disrupting another. For example, policies aimed at destabilizing social norms will likely require changing a community's empirical and normative expectations, whereas policies aimed at disrupting a social custom will likely require altering the relevant incentives or providing better means to satisfy some common needs.

Our research methodology includes the development and administration of social norms surveys designed specifically to measure respondents' personal normative beliefs, empirical expectations, normative expectations, and legal knowledge. We assess conditionality of preferences (and behavior) using vignettes, in which we vary the strength and congruence of social expectations. These tools allow us to accurately measure the beliefs and expectations that drive collective practices, providing powerful insights into the types of policy interventions that may be effective at inducing behavioral change.

In the rest of this chapter, we focus on corrupt practices as interdependent behaviors. In our view, social expectations play a powerful role in sustaining corrupt practices under conditions of systemic corruption. We turn to the role of shared expectations in sustaining corrupt practices now.

b. Social Dilemmas and Social Expectations

One standard theoretical characterization of corruption is as a principal-agent problem (Rose-Ackerman 1978; Klitgaard 1988). A simple version of this model assumes that an honest "principled" principal (e.g., a public body) contracts with a self-interested agent with exogenous preferences (e.g., a corrupt politician). A divergence of interests and asymmetric information between the principal and the agent generates a familiar agency problem (i.e., moral hazard) that gives the agent the opportunity to successfully pursue their own self-interest at the expense of the principal's (or public's) interest. Given that there are honest "principled principals" and that agents have self-interested exogenous preferences, anti-corruption policy inspired by this approach aims to alter the expected costs (being caught) and benefits (not being caught) of participating in corruption. In practice, this has meant a focus on formal institutions, and in particular, those mechanisms that allow the principal to monitor, detect, and punish unethical behavior on the part of the agent. The right sorts of formal institutions change the relative payoffs faced by the agent such that the agent's interest becomes aligned with the principal's interest (or so the argument goes).

The admittedly crude version of the principal-agent theory presented here emphasizes the role of formal mechanisms in producing legal/economic incentives that motivate self-interested individuals to act honestly rather than dishonestly. But social incentives are also important, since in many cases the relevant system of incentives that individuals face is social, in large part shaped by their first-order expectations of others' behavior (empirical expectations) and/or second-order expectations about their beliefs (normative expectations). Variations in the precise characteristics of these social expectations, such as their accuracy (i.e., whether normative expectations truly reflect the prevalence of personal normative beliefs in the community), their composition (i.e., whether either, neither, or both present), and the relation in which they stand to one another (i.e., whether they are in harmony or conflict), will have significant implications for corrupt practices.

Consider empirical expectations under conditions of systemic corruption. In high corruption societies, corruption is conspicuous. Some corrupt practices are overt and directly observable, especially nonelite corruption (e.g., petty bribery, grease payments) that involve impersonal exchange and relatively transparent markets. The use of the services provided by these markets is practically unavoidable, as they are ubiquitous and deeply embedded into the practicalities of everyday life, offering a relatively efficient private alternative to (at times untenably) cumbersome bureaucratic processes. Other practices are covert yet nonetheless evident, in particular elite forms of corruption (e.g., embezzlement) that explain the otherwise inexplicably lavish lifestyles enjoyed by government officials while on ostensibly modest public salaries (without legal or other repercussions, too).

Under these conditions, most people naturally come to hold high empirical expectations: they believe that most of those around them will participate in corruption, and this has profound implications for the trade-offs they face when deciding to participate in corruption. On a general level, this is the trade-off at the core of cooperative action, that is, the tension between relative riskiness of social cooperation and the relative safety of anti-social action. Whether we choose to cooperate with others (by, e.g., refraining from corruption, refusing to opportunistically exploit, agreeing to play by the rules, etc.) or whether we choose the relative safety of the anti-social action (by, e.g., participating in corruption, choosing to opportunistically exploit, not agreeing to play by the rules) at the expense of foregoing the larger benefits available via social cooperation ultimately comes down to what we believe others will do—will they cooperate with us or will they exploit us?

We can formalize this tension as an Assurance Game with multiple equilibria (see Table 1.1) (Nichols 2003; Dixit 2018). The payoff structure is such that when everyone refuses to bribe (mutual cooperation), players coordinate on the superior low corruption equilibrium where bribery behavior is rare (5, 5); when everyone bribes (mutual defection), players coordinate on the inferior high corruption equilibrium, where bribery behavior is rampant (3, 3).

Table 1.1 Bribery as an Assurance Game

	Cooperate/Refuse to Bribe	**Defect/Bribe**
Cooperate/Refuse to Bribe	5, 5	0, 3
Defect/Bribe	3, 0	3, 3

© Cristina Bicchieri, Raj Patel, and Leena Koni Hoffmann.

In an Assurance Game, unlike a Prisoner's Dilemma, individual and collective interests merge as the optimal choice for each player is also the socially optimal choice for all players, and there is no conflict of preferences as all players prefer to coordinate on the superior low corruption equilibrium (mutual cooperation Pareto dominates mutual defection). Given the relative payoffs, cooperation is the payoff-dominant strategy (maximizes payoff but risks exploitation) and defection is the risk-dominant strategy (secures a smaller but safer payoff). The payoff structure of an Assurance Game is such that players are left best-off when they cooperate if others cooperate (coordination on mutual cooperation/low corruption equilibrium), second best-off when they defect when others defect (coordination on the mutual defection/high corruption equilibrium), and worst-off when they fail to coordinate (they are exploited/non-coordination).

Whether players choose to cooperate will depend on their expectations of the other players' behavior: if they expect that the other player will cooperate, there is no reason for them to defect (and vice versa: if they expect the other player will defect, there is no reason for them to cooperate). The riskiness of payoff-dominant strategy stems from the fact that its payoff is a product of joint action (i.e., securing it requires all players to cooperate) and failure to achieve joint action runs the risk of being "suckered" (i.e., having one's cooperated efforts exploited); cooperation can go either way, in other words, and so it is the best outcome if successful and the worst outcome if it fails. There is no such risk in defection, since the payoff is not dependent on joint action, and so provides the smaller but guaranteed payoff independently of what others do.

Since cooperation offers the chance to obtain the best outcome but runs the risk of exploitation in case of failure, the best strategy from the perspective of each player is to coordinate with other players: cooperate if others cooperate (payoff dominance), and defect if others defect (risk dominance). Notice also that there is no dominant strategy—rational players could prefer either payoff dominance or risk dominance depending on their empirical expectations. As a general rule, high empirical expectations create a relatively riskier strategic landscape, as they imply a generally non-cooperative environment (and the converse is true for low empirical expectations).

Understood in this way, systemic corruption is the bad equilibrium of an Assurance Game and the social dilemma of corruption is a coordination problem (equilibrium selection or equilibrium shift), the solution to which requires setting expectations such that players expect others to cooperate so that players can coordinate on the "superior" low corruption equilibrium, or resetting expectations such that players trapped at the bad equilibrium can shift to the good equilibrium. The goal of anti-corruption policy, then, is the attempt to move a society from the bad equilibrium to the good equilibrium.

Table 1.2 Bribery as a Prisoner's Dilemma

	Cooperate/Refuse to Bribe	Defect/Bribe
Cooperate/Refuse to Bribe	3, 3	0, 5
Defect/Bribe	5, 0	1, 1

© Cristina Bicchieri, Raj Patel, and Leena Koni Hoffmann.

The Assurance Game provides a relatively optimistic picture of the problem. A competing interpretation of the social dilemma is as the lone equilibrium in a Prisoner's Dilemma (see Table 1.2). Rather than a coordination problem, there is a more fundamental problem of cooperation due to a sharp divergence of individual and collective interests. The best outcome for all players (mutual cooperate) is not the best outcome for each individual player (defection when others cooperate, i.e., exploitation), so choosing the socially optimal outcome means choosing "less rather than more" (Skyrms 2004: 3) relative to the individually optimal outcome. While exploitation secures the highest payoff, being exploited leaves the player with the lowest payoff and is the worst outcome. The looming temptation to exploit others (when they cooperate) and the fear of being exploited by them (when they defect) mean each player has an incentive to defect regardless of what the other player does, leaving all worse-off as a result. Note the stark contrast with the Assurance Game: In the Assurance Game, the fact that others cooperate supplies a reason to cooperate as mutual cooperation secures the highest payoff. In the Prisoner's Dilemma, the fact that others cooperate supplies a reason to defect as exploitation secures the highest payoff. This difference has profound implications for the prospects of social cooperation.

Situations that resemble a Prisoner's Dilemma are ubiquitous in corruption-related contexts. Consider a firm deciding whether to bribe a state official to receive a lucrative contract. Since the value of a bribe is inversely proportional to the total number of bribes, the temptation to bribe the official is highest when the rest of the competing firms do not offer a bribe (the allure of exploitation). But the firm does not want to be left at a disadvantage in the case that another firm offers a bribe, so they are motivated to bribe if the other firms bribe, too (the fear of being exploited). The allure of exploitation and the fear of being exploited supplies the firm with reason to bribe whether the other firms bribe or not which exhausts the possible choices each firm has; thus every firm has incentive to bribe regardless of what the other firms do. This makes each individual bribe essentially worthless—for if everyone pays a bribe, nobody gains an advantage—and they would have been better-off collectively refusing to bribe (i.e., cooperating).

Corruption thought of as the non-cooperative equilibrium of a Prisoner's Dilemma paints a rather grim picture—each player is incentivized to take the anti-social action regardless of what the other player does, there is no cooperative equilibrium to which players can hope to move, and the standard intuitive solution (i.e., prosocial punishment of exploitation) are in effect public goods, and thus suffer from familiar second-order collective action problems associated with their provision (Ostrom 1998). Indeed, one of the more promising solutions to a Prisoner's Dilemma is in fact to turn it into an Assurance Game through repeated interactions on a range of issues, as the relatively prosocial preferences reflected in the payoff structure of the Assurance Game allow for the cooperative equilibrium.

Whether the social dilemma of corruption is better understood as an Assurance Game or a Prisoners' Dilemma is an open question still subject to debate (Rothstein 2010; Dixit 2018). We do not weigh in here. Our focus is on how the success of social cooperation turns on the presence of mutual beliefs, a point which seems especially salient in the context of corruption.

Consider bribery related to examination malpractice. In some parts of the world, it's common for parents to bribe examination officials to secure high pass marks for their children in state or national exams.[2] Assuming that the strategic situation resembles an Assurance Game, whether a parent opts to bribe will depend on their expectations about the bribery behavior of the other parents (i.e., on their empirical expectations). When empirical expectations are low and the prevailing perception is that bribery is rare, parents have reason *not* to bribe (i.e., they should choose the payoff-dominant strategy), for low empirical expectations mean that mutual cooperation is possible, and if all parents successfully refrain from bribing (and mutual cooperation is achieved), they successfully coordinate on the superior low corruption equilibrium and secure the highest payoff. The benefits of cooperation in this context might be thought of in terms of the interests that the parents share in securing the significant private benefits (e.g., a high-quality education for their child) and social benefits (e.g., the public good type benefits that flow from having a competent, well-educated community) that are impossible to provide for without the requisite high standards of academic integrity and excellence.

Conversely, when empirical expectations are high, and the prevailing perception is that bribery is common, parents have reason to bribe (i.e., choose the risk-dominant strategy). One reason comes from concerns over fairness: refusing to bribe when the other parents bribe leaves one's child at a disadvantage relative to the other children— bribing is a means to bridge the gap and close what may be perceived as an unfair advantage. In addition, high empirical expectations may alter each parent's risk perceptions in ways that accentuate the precarity of social cooperation, providing further reasons to choose risk dominance over payoff dominance. More specifically, when parents believe that most of the other parents will bribe, they perceive their chances of finding honest parents (as potential cooperators) are lower, and their chances of being exploited are higher. High empirical expectations mean that the strategic environment has low cooperation rates, thus making cooperation risky, in turn making salient the risk of exploitation. Exploitation aversion, which in this case is motivated both by the material incentives faced by each parent (exploitation is the worst-case scenario for any given parent) and by the general psychological desire that people generally have in not being exploited, would therefore provide further motivation to bribe rather than cooperate.

Thus whether parents end up at the low corruption equilibrium or become trapped in the high corruption equilibrium turns on their mutual empirical expectations, given the way these expectations shape their incentives and influence their risk environment. When empirical expectations are high, parents get trapped at the high corruption equilibrium, where honesty is costly relative to dishonesty, where the environment is non-cooperative, and where exploitation aversion is especially salient in strategic decision-making (given the risk of becoming "suckered" is high). By contrast, when empirical expectations are low, parents achieve coordination on the low corruption equilibrium, where dishonesty is relatively costlier than honesty, where the environment is generally cooperative, and where concerns over exploitation need not be as salient as the general expectation is that others will cooperate. Variation in the initial empirical expectations is decisive in determining whether a society becomes mired in its collective action problems (high corruption) or whether it creates the conditions in which it can successfully solve them (low corruption).

The Assurance Game presents a useful theoretical account of the strategic structure of the problem. But note that, as an empirical matter, the equilibrium forces that sustain the "bad" behavior at the high corruption equilibrium and the costs involved in moving to the low corruption equilibrium will vary from one practice to the next. This reflects the variety of reasons that motivate individuals to participate in the corruption, and the different incentives and constraints they face in abandoning old behaviors and adopting new ones. In many cases, empirical expectations are enough to sustain a corrupt practice. But in other cases, social norms prescribe or proscribe corrupt practices, meaning that normative expectations also have a role to play in behaviors related to corruption.

Consider the ways in which normative expectations surrounding corruption vary across high corruption and low corruption societies regarding petty bribery. In low corruption societies, corruption is by definition rare and widely condemned, and so there is harmony between low empirical expectations (e.g., "petty bribery is rare") and a supporting normative expectation (e.g., "I believe that others in my community believe that petty bribery is unacceptable"). Taken together, these expectations typically support a strong and widely followed social norm against petty bribery.

In high corruption societies, the situation is more complicated. Corruption is by definition common, and so people hold high empirical expectations about corrupt practices in general. But what about normative expectations? One mounting body of evidence suggests that people living under systemic corruption around the world (including high corruption societies in Africa, Latin America, and the post-Soviet states) widely condemn it (Krastev 2001; Karklins 2005; Persson, Rothstein and Teorell 2013; Rothstein 2021; Agerberg 2022). If this is right, and people generally hold accurate beliefs about the distribution of personal normative beliefs in their community, we might expect to find negative normative expectations across a range of corrupt practices, which would in turn imply a conflict between the empirical expectation (e.g., "petty bribery is common here") and the normative expectation ("I believe that others in my community believe that petty bribery is unacceptable"). If this were the case, this conflicting expectation would support a weak and routinely violated social norm against petty bribery which would, over time, give way to a descriptive norm supporting bribery. This is because when empirical and normative expectations conflict, empirical expectations dominate (Bicchieri and Xiao 2009), and high empirical expectations that conflict with the relevant normative expectation imply widespread transgressions of the norm, which undermines the prescriptive force of the conflicting normative expectations. Over time, this may undermine normative expectations to such an extent that they no longer hold any normative weight at all (Bicchieri 2016: 85).

Despite this mounting evidence, we still have good reasons to exercise caution in assuming widespread condemnation means universal condemnation of corruption for at least two reasons. First, social desirability concerns may be especially salient in this context given how normatively charged the phenomenon of corruption is and the sheer prevalence of anti-corruption messaging and programming in high corruption countries around the world today. Second, we should not assume that widespread condemnation of corruption *in general* translates neatly to negative normative expectations toward a corrupt practice *in particular*. While some practices seem to be universally condemned (e.g., petty bribery involving traffic law enforcement) (Hoffmann and Patel 2017), others seem to invite mixed evaluations (e.g., clientelistic vote buying) (Hoffmann and Patel 2022), and yet others are even seen in a positive light (e.g., petty bribery in healthcare) (Hoffmann and Patel 2017).

What explains this variation? The answers to this question are as diverse as the factors that might influence our normative evaluations. In some cases, context-specific features of the environment, such as who is being bribed, where the transaction is taking place, previous experience with the relevant actors involved, and so on, may influence our normative evaluations. In other cases, the relation in which one stands to the corrupt act or practice may influence our moral evaluations. In yet other cases, whether the proceeds from the corrupt act or practice produce shared social benefits (i.e., club or public goods) or if they are exclusively enjoyed privately may influence our normative evaluation, and so on. Whatever the causal story behind them is, the presence of normative expectations and the normative consensus they reflect are important for understanding the characteristics of corrupt practices.

In some cases, the very same transaction might invite positive or negative normative evaluations, as whether a transaction is coercive depends on the background expectations of the parties. For example, offering an individual a state job they were not expecting and do not believe they are entitled to in exchange for their political support may be viewed positively, as the "take-it-or-leave-it" offer adds another option to their available option set. But offering an individual a state job they believe they are already entitled to or were already expecting in exchange for political support may be viewed negatively, as the "or-else …" undertone underscores the coercive element to the transaction—rather than adding to their option set, the offer threatens to take away from it (Maris and Young 2016: 270). These two circumstances would look almost identical from the outside, even though one is coercive while the other is not. Variation in details such as these will naturally result in differing normative expectations toward the relevant practice.

Corrupt practices that are explicitly linked to the provision of social benefits may also invite more nuanced normative evaluations. These cases typically involve the provision of club or public goods or direction of funds toward an institution that has a mission goal of providing club or public goods (such as religious institutions, see Hoffmann and Patel 2021a). Cases like this are especially prevalent in high corruption democracies with clientelist political systems, as under these circumstances the provision of public goods occurs at the sole discretion of the corrupt political elite, who have incentives to supply them strategically in order to maximize chances of electoral victory. For instance, when a politician embezzles state funds which are then partly used to fund a local public good (such as a water treatment project for a village in their district), the initial embezzlement may not appear to be an instance of corruption, especially from the perspective of its beneficiaries. In these cases, whether people consider an action to be corrupt turns on the relationship between the evaluator and the instance of corruption they are evaluating (i.e., whether they are a beneficiary of the action, whether the person committing the act is a member of the in-group or out-group, and so on) (Hoffmann and Patel 2017: 21).

Sometimes normative expectations that are mutually consistent with empirical expectations produce social norms that *support* corrupt practices, such as social norms supporting extortion at traffic police checkpoints in Nigeria (Hoffmann and Patel 2017: 9). From the perspective of a corrupt police department, what appears to be extortion of motorists at a checkpoint externally may be a means to raise funds to finance a local public good or a club good internally, as when proceeds from extortion are pooled and used to pay tribute payments up the chain of command or to augment meager departmental funding.[3] If this is the case, then raising the funds presents a collective action problem for the officers because all officers in the department potentially benefit from the fund regardless of their contributions. While refusing to extort is honest behavior worthy of praise from an outsider's perspective, to the officers it is exploitative behavior worthy of derision, for honest officers are free riding on the cooperative efforts of others. This could explain why officers who refuse to participate invite such moralized vitriol from their fellow officers, such as being called "wicked," "evil," and "mean-spirited" (Hoffmann and Patel 2017: 11). Name-calling and other informal sanctions are intended to prevent free-rider behavior, and so we might think of the social norm as a solution to the collective action problem faced by the dishonest police department.

Before proceeding to the empirical section of the chapter, we note that all the examples mentioned above rely on the assumption that there is a fidelity between the objective consensus (i.e., what the community actually thinks as reflected by the aggregation of personal normative beliefs) and perceived consensus (what community members believe about the personal normative beliefs in their community). This is not a safe assumption in every case, as individuals often err in their estimation of the personal normative beliefs of their community. Disparities between an individuals' normative expectations and the actual prevalence of the personal normative beliefs in the community (the objective consensus) are especially prevalent with behaviors that are widespread but are not openly discussed. In situations like this, the gap between private beliefs and public behavior means that individuals may falsely infer that others in their community implicitly endorse a practice because they observe them participating in it, even if most community members hold negative personal normative beliefs toward it.

Corrupt practices—taboo subjects as they often are—lend themselves to precisely this kind of false inference, leading to perverse circumstances in which the majority of individuals privately reject a behavior but nonetheless falsely believe that the majority of others approve of it. This is an instance of a more general phenomenon called *pluralistic ignorance*, a cognitive state characterized by the belief that one thinks and believes differently than other similarly situated individuals do, even when public behavior is identical (Jackson and Kobis: 4). In this chapter, we use an expanded definition of pluralistic ignorance that focuses on the gap between normative and objective consensus, that is, the "perceived self-other distance" (Eisner et al. 2020, 26). We present a longer discussion of pluralistic ignorance in Section 4.

3. Methodology

This research uses data from two rounds of the Chatham House Africa Programme's Local Understandings, Expectations and Experiences survey, which involved 5,600 households across urban and rural areas in six of Nigeria's thirty-six federal states, namely: Adamawa, Benue, Enugu, Lagos, Rivers, and Sokoto and the capital city of Abuja. Implementation[4] was carried out through a test-run phase and pilot before the full roll-out from October to November 2016 and November to December 2018, respectively.

The survey implementation partner, National Bureau of Statistics (NBS), developed and recently updated its National Integrated Survey of Households (NISH) frame covering all thirty-six federal states in Nigeria and the Federal Capital Territory (FCT) of Abuja, with 200 Enumeration Areas (EAs)[5] per state and in FCT-Abuja. This NISH master sample frame was constructed out of the original master frame of the National Population Commission (NPC) for the Housing and Population Census of 2006, which established 23,280 EAs (30 EAs for each of Nigeria's 768 local government areas [LGAs] and 40 EAs for each of FCT-Abuja's six Area Councils). The 200 EAs that make up the NISH frame are grouped into twenty independent replicates with ten EAs in each replication. The Chatham House Africa Programme's Local Understandings, Expectations and Experiences survey of both 2016 and 2018 drew samples from the NISH frame of 200 EAs.

The demographic, sociocultural, economic, and political dynamics found in the surveyed states offer insights into shared beliefs and expectations of petty bribery in Nigeria, as well as uncovering local specificities. Overall, corruption is considered a widespread phenomenon in Nigeria and the country has maintained a very low ranking in Transparency International's Corruption Perception Index for its control of corruption (Transparency International 2022). Additionally, petty bribery transactions during routine interactions between citizens and public officials are a common and observable practice.

The survey data discussed in this chapter is one aspect of a larger instrument using social norms methodology that contained a series of survey questions[6] regarding their beliefs, understandings, experiences, and expectations about context-specific types of corruption. The sub-national locations of Adamawa, Benue, Enugu, Lagos, Rivers, and Sokoto states and the capital city of Abuja were selected for regional comparisons and to understand the relationship of beliefs about corruption and other contextual factors like poverty, conflict, religion, and gender.

4. Findings

a. Examination Malpractice

i) Personal Normative Beliefs and Social Expectations

Question: Do you think parents should pay for their children to receive a pass mark in a national exam?

Table 1.3 Personal Normative Beliefs

	Positive ("Yes," %)	Negative ("No," %)	Don't know (%)
Adamawa	8.6	90.8	0.6
Benue	6.9	92.2	0.9
Enugu	11.0	84.9	4.1
Lagos	7.1	92.2	0.8
Rivers	3.6	92.0	4.3
Sokoto	14.7	70.7	14.7
FCT-Abuja	6.9	88.3	4.8
Total	8.4	87.3	4.3

© Cristina Bicchieri, Raj Patel, and Leena Koni Hoffmann.

While the significant majority of respondents (87.3 percent) thought that parents should not participate in pass-mark bribery, a non-negligible minority (8.4 percent) thought that it was acceptable to do so.

Two states stand out in particular, with 11 percent of respondents in Enugu and 14.7 percent of respondents in Sokoto holding positive normative beliefs toward pass-mark bribery. Enugu and Sokoto also ranked among the lowest of all states for legal knowledge surrounding pass-mark bribery. Only 84.4 percent of respondents in Enugu and 62.6 percent of respondents in Sokoto thought that pass-mark bribery was illegal. This suggests that there may be ambiguity over the legality of pass-mark bribery in these states.

Question: Why do you think parents should pay for their children to receive a pass mark in a national exam? (Positive normative beliefs).

Question: Why do you think parents should not pay for their children to receive a pass mark in a national exam? (Negative normative beliefs).

Table 1.4 Reasons for Personal Normative Beliefs

	Positive normative beliefs (%)	Negative normative beliefs
Moral reasons	10.7	40.2
Practical reasons	77.3	52.4
Underfunded institution	5.7	0.9
Other	6.4	6.5

© Cristina Bicchieri, Raj Patel, and Leena Koni Hoffmann.

The majority of respondents (77.3 percent) who thought that parents should participate in pass-mark bribery did so for practical reasons. Practical reasons are reasons that appeal to the prudential consequences of a course of action, such as whether an action will help satisfy an immediate need for the agent. One often-cited practical justification for pass-mark bribery is that it closes the relative disadvantage an honest parent's child may have if a significant number of other parents are cheating. A minority of respondents (10.7 percent) thought that parents should participate in pass-mark bribery on moral grounds. Moral reasons are reasons that appeal to overarching normative principles which often motivate agents to act independently of what others do or think. One moral justification for pass-mark bribery is that it fulfills parents' moral obligation to ensure their children's success, even if doing so requires participating in unethical behavior.

A slim majority of respondents (52.4 percent) who thought that parents should not participate in pass-mark bribery did so for practical reasons. These respondents thought that parents should not participate in pass-mark bribery because the practice leads to undesirable outcomes, such as declining education standards or perverse incentive structures for students. A significant minority of respondents (40.2 percent) thought that parents should not participate in pass-mark bribery on moral grounds.

Question: Do you think parents should pay for their children to receive a pass mark in a national exam?

Question: Out of ten people in your community whose children attended a public secondary school last year, how many of them do you think paid for their children to receive a pass mark in a national exam? (Empirical expectation).

Question: Out of ten people in your community whose children attended a public secondary school last year, how many of them do you think said that the parents of a student should pay for their children to receive a pass mark in a national exam? (Normative expectation).

Table 1.5 Personal Normative Beliefs and Social Expectations

	Positive ("Yes," %)	Empirical expectations (average, %)	Normative expectations (average, %)
Adamawa	8.6	40	40
Benue	6.9	20	20
Enugu	11.0	40	40
Lagos	7.1	30	30
Rivers	3.6	20	20
Sokoto	14.7	10	10
FCT-Abuja	6.9	10	20

© Cristina Bicchieri, Raj Patel, and Leena Koni Hoffmann.

We found variation in empirical expectations across the states. Respondents in some states had relatively high empirical expectations; for example, respondents in Adamawa and Enugu thought that 40 percent of the parents in their community participated in pass-mark bribery within the last year. Respondents in the remaining states generally had lower empirical expectations. For example, respondents in Sokoto and FCT-Abuja thought that only 10 percent of the parents in their community participated in pass-mark bribery within the last year.

While there was a general congruence between empirical and normative expectations across all states, there was a disparity between respondents' personal normative beliefs and their normative expectations. In some states, the disparity was quite large. For example, respondents in Adamawa and Enugu thought that 40 percent of the people in their community held positive normative beliefs toward pass-mark bribery when in fact only 8.6 percent and 11 percent did so (respectively). In most of the other states, the disparity was smaller but still present. For example, respondents in Benue and Rivers thought that 20 percent of the people in their community held positive normative beliefs toward pass-mark bribery when in fact only 6.9 percent and 3.6 percent did so (respectively). Sokoto, however, is a notable exception in that there was a general parity between personal normative beliefs and normative expectations. Respondents in Sokoto thought that 10 percent of the people in their community held positive normative beliefs toward pass-mark bribery when in fact 14.7 percent of respondents did so.

The disparity between respondents' personal normative beliefs and their normative expectations suggests pluralistic ignorance. Pluralistic ignorance sometimes means that relatively unpopular behaviors appear more popular than they actually are as individuals mistakenly believe that others in their community hold positive normative beliefs toward the practice. Since normative expectations often imply the threat of informal sanctions, pluralistic ignorance may contribute to higher perceived costs of abandoning pass-mark bribery. We return to this theme in Section 5.

b. Conditionality Measures

Question: Given what X has learned, how likely do you think it is that X will pay for their children to receive a pass mark?

Table 1.6 Vignettes with Varying Social Expectations

	Low normative expectations	**High normative expectations**
Low empirical expectations	X has a child who attends a local public secondary school. X has learned that **very few** of the other parents at this school pay for their children to receive a pass mark in examinations and **very few** people in the community think that it is acceptable for parents to pay for their children to receive a pass mark in national examinations.	X has a child who attends a local public secondary school. X has learned that **very few** of the other parents at this school pay for their children to receive a pass mark in examinations and **almost all** people in the community think that it is acceptable for parents to pay for their children to receive a pass mark in national examinations.
High empirical expectations	X has a child who attends a local public secondary school. X has learned that **almost all** of the other parents at this school pay for their children to receive a pass mark in examinations and **very few** people in the community think that it is acceptable for parents to pay for their children to receive a pass mark in national examinations.	X has a child who attends a local public secondary school. X has learned that **almost all** of the other parents at this school pay for their children to receive a pass mark in examinations and **almost all** people in the community think that it is acceptable for parents to pay for their children to receive a pass mark in national examinations.

© Cristina Bicchieri, Raj Patel, and Leena Koni Hoffmann.

We measured whether pass-mark bribery was conditional on social expectations by manipulating empirical and normative expectations using four vignettes (see Table 1.6). Respondents were provided with a vignette that had one of the four possible conditions: (1) low empirical, low normative; (2) low empirical, high normative; (3) high empirical, low normative; and (4) high empirical, high normative. The four conditions were randomized such that respondents had an equal chance of receiving one of the conditions during survey administration. Respondents were then asked to assess the likelihood that the parent in the vignette would pay the bribe (under the particular empirical and normative expectation conditions they are presented with).

Table 1.7 Mean Probability of Bribery Given Varying Social Expectations

	Condition (1): Low empirical, low normative (probability)	Condition (2): Low empirical, high normative (probability)	Condition (3): High empirical, low normative (probability)	Condition (4): High empirical, high normative (probability)
Adamawa	0.49	0.58	0.66	0.73
Benue	0.44	0.53	0.62	0.69
Enugu	0.49	0.58	0.66	0.73
Lagos	0.53	0.62	0.70	0.77
Rivers	0.46	0.56	0.65	0.72
Sokoto	0.57	0.65	0.73	0.79
FCT-Abuja	0.51	0.60	0.69	0.76
Total	0.49	0.59	0.67	0.75

© Cristina Bicchieri, Raj Patel, and Leena Koni Hoffmann.

Table 1.7 presents the predictive probabilities from the vignettes. Our results suggest that while respondents condition the likelihood of bribe payment on both empirical and normative expectations, empirical expectations may be especially influential in pass-mark bribery.

In particular, we found relatively modest increases in the chances of bribe payment moving from low normative expectation conditions (1 and 3) to high normative expectation conditions (2 and 4). When respondents were presented with condition 1 (low empirical low normative), the chances of bribe payment were 49 percent. Chances of bribe payment increased by 10 percent in condition 2 (low empirical high normative) relative to condition 1. Similarly, chances of bribe payment increased by 8 percent in condition 4 (high empirical high normative) relative to condition 3 (high empirical low normative).

In contrast, we found relatively substantial increases in the chances of bribe payment moving from low empirical expectation conditions (1 and 2) to high empirical expectation conditions (3 and 4). Chances of bribe payment increased by 18 percent in condition 3 (high empirical low normative) relative to condition 1 (low empirical low normative). Similarly, chances of bribe payment increased by 16 percent in condition 4 (high empirical high normative) relative to condition 2 (low empirical high normative). The most substantial difference, however, was found between the two congruent social expectation conditions (4 and 1) in which the chance of bribe payment increased by 26 percent in condition 4 (high empirical high normative) relative to condition 1 (low empirical low normative). Notably, respondents predicted the highest chances for bribe payment under the two high empirical expectation conditions (3 and 4).

5. Discussion and Policy Implications

In this section, we limit our discussion to one of our central findings, that is, the presence of pluralistic ignorance, and speculate as to its broader significance for anti-corruption effort surrounding pass-mark bribery (but see Hoffmann and Patel 2021b for a broader discussion).

As we noted in Section 2, pluralistic ignorance is a situation in which the private beliefs of a group differ from the public beliefs that seem to be supported by group behavior. On our expanded definition, these are situations characterized by a discrepancy between the perceived consensus (reflected by group member's second-order normative expectations) and the objective consensus (reflected by their personal normative beliefs), often because people falsely infer that others do not think as they do, even when public behavior is identical. Across all states (except Sokoto), we found that respondents' normative expectations about the prevalence of positive normative beliefs toward pass-mark bribery (perceived consensus) systematically overestimated the actual prevalence of positive normative beliefs within the community (objective consensus) (see Table 1.5). In other words, respondents thought that there was a higher percentage of group members who held positive normative beliefs toward pass-mark bribery than was actually the case. The distance between perceived consensus and objective consensus was greatest in states where the behavior was perceived to be more frequent (i.e., where empirical expectations are high). Respondents in Adamawa and Enugu, for example, thought that almost half of their community were in favor of pass-mark bribery (when in fact only 8.6 percent and 11 percent were, respectively).

As noted in Section 2, pluralistic ignorance is not uncommon under conditions of systemic corruption. The ubiquity of corrupt practices provides fertile ground for individuals to falsely infer that those around them find corruption acceptable or desirable. This is true even with respect to practices that are universally condemned (e.g., pluralistic ignorance surrounding traffic law enforcement corruption [Hoffmann and Patel 2017, 12]). Pluralistic ignorance can impede anti-corruption efforts by raising the perceived costs of collective action or even making it seem infeasible. The belief that many of those around them find corruption acceptable or desirable may leave individuals with the impression that there are not enough likeminded individuals in their community with which they can cooperate to enact social change. Thinking that almost half of the parents in the community will participate in pass-mark bribery—as respondents in Adamawa and Enugu do—can be demoralizing, ultimately leading to a fatalism toward corruption and a sense of futility regarding the prospects of anti-corruption efforts.

It is also true that, over time, individuals tend to shift their private beliefs toward what they perceive to be the prevailing group consensus as a means to resolve the conflict between private beliefs and public behavior (Prentice and Miller 1993; Eisner et al. 2020). This may be because shifting one's private belief toward the perceive consensus is the most attractive option available. Attempting to change the group's opinion may appear to be an insurmountable task and rejecting the group entirely may be prohibitively costly, and both are inherently risky in general as they require revealing one's deviation from the group's consensus (Bjerring, Hansen, and Pedersen 2014).[7] This has the perverse consequence that, if left unchallenged, the perceived consensus may become the objective consensus even if widely unpopular. This concern may be particularly relevant in Adamawa and Enugu, where the gulf between normative expectations and personal normative beliefs is particularly wide.

Dispelling pluralistic ignorance is an important step toward creating the conditions under which collective efforts against corruption may be successful. One way to bridge the gap between perceived and actual consensus is through deliberation among the relevant community (e.g., the parents of a particular school or within a particular school district) (Bicchieri and Mercier 2014: 63; Bicchieri 2016: 155). Deliberation allows for open conversation on taboo subjects, exposing the participants to the group's true beliefs and thus to the widespread agreement amongst them. This would in effect expose the distance between perceived consensus and actual consensus, and shift normative expectations such that they are consistent with the personal normative beliefs of the community.

Deliberation can be risky, however, and care must be taken to structure the discussion. The effectiveness of deliberation rests on the ability of participants to speak openly about pass-mark bribery. But there may be conditions under which individuals will not feel free to do this. For example, participants in Adamawa and Enugu might feel reluctant to speak openly, given the implied polarization of the perceived consensus (40 percent approve of pass-mark bribery, suggesting that 60 percent disapprove of it).[8] Revealing one's private beliefs may appear to be a daunting task in this context as it would signal open disagreement with almost half of the room. Power dynamics may also undermine the effectiveness of deliberation, if, for example, those in less powerful social positions do not feel free to challenge the arguments from the more powerful social positions. In cases like this, deliberation may even backfire, as individuals may choose to publicly signal their commitment to a practice rather than reveal their true beliefs about it. The use of external agents, such as respected leaders, to facilitate and guide the discussion may help overcome these challenges, by ensuring that everybody has a chance to speak and is comfortable in voicing their opinions (Bicchieri 2016: 156).

Resolving pluralistic ignorance is particularly pertinent in cases where the relevant behavior is conditional on normative expectations (i.e., a social norm). Our conditionality measures show that pass-mark bribery is such a behavior, and it could be the case that there is a social norm of varying strength against pass-mark bribery across all of the states.[9] Even respondents in Adamawa and Enugu, where empirical expectations are high, could plausibly hold the following beliefs:

1. Personal normative belief: I believe parents should not bribe examination officials.
2. Normative expectation: I believe the majority of people in my reference network think that one should not bribe examination officials.
3. Empirical expectation: Most parents in my reference network do not bribe examination officials.

This set of beliefs, coupled with our finding that pass-mark bribery is conditional on social expectations, suggests that there is a social norm against bribery. If this is right, then dispelling pluralistic ignorance could be part of a broader strategy aimed at strengthening the social norm by, for example, lowering empirical expectations and creating the right normative expectations.

This may be particularly effective in states with high empirical and normative expectations (e.g., Adamawa, Enugu, and Lagos). In these states, social expectations suggest a weak norm that is not widely followed—supported by just over half of the community (60 percent) and violated by just under half of (40 percent). These social expectations verge on outright conflict, and we would expect the norm to become weaker over time were empirical expectations to rise. This is because of the ways in which rising empirical expectations shape incentives and have a self-fulling tendency through which persistent violations become widespread violations. As empirical expectations rise, they may further undermine normative expectations, even to the point where the norm loses its normative grip and normative expectations disappear. This would mark a transition from a social norm against pass-mark bribery into a descriptive norm that motivates it, as the new behavior would be conditional on high empirical expectations alone.

A strategy aimed at strengthening the norm in these states must also include interventions aimed at lowering empirical expectations. Behavior must change; otherwise normative expectations will consistently be undermined by perceptions of violations. Since these bribery transactions (in this context) are often done in secret, it is difficult for parents to directly observe a lower incidence of pass-mark bribery (and therefore update their empirical expectations accordingly). Indirect observation is imperfect at best, as one cannot conclude nefarious activity with much certainty from the fact that a child seemingly overperforms on an examination. In effect, parents need a coordination device so that they can coordinate on the low-corruption equilibrium of the Assurance Game described in Section 2. A social norm that effectively sanctioned violations would serve as a coordination device. Other tools, such as the use of public pledges, may also serve to coordinate expectations (Sally 1995).

6. Conclusion

The drastically different incentives that people face when under conditions of systemic corruption are in large part due to the relevant social expectations they hold. Understanding the characteristics of these social expectations, as well as the behavioral rules they give rise to, is therefore crucial in curbing corrupt practices. In this chapter, we introduced a framework—the social norms framework—that aims to render these invisible rules visible, with the ultimate aim of producing policy to curb such practices.

Notes

1. In this chapter, we use the terms "high corruption" and "systemic corruption" interchangeably. High corruption societies or conditions of systemic corruption refer to conditions in which corruption is so embedded into the social reality of everyday life that it is the expected action across a range of diverse circumstances and contexts.
2. In this section, our discussion of examination malpractice is theoretical. We return to an empirical discussion of the topic in Section 4.
3. There is some evidence that at least some proceeds from extortion are used in this way (see, e.g., https://www.bbc.com/news/world-africa-11001624).
4. The survey primarily used qualitative data collection methods with the support of a network of Nigeria-based researchers. The data presented in this chapter was collected during research activities conducted between September to December 2016 and October to December 2018. The survey teams were led by the following Nigeria-based researchers: Dr. Anthony Ajah of the University of Nigeria, Nsukka, Dr. Kemi Ogunyemi of the Pan-Atlantic University, Lagos, Professor Elizabeth Adebayo of the Modibbo Adama University of Technology, Yola, Dr. Tukur Baba and Dr. Sulaiman Kura of the Usmanu Danfodiyo University, Sokoto, Professor Euginia Member George-Genyi of the Benue State University, Makurdi, Dr. Tubodenyefa Zibima of the Stakeholder Democracy Network and Professor Daisy Onyige of University of Port Harcourt, Rivers, and Ms. Rakiya Mohammed of the National Bureau of Statistics.
5. Enumeration Areas (EAs) are geographic units demarcated for the purpose of data collection.
6. The survey questions in both 2016 and 2018 were translated and administered in the following languages: Yoruba, Igbo, Hausa, Tiv, Ikwere, Pidgin English, Fulfulde, Idoma, Igede, and Ogoni (Khana).
7. In strategic terms, just like players in an Assurance Game outlined in Section 2, individuals in a situation of pluralistic ignorance may prefer to capture the benefits of coordination rather than incur the costs of non-coordination, even if coordination happens on a suboptimal equilibrium (i.e., the perceived consensus).
8. This assumes that individuals take evaluation of normatively charged practices (such as pass-mark bribery) in binary terms (i.e., approve or disapprove). Strictly speaking, of course, this is not a valid inference, as the absence of minority approval does not prove the presence of majority disapproval. This is because these two options do not exhaust the possible stances one might take (one may be indifferent, for example). Nonetheless, given that pass-mark bribery raises explicitly moral questions (e.g., relating to fairness, obligations we have to our children, and so on), and its harmful consequences are social and pervasive (e.g., declining education standards leave everyone worse-off), it is reasonable to think that people would perceive evaluative judgments in these binary terms.
9. Further empirical investigation into the perceived consensus and whether the community would sanction violations would make this case stronger.

References

Agerberg, Mattias. 2022. "Messaging About Corruption: The Power of Social Norms." *Governance* 35, no. 3: 929–50.

Bicchieri, Cristina. 2006. *The Grammar of Society: The Nature and Dynamics of Social Norms*. Cambridge: Cambridge University Press.

Bicchieri, Cristina. 2016. *Norms in the Wild: How to Diagnose, Measure, and Change Social Norms*. Oxford: Oxford University Press.

Bicchieri, Cristina, and Carlo Rovelli. 1995. "Evolution and Revolution: The Dynamics of Corruption." *Rationality and Society* 7, no. 2: 201–24.

Bicchieri, Cristina, and John Duffy. 1997. "Corruption Cycles." *Political Studies* 45, no. 3: 477–95.

Bicchieri, Cristina, and Yoshitaka Fukui. 1999. "The Great Illusion: Ignorance, Informational Cascades, and the Persistence of Unpopular Norms." In *Experience, Reality, and Scientific Explanation*, 89–121. Dordrecht: Springer.

Bicchieri, Cristina, and Erte Xiao. 2009. "Do the Right Thing: But Only if Others Do So." *Journal of Behavioral Decision Making* 22, no. 2: 191–208.

Bicchieri, C., and Mercier, H. 2014. "Norms and Beliefs: How Change Occurs." *The Complexity of Social Norms*: 37–54.

Bjerring, J.C., Hansen, J.U., and Pedersen, N.J.L.L., 2014. "On the Rationality of Pluralistic Ignorance." *Synthese* 191: 2445–70.

Dixit, Avinash. 2018. "Anti-corruption Institutions: Some History and Theory." In *Institutions, Governance and the Control of Corruption*, 15–49. Cham: Palgrave Macmillan.

Eisner, L., D. Spini, and N. Sommet. 2020. "A Contingent Perspective on Pluralistic Ignorance: When the Attitudinal Object Matters." *International Journal of Public Opinion Research* 32, no. 1: 25–45.

Gambetta, Diego. 2000. "Can We Trust Trust." *Trust: Making and Breaking Cooperative Relations* 13, no. 1: 213–37.

Heywood, Paul M. 2017. "Rethinking Corruption: Hocus-Pocus, Locus and Focus." *Slavonic and East European Review* 95, no. 1: 21–48.

Hoffmann, Leena Koni, and Raj Navanit Patel. 2017. *Collective Action on Corruption in Nigeria: A Social Norms Approach to Connecting Society and Institutions*. London: Chatham House.

Hoffmann, Leena Koni, and Raj Navanit Patel. 2021a. *Collective Action on Corruption in Nigeria: The Role of Religion*. London: Chatham House.

Hoffmann, Leena Koni, and Raj Navanit Patel. 2021b. *Pass-mark Bribery in Nigerian Schools*. London: Chatham House.

Hoffmann, Leena Koni, and Raj Navanit Patel. 2022. *Vote-selling Behavior and Democratic Dissatisfaction in Nigeria: Is Democracy Really for Sale?*. London: Chatham House.

Jackson, David, and Nils Köbis. 2018. "Anti-corruption Through a Social Norms Lens." *U4 Issue* 7.

Klitgaard, Robert. 1988. *Controlling Corruption*. London, England: University of California Press.

Köbis, Nils C., Daniel Iragorri-Carter, and Christopher Starke. 2018. "A Social Psychological View on the Social Norms of Corruption." In *Corruption and Norms*, 31–52. Cham: Palgrave Macmillan.

Köbis, Nils C., et al. 2015. "'Who Doesn't?'—The Impact of Descriptive Norms on Corruption." *PloS one* 10, no. 6: e0131830.

Köbis, Nils C., et al. 2022. "Social Norms of Corruption in the Field: Social Nudges on Posters Can Help to Reduce Bribery." *Behavioural Public Policy* 6, no. 4: 597–624.

Köbis, Nils, Jean-François Bonnefon, and Iyad Rahwan. "Bad Machines Corrupt Good Morals." *Nature Human Behaviour* 5.6 (2021): 679–85.

Krastev, I. 2001. A Moral Economy of Anti-Corruption Sentiments in Transition (No. 008). wiiw Balkan Observatory Working Papers.

Krastev, Ivan. 2005. "Corruption, Anti-corruption Sentiments, and the Rule of Law." In *Rethinking the Rule of Law after Communism*, edited by A. Czarnota, M. Krygier and W. Sadurski, 323–41. Central European University Press.

Kubbe, Ina, and Annika Engelbert, eds. 2017. *Corruption and Norms: Why Informal Rules Matter*. Cham, Switzerland: Springer.

Mares, I., and Young, L. 2016. "Buying, Expropriating, and Stealing Votes." *Annual Review of Political Science* 19: 267–88.

Marquette, Heather, and Caryn Peiffer. 2015. "Collective Action and Systemic Corruption." ECPR Joint Sessions of Workshops, University of Warsaw 29.

Marquette, Heather, and Caryn Peiffer. 2018. "Grappling with the "Real Politics" of Systemic Corruption: Theoretical Debates Versus "Real-World" Functions." *Governance* 31, no. 3: 499–514.

Marquette, Heather, and Caryn Peiffer. 2019. "Thinking Politically About Corruption as Problem-Solving: A Reply to Persson, Rothstein, and Teorell." *Governance* 32, no. 4: 811–20.

Nichols, Philip M. 2003. "Corruption as an Assurance Problem." *Am. U. Int'l L. Rev.* 19: 1307.

Ostrom, E. 1998. "A Behavioral Approach to the Rational Choice Theory of Collective Action: Presidential Address, American Political Science Association, 1997." *American Political Science Review* 92, no. 1: 1–22.

Persson, Anna, Bo Rothstein, and Jan Teorell. 2013. "Why Anticorruption Reforms Fail—Systemic Corruption as a Collective Action Problem." *Governance* 26, no. 3: 449–71.

Persson, Anna, Bo Rothstein, and Jan Teorell. 2019. "Getting the Basic Nature of Systemic Corruption Right: A Reply to Marquette and Peiffer." *Governance* 32, no. 4: 799–810.

Prentice, D. A., and D. T. Miller. 1993. Pluralistic Ignorance and Alcohol Use on Campus: Some Consequences of Misperceiving the Social Norm." *Journal of Personality and Social Psychology* 64, no. 2: 243.

Rose-Ackerman, Susan. 1975. "The Economics of Corruption." *Journal of Public Economics* 4, no. 2: 187–203.

Rothstein, Bo. 2007. "Anti-Corruption—A Big Bang Theory." *QoG WORKING PAPER SERIES* 2007, no. 3: 3.

Rothstein, Bo. 2011a. "Anti-Corruption: The Indirect 'Big Bang' Approach." *Review of International Political Economy* 18, no. 2: 228–50.

Rothstein, Bo. 2011b. *The Quality of Government: Corruption, Social Trust, and Inequality in International Perspective*. Chicago: University of Chicago Press.

Rothstein, Bo. 2014. "What Is the Opposite of Corruption?." *Third World Quarterly* 35, no. 5: 737–52.

Rothstein, Bo. 2021. *Controlling Corruption: The Social Contract Approach*. USA: Oxford University Press.

Sally, D. 1995. "Conversation and Cooperation in Social Dilemmas: A Meta-Analysis of Experiments from 1958 to 1992." *Rationality and Society*, 7, no. 1: 58–92.

Skyrms, Brian. 2004. *The Stag Hunt and the Evolution of Social Structure*. New York: Cambridge University Press.

2

Rules, Risk, and Agreement

Justin P. Bruner

1. Introduction

What does it mean to divide fairly? We consider the simple case where several indivisible items must be allocated to two individuals. While our claimants may not value items similarly, the parties are otherwise symmetrically situated: neither party is particularly needy, and goods are manna from heaven (i.e., no individual is any more deserving than her counterpart). How should items be distributed in such a case? One popular approach begins with a *fairness rule*, a procedure or algorithm that determines how to allocate the various goods to our two claimants. *Normative criteria* are then invoked to compare different fairness rules. For instance, some rules (see Section 3) satisfy the envy-free criterion (Foley 1967), meaning the division selected by the rule is one where no individual believes their share is worse than the share of any other agent.[1] Prior work has compared fairness rules and explored the logical relationship between normative criteria (Young 1995; Brams, Edelman, and Fishburn 2001).

Our goal in this chapter is to outline and develop an alternative approach to the study of fair division (and normative economics more generally) that draws inspiration from the social contract tradition. Briefly, contractarians take the ideal rules, principles, or institutions to be those rules, principles, or institutions rational individuals would agree to in certain circumstances (Rawls 1971; D'Agostino, Gaus, and Thrasher 2011; Moehler 2018; 2020; Thrasher 2019). We use this contractarian model and a series of computer simulations to explore the problem of fair division and uncover that a somewhat overlooked fairness rule—maximum Nash welfare—receives ample support. Furthermore, we explore the fragility of agreement and consider whether consensus still exists when individuals have different attitudes toward risk and, alternatively, have drastically different beliefs about the extent to which their interests overlap. We find that agreement is not undermined, and the maximum Nash welfare rule continues to secure broad support.

We proceed as follows. In Section 2 we more rigorously introduce the fair division problem. We additionally motivate and expound upon our contractarian approach. In Section 3 we introduce five canonical fair division rules and outline a simple computer simulation which is then explored in detail in Section 4, and Section 5 concludes.

2. Fair Division and Agreement

For our purposes, a fair division problem involves g indivisible goods that must be allocated in some fashion to n parties.[2] We consider the simplest case where $n = 2$ and there are always more contested items than claimants ($g > 2$). Furthermore, it is not possible for individuals to share goods and cash transfers between parties are prohibited.[3] We provide a simple example involving six indivisible items and two claimants, Aiko and Bing. Below we introduce utility functions[4] for Aiko and Bing.

Table 2.1 Fair Division Problem Involving Six Items and Two Individuals (Aiko and Bing)

	1	2	3	4	5	6
Aiko's utility	0.87	0.92	0.64	0.67	0.10	0.05
Bing's utility	0.12	0.24	0.79	0.31	0.84	0.52

© Justin P. Bruner.

An allocation is represented as a vector: (124, 356) refers to the division where items 1, 2 and 4 are allocated to Aiko and the remaining three items to Bing. Note that this allocation ensures both Aiko and Bing receive their most-preferred items, and as a result this allocation is envy-free: Aiko prefers her share to Bing's share and vice versa. (12, 3456) and (134, 256) are also envy-free allocations. An envy-free fairness rule could implement any of the above divisions. Another popular normative criterion is the *maximin share* criterion (Budish 2011). Aiko's *maximin value* is the maximum value she can secure if for each way of partitioning g items she takes the share of lesser value. A fairness rule is said to satisfy the maximin share criterion if it always selects an allocation that ensures all individuals receive a share whose value is no less than their maximin value.

As mentioned, these criteria (and many others) are routinely appealed to when assessing and comparing fairness rules. As one might expect, trade-offs exist, and no fairness rule satisfies all sensible criteria (we discuss this more in Section 3, and Bouveret et al. (2016) provide a helpful overview). One must then weigh the importance of different criteria. Unfortunately, this is a matter of great controversy. In this sense, fair division is similar to related areas in normative economics (such as bargaining and voting theory) where disagreement over the importance of various criteria explains long-standing disagreement as to which rule is best.[5]

In this chapter we do not invoke some normative criterion but instead appeal to a notion familiar to those in the social contract tradition: agreement. That is, we consider which fairness procedure rational and self-interested individuals would agree to. Yet agreement is hard to come by because self-interested parties will likely endorse whichever procedure benefits them in the current case. How, then, can agreement be achieved? Consider this somewhat fanciful example.

Tomb Raiders

Indiana and Lara are world-trotting treasure hunters. After years of fierce rivalry, the two decide to partner up. To ease tension, they want to lay down rules that dictate how they will divvy up rare artifacts retrieved during their expeditions (rules are enforced by a third party: Sean C., Indiana's estranged—and thus impartial—father). Each excursion is shrouded in mystery: it is unclear how many valuable items they will recover, nor can they predict whether they will unearth jewelry, scrolls or something else entirely.

What is distinctive about this scenario is that Indiana and Lara must agree to an allocation rule under conditions of ignorance. Moreover, the chosen procedure is to be applied not just to their next trip but to all future excursions. In light of this uncertainty, it is sensible to think that Indiana and Lara are able to agree to the same fairness rule. This familiar line of thought is found in James Buchanan and Gordon Tullock's discussion of the so-called veil of uncertainty.[6] Deprived of vital information, our rational and self-interested treasure hunters will endorse rules "that maximize utility in a series of collective decisions with their own preferences [...] being more or less randomly distributed" (1962, 78).[7] Rawls, in an early articulation of what would eventually become the veil of ignorance, has a similar approach. In his 1958 article he considers choice of principle where each individual understands the principle is "binding of future occasions" and thus individuals will be wary of proposing a principle that is to their immediate advantage because he will be "bound by it in future circumstances the peculiarities of which cannot be known, and which might well be such that the principle is then to his disadvantage" (1958, 171).

One common worry is that agreement is fragile and will only occur in highly idealized circumstances. For instance, the parties may fail to agree on a rule because they have different risk attitudes. Moreover, individuals may have different beliefs regarding the consequences of adopting various rules. As Buchanan himself acknowledges, "once subjectivity is allowed," the individuals may fail to come to a consensus and instead endorse "alternative institutions or rules." Worries surrounding the possibility of dissensus, of course, go well beyond Buchanan's specific model of the social contract and extend to the writings of Gauthier, Harsanyi, Rawls, and other contract theorists. Harsanyi's argument for utilitarianism, for example, is predicated on the assumption that individuals have identical empathetic preferences. In Section 4, we find that consensus is achieved in nonideal circumstances. Thus, our results suggest that the contractarian approach is more resilient than previously thought.

3. Fairness Rules and Simulation Set-up

In this section we introduce our fairness rules. Out of necessity, we limit the menu of rules to just those procedures that have garnered significant attention in the literature. A more exhaustive analysis is a task for a later date. We then describe the set-up of our computer simulation.

As a way of brief overview, we consider five fairness procedures. As will become clear, these rules vary in several respects. Some require a cardinal utility function, while others only demand an ordinal ranking of items. Many fairness rules are decentralized in the sense that they can easily be implemented by the claimants themselves. Others are computationally demanding and may require the involvement of a central planner or an arbitrator. Either way, these rules specify how indivisible goods are allocated to individual claimants. We briefly outline each and discuss their normative properties.

To demonstrate our first procedure, the **descending demand rule** (Herreiner and Puppe, 2002), we return to the example from Section 2. Consider Aiko and Bing's ranking of possible shares, from best to worst. The best share for Aiko is (123456)—that is, she secures all of the contested objects. The second-best share for Aiko is (12345), third-best is (12346), and so on. Let a share's "rank" be the number of steps it is above Aiko's least preferred share (the null set) in her ordinal ranking of shares. Descending demand selects the allocation that maximizes the rank of the share held by the worse-off agent.[8] This fairness rule is efficient (it always returns a pareto efficient allocation). It is also considered to be egalitarian in flavor as it maximizes the position (rank) of the worse-off individual.

Unlike descending demand, the **maximum Nash welfare rule** (MNW) requires more than just an ordinal ranking of possible shares. Both agents disclose their cardinal utility function and the allocation with the greatest Nash welfare is selected, where Nash welfare is the product of the agents' utilities. Thus, MNW is analogous to the Nash solution from axiomatic bargaining theory (Nash 1953). MNW has a number of desirable properties (Caragiannis et al. 2019). In addition to efficiency, it satisfies the maximin share criterion (Section 2).[9] Furthermore, although MNW does not satisfy the envy-free criterion, MNW does satisfy the somewhat weaker "envy-free up to one good" criterion.[10] For a better handle on MNW and the division it recommends, briefly consider related work in bargaining theory. The Nash solution holds a prominent place in axiomatic bargaining theory, and Shiran Rachmilevitch (2016) has shown that the Nash solution strikes a balance between the utilitarian and egalitarian divisions, lying somewhere between these arrangements on the pareto frontier. Moreover, Geoffroy de Clippel (2007) proved the Nash solution ensures each participant at least one half of their maximum possible utility.

The most intuitive fairness rules we consider are **Strict Alternation** (SA) and **Balanced Alternation** (BA). Both are examples of a "picking sequence rule" (Brams and Taylor 2000). These rules select an allocation by simulating a sequence of moves made by the parties. Agents claim items for themselves in a predetermined order (known as a picking sequence). One natural picking sequence is "strict alteration." Under SA, Aiko claims an item, then Bing makes a claim, and so on until there are no more unclaimed objects.[11] In other words, SA involves a kind of turn taking. Note, however, that as the first mover, Aiko has a distinct advantage. BA attempts to correct for this. Consider a division problem involving four items. If in the first two moves of the sequence Aiko gets "first pick" (Aiko-Bing), then in the latter two moves of the sequence Bing should get "first pick" (Bing-Aiko). The sequence is thus Aiko-Bing-Bing-Aiko. As Steven Brams puts it, BA ensures the parties "take turns taking turns." This logic can easily be extended to cases involving more than four items, meaning our claimants "take turns taking turns taking turns" and so on. When eight items are in dispute, for example, BA implements the following picking sequence: Aiko-Bing-Bing-Aiko-Bing-Aiko-Aiko-Bing.[12]

Although intuitive, neither SA nor BA ensures the selection of an envy-free allocation. While this is a limitation, the virtue of picking sequence rules is their simplicity and the ease with which they can be implemented in the absence of a social planner or referee.

Finally, the **undercut method** is the most complicated procedure we consider and begins with both claimants announcing their most preferred item (Brams, Kilgour, and Klamler 2012). If these items are distinct, both claimants receive their desired object. If they desire the same item, the object goes into the "contested pile" (CP). This continues until all objects are either owned by an agent or are placed in the CP. If there are no objects in the CP, the procedure terminates. If the CP is non-empty, one agent proposes a division of the CP. Her counterpart must accept the proposal or "undercut" the offer. This method of dividing the CP is the discrete analogue of the popular divide-and-choose cake-cutting protocol (Brams and Taylor 1996) and Brams, Kilgour, and Klamler prove that under certain conditions there is an envy-free split of the CP.

With all five fairness rules on the table, we now turn to the question of which rule rational agents would agree to. As discussed in Section 2, individuals are interested in selecting the fairness rule that maximizes expected utility over a series of interactions. Importantly, claimants do not know crucial details relating to the fair division problem. That is, agents do not know which items are on offer and how desirable said items are. We consider L evenly spaced utility levels. Our g indivisible items are then each placed at a particular utility level. We rule out the case of indifference, meaning there are a total of possible ways to order g indivisible goods, each of which correspond to a different cardinal utility function. In the case of $g = 3$ and $L = 10$ there are a total of 720 possible utility functions. We assume that behind the veil individuals take all utility functions to be equally likely.[13] Furthermore, we assume independence: that is, the valuations for both agents are determined by independent draws from a uniform distribution over the space of all utility functions. In Section 4.2 we relax the independence assumption and allow for cases where individuals frequently have (dis)similar rankings of goods.

Parties now have enough information to determine the average expected utility associated with each of our five fairness rules. Before we discuss our findings, a quick word about interpersonal utility comparisons. For our purposes, interpersonal comparisons are unnecessary: the fairness procedures in question do not require such comparisons, and each claimant is purely concerned with *her* utility across a series of interactions. So, in this sense, the problem we explore here is different from that of the typical utilitarian social planner. This is an important way in which our approach differs from recent work in the social contract tradition (Binmore 2005; Vanderschraaf 2018).

4. Results

In this section we introduce and discuss our main findings. We see that MNW secures the highest expected utility and, somewhat surprisingly, claimants agree to the same rule under a variety of different conditions.

4.1 General Results

We determine the expected utility for five different fairness procedures (MNW, undercut, descending demand, SA, BA) for $g = 3, 4, 5, 6, 7, 8$. Results are displayed in Figure 2.1. For each value of g we generate 100,000 fair division problems. For ease of comparison, we consider for each rule the payoff an individual receives across the 100,000 fairness problems. We then consider the ratio of this number to the sum of the maximum possible payoff (i.e., the payoff the agent secures if they receive all of the contested items) across all 100,000 division problems. We observe that for all five fairness methods, the ratio of total actual payoff to maximum payoff is greater than 0.5, meaning the claimants on average receive more than half of the value of the set of contested items. Individuals secure greater than half the value of the set on average because they and their counterpart do not always value items in a similar fashion. Furthermore, as the number of contested items increases, individuals secure an increasingly larger fraction of the maximum payoff.

The fairness rule with the highest expected utility is maximum Nash welfare. In some sense this is not too surprising because MNW maximizes the product of utilities. The descending demand protocol also does rather well, beating out all picking procedures and the undercut method. As mentioned, the descending demand protocol is egalitarian in spirit because it maximizes the ordinal rank of the bundle held by the worse-off agent. It is therefore somewhat surprising that descending demand does so well.

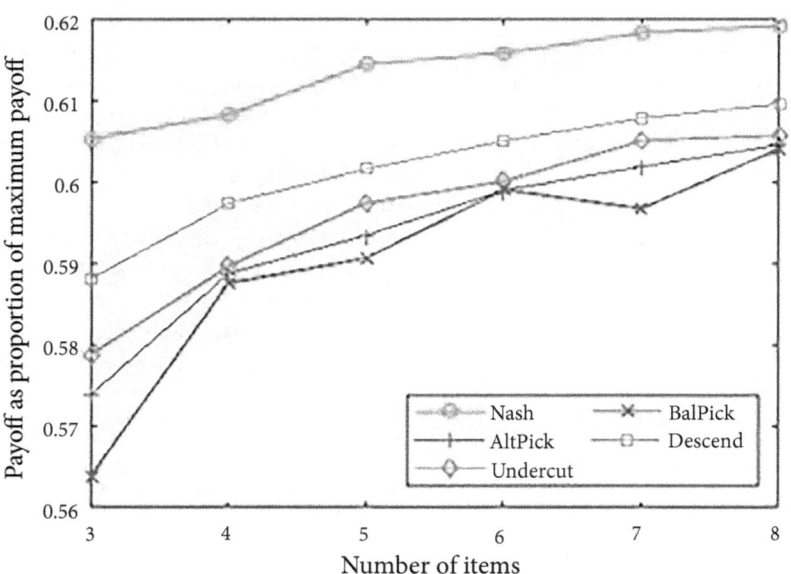

Figure 2.1 Expected utility and fairness rules. © Justin P. Bruner.

4.2 Correlation

We have assumed valuations are randomly assigned to both agents. Yet this is somewhat unrealistic. Our intrepid treasure hunters from Section 2 may have identical tastes (both value jewelry), or they may possess preferences that nicely complement those of their partner (Lara prefers runes, Indiana prefers jewelry). Moreover, Lara and Indiana could have different subjective beliefs about the extent to which their interests overlap. Lara may think she and Indiana are similar, while Indiana may believe that the two treasure hunters have different preferences.[14] We consider such scenarios in this

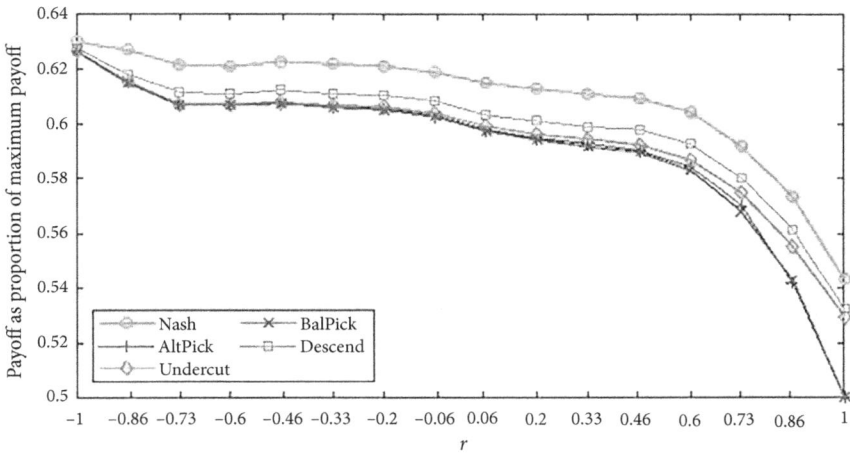

Figure 2.2 Expected utility and fairness procedures for various correlation levels (six items). © Justin P. Bruner.

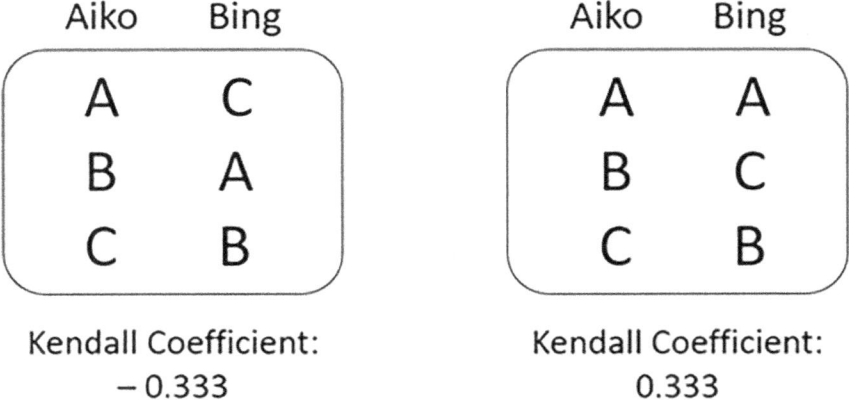

Figure 2.3 Two preference profiles and corresponding Kendall coefficient score. © Justin P. Bruner.

section and find that despite these complications, Lara and Indiana still find MNW to be the most attractive rule.

To begin, we quantify the similarity between the claimants' ordinal rankings. To do so, we use the Kendall rank correlation coefficient. This popular measure is calculated by taking the total number of concordant pairs, subtracting from this the total number of discordant pairs, and then dividing by the total number of distinct pairs (see Figure 2.3 for an example). When ordinal rankings are similar, the Kendall coefficient is high (and the coefficient is 1 in the case of identical rankings). The Kendall coefficient is negative when orderings are dissimilar.

Individuals do the worst when they have identical ordinal rankings and best when the Kendall coefficient is strongly negative (Figure 2.2).[15] This relationship is expected: if claimants have complementary tastes, then both agents are likely to receive those items they value most highly. Somewhat surprisingly, the analysis from Section 4.1 remains relatively unchanged. MNW secures the highest expected utility and does so for all possible Kendall coefficient values. Parties agree to the same fairness rule even though some may anticipate that they and their counterpart have near-identical valuations of the contested items, while others expect that they and their counterpart do not have the same preference ordering. Furthermore, the ordering of fairness rules by expected utility we uncovered in the past section (MNW, descending demand, undercut, SA, BA) holds for all Kendall coefficient values.

4.3 Risk-Aversion and Rules

Relatedly, one may worry that agreement is not possible if some claimants are risk averse while others are risk neutral. A risk-averse agent may find descending demand to be an attractive rule because it ensures that the rank of the share held by the worse-off individual is maximized.[16] A risk-neutral agent, on the other hand, will be drawn to MNW.

To address these concerns, we draw on rank-dependent expected utility theory (REU), a generalization of expected utility theory (EU).[17] REU has recently received substantial attention in the philosophical literature and is a simple framework we can use to determine whether consensus is achieved when claimants have different risk attitudes. According to EU, the *expected utility* of a gamble is the sum of utilities for all outcomes weighted by the probability those outcomes obtain. Under REU, the probability weighting depends not only on the probability of the outcome but additionally on the outcome's *rank*, where rank refers to the outcome's position in the overall lottery (Quiggin 1982; Buchak 2013). In some versions of REU (such as Lara Buchak's risk-weighted expected utility theory), the agent is represented as having not only a utility and probability function but also a special risk function that captures the "tradeoffs they are willing to make in the face of risk" (Buchak 2014: 1,110). Risk-averse individuals are more concerned with what happens in worse outcomes than better outcomes, while risk-inclined individuals put more weight on better outcomes.

In a recent article, Buchak contends that a rank-dependent expected utility maximizer will endorse the so-called Gini social welfare function (SWF) behind Harsanyi's version of the veil of ignorance (Buchak 2017).[18] The Gini SWF is a sub-

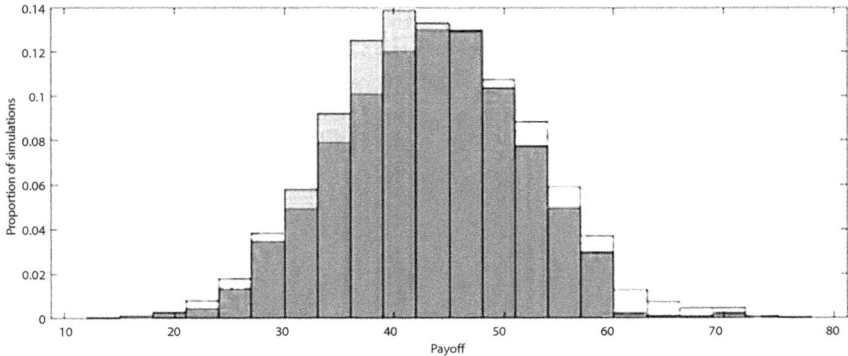

Figure 2.4 Distribution of individual payoff for MNW (white) and descending demand (light gray). For $g = 6$, $L = 21$ and 1,000 fair division problems. © Justin P. Bruner.

family of a larger class of functions known as rank-weighted functions. Rank-weighted SWFs sum individual utilities subject to a vector of decreasing weights.[19] Returning to our treasure hunters, Indiana is now an REU maximizer. He does not know vital information about the fair division problem and selects a fair division rule that maximizes his rank-dependent expected utility given this uncertainty. This is akin to selecting the society-wide distribution of welfare which maximizes the Gini SWF, where each citizen is Indiana confronted by a different fair division problem.

Which fairness rule would an REU maximizer select? Descending demand may strike Indiana as especially appealing because an REU maximizer is concerned with worse outcomes. Somewhat surprisingly, MNW still does best. To see why, consider Figure 2.4, which compares the two fairness rules. MNW often produces extreme outcomes: MNW is more likely than descending demand to generate bad outcomes, and MNW is significantly more likely than descending demand to lead to better outcomes. Additionally, note that MNW and descending demand are equally likely to produce *extremely* bad outcomes. As a result, a risk-averse agent will be drawn to MNW. Although our treasure hunters may have different risk attitudes, they nonetheless agree to use MNW.

5. Concluding Remarks

The traditional approach to fair division begins with several sensible normative criteria, and disagreement over the relative importance of said criteria explains long-standing disagreement over fairness rules. We outline a new approach which places agreement front and center. We consider self-interested individuals faced with a recurring class of problems and ask what rule they find most attractive. Of course, consensus is unlikely if our agents have prior knowledge of the fair division problem. Instead, we assume the future is hazy and individuals must maximize in light of this uncertainty. We find that behind the veil of uncertainty the maximum Nash welfare rule is endorsed.

Moreover, this chapter suggests that the contractarian approach is more versatile and robust than previously thought. As we have seen, models of agreement from the social contract tradition can be brought to bear on fair division problems, and there is no reason to think the contractarian approach cannot be extended to other areas of normative economics such as bargaining[20] or voting theory. Furthermore, we've seen that agreement is by no means fragile. Participants endorse the same fairness rule even though they have different attitudes and beliefs. Agreement is possible when the veil is translucent.

Notes

1. Note that there need not always exist an envy-free allocation, so a rule is said to satisfy the envy-free criterion if it selects an envy-free allocation should one exist.
2. Lang and Rothe (2016) provide accessible introductions to fair division problems.
3. These two assumptions are typically made in the literature.
4. Throughout we assume utility functions are *additive*. A utility function is said to be additive if the utility of a set of items is equal to the sum of the utilities of each item separately. Additivity is a common assumption in the fair division literature and rules out interdependencies between objects.
5. See Don Saari and Matthias Risse's debate over the importance of two conditions that underlie the Borda count in social choice theory (Risse 2005; Saari 2006). In bargaining theory, consider the debate over the normative significance of the IIA condition (Braithwaite 1955; Gauthier 1986; Young 1995; Moehler 2018).
6. For a discussion of the differences between Rawls and Buchanan, see Thrasher and Gaus (2015). See Mueller (2003, 617–19) as well as Thrasher and Gaus (2017) for more on the veil of uncertainty.
7. One might wonder how this squares with a famous paper by M. E. Yaari and M. Bar-Hillel (Yaari and Hillel 1984), which finds that experimental subjects tend to support divisions corresponding to the maximin division (and thus will not, as Buchanan and Tullock suggest, be drawn to utility-maximizing arrangements). Interestingly, more recent experimental work (Herne and Mard 2008) has established that egalitarian principles are more likely to be supported when subjects are asked to select principles that govern the affairs of others (as the experiments in Yaari and Hillel do). Experiments more directly investigating behavior behind the veil, however, by and large indicate that individuals select utilitarian principles (Frohlich and Oppenheimer 1993; Bruner 2018).
8. In particular, Herreiner and Puppe (2002) provide a decentralized procedure two individuals can implement that will identify the allocation that maximizes the rank of the share held by the worse-off agent.
9. Specifically, MNW always satisfies the maximin share criterion for two claimants. If more than two claimants are involved, the MNW satisfies a weaker version of the maximin share criterion.
10. This means that while Aiko can envy Bing, envy dissipates if we remove one good from Bing's share (Lipton et al. 2004).
11. The first mover is determined by a flip of a coin. Also, these picking sequence rules simulate a process where individuals are "unsophisticated" in the sense that they simply pick the best item on offer.

12 In the case of three or six items, we use a truncated version of the longer picking sequence (Aiko-Bing-Bing and Aiko-Bing-Bing-Aiko-Bing-Aiko, respectively).
13 In other words, the claimants are deprived crucial knowledge of the fair division problem, such as what items are up for dispute and the value of said items. This is equivalent to them not "knowing their utility function."
14 Moreover, this section and the next push back against a common criticism made against the contractarian, namely, that the modeling assumptions underlying the veil reduces the situation to that of an individual choice, moving us away from a group of individuals tasked to iron out an agreement (see, for instance, Hampton 1980). Yet as we shall see, we can allow for real differences between the agents behind the veil and still recover agreement on fairness rule.
15 The dataset used to produce this figure is the same data set used to generate Figure 2.1. For each simulation we conducted for Figure 2.1, we calculate the Kendall correlation coefficient and then reorganize the dataset to highlight the relationship between correlation coefficient and expected payoff.
16 There is now a large literature exploring risk-aversion and agreement. For recent contributions see Buchak (2017), Stefánsson (2021), and Nebel (2020). Much criticism has been levied at Rawls for purportedly assuming that individuals are infinitely risk averse (for a recent example, see Jehle and Reny 2011). Yet Rawls himself is explicit: individuals are not swayed by "special psychologies [and] are not moved by such desires and inclinations" (JF, 108). For more on Rawls and the criticisms he received for using nonstandard decision theory, see Moehler (2018).
17 Note that under standard EU theory agents with different risk attitudes behave in identical ways when choosing a fairness rule because standard EU theory does not allow individuals to have different preference over the global properties of gambles (Buchak 2013).
18 The Gini SWF is considered by some to be egalitarian in flavor (Adler 2019) because the welfare of those at the low end of the distribution are given substantially more weight than their better-off peers (although see Buchak, 2017, who classifies the Gini SWF as a prioritarian SWF). Since a risk-averse REU maximizer is more concerned with what happens in worse outcomes than better outcomes, it is no surprise that such an agent favors the Gini SWF.
19 See chapters 3 and 4 of Adler (2019) for more on rank-weighted SWFs.
20 For work in this direction, see Pivato (2009).

References

Adler, M. 2019. *Measuring Social Welfare: An Introduction*. New York: Oxford University Press.

Binmore, K. 2005. *Natural Justice*. New York: Oxford University Press.

Bouveret, S., Y. Chevaleyre, and N. Maudet. 2016. "Fair Allocation of Indivisible Goods." In *Handbook of Computational Social Choice*, edited by F. Brandt, V. Conitzer, U. Endriss, J. Lang, and A. Procaccia. New York: Cambridge University Press.

Braithwaite, R. 1955. *Theory of Games as a Tool for the Moral Philosopher*. Cambridge: Cambridge University Press.

Brams, S., and A. Taylor. 1996. *Fair Division: From Cake Cutting to Dispute Resolution*. Cambridge: Cambridge University Press.

Brams, S., and A. Taylor. 2000. *The Win-Win Solution: Guaranteeing Fair Shares to Everybody*. New York: Norton.

Brams, S., D. Kilgour, and C. Klamler. 2012. "The Undercut Procedure: An Algorithm for the Envy-Free Division of Indivisible Items." *Social Choice and Welfare* 39: 615–31. https://doi.org/10.1007/s00355-011-0599-1.

Brams, S., P. Edelman, and P. Fishburn. 2001. "Paradoxes of Fair Division." *Journal of Philosophy* 98, no. 6: 300–14.

Bruner, Justin. 2018. "Decisions Behind the Veil." In *Oxford Studies in Experimental Philosophy*, vol. II. Oxford: Oxford University Press.

Buchak, Lara. 2013. *Risk and Rationality*. Oxford: Oxford University Press.

Buchak, Lara. 2014. "Risk and Tradeoffs." *Erkenntnis* 79: 1091–117.

Buchak, Lara. 2017. "Taking Risks Behind the Veil of Ignorance." *Ethics* 127: 610–44.

Buchanan, James M., and Gordon Tullock. 1962. *The Calculus of Consent*. Ann Arbor: University of Michigan Press.

Budish, Eric. 2011. "The Combinatory Assignment Problem: Approximate Competitive Equilibrium from Equal Incomes." *Journal of Political Economy* 119, no. 6: 1061–103.

Caragiannis, I., D. Kurokawa, H. Mouolin, A. Procaccia, N. Shah, and J. Wang. 2019. "The Unreasonable Fairness of Maximum Nash Welfare." *ACM Transactions on Economics and Computation* 7, no. 3.

de Clippel, G. 2007. "An Axiomatization of the Nash Bargaining Solution." *Social Choice and Welfare* 29: 201–10.

D'Agostino, F., G. Gaus, and J. Thrasher. 2011. "Contemporary Approaches to the Social Contract." In *The Stanford Encyclopedia of Philosophy*, edited by Edward N. Zalta (Winter 2011 ed.).

Foley, Duncan. 1967. "Resource Allocation and the Public Sector." *Yale Econ Essays* 7, no. 1: 45–98.

Frohlich, N., and J. Oppenheimer. 1993. *Choosing Justice: An Experimental Approach to Ethical Theory*. Berkeley: University of California Press.

Gauthier, D. 1986. *Morals by Agreement*. Oxford: Oxford University Press.

Hampton, J. (1980) Contracts and choices: Does Rawls have a social contract theory? *The Journal of Philosophy*, 77(6): 315–338.

Harsanyi, John. 1977. "Morality and the Theory of Rational Behavior." *Social Research* 44, no. 4.

Herne, K., and T. Mard. 2008. "Three Versions of Impartiality: An Experimental Investigation." *Homo Oeconomicus*, 25: 27–53.

Herne, K. and M. Suojanen. 2004. "The Role of Information in Choices over Income Distributions." *Journal of Conflict Resolution* 48, no. 2: 173–93.

Herreiner, D., and C. Puppe. 2002. "A Simple Procedure for Finding Equitable Allocations of Indivisible Goods." *Social Choice and Welfare* 19, no. 2: 415–30.

Jehle, G. A., and P. J. Reny. 2011. *Advanced Microeconomic Theory*. 3rd edition. Essex: Pearson.

Lang, J., and J. Rothe. 2016. "Fair Division of Indivisible Goods." In *Economics and Computation*, edited by J. Rothe. Heidelberg: Springer Berlin.

Lipton, R. J., E. Markakis, E. Mossel, and A. Saberi. 2004. On approximately fair allocations of indivisible goods. In Proceedings of the 6th ACM Conference on Economics and Computation (EC'04). 125–31.

Moehler, M. 2018. *Minimal Morality: A Multilevel Social Contract Theory*. Oxford: Oxford University Press.

Moehler, M. 2020. *Contractarianism*. Cambridge: Cambridge University Press.

Mueller, D. 2003. *Public Choice III*. Cambridge: Cambridge University Press.

Muldoon, R., C. Lisciandra, M. Colyvan, et al. "Disagreement Behind the Veil of Ignorance." *Philos Stud* 170: 377–94. https://doi.org/10.1007/s11098-013-0225-4.

Nash, J. 1953. "Two-Person Cooperative Games." *Econometrica* 21: 128–40.

Nebel, J. 2020. "Rank-Weighted Utilitarianism and the Veil of Ignorance." *Ethics* 131: 87–106.
Pivato, Marcus. 2009. "Twofold Optimality of the Relative Utilitarian Bargaining Solution." *Social Choice and Welfare* 32: 79–92.
Quiggin, J. 1982. "A Theory of Anticipated Utility." *Journal of Economic Behavior and Organization* 3(4): 323–343.
Rachmilevitch, S. 2015. "The Nash Solution Is More Utilitarian than Egalitarian." *Theory Decis* 79: 463–78.
Rachmilevitch, S. 2016. "Egalitarian–Utilitarian Bounds in Nash's Bargaining problem." *Theory Decis* 80: 427–42. https://doi.org/10.1007/s11238-015-9510-3.
Rawls, John. 1958. "Justice as Fairness." *The Philosophical Review* 67(2): 164–94.
Rawls, John. 1971. *A Theory of Justice*. Cambridge, MA: Harvard University Press.
Risse, M. 2005. "Why the Count de Borda Cannot Beat the Marquis de Condorcet." *Social Choice and Welfare* 25: 95–113.
Saari, D. 2006. "Which Is Better: The Condorcet or Borda Winner?" *Social Choice and Welfare* 26: 107–29.
Stefansson, H. O. 2021. "Ambiguity Aversion Behind the Veil of Ignorance." *Synthese* 198: 6159–82.
Sugden, R. 1982. *The Political Economy of Public Choice: An Introduction to Welfare Economics*. New York: John Wiley and Sons.
Sugden, R. 2018. *Community of Advantage: a Behavioral Economist's Defense of the Market*. Oxford: Oxford University Press.
Thrasher, J. 2019. "Constructivism, Representation and Stability: Path-Dependence in Public Reason Theories of Justice." *Synthese* 196: 429–50.
Thrasher, J., and G. Gaus. 2015. "Rational Choice and the Original Position: The (many) Models of Rawls and Harsanyi." In *The Original Position*, edited by Timothy Hinton. Cambridge UK: Cambridge University Press.
Thrasher, J., and G. Gaus. 2017. "On the Calculus of Consent." In *The Oxford Handbook of Classics in Contemporary Political Theory*, edited by Jacob Levy. Oxford: Oxford University Press
Vanderschraaf, P. 2018. *Strategic Justice: Convention and Problems of Balancing Divergent Interests*. Oxford: Oxford University Press.
Yaari, Menahem, and Maya Bar-Hillel. 1984. "On Dividing Justly." *Social Choice and Welfare* I: 1–24.
Young, Peyton. 1995. *Equity: In Theory and Practice*. Princeton: Princeton University Press.

3

Does Equality Matter for Its Own Sake?: An Experimental Examination of the Leveling-Down Objection

Christopher Freiman and Adam Lerner

As Derek Parfit puts it (1997: 220), *telic egalitarianism* is the view that "it is in itself bad, or unfair, if some people are worse off than others through no fault or choice of theirs." Parfit offers what is probably the most common and compelling argument against telic egalitarianism: the *leveling-down objection*. In Parfit's words,

> If inequality is bad, its disappearance must be in one way a change for the better, however this change occurs. Suppose that, in some natural disaster, those who are better off lose all their extra resources, and become as badly off as everyone else. Since this change would remove the inequality, it must be in one way welcome, on the Telic View. Though this disaster would be worse for some people, and better for no one, it must be, in one way, a change for the better. Similarly, it would be in one way an improvement if we destroyed the eyes of the sighted, not to benefit the blind, but only to make the sighted blind. These implications can be more plausibly regarded as monstrous, or absurd.
>
> (1997: 211)

When equalization worsens some and betters none, there's no reason to equalize. So we can infer that equality has no intrinsic value. Larry Temkin, a defender of egalitarianism, says that the problems raised by the leveling-down objection "have tremendous force, and I believe they underlie the thinking of most nonegalitarians" (1993: 248). He calls the leveling-down objection "the main argument of most antiegalitarians" (1993: 282).

A number of egalitarians agree with Parfit that leveled-down worlds are in no way better than Pareto-superior worlds but argue that egalitarianism, correctly specified, doesn't imply leveling down.[1] Others allow that leveled-down worlds are in one way better than Pareto-superior worlds (namely, they are more equal) but reject leveling down all things considered. According to this reply, the leveled-down world is in one way better than the Pareto-superior world because equality carries *some* moral weight—it just happens to be outweighed by other values like utility. Here's Temkin (1993: 282): "I, for one, believe that inequality is bad. But do I *really* think that there is some respect in which a world where only some are blind is worse than one where all are? Yes. Does this mean I think it would be better if we blinded everybody? No. Equality is not all that matters." Call this the *pluralist reply*. The philosophers who have offered variations of the pluralist reply make up a "who's who" of egalitarians, including Temkin, Harry Brighouse and Adam Swift (2006: 493), G. A. Cohen (2008a), T. M. Scanlon (1976: 9–10), and Amartya Sen (1992: 92–3).

This chapter offers an original challenge to the pluralist reply to the leveling-down objection (Section 1). Drawing on new experimental results, we argue that the judgment that leveling down is in some way good is implicitly driven by the (false) belief that leveling down is beneficial for those who are worse off (Sections 2 and 3). Thus, a concern for the welfare of the worse-off, rather than for equality itself, is responsible for people's pro-equality intuitions in cases of leveling down. As such, these intuitions do not provide support for the claim that equality is intrinsically valuable (Section 4).

1. Leveling Down and the Pluralist Reply

To illustrate the challenge posed by the leveling-down objection, Cohen offers a case in which society's only choice is between an equal distribution of manna and a Pareto-superior unequal distribution. He says, "Equality at that higher level is here *strictly* unattainable: its unattainability is dictated entirely exogenously with respect to human will" (2008a: 316). Thus, the feasible set is: Distribution I, in which A has 5 and B has 5, or Distribution II, in which A has 7 and B has 6. Cohen states (2008a: 317), "Many would concur with the relational egalitarian intuition that says there is an injustice if society chooses Distribution II, in which A has more manna than B through no fault or merit or choice of either." Cohen does not claim that I is preferable to II all things considered—other moral considerations such as welfare may override our reason to equalize. Rather, on his view, there is always *pro tanto* reason to prefer equality even if inequality is justified all things considered.[2]

Note that Cohen is here offering an empirical claim about the distribution of intuitions: he asserts that "many" would object to the Pareto-superior condition. This and related claims about intuitive assessments of cases have significant philosophical implications for a view like Cohen's, given his explicit methodological commitment to bring philosophical theory into alignment with "pertinent prephilosophical judgment."[3]

Although Cohen's remarks suggest that he accepts the philosophical significance of folk morality, one might challenge Cohen on the grounds that the moral intuitions of professional philosophers are more trustworthy than those of laypeople. We offer two replies. First, at a minimum, an examination of the moral intuitions of laypeople could give rise to an *internal* critique of Cohen's view.

Indeed, Cohen is far from alone in asserting that political philosophy attempts, among other things, to systematize prephilosophical judgment.[4] For instance, David Miller states (2003: 51), "A theory of justice brings out the deep structure of a set of everyday beliefs that, on the surface, are to some degree ambiguous, confused, and contradictory." In the same vein, John Rawls writes (1999: 41), "One may regard a theory of justice as describing our sense of justice ... A conception of justice characterizes our moral sensibility when the everyday judgments we do make are in accordance with its principles." One reason for thinking that everyday judgment is relevant for political philosophy in particular is that principles of justice may need to serve the practical function of gaining allegiance from nonphilosophers who will be governed by such principles. To put the point in Rawls's words, we have reason to seek a conception of justice "which is congenial to the most deep-seated convictions and traditions of a modern democratic state" (2005: 300).

Second, it's simply not clear that philosophers enjoy a general epistemic advantage over the folk, at least when it comes to avoiding cognitive bias. A recent comprehensive experimental study conducted by Joachim Horvath and Alex Wiegmann (2021) found that subjects with a postgraduate degree in philosophy with a specialization or competence in ethics were significantly affected by various biases when evaluating a variety of moral dilemmas. While ethical experts were less susceptible to bias than laypeople in two of five cases, this result would support at most a very limited version of the expertise defense, whereby philosophers "need not worry about just a few cases and a few human biases—and even that modest hypothesis can only be upheld on the basis of sufficient empirical research" (Horvath and Wiegmann 2021: 16). Thus, to claim an epistemic advantage for philosophers over the folk with respect to a particular kind of case, one must mobilize empirical research in defense of that claim. The burden of justification, then, would rest with those who contend that folk judgments about leveling down cases ought to be disregarded in favor of attending exclusively to philosophers' judgments.

In what follows, we argue that the pluralist reply fails. We contend that the judgment that leveled-down conditions are in some way better than Pareto-superior conditions is driven, implicitly, by the false belief that the leveled-down conditions benefit the worse-off (and thus are not genuine cases of leveling down).

We believe there is an overlooked factor implicitly influencing people's beliefs about whether there is a *pro tanto* reason to level down—namely, the possibility that worsening the better-off can benefit the worse-off. As a number of egalitarian philosophers have pointed out, decreasing the welfare of the better-off can increase the welfare of the worse-off.[5] A society in which everyone suffers from the same problem may be more likely to display greater empathy, solidarity, and fellowship. Indeed, Cohen himself (2008b) stresses the ways in which equality promotes community. Likewise, it may be more likely to devote resources to ameliorating the shared condition. Disadvantaged persons are also likely to fare better in direct competitions for jobs, credentials, prizes, and so on with others who share the disadvantage. Thus, we think it is plausible that the judgment that a world in which everyone is (e.g.) blind or needy is in some way better than a world in which most are sighted or prosperous is due to an implicit assumption that such a world *benefits* the blind and needy. If we are right, then this judgment would not support an egalitarian principle according to which equality is intrinsically valuable.

Our hypothesis implies that people who have egalitarian intuitions about leveled-down worlds are mistaken about why it is they have the intuitions they have. Whereas they claim that their intuitions are driven by a concern with equality, we claim that their intuitions are driven by a concern for the worst-off. Our position may sound uncharitable. In order to be justified in denying that people have insight as to the causes of their own intuitions, we must have good reason to think that people's judgments about the causes of their own intuitions are unreliable. We do.

2. The Role of Experimental Political Philosophy

One of the most prominent themes arising out of the last forty years of empirical work in social psychology is that people are often radically mistaken about why it is they believe what they believe, desire what they desire, and behave as they behave. Rather than enjoying privileged access to the causes of their behavior, people attempt to infer those causes after the fact, often leading them to confabulate reasons for acting as they did that have nothing to do with the actual causes of their behavior. The most widely cited illustration of this phenomenon comes from Richard Nisbett and Timothy Wilson (1977). In one of many similar experiments, Nisbett and Wilson presented participants with four pairs of pantyhose and then asked participants to tell them which pair they liked most. When asked to explain why they preferred one pair of pantyhose over the others, participants cited intrinsic properties of the pantyhose. Unbeknown to the participants, however, the pantyhose were all identical with respect to their intrinsic properties. The explanations participants provided for why they preferred one pair of pantyhose over another could not be true, for they invoked differences between pantyhose that did not exist. The actual explanation for why participants preferred the pantyhose had to do with the extrinsic properties of the pantyhose—participants preferred pantyhose that appeared on the right side of the display over those that appeared on the left.

Since Nisbett and Wilson, numerous other examples of post hoc rationalization have been found across a variety of domains, including the moral domain.[6] These findings suggest that the best way to find out why people have the moral intuitions they do about a given hypothetical case is not always (if ever) to ask them why they have those intuitions. A better approach is to devise a series of cases that are the same in every respect to the original case but in which the factor that is thought to play a role in people's moral judgments is absent or varied in some systematic way. When there is a difference in people's intuitions between any given pair of cases, this difference can be attributed to the difference in the features of the cases, and this can in turn lend support to a particular explanation of why it is that people have the intuitions they do about those cases.

This approach is just the method of cases already familiar to those working in moral and political philosophy. Taken alone, however, the method of cases is of limited epistemic value. The success of the method of cases as a way of arbitrating between competing explanations of people's moral intuitions depends on the extent to which it is possible to devise cases that completely isolate the factors relevant to assessing the competing explanations. It is not always possible to do this in any natural manner. For instance, without receiving some bit of philosophical training, people often misinterpret determinism to imply epiphenomenalism. It follows that, in order to discover whether people believe determinism is compatible with moral responsibility, one cannot simply ask people for their intuitions about "causally determined" agents; if people deny that causally determined actors are morally responsible, this may be because they believe epiphenomenalism is incompatible with moral responsibility—not because they believe determinism, properly understood, is incompatible with moral responsibility.

One way to get around this difficulty is to supplement the method of cases with additional methods of investigation. One such method is *mediational analysis*. Mediational analysis is a statistical technique that allows one to see whether an apparent effect, such as the effect of causal determinism on people's intuitions about whether that person can be morally responsible, can be explained just as well by other factors, such as how strongly people believe that causal determinism implies epiphenomenalism. Indeed, Eddy Nahmias and Dylan Murray (2010) have found that people's tendency to believe that causally determined agents are less morally responsible than agents who are not causally determined seems to be fully mediated by how strongly they believe that causal determinism implies either epiphenomenalism or fatalism. Likewise, Chandra Sripada (2012) has found that people's tendency to attribute less free will to manipulated agents than unmanipulated agents is fully mediated by how strongly they believe those agents failed to act in accord with their deeper values or suffered from a lack of morally relevant information.

Mediational analysis is a special type of *regression analysis*. Regression analyses allow one to investigate correlations between variables and, on the basis of those correlations, make estimates regarding what the level of the dependent variable would be at various levels of the predictor variables. In mediational analysis, for instance, one estimates whether a given predictor variable would be significantly correlated with the dependent variable even if another predicted variable—the proposed mediator—were held fixed.

In this study, we use mediational analysis and regression analysis more generally in the service of political philosophy. With these statistical techniques, we investigate whether people's tendency to believe there is some respect in which leveled-down worlds are better than non-leveled-down worlds can be explained by how strongly they believe that the worst-off in leveled-down worlds would be better off in leveled-down worlds than in non-leveled-down worlds. If found, this result would undermine a crucial source of support for the pluralist reply to the leveling-down objection. Our approach here fits within the broader tradition of experimental philosophy, which makes use of experimental methods to investigate laypeople's beliefs about philosophical issues (among other things).

3. Methods

Our claim, then, is that the judgment that leveled-down worlds are in some way better than Pareto-superior worlds is driven by an implicit concern for the welfare of the worst-off. To assess this claim, we conducted an experiment. We asked 178 participants to consider both an "unequal world" in which *some* people suffer from a genetic disease and an "equal world" in which *all* people suffer from that disease.[7] Participants were told that those with the disease do not develop any of the associated symptoms until the age of forty, at which point they rapidly develop the whole range of symptoms over several weeks. Participants were also told that everyone who has the disease lives out a normal life span, dying at the age of approximately eighty. Our independent variable was the kind of symptoms the disease caused: half of the participants were told that the disease caused people to become permanently deaf, while the other half were told that the disease caused people to become permanently deaf, blind, mute, and paralyzed, as well as to experience intense physical pain.

After considering one of these two pairs of worlds, participants were asked to report how strongly they agreed or disagreed with the following four statements:

1) "The equal world is, in some way, better than the unequal world."
2) "The unequal world is, in some way, worse than the equal world."
3) "People with the disease in the equal world would, in some way, have better lives than people with the disease in the unequal world."
4) "People with the disease in the unequal world would, in some way, have better lives than people with the disease in the equal world."[8]

Participants reported their level of agreement with each statement on a 7-point Likert scale (1 = *strongly disagree* and 7 = *strongly agree*).[9]

4. Predictions

Our first dependent variable was an average of each participant's level of agreement with statements (1) and (2). This variable represents the strength of participants' agreement with the pluralist egalitarian intuition that there is some reason to prefer a leveled-down world to a Pareto-superior world in which everyone is unequally better off. Our second dependent variable was a binary dependent variable: whether participants had an average response to statements (1) and (2) that was equal to or greater than 4—the midpoint on the scale between "strongly disagree" and "strongly agree"—or whether participants had an average response that was less than 4. This variable represents whether participants agreed with the egalitarian intuition at any level whatsoever.

We predicted that (i) participants would be more likely to agree with the egalitarian intuition (i.e., to have an average response to the first two statements that is at or above 4) when the disease caused only deafness, and (ii) participants would more *strongly* agree with the egalitarian intuition (i.e., the mean response to the first two statements would be higher) when the disease caused only deafness. We made these predictions based on the assumption that people would be more likely to believe that those who had the disease in the equal world would be better off than those who had the disease in the unequal world, but only when the disease causes deafness alone; one can easily imagine a number of changes that could be made to the world to improve the lives of deaf people, but it is difficult to imagine changes that could be made to improve the lives of people who were deaf, blind, mute, paralyzed, and suffering from intense pain.[10]

Our third variable of interest was each participant's level of agreement with statement (3). This variable reflects how strongly participants believed that those who had the disease in the equal world would, in some respect, have better lives than those who had the disease in the unequal world. In the event we found support for the predicted effect of disease type on the strength of people's agreement with the egalitarian intuition, we predicted that this variable would fully mediate this effect; we predicted that once we controlled for differences in people's beliefs about how much better the lives of the afflicted would be in the equal world, people would be just as inclined to have the egalitarian intuition when they believed the disease was less severe as they would when they believed the disease was more severe. If this mediational analysis turned out as we predicted, it would provide strong evidence for the claim that people who have the egalitarian intuition do so because they implicitly believe that people who suffer from the disease will have better lives if everyone suffers from that disease.

Lastly, we predicted that our data would support the following statistical inferences. First, when it is assumed that people deny that those with the disease would be better off in the equal world—as they must if the scenario is to present a true test of whether people are (pluralist) telic egalitarians—the estimated mean value of our first dependent variable should be less than 4, reflecting widespread disagreement with the egalitarian intuition. Second, when the same assumption is made about people's beliefs concerning the well-being of the worst-off, the estimated percentage of people who report any level of agreement with the egalitarian intuition should be less than 50 percent. If our data support these estimates, this would provide even stronger support for our hypothesis; if most people would relinquish the egalitarian intuition upon learning that the worst-off would be no better off in the equal world than in the unequal world, then people's initial inclination to agree with the egalitarian intuition would seem to be driven by a concern for the worst-off in society rather than a concern for equality *per se*.

5. Results

As predicted, the mean level of agreement with the egalitarian intuition was significantly higher when the disease caused only deafness ($M = 3.99$, $SD = 1.81$) as opposed to deafness, blindness, muteness, paralysis, and extreme pain ($M = 3.16$, $SD = 1.86$), $t(176) = 3.04$, $p = .003$, $d = 0.456$. People were also more likely to agree with the egalitarian intuition (at any level) when the disease caused only deafness: 61.2 percent of people agreed with the egalitarian intuition when the disease caused only deafness, whereas only 40.9 percent agreed with the egalitarian intuition when the disease was more severe. This difference was significant, $\chi^2 (1, N = 178) = 7.33$, $p = .007$, and it had a small-medium effect size, $\varphi = .20$).

Because we found support for our first prediction, we went on to test our second prediction. Our second prediction was that the effect of disease severity on the strength of people's egalitarian intuitions would be fully mediated by differences in people's beliefs about how well off those with disease would be in the equal world as opposed to the unequal world. As predicted, people's beliefs about how well those with the disease would do in the equal world were strongly correlated with how strongly participants agreed with the egalitarian intuition, $\beta = 0.698$, $t(175) = 11.74$, $p < .001$, and this relationship fully mediated the initial effect of disease severity on the strength of people's egalitarian intuitions, $z = 4.89$, $p < .001$. To put the point differently, when holding fixed people's beliefs about how much better off those with the disease would be in the equal world than in the unequal world, people were no more inclined to agree with the egalitarian intuition when the disease was less severe than when it was more severe, $\beta = -0.039$, $t(175) = -0.654$, $p = .514$.

Our final two predictions concerned the statistical inferences we could make based on the regression equations that best fit our data.[11] We predicted that when assuming people deny that those with the disease in the equal world would live better lives than those in the unequal world (i.e., when each person's response to statement (3) was assumed to be *strongly disagree*), the estimated mean response to the egalitarian intuition would be to disagree with it, and less than 50 percent of people would agree with it. We found support for both of these claims. Our data suggest that if people were to strongly disagree with the claim that those in the equal world would live better lives than those in the unequal world, the mean response to the egalitarian intuition would be 1.81, 95 percent CI [1.48, 2.15]. That is to say, the mean response would be to disagree. Our data further suggest that if people were to strongly disagree with the claim that those in the equal world would live better lives, then only 14.1 percent of participants would agree with the egalitarian intuition, 95 percent CI [7.9%, 24.0%]. Put another way, the majority of participants would reject the egalitarian intuition.

6. Discussion

We think these results corroborate Parfit's suggestion that the appeal of egalitarianism rests not on a concern for equality as such but rather on a concern for the badly off. Parfit notes that we do have an intuitive preference for equal distributions in some cases, for example, for a distribution of everyone at 145 rather than the optimific distribution of half at 100 and half at 200. Yet rather than endorsing the intrinsic value of equality, Parfit (1997: 212) suggests that our intuitive preference for equal distributions in a variety of cases can be given "a different explanation. Rather than believing in equality, we might be especially concerned about those people who are worse off."

Our findings, then, give us reason to favor a fundamentally nonrelational principle of distributive justice that preferentially distributes benefits to the worst-off. There are a number of such principles. For instance, on a prioritarian view, a benefit has greater moral value the worse off the beneficiary is in absolute terms.[12] A sufficientarian will prioritize gains to those below a threshold of adequate resources or welfare.[13] John Rawls' difference principle distributes resources in the way that maximally benefits the members of the worst-off class.[14] And utilitarians will note that distributing a resource to the poor rather than the rich tends to maximize utility due to the diminishing marginal utility of wealth.

Our results don't enable us to arbitrate between these kinds of principles. However, they do suggest that insofar as we have reason to bring about more equal distributions, the reason is due to equality's tendency to benefit the badly off. Thus, if people's ostensibly egalitarian intuitions about leveled-down worlds provide support for any principle of justice at all, it is a fundamentally nonrelational principle rather than a fundamentally relational principle like egalitarianism.[15]

Notes

1. See, e.g., Mason (2001); Christiano (2007).
2. Cohen offers another scenario in which manna falls from heaven and is shared equally. An additional unit of manna falls to Jane, who proceeds to burn it for the sake of equality. Cohen (2008a: 318) contends that Jane's act of leveling down is not "merely foolish" but just.
3. Ibid., 3.
4. For additional discussion, see Freiman and Nichols (2011). Critical to this approach is the idea of *systematizing* common sense moral judgments via reflective equilibrium. See Rawls (1999: 43). For a discussion of this point in the context of experimental political philosophy in particular, see Freiman and Lerner (2015: 3186).
5. See, e.g., Brighouse and Swift (2006); Scanlon (2003); Eyal (2013). Eyal suggests that these instrumental considerations imply that cases of leveling down resources are sometimes better in virtue of promoting utility. Interestingly, though, he believes that our *intuitions* about these cases are insensitive to such considerations. For replies to arguments alleging that leveling down tends to benefit the worst-off, see Freiman (2014); Freiman (2017: 101–19).
6. See, e.g., Sripada (2012); Hauser et al. (2007); Hall, Johansson, and Strandberg (2012).
7. Adult participants (102 men, 75 women, 1 unidentified, M_{age} = 33.3 years, age range: 18–72 years) were recruited online through Amazon's Mechanical Turk (www.mturk.com) for a survey on "Opinions about Medical Conditions." All participants reported living in the United States. Participants were compensated $0.50 upon completion of the survey.
8. The order of these statements was randomized between participants. Question #4 was a filler question.
9. On a separate page, participants were asked to recall how many people in the equal world get the disease, how many people in the unequal world get the disease, and what happens to people who get the disease. Twenty-two participants got one of these three questions wrong; the responses from these participants were not included in the statistical analyses below.
10. One might object that these people fail to live even a minimally decent life and thus fail to meet a threshold of sufficiency. We find this plausible, but we don't think it undermines our critique. Even if people in the second scenario fall below the threshold of sufficiency, the (telic) egalitarian is committed to the claim that a world in which *all* are below sufficiency is in one way better than a world in which some are below sufficiency and some are above because the latter is more equal. We owe thanks to Matthew Lindauer for raising this concern.

11 One regression equation predicted the strength of people's agreement with the egalitarian intuition at a given level of the proposed mediator, while the other predicted the percentage of people that would agree with the egalitarian intuition at a given level of the proposed mediator. Because including the proposed mediator in the regression model rendered the effect of disease severity nonsignificant, we dropped the term representing the effect of disease severity from our final regression equations. The resulting regression equations were $\hat{y}_{strength}$ = 1.20 +.618x and $\hat{y}_{percentage}$ = 1/{1+$e^{-(.647x-2.453)}$}. These regression equations both explained a significant portion of the variance in their respective dependent variables, R^2 =.47, $F(1, 176)$ = 154.24, p <.001; Nagelkerke's R^2 =.38, χ^2 (1, N = 178) = 58.78, p <.001.
12 See, e.g., Parfit, "Equality and Priority."
13 Harry Frankfurt, "Equality as a Moral Ideal," *Ethics* 98 (1987), 21–43; Roger Crisp, "Equality, Priority, and Compassion," *Ethics* 113 (2003); Christopher Freiman, "Why Poverty Matters Most: Toward a Humanitarian Theory of Social Justice," *Utilitas* 24 (2012): 26–40.
14 See Rawls, *A Theory of Justice*, 1999.
15 We are grateful to Matthew Lindauer and an anonymous referee for their helpful comments on an earlier version of this chapter.

References

Brighouse, H., and A. Swift. 2006. "Equality, Priority, and Positional Goods." *Ethics* 116: 471–97.

Christiano, T. 2007. "A Foundation for Egalitarianism." in *Egalitarianism: New Essays on the Nature and Value of Equality*, edited by Nils Holtug and Kasper Lippert-Rasmussen, 41–82. New York: Oxford University Press.

Cohen, G. 2008a. *Rescuing Justice and Equality*. Cambridge: Harvard University Press.

Cohen, G. 2008b. *Why Not Socialism?* Princeton: Princeton University Press.

Crisp, R. 2003. "Equality, Priority, and Compassion." *Ethics* 113: 745–63.

Eyal, N. 2013. "Leveling Down Health." in *Inequalities in Health: Ethics, Measurement, and Policy*, edited by Eyal, et al., 194–213. New York: Oxford University Press.

Frankfurt, H. 1987. "Equality as a Moral Ideal." *Ethics* 98: 21–43.

Freiman, C. 2012. "Why Poverty Matters Most: Toward a Humanitarian Theory of Social Justice." *Utilitas* 24: 26–40.

Freiman, C. 2014. "Priority and Position." *Philosophical Studies* 167: 341–60.

Freiman, C. 2017. *Unequivocal Justice*. New York: Routledge.

Freiman, C., and A. Lerner. 2015. "Self-Ownership and Disgust: Why Compulsory Body Part Redistribution Gets Under Our Skin." *Philosophical Studies* 172: 3167–90.

Freiman, C., and S. Nichols. 2011. "Is Desert in the Details?" *Philosophy and Phenomenological Research* I82: 121–33.

Hall, L., P. Johansson, and T. Strandberg. 2012. "Lifting the Veil of Morality: Choice Blindness and Attitude Reversals on a Self-Transforming Survey." *PLoS ONE* 7, no. 9: e45457.

Hauser, M., F. Cushman, L. Young, R. Kang-Xing Jin, and J. Mikhail. 2007. "A Dissociation Between Moral Judgments and Justifications." *Mind & Language* 22: 1–21.

Horvath, J., and A. Wiegmann. 2021. "Intuitive Expertise in Moral Judgments." *Australasian Journal of Philosophy*. DOI: 10.1080/00048402.2021.1890162.

Mason, A. 2001. "Egalitarianism and the Levelling Down Objection." *Analysis* 61: 246–54.
Miller, D. 2003. *Principles of Social Justice*. Cambridge: Harvard University Press.
Nahmias, E., and D. Murray. 2010. "Experimental Philosophy on Free Will: An Error Theory for Incompatibilist Intuitions." In *New Waves in Philosophy of Action*, edited by J. Aguilar, A. Buckareff, and K. Frankish, 189–216. New York: Palgrave-Macmillan.
Nisbett, R., and T. Wilson. 1977. "Telling More Than We Can Know: Verbal Reports on Mental Processes." *Psychological Review* 84: 231–59.
Parfit, D. 1997. "Equality and Priority." *Ratio* 10: 202–21.
Rawls, J. 1999. *A Theory of Justice*. Cambridge: Harvard University Press.
Rawls, J. 2005. *Political Liberalism*. New York: Columbia University Press.
Scanlon, T. 1976. "Nozick on Rights, Liberty, and Property." *Philosophy and Public Affairs* 6: 3–25.
Scanlon, T. 2003. "The Diversity of Objections to Inequality." In *The Difficulty of Tolerance*, 202–18. Cambridge: Cambridge University Press.
Sen, A. 1992. *Inequality Reexamined*. Oxford: Oxford University Press.
Sripada, C. 2012. "What Makes a Manipulated Agent Unfree?." *Philosophy and Phenomenological Research* 85: 563–93.
Temkin, L. 1993. *Inequality*. New York: Oxford University Press.

4

What Does Labor Mixing Get You?

Shaun Nichols and John Thrasher

> *The first person who, having enclosed a plot of land, took it into his head to say "this is mine," and found people simple enough to believe him, was the true founder of civil society.*
>
> —Rousseau

How does one come to acquire property, that is, rightful ownership in something that was previously unowned and, by so doing, exclude all others from its rightful use? The distinction between mine and thine also creates the distinction between use and theft and, as Rousseau noted, is the true source of human inequality (1755, 69). One prominent answer to this question is that one can rightfully acquire ownership of something that was previously unowned by improving it through one's labor. One can come to own an unowned plot of land, for instance, by farming or building on the land. The classic philosophical source for this view is Locke's *2nd Treatise on Government*. There, Locke argues that since we own ourselves and our labor, once we "mix" our labor with a thing, we make it our own.

> The labour of his body, and the work of his hands, we may say, are properly his. Whatsoever then he removes out of the state that nature hath provided, and left it in, he hath mixed his labour with, and joined to it something that is his own, and thereby makes it his property. It being by him removed from the common state nature hath placed it in, it hath by this labour something annexed to it, that excludes the common right of other men: for this labour being the unquestionable property of the labourer, no man but he can have a right to what that is once joined to, at least where there is enough, and as good, left in common for others.
>
> (Locke 1681, §27)

Leaving aside the so-called "Lockean proviso" about leaving "enough, and as good" in common for others, the basic idea seems to be that once someone has labored and improved something, for another to use it without their consent would be

---

We would like to thank Matthew Lindauer and Rachana Kamtekar for helpful comments on an earlier draft.

equivalent to that person stealing their labor. Recent research on lay intuitions about ownership supports this Lockean claim; people do indeed think that labor mixing generates rightful ownership (e.g., Kanngiesser and Hood 2014; Rochat et al. 2014; Levene, Starmans, and Friedman 2015). In this chapter, we explore a more subtle question about ownership and labor mixing—namely, does mixing one's labor with an object entail ownership of that object and if so, to what extent and under what circumstances?

In modern political philosophy, one of the earliest ideas about rightful acquisition of property is the First Possession Theory. On this view, one comes to rightfully own an object by virtue of being the first one to possess it (e.g., Pufendorf 1673). There is some evidence that lay subjects also regard first possession as sufficient for ownership (Friedman 2008). However, as we review below, several studies have pitted first possession against mixed labor, and in the studies, labor mixing seems to be a more powerful determiner of judgments of rightful possession. For instance, a cross-cultural (US, China, Vanuatu, and Brazil) developmental study on intuitions about ownership found that people's judgments about rightful ownership are more strongly determined by labor mixing than by other candidate principles, like first possession (Rochat et al. 2014). In this study, one condition tested judgments of rightful possession in a circumstance involving "first contact," where one child sees the object first and calls out, but the other child touches it first. Contrary to the author's predictions, across ages and culture, children responded at chance as to whether the person who first touches the object was the rightful owner (478, 480). Rochat and colleagues also included a labor-mixing condition in which one child creates a toy; this child ends up in a dispute with another child about who owns the toy. In that case, there was a pronounced effect: five-year-old children, across cultures, tended to attribute ownership to the creator (477).

One potential drawback to the Rochat et al. study is that it evaluated labor mixing and first possession in separate conditions. In contrast, Levene and colleagues (2015) pitted first possession against labor-mixing in a single condition using a clever manipulation. Participants were presented with the following vignette:

> People sometimes visit a local landfill looking for things that can be salvaged and sold. Mike is on a large hill at the landfill. He sees a big metal can 20 feet away. Mike decides to crush it into an ashtray. However, crushing the can just right won't be easy. He picks up a heavy rock, walks a little bit closer, and throws it at the can. The rock crushes the can into an ashtray! Mike walks towards the ashtray. Before he reaches it, another man named Dave runs over and picks it up. The two argue about who gets to keep the ashtray.
>
> Participants were then asked, "who does the ashtray belong to?"
>
> (Levene et al. 2015, 105)

Participants tended to say that the ashtray belong to the agent when he succeeded in making it an ashtray, but not when he didn't (105). Summarizing the studies, the authors write, "Participants ascribed ownership to agents who successfully created, but were less likely to ascribe ownership to agents who modified objects but failed to create" (108).

These studies all suggest that putting labor into an object exerts a powerful role in lay intuitions about ownership. But what exactly comes to fall under the laborer's ownership? Robert Nozick suggests that perhaps what one comes to own is the value that was added to the object, but not necessarily the object itself. He writes:

> Perhaps the idea … is that laboring on something improves it and makes it more valuable; and anyone is entitled to own a thing whose value he has created. … Ignore the fact that laboring on something may make it less valuable (spraying pink enamel paint on a piece of driftwood that you have found). Why should one's entitlement extend to the whole object rather than just to the *added value* one's labor has produced?
>
> (Nozick 1974, 175)

The question here is of some philosophical significance. Theories of property are supposed to give an account of rightful acquisition of an object, not simply rightful acquisition of the value added by one's labor. What do people do that secures their rightful possession of whole objects, like animals, minerals, and tracts of land? Nozick is pointing out that without further elaboration, the labor mixing theory does not explain why mixing one's labor with an object would yield rightful acquisition of the entire object.

In cognitive science, of course, we are not doing fundamental normative political philosophy. We are not directly determining the correct conditions under which a person gains rightful possession of an object. But many of the arguments that political philosophers use in these debates draw on our intuitions about cases. Both Locke and Nozick, for instance, appeal to intuitions about the plausibility of cases as evidence. Since those intuitions likely depend on broader common-sense intuitions, which, in turn, are related to the beliefs about the legitimacy of actual political institutions, it's worth investigating common-sense intuitions on the matter. In the following three preregistered[1] studies, we explore intuitions about labor mixing. In particular, we examine people's judgments that bear on whether mixing one's labor with an object generates rightful possession of the whole object.

Study 1

To address Nozick's question, we need to see if people judge there to be a difference between the value added to something by one's labor and ownership of the object as a whole. We can investigate this issue first by capitalizing on earlier work on mixed labor. Across several studies, Kanngiesser and Hood (2014) investigated the role of value in intuitions about labor mixing and ownership. They use the following kind of vignette:

> Mary owns some [material]. Sarah takes the [material] and [turns it into a piece of artwork]. Mary likes the [artwork/materials] and wants to keep it. Sarah also likes the [artwork] and wants to keep it.
>
> (355)

Participants were asked, "who owns the artwork" (355). The study varied the value of the material involved. They found that when the material was not very valuable (e.g., clay), people were more inclined to attribute ownership of the artwork to the artist than they were when the material was quite valuable (e.g., gold) (356). This suggests that labor mixing does matter for ownership but is qualified by the antecedent value of the object.

In these studies, at least when the value of the material is low, participants tend to say that the artwork belongs to the person who made the artwork rather than the person who owned the material. Kanngiesser and Hood (2014) also included a control condition, in which the second agent "looks at" the material, and there is no mention of labor mixing. Not surprisingly, in that condition almost no one said that the material belonged to the agent who merely looked at it. Note that in this study, participants are only asked who owns the material in a condition where there is no artwork. In our study, we simply ask all participants both questions—we ask who owns the artwork and who owns the material. This allows us to explore whether the rightful possession of the artwork entails the rightful possession of the whole object, including the material.

Methods

Participants

For the study 150 participants were recruited on Prolific: 70 female, 78 male, 2 participants indicated "other." Mean age = 26.6. Seven participants missed the attention check, leaving $N = 143$ participants for analysis.

Design, Materials, and Procedure

The study has a within subjects design with two conditions, corresponding to two dependent variables. Participants were presented with the primary vignette from Kanngiesser and Hood (2014, 355). Their study showed that the value of the material mattered, and only when the material was of low value did participants attribute ownership of the artwork to the artist. Hence our vignette used only a low value material. The full vignette is:

> Mary owns some clay. Sarah takes the clay and turns it into a piece of artwork. Mary likes the artwork and wants to keep it. Sarah also likes the artwork and wants to keep it.

Following this, participants were asked two questions about rightful possession:

> Who owns the clay?
>
> Who owns the artwork?

Responses were given on a 1 (Definitely Mary)–6 (Definitely Sarah) scale. The order of the questions was randomized.

Following responses to the two DVs, participants were asked to explain their answer, and then were given a basic attention check in which they had to indicate disagreement with the statement: "March comes before April alphabetically" (1—Strongly disagree, 6—strongly agree). Following our preregistration, the seven participants who failed this attention check were excluded from analysis.

Results and Discussion

Participants were significantly more likely to say that the artwork belonged to the agent who contributed labor ($M = 4.34$) than that the clay belonged to that agent ($M = 1.61$) ($t(142) = 18.8$, $p < .0001$, Cohen's $D = 1.57$). Indeed, as is evident from Figure 4.1, participants tended to say that the artwork belonged to the agent who contributed labor and the clay belonged to the other agent.

These results indicate that people don't make a direct inference that mixing one's labor with an object yields rightful possession of that object. Even though Sarah is said to own the artwork, she is not said to own the clay out of which the artwork is made. This is a rather striking position. The artwork is composed out of the clay, and participants maintain that the clay belongs to one person and the artwork belongs to another. Thus, producing an artwork does seem to be sufficient for generating the intuition that one owns the artwork. But it is not sufficient to generate the intuition that one thereby owns the material.

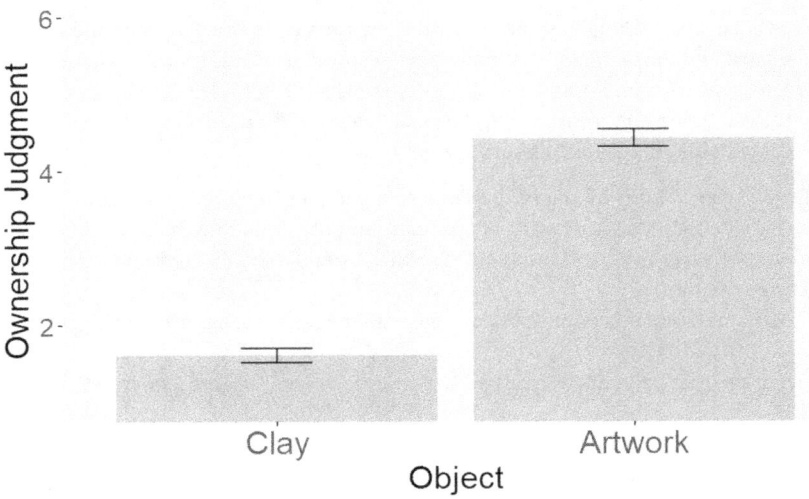

Figure 4.1 Average ownership scores in Study 1, with error bars reflecting the standard error of the mean. Scale from 1 (Definitely Mary [the original owner of the material]) to 6 (Definitely Sarah [the person who contributed labor to produce the artwork]). © Shaun Nichols and John Thrasher.

Study 2

In the previous study, we found that in a case of transfer of ownership, participants tend to think that mixing one's labor with an object generates ownership of the product of that labor but does not generate ownership of material on which that labor was conducted. This shows that participants are sensitive to the distinction that Nozick makes. That is, they recognize the difference between owning the value one adds to an object and owning the object itself. But Study 1 doesn't directly test whether this judgment holds in cases of unowned objects since the clay in Study 1 is already owned by Mary. In our second study, we want to investigate the issue in the context of something more closely resembling the original acquisition of unowned objects.

Methods

Participants

For this study, 150 participants were recruited on Prolific: 58 female, 91 male, 1 participant indicated other. Mean age = 27.7. Five participants missed the attention check, leaving $N = 145$ participants for analysis.

Design, Materials, and Procedure

The study has a within subjects design with two conditions, corresponding to two dependent variables. Participants were presented with the following vignette:

> Mark is a painter, hiking in some uncharted territory. He is struck by the silhouette of a hawk and looks around for materials to capture it. He sees a rock with a flat side near the river and uses some clay from the riverbank to sketch the silhouette on the rock. He's very pleased with the result. He doesn't have room in his pack to take it with him but plans to return the next day to get it.
>
> The next day, John is hiking in the same area and sees the same rock. He doesn't see the side that Mark's drawing is on. But John notices that the rock has a small amount of silver in it, and estimates it's worth around $80. He picks up the rock to take with him.
> Mark arrives at this point and sees John with the rock that has his drawing on it.

Following this, participants were asked two questions about rightful possession:

> Who does the drawing belong to?
>
> Who does the rock belong to?

Responses were given on a 1 (Definitely John)–6 (Definitely Mark) scale. The order of the questions was randomized.

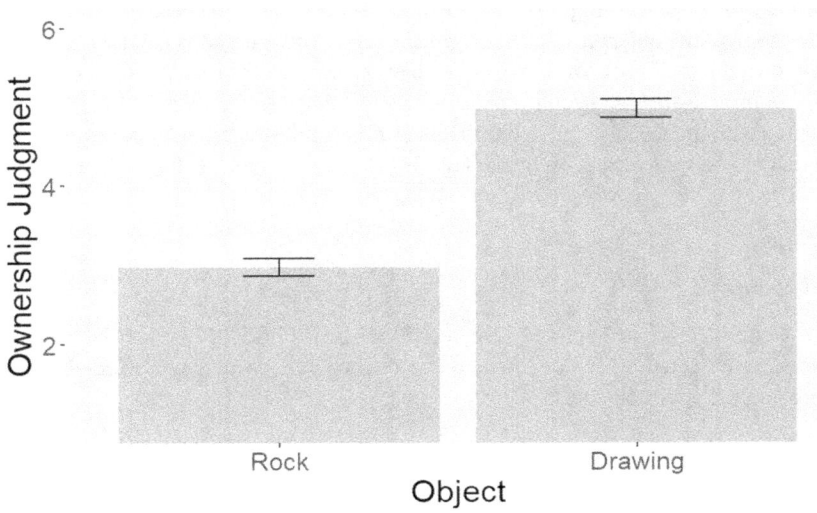

Figure 4.2 Average ownership scores in Study 2, with error bars reflecting the standard error of the mean. Scale from 1 (Definitely John [the person who picked up the rock]) to 6 (Definitely Mark [the person who contributed labor to produce the drawing]). © Shaun Nichols and John Thrasher.

Following responses to the two DVs, participants were asked to explain their answer, and then were given the same attention check as in Study 1. Following our preregistration, the five participants who failed this attention check were excluded from analysis.

Results and Discussion

Participants were significantly more likely to say that the drawing belongs to the agent who contributed labor ($M = 5.0$) than that the rock belonged to that agent ($M = 2.97$) ($t(144) = 12.68$, $p < .0001$, Cohen's $D = 1.05$). Indeed, as is evident from Figure 4.2, participants tended to say that the drawing belonged to the agent who contributed labor and the rock belonged to the other agent.

As in Study 1, we found that people distinguish between ownership of the value that was added to the object (the drawing) and the object itself (the rock). While participants said that the artist retained rightful ownership of his drawing, they did not extend rightful ownership to the whole object. Once again this suggests a significantly nuanced view about the relation between labor mixing and rightful ownership.

Study 3

In the previous study, we found that even in the context of something resembling original acquisition, participants show a divided verdict, such that a person who mixes his labor with an object might thereby own the value he added to the object without coming to own the object itself. But this might seem a little paradoxical. How can one person own the drawing on a rock and another person own the rock itself? In our final study, we investigate how people would resolve this apparent conflict. Participants are presented with the scenario much like that in Study 2, and we explored how participants who rendered a split verdict on ownership would prefer to resolve the conflict.

Methods

Participants

For this study 150 participants were recruited on Prolific: 95 female, 54 male, 1 participant indicated other. Mean age = 24. Twenty-four participants were excluded for missing the attention check.

Design, Materials, and Procedure

All participants were presented with the following vignette:

> Gary is a sculptor, hiking in some uncharted territory. He is struck by the beauty of a vista. He finds a rock and uses some tools to chisel out a detailed and subtle depiction of the scene. He's very pleased with the result. He doesn't have room in his pack to take it with him but plans to return the next day to get it.
>
> The next day, Eric is hiking in the same area and sees the same rock. He doesn't see the side that Gary's sculpture is on. But Eric notices that the rock has a small amount of silver in it, he picks up the rock and estimates the silver is worth around $80. He sets the rock down to open his pack to put the rock in it.
>
> Gary arrives at this point and sees Eric and the rock with the sculpture he made.

Following the vignette, participants were asked to assign ownership for the sculpture and for the rock:

> Who would you say the sculpture belongs to?
> Gary
> Eric
>
> Who would you say the rock belongs to?
> Gary
> Eric

Finally, participants were asked the question of interest, regarding how to resolve a conflict in ownership.

Which of these do you think is the most appropriate thing to happen with this rock that has the sculpture on it:

Gary gets to keep it
Eric gets to keep it
Gary gets to keep it after giving Eric some money
Eric gets to keep it after giving Gary some money

They were asked to select one of the above options, which were counterbalanced for order.

Following responses to this question, participants were given the same attention check as in Study 1. Following our preregistration, the twenty-four participants who failed this attention check were excluded from analysis.

Results and Discussion

A majority of participants (67/126) rendered a split verdict on ownership. That is, they maintained that the sculpture belonged to the first person, and the rock belonged to the second person. Following our preregistration, we collapsed the responses to the resolution dependent measure into two categories. One category ("Compromising") included both options in which one person gets to keep the object after paying the other person money; the other category ("Uncompromising") included both options in which ownership was simply assigned to one person. The number of participants who selected a Compromising response ($N = 46$) was greater than the number of participants who selected and Uncompromising response ($N = 21$) (see Figure 4.3). Following our preregistration, we conducted chi-square goodness of fit test, which revealed a significant difference from what would be expected by chance ($\chi^2 = 9.3284$, $df = 1$, p-value $= 0.002$, Cramer's $V=.37$).

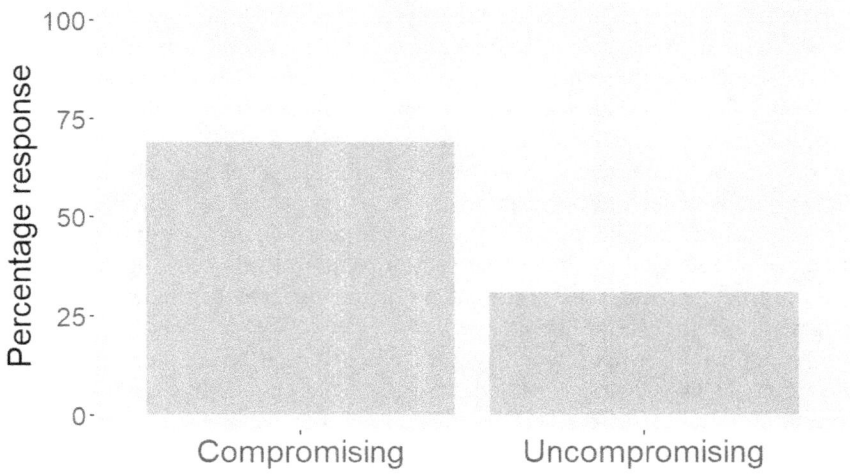

Figure 4.3 Percentage response in each category in Study 3. © Shaun Nichols and John Thrasher.

General Discussion

In political philosophy, it is a vexed question how an individual obtains rightful ownership of an object. Locke's labor mixing theory provides one of the most interesting and widely discussed accounts. According to the Lockean theory, I acquire an object by mixing my labor with it. One natural way to elaborate this theory is that the reason I acquire the object by mixing my labor with it is that my labor increases the value of the object. Empirical studies on lay judgments about rightful possession provide evidence that people do take labor mixing to contribute to rightful possession (e.g., Kanngiesser and Hood 2014; Rochat et al. 2014; Levene et al. 2015).

As we saw above, Locke argues that insofar as one mixes one's labor with an object that is clearly not owned by someone else (i.e., it is in the commons), then it becomes one's legitimate property. We can agree with Locke that it certainly does seem intuitive that, *ceteris paribus*, I own the fruits of my labor. However, insofar as the object itself is not the fruit of my labor, does my increasing the value of the object entail that I thereby acquire rightful ownership of the object? Locke seems to think so, but recall Nozick's astute question. Why don't I just own the value added to the unowned object, rather than the object itself? Our studies indicate that people are more Nozickian in this sense than Lockean: they do not infer directly from labor mixing to rightful ownership of an object. Nevertheless, the core Lockean insight remains since our studies confirm previous results that by mixing my labor with an object, I come to own *something*. In particular, I come to own that which I created. But the act of creation itself does not necessarily transfer or secure the ownership of the object itself. By making a sculpture out of clay, I come to own the sculpture, but the ownership of the clay does not follow necessarily.

Previous work shows that ordinary intuitions about rightful acquisition cannot be captured by a simple first possession theory (e.g., Friedman 2008). Our current results show that neither can a simple labor mixing theory capture ordinary intuitions about rightful acquisition. The principles that underlie our ordinary judgments about rightful ownership seem to be more complex and disparate. There is some reason to think that territorial instincts contribute to judgments of rightful ownership (cf. Gintis 2007). However, these innate factors do not fully determine the set of principles that govern our intuitions about rightful ownership. Rather, principles of rightful ownership plausibly depend on the cultural emergence of conventions regarding ownership (pace Gintis 2007). Given the bumpy path of cultural development, it shouldn't be so surprising if it turns out that there is no simple principle that underlies ordinary judgments of rightful acquisition.

Our findings here suggest one way that critics and defenders of the Lockean labor mixing might use empirical methods to make philosophical progress. Some have argued, for instance that the Lockean theory of property as a whole is incompatible with the labor mixing theory of original acquisition (Kogelmann 2021). Others argue that original appropriation in the Lockean sense is more about individuating rather than justifying property rights (van der Vossen 2009). Understanding the relationship between judgments about value and ownership will surely shed some light on these and other debates. More studies along the lines that we have presented here will be needed to decisively settle many of these questions, but there is little reason to think that they can be easily settled without the kind of empirical testing that we do here.

Note

1 Preregistration for Study 1 can be found here: https://aspredicted.org/nv3uu.pdf; preregistration for Study 2 can be found here: https://aspredicted.org/6b6mr.pdf; preregistration for Study 3 can be found here: https://aspredicted.org/va9vz.pdf.

References

Friedman, Ori. 2008. "First Possession: An Assumption Guiding Inferences About Who Owns What." *Psychonomic Bulletin & Review* 15, no. 2: 290–5. https://doi.org/10.3758/PBR.15.2.290.

Gintis, Herbert. 2007. "The Evolution of Private Property." *Journal of Economic Behavior and Organization* 64, no. 1: 1–16.

Kanngiesser, Patricia, and Bruce Hood. 2014. "Not by Labor Alone: Considerations for Value Influence Use of the Labor Rule in Ownership Transfers." *Cognitive Science* 38, no. 2: 353–66. https://doi.org/10.1111/cogs.12095.

Kogelmann, Brian. 2021. "Lockeans Against Labor Mixing." *Politics, Philosophy & Economics* 20, no. 3: 251–72. https://doi.org/10.1177/1470594X211027256.

Levene, Merrick, Christina Starmans, and Ori Friedman. 2015. "Creation in Judgments About the Establishment of Ownership." *Journal of Experimental Social Psychology* 60 (September): 103–9. https://doi.org/10.1016/j.jesp.2015.04.011.

Nozick, Robert. 1974. *Anarchy, State, and Utopia*. New York: Basic Books.

Pufendorf, Samuel. 1673. *The Whole Duty of Man, According to the Law of Nature*. Indianapolis, IN: Liberty Fund.

Rochat, P., E. Robbins, C. Passos-Ferreira, A. D. Oliva, M. D. Dias, and L. Guo. 2014. "Ownership Reasoning in Children Across Cultures." *Cognition* 132, no. 3: 471–84.

Rousseau, Jean-Jacques. 1755. "Discourse on the Origin of Inequality." In *The Basic Political Writings*, edited and translated by Donald A. Cress, 25–110. Hackett Publishing.

Vossen, Bas van der. 2009. "What Counts as Original Appropriation?" *Politics, Philosophy & Economics* 8, no. 4: 355–73. https://doi.org/10.1177/1470594X09343074.

5

Segregation and the Portfolio Theory of Identity

Ryan Muldoon

1. Introduction

Political philosophy often abstracts away from questions about how and on what terms citizens interact with each other. But there are many fascinating political questions that only manifest themselves at this very local level. When we understand concepts like citizens respecting the rule of law, or embracing a sense of justice, we often think of this in terms of the relations citizens have to the formal institutions of the state—that citizens will not break the laws, or that state institutions will treat citizens with equal respect, and so on. But there is much else that is valuable to consider, as we still can have large-scale civic consequences from a series of permissible choices made by individuals who remain committed to a political conception of justice. One that has long had salience in real political discussions is residential segregation. Segregation is philosophically interesting both as a first-order local phenomenon and for its second-order nonlocal effects on politics. That is, we can identify features of a segregated community that fail to realize civic ideals, or that undermine the equality of citizens as a local challenge for an account of justice, but even if we only care about national-level issues of justice, considerable social science has shown that segregation fuels democratic dysfunction and can undermine rights protection.[1]

The spatial arrangement of citizens is important for several reasons. Perhaps most obviously, many core services (whether provisioned by the state, by community organizations, or by private enterprise) are provisioned spatially. Schools, police and fire protection, water and sanitation, roads and transit, and telecommunications all cover specific places. This is unlike, say, setting income tax policy. Where you are and who you are near shape the quality and availability of service. Likewise, citizens are shaped by their local environments and their neighbors.[2] There is robust evidence that segregation is linked to discriminatory behaviors and attitudes, both by preventing inter-group contact and by shaping between-group perceptions.[3] There is increasing evidence of a link between segregation and partisan polarization.[4] If we abstract away from the spatial arrangement of citizens, we would miss these important dynamics that shape questions of both local justice and national justice.

Of course, if we were to look at the history of residential segregation in the United States, we would see a series of laws passed at the local, state, and federal level that combined to enforce racial segregation with the coercive power of the state.[5] These were laws that were passed with the clear policy goal of achieving racial segregation. These laws were unfortunately effective in achieving their aims—segregation increased in this period, and this residential segregation has had long-run deleterious effects on even ameliorative efforts to enhance civic equality. While much could be done to analyze how these unjust laws were treated as legitimate, it is well-established that laws such as these serve to directly undermine core liberal rights and were done with the assumption that citizens were not fully equal. I'd like to step back from the analysis of overtly unjust actions, and instead focus on a somewhat gray area between ideal and nonideal theory in political philosophy. That is, I am interested in considering the behaviors of law-abiding citizens who are not motivated by racial animus but who are at least somewhat responsive to the composition of their neighborhood. Primarily, this will be operationalized as people who are uncomfortable with being too much in the minority—where "too much" may be set at different levels. This may be contrasted against someone who is entirely insensitive to differences in people's personal characteristics. I consider this a gray area between ideal and nonideal theory insofar as we can stipulate that the agents that we consider are all following the laws in good faith, follow the (formal) demands of justice, and endeavor to treat everyone with equal respect. Indeed, any individual choice is innocuous, and not driven by animus. It's also a straightforward exercise of the core liberal right of association. All this requires is that citizens have both equal basic respect for other citizens and additional affinities for particular groups. However, a series of these permissible choices, following psychologically common dispositions, can in aggregate serve to generate unjust outcomes, like residential segregation and its many civic consequences.

Thomas Schelling developed an early and influential model of emergent residential segregation based on a chessboard. Schelling randomly placed pennies and dimes on the squares of the board, leaving a few squares unoccupied. This chessboard with pennies and dimes is meant to represent a grid of homes, and pennies and dimes represent two distinct groups (for instance, two racial groups). In each time period, each piece on the board considers the eight squares surrounding it and evaluates the fraction of its neighbors as being in its same group. Each piece—we'll call them agents—has a threshold of comfort with their neighborhood. The idea is that while people may not object to integrated neighborhoods (or even prefer them), they may dislike being in too small of a minority. For instance, perhaps pennies like neighborhoods that are composed of at least 35 percent pennies. Dimes might prefer a neighborhood of at least 50 percent dimes. In each timestep for the model, the modeler considers each coin and evaluates whether its neighborhood satisfies its comfort threshold or not. If it does, the coin stays put. If not, it moves to a random empty space (or the first available in some search process). The model proceeds through more timesteps until no one wants to move anymore.

What Schelling found is that under a very wide range of thresholds—even as low as 35 percent—the chessboard will end up fully segregated. This is because of what Schelling called a chain reaction, or a tipping point phenomenon. If our movement decisions are all based on the demographic composition of our neighborhood, Alice's movement decision will impact Bob's, which will impact Carol's. This is because when Alice moves out of her neighborhood, that will shift its makeup, and some former neighbors who were previously happy may become unhappy. As she moves into a new neighborhood, a similar issue will arise. Her move will shift the relative numbers of different groups, and this can cause people from the other group to go below their comfort threshold. This will induce them to move in the next round.

As Muldoon et al. (2012) note, if we slightly expand one's view of a neighborhood to expand beyond just one's eight immediate neighbors, using a radius-defined neighborhood, segregation can be generated even when people *want to be in the minority*. In this model, there's no comfort threshold—every extra neighbor that's of a different type is valued. So even decision rules compatible with an active preference for integration can drive a population to segregate. The macro-level phenomenon of segregation is indeed so robust that it's essentially impossible to infer the motives that led to it if all one has to go by is the end result. There are simply too many decision rules (whether threshold-based or not) that will result in a chain reaction of decisions that will lead to segregation. A sharply segregated town could be caused by movement decisions motivated by aggressively racist attitudes, or people who just don't want to be too far in the minority, or even people who much prefer to be in the minority and want to be around people who are different than them.

It is worth noting that one interesting feature of standard segregation models is that they tend to assume that agents all have a single (relevant) property, which everyone uses as the informational basis for their movement decisions. The standard property to rely on is race. This is done with good reason in models of segregation—in general, these models are attempts to explore the dynamics of racial segregation. But fairly obviously, one's race is merely one of many characteristics that contribute to any classification of one's social identity. While this is no great revelation, it does give us reason to pause and reconsider what it means for the Schelling model and its many variants to assume that agents to make decisions on the basis of a single agent property. If we interpret this assumption, it would mean that there is a robust agreement across all agents that the only feature of their neighbors they have reason to care about is race. Perhaps that is true in certain times and places—after all, we do see a great deal of racial segregation. But this ignores a relevant source of agency and diversity. People can conceive of themselves in myriad ways, and further, they can categorize or evaluate others in a variety of ways as well.

If we step back and consider these results, emergent segregation is in part brought on by a more general uniformity in how agents see the world. That is, it is the widespread agreement that we (only) conceive of ourselves and others in terms of race that does the work of driving us to segregate on race, *even if we prefer the opposite*. It's important to note here that, regardless of any beliefs one might have on the status of a racial categories as natural or social kinds, how one constructs one's social identity, and sees the identities of others, is *not* a natural fact. Social identities are up to us. We likely constrain each other in our capacity to realize particular social identities, as a social identity will involve social recognition, but these identities are things that can vary though time and place, and are functions of our particular sets of social arrangements.

Notably, it is also pretty evident that our social identities are complex. I can usefully categorize myself or others along several dimensions. Our institutional arrangements formally recognize our race, gender, religious affiliation, marital status, age (which we often clump by fairly arbitrary generational lines), employment status, among other things. We often make evaluative distinctions around our political affiliations, our wealth, our educational attainment, our musical tastes, and so on. Notably, many of us vary in what we consider to be the most important attributes of ourselves or others. This is aside from questions of what those evaluative judgments might be—just which sorts of characteristics ought to be the most salient for our judgments. We might expect to find robust disagreement about these questions of social identity in a diverse liberal political order, given what Rawls called "the burdens of judgment"—the idea that well-meaning people who properly exercise their reason will still disagree about, for instance, fundamental values, how to interpret evidence, and how to weigh competing considerations (Rawls 1996, 54–7).

To make this idea more concrete, such that we can operationalize it in a model, what I suppose instead here is a simplified version of what we might call a portfolio theory of identity. Instead of having a single trait on which one hangs their social identity, we can imagine that people have many traits. One's social identity is built out of N traits, each of which is constrained to have M possibilities. This gives an individual a portfolio from which they can construct a self-conception. We might suppose that in different contexts, we might present different versions of ourselves and make different sorts of assessments of others. In doing so, we can find ourselves in different in-groups or out-groups. In a work setting, for instance, Alice the experimental philosopher may have less in common with Bob the literary theorist than with Carol the experimental economist. But Alice and Bob are both Bills fans, and so while watching a football game, Carol the Patriots fan may find herself less favored than before. We can also imagine that we can make all-things-considered judgments about others in at least some contexts. For instance, we might think that we do this when considering preferences over neighborhood composition.

What I will argue is when we shift to all-things-considered judgments over more complex social identities, we find a significantly larger space of possibilities for stable integrated states. This is true under several different ways of characterizing "all-things-considered" judgments. The primary reason for this is that these more complex social identities work to blunt the onset of a chain reaction of people moving. The paper will proceed as follows. Section 2 of the chapter will describe the model. Section 3 discusses the results. Section 4 offers a discussion of what we can learn from this approach. Section 5 concludes.

2. The Segregation Model

I develop an extension of the agent-based Schelling Segregation model implemented in Netlogo 6.1.1. The model consists of a "town" constructed on a 35 × 35 grid torus.[6] Each location on the grid represents a single home, and 900 agents individually occupy a random subset of the available homes.[7] Each agent is randomly assigned a set of attributes that comprise its social identity. These attributes are assigned independently. The number of attributes N and the number of possibilities per attribute M are global variables set as model parameters.

The model operates in discrete time, where all agents make assessments in each timestep of the model about whether they are unhappy with their neighborhood composition or not. Unhappy agents will move to a random unoccupied home. Agents make this decision sequentially, but the order in which they make their movement decisions is randomized between timesteps. All agents determine their happiness by relying on a Schelling-style threshold judgment about their neighbors. They look at the neighbors that reside in the eight homes that surround their own and assess whether there is a high enough proportion of agents who are similar to themselves. If there are, they remain where they are. If there are not, they are unhappy, and they move. That is, the agents all follow a threshold function for determining their movement decision, as with the original Schelling model. The similarity threshold is set as a model parameter, so all agents share the same threshold.

Where this model extends the original Schelling model is in the determination of agent similarity. There are three kinds of identity comparisons that agents might make, the choice of which is a global model parameter: a "Priority" judgment, a "Matches" judgment, or a "Manhattan" judgment. I will explain each shortly.

The segregation model proceeds in subsequent timesteps until there are no agents who are unhappy with their neighborhood. If that equilibrium condition is reached, the model run ends.

2.1 Three Approaches to Identity Comparisons

As mentioned, I consider three different extensions of the Schelling model, each of which differs in how agents make similarity judgments. While each assumes that agents have multiple attributes from which one could construct a social identity, each approach does this in a different way. Each approach aims to embody a recognizable and plausible set of liberal values. This allows us to model individuals who can be understood as adhering to the requirements of justice, while exercising associational rights. This exercise of associational rights is entirely consistent with mainstream liberal theories, and allows us to model straightforward ways in which the burdens of judgment and associational rights may interact among well-intentioned agents.

2.1.1 The Priority Model

The simplest option is a "priority" judgment. On this approach, while everyone has N attributes, each agent has a private assessment about which one of those N attributes they consider to be important in this context. The agent then makes similarity judgments on that attribute only. So, if we imagine that Alice, Bob, and Carol have a race, a favorite sports team, and a religion, under a "priority" scheme, it may be the case that Alice and Carol think it's most important to have at least some neighbors that share one's sports fandom, while Bob thinks it's most important to have at least some neighbors that share one's religion. On this scheme, Alice and Carol would act on the same information, and so their decisions will be correlated with each other. But while Bob's move may inform Alice's and Carol's, he's responding to different information than they are altogether. It is important to note that, on this setup, Alice would care only about whether enough of her neighbors cheered for the same team. She doesn't care about (or have a means to learn within the confines of the model) their priority for judging others.

The priority model is a natural extension of the original Schelling model. It retains the simplicity of the basic model, but just supposes that there is a disagreement in the population over what the most important characteristic of one's social identity is. We might see this as a straightforward interpretation of the burdens of judgment as it applies to our assessments of a population complying with the demands of justice, while exercising their liberal rights as aligned with their values. From the perspective of any single agent, they simply want to make sure that there is enough some kind of person in their neighborhood. So, maybe it's enough Bill's fans, or maybe it's enough Muslims, or perhaps it's enough Democrats, or enough black people that the agent feels comfortable in their home environment. Note that unless the threshold is set high, this does not require a *majority*. It just requires enough people of one's type to feel comfortable.

2.1.2 The Match Model

The second way of making a social identity comparison is a "match" judgment. The matching model adds an additional global model parameter, which sets how many attribute matches one wants with one's neighbors. So, if we have, say, 5 attributes to our identity, we may decide that enough of our neighbors need to share at least 2 attributes with us, though we don't particularly care *which* attributes we share with them, and we do not need to have the same attributes shared amongst all of our neighbors. We can see that this "matches needed" parameter determines the stringency of this judgment. If we set the number of matches needed to 1 and the number of agent attributes to 1, this is just the same as the original Schelling model. But we can now generalize it in two dimensions—first by increasing the number of attributes, and then by increasing the number of attribute matches required. On that first dimension, as we increase the number of attributes, if we need only one match, then this is a weaker similarity criterion than either the base Schelling model or the priority model. There are just more ways to be like your neighbor. However, as the number of matches needed increases, the stringency of this criterion is dramatically increased. Indeed, unless the number of attributes is large, having many matches required quickly becomes impossible to satisfy, and will inspire constant agent movement.

If we consider the 1 or 2 match case, however, we can see that this bears a great deal of resemblance to Kwame Anthony Appiah's approach to non-universal shared identity that he develops in chapter 7 of *Cosmopolitanism*. He notes "the points of entry ... are things that are shared by those in the conversation. They do not need to be universal; all they need to be is what these particular people have in common" (Appiah, pp. 97). Our shared identity, or our connection with others that allows us to see them as part of an in-group, can be varied and shaped by the points of connection we have with any particular other individual (Appiah, pp. 98). Appiah's account, then, is an important precursor to the portfolio theory of social identity sketched earlier, and most harmonizes with the 1 or 2 match model of shared identity, especially when paired with a large number of attributes to one's social identity. The more attributes we have, and the fewer number of matches we require, the more likely it is we will find ourselves at home no matter who our neighbors are. While our bases for connection will be different across our different neighbors, we will have a way to have a connection to most if not to all. This is an appropriately cosmopolitan view of shared social identity. We can likewise find a parallel in the sociology literature around "bridging social capital"—where bridging refers to cross-cutting identity connections based on (for instance) club or associational affiliation.

As we ramp up the match requirements, we can see that a very different civic model emerges. With many match requirements, this is more like a thick model of shared culture. In sociological terms we might conceive of this as a high degree of bonding social capital—rather than scant, contingent connections that may vary between neighbors with bridging capital, we assume a sort of family resemblance idea of shared attributes among neighbors. On this view, we want a robust set of shared attributes to facilitate mutual understanding and harmony within the community. In political terms, this may look increasingly like a communitarian ideal, or other views that have a thick "common good" conception of civic relations at their core. This still admits of some amount of diversity, but that diversity is heavily constrained by the shared attributes requirement.

So, where the "priority" approach may be thought of as a generalization of the original Schelling model that remains focused more on individual "consumer choice" among neighborhoods, the "matches" approach helps us assess differences across a sliding scale of civic ideals, from a thin cosmopolitan/Open Society liberal vision, toward an increasingly thick conception of ideal civic life that can take on communitarian or perfectionist attributes. Agents using this matching model are (on the thin account) cosmopolitan in their willingness to find any sort of connection to their neighbors, and deeming that sufficient for having a similar identity. On the thick account, agents desire to live around enough people who are substantively similar to them on a number of dimensions.

2.1.3 The Manhattan Model

The last approach to making similarity judgments notably deviates from the first two, and requires a bit more care in interpretation. On the "Manhattan" approach, agents don't require that their neighbors have *any* attributes that match their own. Instead, they care about their perceived *social distance* from their neighbors. This social distance is interpreted as the Manhattan distance between the two attribute profiles of two agents. This is the sum of the absolute difference between the measures of each attribute. So, suppose that Alice and Bob each have five attributes, and each attribute can be assigned a number in some metric space (say, the integers). The Manhattan distance between them is the sum of the absolute difference between each attribute of Alice and Bob. If Bob's attributes are represented as (1,5,2,1,4) and Alice's attributes are represented as (2,4,1,2,3), Alice and Bob would have a social distance of 1+1+1+1+1, or 5. This is because each of their attributes are 1 unit apart.

Since this approach no longer relies on matching attributes, and instead uses a more general concept of social distance, it is important to note that this means that individuals must have some kind of way to *measure* social distance. That means that there needs to be a standard metric across different attributes, such that we can sensibly place options for those attributes in relation to each other. So, how Alice perceives "distance" between, say, religious affiliations would be commensurate with how Alice perceives racial distance, or distance between sports fandoms. This is a nontrivial assumption. What makes this assumption easier to manage is that there is no particular reason for why this distance metric needs to be inter-personally consistent. Alice and Bob can have different measurements for this. Furthermore, as with other considerations in our model, we can treat this not as something that Alice or Bob explicitly calculate but rather as a rational reconstruction of their all-things-considered final judgment about social distance. Using Manhattan distance allows us to present a consistent all-things-considered judgment without having to make arbitrary assumptions about how different identity attributes stand in relation to each other. Each can be treated as an independent vector space. This is valuable both because it allows us to consider arbitrary identity attributes, and it allows us to be silent on contentious questions of relations between different attributes of one's social identity. In a liberal society we would almost certainly disagree about those relations, and utilizing this distance measure allows us to respect that disagreement.

To be able to use Manhattan distance in the model, we need a threshold for judging whether an agent's neighbors are similar enough or not. To do this, we introduce a normalized similarity metric defined on the unit interval. The similarity metric is a scale that runs from total match on each attribute (1) to maximum distance on all attributes (0). This normalization allows for a consistent measure independent of other model parameter settings. So, on this all-things-considered judgment of social distance, agents are willing to live in neighborhoods where there are enough neighbors who they perceive as close to them in identity, but will move otherwise.

So, a Manhattan model of social distance, while a bit more laden with assumptions on how we can calculate social distance, allows us to consider a more flexible model of social distance, where we can consider ourselves to be similar to each other without ever being the same on any particular dimension. We might think of this as one way of operationalizing an idea of limited tolerance.[8] Citizens accept a form of pluralism and can be tolerant of others, but this tolerance may only extend so far—at least with respect to their immediate living conditions. On this model, citizens would need some sufficient threshold of fellow neighbors to be in the range of beliefs or behaviors that they find congenial, such that they would be comfortable with others being outside of that zone. A more generous similarity threshold would model a more tolerant society.

Thus, we have three distinct measures of social identity, all of which can be simply operationalized in the context of a Schelling Segregation model, and each of which offers a way of capturing common ideals in liberal thought. The first allows a more individual "consumer choice" model of private judgment, but is paired with a conception of the burdens of judgment in which we may reasonably and permissively disagree about how one ought to go about making such judgments about neighborhoods. The second allows us to capture a range of liberal views between a cosmopolitan conception of contingent and thin shared identity, all the way toward a far more robust conception of thick shared identity. The third allows us to examine a constrained tolerance model based on a more flexible understanding of social distance.

Now, we can turn to the question of how these conceptions of social identity can have appreciable effects on questions of local justice.

3. Model Results

To explore the consequences of this portfolio theory of identity, and the three associated ways of operationalizing a notion of social distance that comport with traditions in liberal thought, I ran a series of agent-based model experiments in Netlogo 6.1.1 using the Behaviorspace tool to investigate parameter space. For all reported results, I ran each parameter combination 500 times and present the average. Since the model is not guaranteed to end, I limited each model run to 250 timesteps. If we interpret each timestep as taking somewhere between a week and a month, this would give us a range of five to twenty years for the maximal length of time under consideration. Given that this model is assuming a fixed population with no in- or out-migration, extending the time frame too far out would run into interpretational challenges. Models that settled into an equilibrium typically did so within the range of 10–50 rounds, so a matter of a few months to 5 or so years.

Like the original Schelling model, the core outcome that we are interested in considering is racial segregation. However, in our richer modeling environment, we need to carefully operationalize this in a way that allows for comparisons across all of the cases we consider, and makes sense in a context where there can be more than two options for racial groups. Because we are interested in a variable number of possible racial groups, standard measures of segregation, like the Index of Dissimilarity or and Exposure Index, are poor choices as they are standardly defined for two racial groups. So, we will instead rely on the Entropy Index, which allows us to measure the spatial distribution of an arbitrary number of groups.

For an individual neighborhood i, an entropy index h is calculated by

$$h_i = -\sum_{j=1}^{k} p_{ij} \ln p_{ij}$$

where k represents the total number of racial groups, and p_{ij} is the proportion of the jth racial group in neighborhood i.

I follow White (1986) in constructing a city-wide entropy index, which is defined as

$$H = (\hat{H} - \bar{H})/\hat{H}$$

where $\hat{H}$ is the entropy index for the city as a whole, and $\bar{H}$ is the average entropy of all neighborhoods.

The measure is defined such that when H is 0, the city has uniform distributions of racial groups (each neighborhood has the same composition as the city as a whole), and when it is 1, racial groups are fully isolated (each neighborhood has only one racial group). So, lower numbers represent more racial integration, and higher numbers represent more racial segregation.

This index will give us a consistent measure of city-level segregation across all investigations of our extended model. Since within the formal model itself, "race" is simply an interpretation imposed on an element of a vector, this approach generalizes to any attribute of a social identity that we may wish to investigate.

With our outcome measure clearly defined, we can now turn to the core findings of the model. Most importantly, it is clear that once we introduce a more extended notion of social identity, we find a number of ways to generate stable integrated states of the model, regardless of which mode of judgment we have agents employ for determining their comfort with their neighbors.

First, let us turn to our simplest approach making similarity judgments—the Priority judgment. Recall that agents all randomly select one attribute of social identity that they deem to be most important to them in their choice of residential neighborhood, and then apply their similarity threshold to ensure that enough of their neighbors are like them on their priority attribute.

As we can see in Figures 5.1 and 5.2, increasing the number of identity-relevant attributes greatly diminishes the level of segregation in a city. This pattern is consistent regardless of how the number of options there are per attribute, or how we set agents' similarity thresholds.

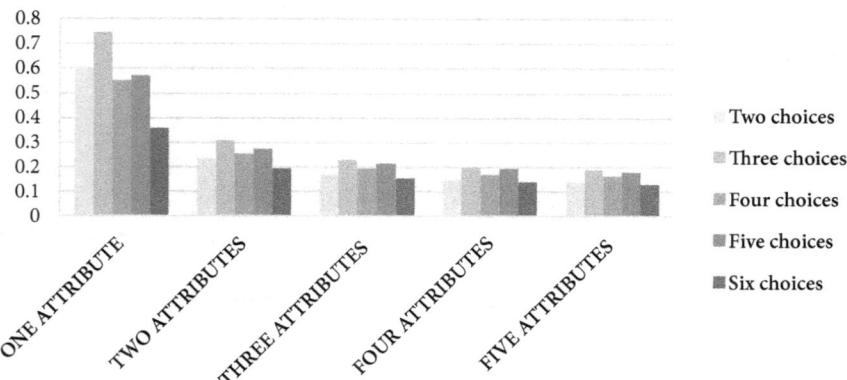

Figure 5.1 On the priority model, adding even one agent attribute dramatically reduces segregation. © Ryan Muldoon.

EFFECT OF SIMILARITY THRESHOLD ON SEGREGATION

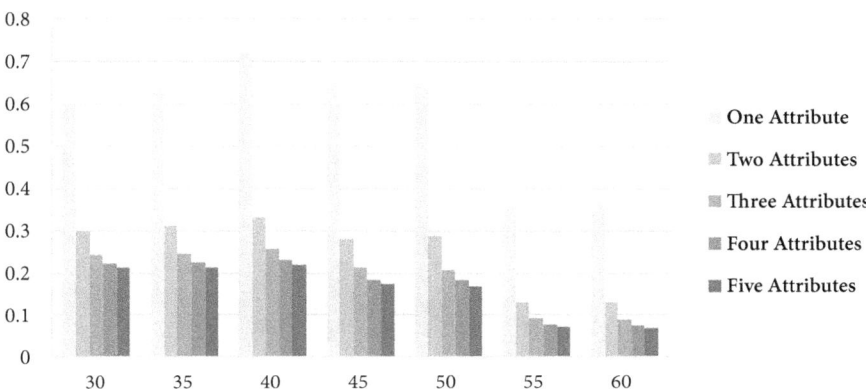

Figure 5.2 On the priority model, even with high similarity thresholds, more attributes sharply reduce segregation. © Ryan Muldoon.

Turning our attention to the Match judgment, as can be seen in Figure 5.3, we find that we can achieve quite integrated states until the demandingness of agents' considerations of similarity gets too high. That is, as we increase the number of attribute matches required for another agent to be seen as similar, the more difficult it is to find agents who satisfy those criteria. This interacts with one's threshold of comfort and the number of available options per attribute. This has the interesting effect of dramatically reducing the incidence of segregation across the full range of parameters of the model compared to the base Schelling model, but this does not mean that we always find stable integrated states. Instead, under a wide range of conditions, the model simply cannot equilibrate. That is, at least some people are reliably unhappy and keep moving in an attempt to satisfy their residential preferences, which in some instances are simply impossible to jointly satisfy. In Figure 5.3, we see that when agents have a total of ten attributes, each with two options, matching is trivial with one to three matches required, but becomes unachievable beyond six matches with a 35 percent threshold.

It is worth noting that, as with the Priority extension to the Schelling model, the Match extension is aided by the fact that as you add more identity attributes, any given attribute will be less likely to be the subject of an agent's judgments, so it can more readily be dispersed through the population. This is because the Schelling chain reaction of movements is undermined by the more diverse informational basis of agent movement choices.

Manhattan distance judgments of social similarity show us an expected pattern. More demanding views of social similarity—where one requires a Manhattan distance within 10 percent of the possible variation in social identities, for instance—have notably higher rates of segregation than more permissive views of social similarity. Likewise, higher thresholds for the proportion of one's neighbors that satisfy this

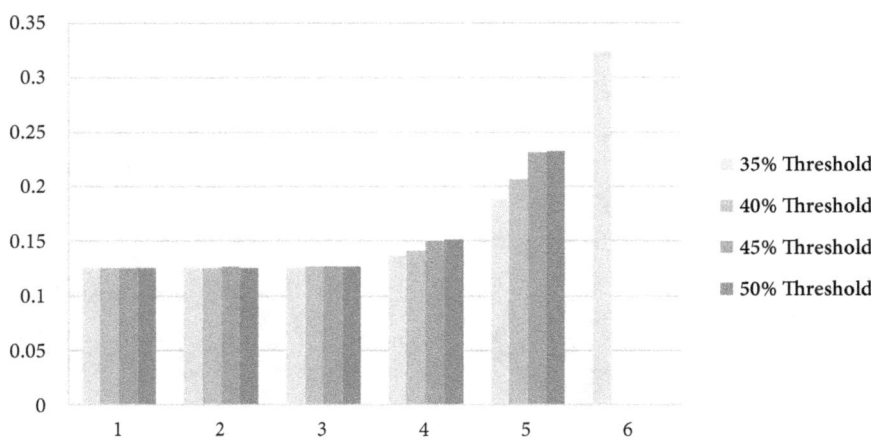

Figure 5.3 On the match model, segregation is much lower, but as similarity judgments require more attributes to match, this becomes too demanding such that the model cannot equilibrate. © Ryan Muldoon.

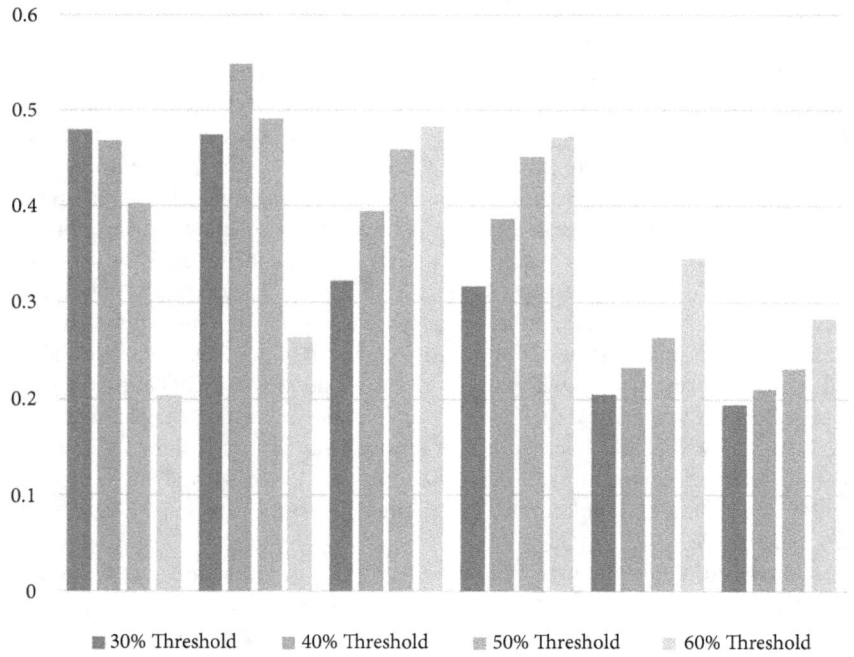

Figure 5.4 On the Manhattan model, we again see lower levels of segregation than the base model. On this model, more restrictive social distance and higher threshold requirements both result in higher rates of segregation. © Ryan Muldoon.

similarity criterion are associated with more segregated cities. Figure 5.4 highlights these relationships, though the pattern in the first two groupings (for a Manhattan similarity range of 10 percent and 20 percent) is skewed in part because the pairing of a narrow model of similarity with a high demand for similar neighbors led to model runs that would never equilibrate, leading to model completions that were more integrated, but with agents unhappy and looking to move.

4. Discussion

We began with the classic Schelling model of segregation, in which agents who otherwise follow the dictates of justice exercise their associational rights, to make sure that they are not "too much" in the minority. But even though each movement was by itself socially innocuous, the aggregate of their behavior results in stark segregation. As discussed, this reliably leads to social and political dysfunction. This offers us a clear example of how individually permissible choices can add up to something that leads to multiple forms of civic harms and injustice: more inter-group conflict, loss of trust, and disparate provision of services. These undermine civic equality, as the bare fact of segregation works to undermine the functioning of democratic procedures. Thus, we have very good reason to study models such as these, to better understand how our interests in justice and equality can be helped or hindered by the structures of citizen interaction. This case is only reinforced if we have reason to think that there are significant social gains to be had beyond just avoiding injustices in diverse, integrated societies (Muldoon 2016; 2018).

What we find is that, if we shift toward a concept of a portfolio theory of our social identity, we create more space for integrated states that are better realizations (and facilitators) of civic equality than what was possible under a standard Schelling model. This is true under several ways of operationalizing the concept of social distance, each with a relevant interpretation within mainstream liberal theory. That is, we find that a core driver of the Schelling result was *sameness* as much as racial diversity. The Schelling result is driven by a shared salient social categorization—people are categorized by race only—that allows for a chain reaction of common choices based on common information. But we can instead draw from liberal theory to offer a richer account of social identity and social categorization.

This offers a much more optimistic set of possibilities than one might otherwise come away from studying classic models of segregation. Indeed, a stark result of previous models was that even if citizens *wanted* to be in the minority, they would end up segregated. Segregation was a robust finding across many ways of assessing movement decisions. Here, we achieve integrated states even in cases where individual agents have more stringent requirements for the composition of their neighborhoods.

How should we understand these results? In one sense, this paints a rather optimistic picture. We find that we can achieve good macro-scale outcomes without requiring that individual citizens be perfectly free of bias. Indeed, we can suppose that citizens are mildly tribalistic and have in-group preferences, and still ensure that we maintain democratically healthy cross-exposure and a concrete instantiation of equal treatment. This result merely depends on a modeling shift toward greater representational realism. That is, we get this result not because we assume people are nicer but because we assume that people have more complex social identities than earlier models allowed for. So, a move toward a recognition that individual diversity is multi-dimensional allows us to break the chain reaction phenomenon that drives Schelling models. In this way, human diversity helps provide the resources for resolving political challenges that diversity can generate.

This approach is useful as it allows us to think about the space of political possibilities that does not rely on an extremely stringent ideal theory. In fact, this allows us to reason more directly about nonideal cases, where we can study people with normal levels of moral motivation. Finding ways that diversity can help us address serious political challenges gives liberal societies more room to become more diverse.

The other way that we may look at these results is that they provide evidence for the fact that a portfolio theory of identity must not be operative in real residential decisions. After all, most American cities are quite segregated by race. I think there are two responses to this. First, we can recall that the United States was, for several decades, under a legal regime that more or less required residential segregation, and after this legal regime ended, citizens were not randomly assigned new homes. Instead, the housing patterns that were generated by unconstitutional rights violations remained in place. We are in some sense trapped by our past. If we suppose that agents are as I have previously described them, it may be the case that we would slowly reduce the rate of segregation. Indeed, Elbers (2021) finds that multigroup racial segregation has declined by a third since 1990, even if the total level of segregation remains high. There may be room to think that we are seeing movement toward more integrated spatial housing patterns, from a segregated baseline. This trend would be extraordinarily unlikely to occur if our primary consideration for neighborhood choice was racial composition. Second, it is likely the case that one of our modeling assumptions is fairly strong: we assume that identity attributes are independently distributed. It is worth considering this assumption in greater detail.

Agents in the model have a variable number of attributes that contribute to their social identities. Each is independently distributed. But we know that in most real populations, there are correlations between various identity attributes. So, one approach could be that we could jointly distribute traits, to provide clusters of properties of various sorts. This would induce a higher rate of segregation, and perhaps this could better describe what we see in, for instance, American cities. However, I would argue that a model like that doesn't help to clarify the crucial lesson that we can take from what our present model provides: as we expand the dimensionality of our judgments (whether individually or in aggregate), we can avoid the pathologies of intentional or unintentional herding behaviors that can work to undermine the real value of our civic equality, and set the stage for poor functioning of democratic processes that assume balanced inputs. A remarkable thing to notice from the simulation results is that as soon as just one more attribute is added to the space of our social identities, we see a significant decline in segregation. There is a declining marginal value in adding more attributes in terms of reducing segregation rates. This suggests that the expansion in the informational base of our choices does not need to be too large. So even in a world of highly, but not perfectly, correlated identity attributes, just having enough of them will boost the informational base of our aggregated choices sufficiently to reduce segregation. This is even supposing that people have reasonably high in-group preferences.

Another way to put this would be to say that if we hoped to get a descriptively accurate model of residential segregation calibrated to actual moves in actual cities, we would likely want to carefully study the joint distributions of different traits. But if we want to learn about the set of options we might have to reduce segregation, we can rely on the simpler model presented here, and focus instead on the idea of informational bases of choices, rather than the particular details of particular traits.

A fruitful way of interpreting this model as a tool in political philosophy is in considering the value of cross-cutting connections in a diverse liberal order. By enriching the model of citizens as having multiple bases of social identity formation, we get a wealth of new resources for thinking about the social underpinnings of a stable liberal order in a diverse society. Rather than needing to suppose a high degree of normalization among citizens, we can *use* the diversity of citizens to see how even with in-group affinities and limited tolerance, we can have a robust web of connections among individuals. Interestingly, this approach helps us see that a robust liberal political order doesn't need to aim to reduce or eliminate sources of disagreement or overcome factionalization. It can instead do well by *encouraging* novel factions. As we increase the elements of our social identities that we might use to categorize each other, we increase the ways we can consider ourselves similar to more people. The crucial thing to foster is that we want these various in-group affinities and factions to be as cross-cutting as we can manage. My cheering for the Buffalo Bills unites me with fellow fans, with whom I can share joys or sorrows as the season progresses, even as I likely disagree vehemently with many about politics, and our professions vary tremendously. Meeting other parents at the playground likewise gives us a common social identity that lets us engage with each other as an in-group. And so on. Stitching ourselves together in this way allows us to foster democratic respect on the basis of contingently shared social identities. Instead of reasoning "as citizens" to find shared connections, we can do so on the basis of rich and varied civic and private lives.[9] This kind of approach offers more resources to both the theorist and real individuals to support a robust liberal order for people like us.

5. Conclusion

In this chapter, I introduced a series of extensions of the Schelling Segregation model, each of which operationalizes a different way of understanding what I call a portfolio theory of identity. Each operationalization—Priority, Matching, and Manhattan Distance—comports well with established liberal accounts of civic connection. Under each of these operationalizations, I demonstrate that there is a wide range of conditions under which we should expect stable integrated states, rather than segregation. This is entirely because the expansion of the informational basis for movement decisions prevents a chain reaction of correlated movement decisions.

I've argued that this model remains importantly idealized, as attributes of agent identities are independently distributed. In real populations, these would be correlated with each other. However, this idealization allows us to focus on the benefits of an enriched informational base, which would remain valuable in the nonidealized case, so long as attributes aren't perfectly correlated with each other.

This idealization helps us identify an interesting tool for a liberal community, which is fostering more varied and cross-cutting elements to citizens' social identities. Such cross-cutting identities allow a liberal community to grow a dense web of social connections, even if the community is rather diverse, and people retain significant in-group affinities. Having a robust patchwork of diverse social identities and affinity groups provides an avenue for robust informal support for formal liberal institutions that is worth more detailed investigation. Much more work can be done exploring the degree to which cross-cutting connections in a diverse order may provide a robust foundation for formal liberal institutions without needing as many optimistic idealizing assumptions for how citizens reason. Just from this work, we see that *more bases for in-group/out-group judgments*—more bases for disagreement—actually make it easier for us to achieve a civically desirable outcome.

A Schelling segregation phenomenon is an important challenge to a liberal political order. It shows how, even where everyone acts permissibly, we can generate unjust informal outcomes that can harm the function of our formal institutional arrangements. Segregation undermines civic equality, frequently leads to disparate treatment by the state, and fosters distrust of out-groups. As previous work has shown, just making people have more enlightened attitudes is not sufficient to solve the problem. Instead, by making individuals more realistically complex, we can convert these differences into resources that a liberal political order can use to become more robust.

Notes

1. For a survey of the literature on segregation's effects on democratic governance, see Muldoon, "Diversity Isn't What Divides Us. Division Is What Divides Us" Knight Foundation, 2018.
2. See Muldoon, "'Reasoning Qua Citizen' and the Dangers of Idealization in Public Reason," *Public Affairs Quarterly*, 36(1): 1–18.
3. Enos, Ryan D. and Christopher Celaya, "The Effect of Segregation on Intergroup Relations," *Journal of Experimental Political Science*, 5(1): 26–38.
4. Brown, Jacob R. and Ryan D. Enos, "The Measurement of Partisan Sorting for 180 Million Voters," *Nature Human Behavior* 5: 998–1008.
5. For an excellent legal history of residential segregation in the United States, see Rothstein, *The Color of Law*, 2017.
6. A torus is simply a plane with both its horizontal edges and vertical edges wrapped around. This gives it a donut shape. Results are not noticeably changed in a plane. The main virtue of using a torus is to avoid any issues with "edge effects" that are more reflections of the technical implementation than a feature in the world.
7. This number can be varied as a model parameter. Its main effect is changing the speed of model runs.

8 For a more detailed model of an operationalization of tolerance in this way, see Muldoon, Borgida and Cuffaro, "The Conditions of Tolerance," *Politics, Philosophy and Economics*, 11(3): 322–44.
9 See Van Schoelandt, "Convergence in the Political Liberal Community," *Public Reason* 11(2): 3–18.

References

Appiah, Kwame Anthony. 2010. *Cosmopolitanism: Ethics in a World of Strangers*. New York: W. W. Norton.

Brown, Jacob R. and Ryan D. Enos. 2021. "The Measurement of Partisan Sorting for 180 Million Voters." *Nature Human Behavior* 5: 998–1008.

Elbers, Benjamin. "Trends in U.S. Residential Racial Segregation, 1990–2020" *Socius* (January 2021).

Enos, Ryan and Christopher Celaya. "The Effect of Segregation on Intergroup Relations." *Journal of Experimental Political Science* 5, no. 1: 26–38.

Muldoon, Ryan. 2018. "Diversity Isn't What Divides Us. Division Is What Divides Us." Knight Foundation.

Muldoon, Ryan. 2018. "The Paradox of Diversity." *Georgetown Journal of Law and Public Policy* 16, no. 1: 807–20.

Muldoon, Ryan. 2022. "'Reasoning Qua Citizen' and the Dangers of Idealization in Public Reason." *Public Affairs Quarterly* 36, no. 1: 1–18.

Muldoon, Ryan. 2016. *Social Contract Theory for a Diverse World: Beyond Tolerance*. New York: Routledge.

Muldoon, Ryan, Tony Smith, and Michael Weisberg. 2012. "Segregation That No One Seeks." *Philosophy of Science* 74, no. 5: 873–83.

Muldoon, Ryan, Michael Borgida, and Michael Cuffaro. 2012. "The Conditions of Tolerance." *Politics, Philosophy and Economics* 11, no. 3: 322–44.

Rawls, John. 1996. *Political Liberalism*. New York: Harvard University Press.

Rothstein, Richard. 2017. *The Color of Law*. New York: Liveright.

Schelling, Thomas. "Dynamic Models of Segregation." *Journal of Mathematical Sociology* 1: 143–86.

Van Schoelandt, Chad. "Convergence in the Political Liberal Community." *Public Reason* 11, no. 2: 3–18.

White, Michael J. "Segregation and Diversity Measures in Population Distribution." *Population Index* 52: 198–221.

6

Empirical Philosophy: How Engaging with Empirical Evidence Is Important for Theory as Well as Practice

Nicole Hassoun

1. Introduction

Historically, philosophy and the natural sciences were continuous (Anstey and Vanzo 2012). Aristotle dissected Hyenas. Descartes spent significant time with his hands in the belly of a cow. Kant gave lectures on geography and anthropology (Appiah 2008). More recently, some philosophers have started to conduct scientific research once again. Such *experimental* philosophers tend to view their efforts as a continuation of philosophy as historically practiced. But, they also see it as radically new since they are adopting the methods of modern science (Alfano and Loeb 2014). Most experimental philosophy models itself on the psychological literature (Horvath and Grundman 2010; Alexander 2012; Fischer and Collins 2015). That is, philosophers conducting experiments often rely primarily on survey questions to figure out what most people, the "folk," think about different philosophical puzzles. (For a review of potentially relevant experimental philosophy and examples, see: Hassoun 2014; Knobe 2007a; b; Kauppinen 2007). This chapter suggests that philosophers need other kinds of empirical evidence to answer different kinds of questions (Woolfolk 2013; Hassoun 2014; Hassoun 2016; Andow 2016; Polonioli 2017). Moreover, this chapter considers how experimental philosophers should pursue empirical work. It argues, for instance, that philosophers who conduct experimental, and other empirical, research (henceforth simply *experimental philosophers*) should consider adopting sociological, anthropological, historical, and other scientific methods to answer important questions. Empirical inquiry has its limits. Still, it can help make philosophical arguments and evaluate practical proposals for positive change. Good action-guiding theories must comport with sound practice. In other words, no one

The material in this chapter is largely drawn from Chapter 6 of my book *Global Health Impact: Extending Access on Essential Medicines for the Poor* (Oxford University Press, 2020), "Beyond Experimental Political Philosophy: Evaluating Global Health Impact Certification," but it also includes some text from my article "Thoughts on Philosophy and the Science of Well-Being," *Res Philosophica*, Volume 96, Issue 4, October 2019, pp. 521–8, https://doi.org/10.11612/resphil.1803. I am grateful to these publishers for permission to use this material.

should implement such theories in the actual world if they will not have good, or at least acceptable, results. So, it is important to consider what works in practice as well as theory, even if philosophers do not want to engage in empirical research themselves.

In considering how philosophers should engage with theoretical and empirical work, I am not trying to win a verbal debate about what qualifies as *philosophy* or even *experimental philosophy*. I only argue that philosophers often have reason to engage with, if not do, new empirical work. I focus, in particular, on arguing that experimental philosophers should consider new methods from a variety of disciplines to help evaluate practical theories. I do not discuss how experimental philosophers should choose these methods here—though, see Hassoun (2010). I do not care if someone prefers to call the empirical work I suggest these philosophers do something else besides *experimental philosophy*. I will persist, however, in referring to it as *experimental philosophy* not only because of philosophy's historical roots but because of how I think philosophy should inform science. I believe that philosophical theory often advances good science. This theory does not just provide "stimulus, challenge, [and] interest" (Appiah 2008, 19). It is often important for examining, creating, and applying scientific methodology.

So, this chapter also argues that empirical inquiry often requires philosophical investigation. It contends that researchers must use the right methods in testing such theories before putting them into practice. Different methodologies have different limitations and are better and worse for different purposes. Still there are ways of addressing potential problems with this chapter's proposed methodology where they are likely to occur. Philosophical debate can help ensure researchers use good methods for the right purposes. Moreover, ethical evaluation can ensure that empirical inquiry is permissible.

This chapter proceeds as follows. Section 2 argues that philosophers should engage with different kinds of empirical evidence even if they do not want to do science themselves. They can build, arbitrate between, and criticize theories by appeal to empirical evidence. I believe that, upon reflection, few will object to this point. Still, making it sets the stage for subsequent sections' arguments. Moreover, the argument I provide is novel. Most defend using empirical evidence in philosophy by explaining how the evidence allows researchers to challenge appeals to intuition. Some suggest it helps them figure out how the mind works or create less culturally biased theories (Knobe and Nichols 2008). I argue, instead, that such evidence can help ensure that theories have good, or at least acceptable, results when implemented (Lindauer 2020). (Many take this as a desiderata for good action-guiding theories that tell people what to do in the actual world.) Moreover, I suggest that empirical evidence is necessary to establish many philosophical arguments' conclusions unconditionally. In making this case, I also argue that although most experimental philosophy uses psychological methods to address questions about individuals' intuitions, experimental philosophers should consider other scientific methods as well. Section 3 examines empirical evaluation's limitations. It explores some ways of addressing potential problems where they are likely to occur. In doing so, it examines how philosophical inquiry can inform science as well as enrich philosophical theories. Section 4 concludes.

2. Reasons to Engage with Empirical Evidence

Most experimental philosophy utilizes surveys to examine "the folk's" intuitions about a variety of topics, but this section argues that philosophers should consider many other kinds of empirical work (Alfano and Loeb 2014; Hassoun 2014). Traditionally, experimental philosophers have utilized survey methods though they have started to do more sophisticated empirical work and many engage with work by psychologists and (occasionally) other social scientists (Knobe 2007a; b; Kauppinen 2007; Knobe and Nichols 2008; Appiah 2008; Woolfolk 2013). Survey methods can document individuals' beliefs. Researchers also need to know (e.g.) under what conditions these beliefs influence action and whether it is possible to change these conditions (Andow 2016).[1] So, this section argues that there is reason for experimental philosophers to do many new kinds of empirical work. At least, it contends, philosophers often have reason to engage with other kinds of empirical work when they do not have the time, skill, or inclination to do it well themselves.

Some, like David Miller, argue that science and philosophical inquiry always depend on each other (Miller 2001). Miller argues that philosophers often construe reflective equilibrium (arriving at a balance of judgement after deliberation) too narrowly. They, wrongly, reflect only on their own *individual* beliefs. He thinks, philosophers should expand reflective equilibrium to include considered judgments *between* individuals. Miller suggests that:

> Looking at what other people believe about justice, and in particular trying to understand when people disagree and what the ground[s] of their disagreement are, are integral to the process of deciding which of [… one's] … own beliefs deserve to be taken as 'the fixed points (Miller 2001, 56)'.

Others worry about

> standard philosophical methodology, whereby philosophers consult their *own* intuitions from the armchair and assume that they represent ordinary intuitions. While this practice may be appropriate when such an assumption is uncontroversial … philosophers have conflicting intuitions, intuitions that may well have been influenced by their own well-developed theories (Nahmias, Morris, Nadelhoffer and Turner 2006, 34).

At least, when making arguments intended to address those whose beliefs differ from one's own, one should consider others' perspectives.[2] Empirical evidence that others disagree with considered judgments invites reflection on the disagreement's grounds.

Evidence about what people believe is, however, not the only information philosophers interested in developing, or evaluating, action-guiding theories require.[3] Sometimes we require information about how people will act in different circumstances. Under what conditions (if any) will people fulfil their duties? If people understand that they are obligated to do something, will they try to do so? If they try, will their actions have any effect? If not, can researchers modify the choice situation to achieve better moral results? After all, as some utilitarians argue, if the best-case scenario suggests that telling people they are obligated to do something will have primarily negative consequences, it may be better not to tell them. And if that is right, knowing how people will act may have significant consequences for what kinds of moral theories it is fruitful to create.

Insofar as good theories must comport with sound practice (so that they have good, or at least acceptable, results when implemented), philosophers should take different kinds of empirical evidence about the consequences of implementing their recommendations seriously. Many argue that ought-implies-can—that is, that people do not need to do things that they cannot do (Sinnott Armstrong 1984; Copp 2003; Howard-Snyder 2006; Vranas 2007; Talbot 2015). Others maintain that people need fact-sensitive action-guiding theories to decide what they should do, or at least what goals they should aim at, in the actual world (Copp 2003; Howard-Snyder 2006, 27; Valentini 2006; Farrelly 2007).[4] Yet others argue that adequate theories must have good, sustainable consequences (Rawls 1993; Klosko 1994; Vanderschraaf 2006; Sinnott-Armstrong 2019). At least, insofar as good theories must comport with sound practice, different kinds of empirical evidence can help researchers build, arbitrate between, and criticize theories. So, they have reason to take this evidence seriously. Moreover, those interested in gathering data to build, arbitrate between, and criticize theories have reason to gather this evidence.[5]

A different reason to think many kinds of empirical evidence are useful for building, evaluating, and arbitrating between philosophical theories (and, so, that philosophers have reason to take this evidence seriously or gather it themselves) is this: many philosophical theories contain empirical premises that require substantiation to establish their conclusions unconditionally. In some of my work, for instance, I argue that people should purchase ethically labelled goods *if doing so encourages companies to respect rights and start living up to their obligations* (Hassoun 2020). I present some evidence that ethical consumption will affect companies' behavior in these ways and conclude that consumers should engage in ethical consumption. Still, to make a strong ethical case for ethical consumption, empirical evidence is essential to see whether (and under what conditions) people will purchase ethically labelled goods and how companies will respond to this incentive. Empirical evidence is likewise essential to support many other practical conclusions about our moral obligations.

Consider a few concrete examples of theories meriting empirical inquiry to make the case that this inquiry is important for arriving at strong action-guiding ethical theories and, therefore, that philosophers may often benefit from engaging with it. Consider, for instance, a few recent proposals for promoting global justice and health (Wenar 2007; Pogge 2008; Pogge and Hollis 2012). Aidan Hollis and Thomas Pogge, for instance, suggest incentivizing pharmaceutical companies to provide greater access to essential medicines through the Health Impact Fund (HIF). The Health Impact Fund would offer a second (voluntary) patent system for essential drugs and technologies (Pogge and Hollis 2012). Supported by extensive philosophical argument, this system does not give companies a limited monopoly for their inventions. Rather, it rewards inventors based on how much their inventions contribute to ameliorating the global disease burden (Hubbard and Love 2004; Pogge and Hollis 2012). People might also address global health problems by expanding web-based charitable giving (and lending) platforms more broadly. Kiva—an online micro-finance platform that allows people to lend money around the world—might focus, for instance, on giving loans to people to purchase essential medicines. Alternatively, individuals might prefer to give loans to institutions promoting global health (or support global justice in other ways) through a Kiva-like platform.[6] Researchers can test these proposals to see if they work.

Consider how Hollis and Pogge suggest testing the Health Impact Fund. They hope to pilot the proposal for one or two drugs in one country. They want to convince pharmaceutical companies to lower their prices for drugs for a particular disease (e.g., hemophilia) at select treatment centers in exchange for a payment based on drugs' performance in reducing the disease burden on some measure (e.g., how many "bleeds" treatment centers report). To measure health impact, the HIF plans to track sales, evaluate education programs with surveys, and obtain stratified drug usage samples. A successful pilot would demonstrate that researchers can measure and reward companies for drug performance and incentivize investments that increase drug impact. The pilot would observe companies' marketing efforts in response to the payment system and provide essential information on how many dimensions researchers need to measure different drugs' impact in different populations. To carry out the pilot, researchers can secure data from treatment centers, educational centers, and pharmaceutical sales, and Pogge estimates that the pilot will cost at least half a million dollars to complete (Pogge 2013).

Researchers can more easily test the proposal to expand Kiva for health. Since Kiva collects data on loan repayment and what people pay the most attention to in giving aid, researchers might study it easily. Elsewhere, I have worked with economists and computer scientists to examine how people choose to lend money through Kiva using this database (Hassoun, Lubchenco, and Malikov 2016). Controlling for many factors such as borrowers' gender, month, lenders' location, and loan purpose, we take the average income in a country as a proxy for the amount individuals need and funding time as a proxy for the how much individuals care about aiding those in need. The results suggest that people fund loans to those in greater need more quickly than loans to those who need less at least until people receiving aid rise above some income threshold. Moreover, it seems that people care more about helping those further below the threshold. Researchers could create a similar study to see whether people lend (or give) to those with serious health issues. People need to know whether (and, if so, how) such proposals work to embrace, and improve upon, them.

In arguing that empirical evidence is sometimes relevant for creating, evaluating, and criticizing philosophical arguments, I do not claim facts are unchangeable, or that anyone should take people, practices, or institutions as they are (Cohen 1991; Cohen 2002). I am not objecting to ideal theories that only guide action assuming full compliance or that make other simplifying assumptions (Rawls 1980; Valentini 2006; Simmons 2010). I only claim that philosophers should care about some facts (or truths discernible through scientific inquiry) when evaluating theories that rely upon them. Philosophers should attend carefully to the circumstances that must obtain to apply their theories and how people can, and cannot, change these circumstances (Vanderschraaf 2006). At least, those who hope their theories will promote positive change often need to know whether they can do so by changing preferences, practices, or institutions.

Gathering, and/or utilizing, the requisite empirical data does not preclude further philosophical inquiry. People may need to know if it is acceptable to change preferences, practices, or institutions when they can do so.[7] Moreover, when no one can, or must, change these things, philosophers might still argue that they should be different (Gerald 2008; Estlund 2019). However, for this chapter's purposes, the important point is just this: to come to sound conclusions about the real world, researchers must often take into account agents' capabilities and capacities and institutions' strengths and weaknesses.[8]

The conclusion that philosophers sometimes need empirical evidence to support (fact-sensitive) theories does not mean that facts are *always* relevant to philosophical theory or that they are prior to value judgments (Gerald 2003). One may defend a philosophical view that is not fact-sensitive—one may say, for instance, that it is always wrong to engage in (un)ethical consumption independent of the consequences. But, many theories do rely on factual claims that are worth investigating. To give another example from my recent work on global health, I have argued that companies should not lobby for patent protection on essential medicines because doing so often makes it difficult or impossible for people to access these medicines. In doing so, I provided some empirical (as well as theoretical) support for this claim because I did not want to qualify it. I did not just want to claim that companies should not lobby for patent protection on essential medicines *if* that makes it difficult or impossible for people to access these medicines.

It is also compatible with my thesis that, ultimately, all theories must rest on nonfactual claims (Gerald 2003). Facts may never tell people what foundational philosophical principles to embrace.[9] I only claim that researchers *sometimes* need facts that they can only acquire through empirical investigation about much more than individuals' beliefs to build, justify, and criticize philosophical theories.[10]

Moreover, experimental philosophers should broaden their remit because more than individual's beliefs matter for philosophical theory. I do not deny that researchers can benefit from dividing labor between the theoretical and empirical sciences. Empirical, like philosophical, arguments can be better or worse and it is hard to do good empirical work (Woolfolk 2013). When philosophers have the interest, inclination, and capacity, they sometimes contribute to science. Eric Agner and colleagues have found, for instance, that those who are happier are more likely to adhere to medical treatment for at least some diseases (Hassoun 2020). Other experimental philosophers have also examined, and/or worked with, scientists to answer important questions (see, for instance: Cushman, Knobe and Sinnott-Armstrong 2008; Hassoun 2009; Paxton, Figdor and Tiberius 2012; Hassoun, Lubchenco and Malikov 2016; Lindauer and Barry 2017; Wilhelm, Conklin and Hassoun 2018, and the examples below). Still, not everyone is, or should be, an experimental philosopher. Some lack the capacity and training to do good science. Moreover, some purely theoretical research is incredibly important.

However, even those who have no interest in doing experimental philosophy should often engage seriously with new scientific work (Hassoun 2014). Researchers can often build, arbitrate between, and criticize theories by appeal to such evidence partly because it can help people evaluate how proposals work in practice. At least, insofar as researchers must ensure good theory comports with sound practice, they should take many kinds of empirical evidence seriously.

The next section considers testing's limits and argues that, just as researchers often need empirical evidence to construct good theories, they often need theoretical inquiry to conduct good empirical research. Different methodologies have different limitations and are better and worse for different purposes. Theoretical argument can help make the case for using a particular methodology given researchers' objectives. It can also help ensure that researchers are answering the most important questions in a way that is ethically acceptable.

3. The Need for Mid-Level Theory

Although researchers can use many different methods to test proposals for positive change, every methodology has advantages and drawbacks and philosophical theory is necessary for examining, creating, and applying any particular scientific methodology. Consider just one kind of scientific methodology—randomized controlled trials—to see how philosophical evaluation can support scientific evaluation: in these trials, individuals (or sometimes groups) are randomized to a treatment or control condition and then researchers see if there are significant differences in outcomes between the two conditions. This lets researchers control for variation due to extrinsic factors other than the treatment—whether it is a drug, educational program, or other intervention.

Randomized-controlled trials can have high *internal validity*. That is, if the randomly selected population truly represents the study population, the study provides strong evidence that the treatment (or intervention) being tested works *for that population*. However, randomized-controlled trials cannot control for variation that is simply due to chance; randomly selected participants in control and treatment conditions may differ from one another in significant ways. Fortunately, there are some ways to avoid problematic biases due to chance. Matching participants based on potentially confounding factors—like age and location—and selecting randomly from the subsets may help, for instance. (Nonrandom selection makes bias more likely: if one only selects the oldest people or those closest to major metropolitan areas, one has more reason to worry about biasing the sample.)

There are also other ways of dealing with problems that can afflict randomized-controlled trials. Participants in a study may do better because they are happy to be participants or because they receive special treatment in the experiment—undermining the point of randomization (World Health Organization 1998; Peters, Langbein and Gareth 2017). Sometimes studies also find positive results simply because people know they are participating in a study. Researchers call this the Hawthorne or

John Henry effect. Placebo controls may help address the first issue and increasing evaluation's length and scale may help address the second (Hassoun 2010; Peters, Langbein and Gareth 2017).

Even the best randomized-controlled trials that do not suffer from these problems have their limits, however. They may have low *external validity*: their results may not generalize to other areas or larger scales (Peters, Langbein, and Gareth 2017; Al-Ubaydli, List, and Dana 2017; Muralidharan and Niehaus 2017; Banerjee et al. 2017). It is not feasible to select randomly from all the people in a single country, nevermind globally. So, even if a randomized-controlled trial shows that an intervention works in some area, people in different locations might be different (Hassoun 2010). Similarly, it is important that the relevant causal factors do not change between testing and generalization (Basu 2014; Deaton and Cartwright 2017).

Moreover, there are many interesting philosophical assumptions that one must make to accept that randomized-controlled trial results will generalize even in the same population. One must believe, for instance, that the results will generalize for a nonrandomly selected individual, or subpopulation, within the population. Nonrandomly selected individuals may differ in some important ways from most randomly selected individuals (Basu 2014). More generally, to conclude that randomized-controlled trials' results will generalize, even in the same population, one must assume that the study controls for all the relevant factors.

Randomized-controlled studies, like most others, also raise pressing research ethics questions. Must subjects give their informed consent to participate in studies? Can researchers test programs that may harm people? Are the benefits of the study fairly distributed? How can researchers avoid exploiting the global poor in doing research in developing country contexts? And so forth (Nwabueze 2013).

Finally, there is the issue of cost. Must people always test proposals so rigorously before implementing them? Randomized-controlled studies often cost a lot. People may have better ways to use their resources. Such studies may also pose risks to participants and there are potential risks and benefits of implementing proposals without testing too. Researchers need to be sure they evaluate the right things in the right ways (Rosen, Manor, Engelhard, and Zucker 2006; Tollefson 2015; Hammer 2017).

We need further philosophical, as well as empirical, inquiry to address the issues above. Where necessary, researchers can conduct additional randomized-controlled trials (or other empirical studies) to see if their results generalize. Researchers can then systematically review existing studies to come to general conclusions (as medical decision-makers do in healthcare settings). Lacking a complete characterization of relevant background conditions, however, philosophical argument is necessary to decide which are relevant. Philosophical argument can also help make the case for using a different methodology or provide grounds for supporting or criticizing researchers' objectives. It can help ensure that researchers are answering the most important questions in good ways.

Consider how philosophical inquiry might fruitfully inform debates about whether it is acceptable to carry out some research that might be relevant to philosophical arguments about humanitarian interventions—perhaps those for providing health aid in emergency situations. There is little philosophical discussion of scientific research ethics outside medical contexts, but some of the discussion in the biomedical ethics literature is relevant. On the most demanding accounts of what ethical research requires, researchers must not only secure participants' consent but compensate people for the risks of participating in randomized-controlled trials and ensure that their research's benefits are widely distributed (London 2006; Wendler 2017). A lot of debate focuses on what constitutes consent, acceptable risk imposition, and fair distribution of benefits, and what kinds of research institutional review boards should approve (London 2006; Nwabueze 2013). However, different kinds of experiments pose different ethical questions. Is it permissible to create a control group (and withhold immediate aid) to conduct an experimental evaluation of a humanitarian intervention? How can researchers address the risks of experiments creating perverse incentives to delay aid in circumstances where doing so will let researchers conclude that the aid has a larger effect? In some cases, researchers may do better to conduct other kinds of (e.g., quasi-experimental) evaluations (Puri et al. 2017). Further philosophical inquiry is necessary to see what tests are permissible in different circumstances and extend research ethics beyond the medical domain.

Moreover, engaging with empirical work can open up important new avenues for philosophical inquiry. Empirical researchers require "mid-level" philosophical work even to measure many of the things that matter—and creating such mid-level theory would constitute an important contribution to philosophical discourse as well as empirical science.

Let me explain why we need more mid-level philosophical work (as opposed to high-level philosophical theories) to support empirical work with the example of measuring well-being. There are both subjective and objective accounts of welfare in the philosophical literature but few accounts are specified in enough detail for scientists to measure.[11] It is not enough to say, for instance, that welfare is preference satisfaction; one must explain what preferences matter and how to weight different kinds of preference satisfaction against one another in order to develop a philosophically robust measure of welfare as preference satisfaction.

To see why further philosophical work is needed, consider what scientists must do to arrive at a preferentist theory that would be precise enough to measure: it would obviously be very difficult to measure the welfare of every person based on his or her idiosyncratic preferences—researchers would have to figure out a way to elicit all the preferences and then measure their fulfilment over time. Moreover, they would need to know how to weight fulfilment of different preferences to different degrees against one another at different times to even evaluate one person's welfare). Even if researchers only aim to measure aggregate life quality at the population level, they would have to decide whether it was reasonable to say that, in aggregate (and on average in the population), fulfilling all preferences is equally important or they must provide another account of how preferences matter to allow them to measure the contribution of each component. And since they probably cannot ask people about everything they might prefer, researchers must also figure out what preference domains are important to include. It may be incredibly hard to come up with an adequate theory and measure, but a well-justified theory about what constitutes population-level (preferentist) well-being may help researchers create better measures.

Alternately, consider why further mid-level philosophical theory is needed to develop an adequate measure of individual well-being on an alternative, objective list, theory. Let us suppose, just for illustration's sake, that well-being is a function of the quality of one's relationships, knowledge, appreciation, achievements, worthwhile activities, and perhaps other things like the balance of pleasure over pain one experiences over the course of one's life (Hassoun 2015). Suppose, moreover, that researchers are interested in a measure that can tell them how any particular individual is doing.[12] Focusing on this task clarifies some dimensions along which the underlying philosophical theory may require further development.

How would one measure each of the things on the above account of well-being? Researchers might start by examining individuals' relationships. It is likely they will have to say something about the importance of the number of relationships individuals can sustain as well as about their quality. Perhaps it only matters that the person has one good friend, but many think that familial relationships of different kinds are incredibly important. It may matter, for instance, that the person can have children (Braybrooke 1987). Researchers also need to know what constitutes a quality relationship—is this a matter of satisfaction or something more objective? Every choice researchers make will affect the way they construct the measure. Suppose that all that matters is that the person is satisfied with all of the relationships she has and that she has at least some of them. Then researchers could turn to measures of relationship satisfaction such as the Relationship Assessment Scale to at least proxy for this component of well-being or (if they all prove inadequate) construct a new one (Hendrick 1988). With a more complicated theory, researchers not only need to measure the different qualities of relationships. They need to know how to weigh them against each other and the number and/or kinds of relationships the person has. It may even be difficult to measure something that appears simpler like pleasure—some suggest pleasure is just desire fulfilment, others that it is a felt evaluation, and yet others that it is a simple unanalyzable feature of experience that makes the experience attractive (Heathwood 2006; Katz 2016). Similar observations apply to the other components of the account—researchers need to explain what constitutes knowledge, valuable achievement, worthwhile activity, and so forth.[13] Then they can consider what existing measures capture the relevant phenomenon or they can construct new ones that will suffice for the measurement purpose. Moreover, researchers have to explain how to combine these measures into an overall index to say how the individual fares overall on the theory. The underlying philosophical theory will require further development here to be operationalizable.

Some seem to think that we do not need to endorse a theory-based approach to measuring well-being because we can stay neutral between many competing theories or use only an intermediate account that accommodates the core commitments of the main going theories; they maintain that many measures are appropriate proxies for well-being on many theories (Angner 2011; Bishop 2015; Haybron and Tiberius 2015; Hersch 2019; Hersch 2020).

While it is certainly true that measures can work well as proxies for well-being on many different theories, not all measures provide good proxies on all theories. As I have explained above, the differences between theories can matter immensely in constructing good measures. Some components of a measure may be much more closely correlated with well-being than others and some measures may fail to correlate at all. Suppose, for instance, an objective list theory of well-being is correct and that it contains three things—pleasure, important desire satisfaction, and worthwhile achievement. A proxy that considers the extent to which any desires are satisfied may work in some circumstances but produce highly suboptimal results in others. Suppose policy makers can either do something that will give people a lot of pleasure in worthwhile achievements or something that satisfies only base desires. The proxy would suggest pursuing the second option even when the first is better. In any case, having a well-justified theory of what a researcher wants to measure for a purpose is often important for good scientific inquiry, and philosophical inquiry is often important for empirical research just as empirical research is important for philosophical inquiry.[14]

4. Conclusion

This chapter began by arguing that insofar as researchers should make sure good theories comport with sound practice, they should take empirical evidence about policy proposals' effectiveness seriously. At least, those who want to provide, arbitrate between, and/or criticize many action-guiding theories should consider such evidence. Although dividing labor can bring great benefits, I do not see why philosophers cannot do good empirical work. Some might argue that what I propose is no longer experimental, or even empirical, *philosophy*. Even if these critics are right, I do not see why philosophers should not do it.[15] The important question, to my mind, is not "Is this philosophy?" but "What do we want philosophy to be?" Or, better: "What is it important to do?" Even if philosophers do not conduct any empirical research, however, they should engage with new methodologically sophisticated experimental (and other empirical) work in addition to the kinds of survey studies most experimental philosophers have employed so far. I believe philosophers should "sustain a variety of traditions of reflection on questions that matter" (Appiah 2008, 20).[16] Those on the cutting edge are already taking up the challenge.

Like theoretical inquiry, however, empirical research has its limits and addressing these limits can add as much to philosophical inquiry as to scientific analysis. Are proposed studies adequate to their aims, ethical, and are their costs worth the benefits? Further philosophical, as well as empirical, inquiry is necessary to address these questions. Moreover, scientists often require philosophical analysis to conduct good empirical research even for a restricted purpose. Good theories often depend on good empirical work, but good empirical work can also depend on having a good theory. Whether theories merit empirical investigation depends on one's philosophical view. Moreover, when theories merit empirical study, researchers often need philosophical inquiry to clarify what they hope to achieve with empirical research (Deaton 2009). Philosophical inquiry can help ensure that researchers answer the most important questions in ethically acceptable ways. The requisite mid-level theories are philosophically interesting as well as important for good scientific analysis.

Notes

1. Philosophical survey methods may also have some methodological problems. Often the questions are strange—people may fail to understand or interpret them in the right way, many irrelevant contextual factors may influence their responses, and sometimes they may have no real opinion at all (Scholl 2008). Some economists also believe researchers need to give subjects incentives to reveal their true views, ensure confidentiality, and avoid misleading them. They point out that subjects may not reveal their true beliefs if they think others will find out or may give odd answers because they are worried about being deceived. There are methods for addressing some of these problems when they arise (Krosnick and Fabrigar 2006; Karni, Salmon, and Sopher 2008). So, I set these issues aside in what follows.
2. Exactly how relevant one will think evidence about different individuals' beliefs probably depends on one's meta-ethics and how the evidence is used.
3. There are different ways of thinking about what makes a principle action guiding. On one account, "a principle is action-guiding when citizens can use it as a decision-making procedure to help them decide what to do. For this to be the case, two general conditions have to be satisfied. First, the principle must be capable of functioning as a decision-making procedure, which it is when it is capable of delivering coherent, consistent, and determinate verdicts on the justness or unjustness of actions across a range of cases. Second, citizens must be capable of using the principle as a decision-making procedure, which they are when they possess, or it is reasonable to expect them to acquire, the beliefs and abilities needed to derive a prescription from that principle and act in conformity with that prescription. When both of these conditions are satisfied, citizens are capable of using a principle of justice as a decision-making procedure, and so it should be considered action guiding" (North 2016). A weaker account would drop the second condition and broaden the first so that action-guiding principles may be concerned with more than justice. One might say a principle is action guiding if it provides coherent, consistent, and determinate verdicts about the moral status of action in at least some actual cases. That is, it may suffice if the principle applies to actual cases. Even on the weaker account, to know whether a principle is action guiding, one may need to know if the verdicts it provides apply to actual cases. I use something like the weaker account throughout assuming that theories are action guiding when they tell people what to do in the real world.
4. I take it that theories are fact-sensitive when researchers need empirical evidence to build, arbitrate between, and criticize them and theories are action guiding when they tell people what to do in the real world. See discussion in notes above.
5. In arguing that researchers sometimes need empirical evidence to support philosophical arguments intended to guide action, I do not suppose that every action-guiding theory must be implementable (Weinburg 2013). I just claim that philosophers often need empirical evidence to figure out when, and where, their theories likely work well enough. They may have to experiment to figure out what to do (Weinburg 2013). Agents' capabilities and capacities, and institutions' strengths and weaknesses, are sometimes obvious. But, even to know if researchers should experiment, they often need scientific evidence. Moreover, many good experiments are scientific. Researchers must sometimes consider empirical evidence, as well as

theoretical arguments, about what capacities people can secure and maintain and what institutional structures they can implement and sustain.
6   Neha Khanna suggested giving to individuals with health needs via Kiva in conversation, and Kiva discussion boards also advance the idea. Perhaps Kiva, or its micro-finance partners, can work with NGOs, or community health organizations, to offer these loans—some microfinance institutions already offer health insurance.
7   This is so whether one endorses an institutional, or noninstitutional, account of what justice requires.
8   I do not engage with global versions of social constructivism here and know of no one who defends a more limited constructivism sufficient to undercut this chapter's thesis (Mallon 2013).
9   I believe, however, that some fact-sensitive principles are ultimate. I am not convinced that philosophers always need to take the analysis a level deeper to provide a fact-insensitive principle (just as I do not think they always need to provide further fact-sensitive principles).
10 One might accept this conclusion and insist that it is only to design and implement good institutions and laws that people require such information (and questions about what is really just, fair, or right are ultimately fact-insensitive) (Gerald 2003). I will, however, set aside these meta-philosophical disagreements for present purposes and suppose many different kinds of empirical evidence are relevant to establishing some philosopher's claims about what to do.
11 Because this section just aims to explain how the theory-based approach can work once we have a philosophically well-justified theory, it will not explain how we should develop such a theory. That said, empirical research as well as philosophical inquiry may help us make progress in arriving at such a theory. If we have more than one promising theory for a purpose, it may be appropriate to develop multiple measures as well as to inquire into the merits of each theory.
12 This is so, even if that means we need people who can understand both the philosophy and the measurement challenges to make clear exactly what further theory and data we need.
13 How should we quantify knowledge, for example? Most would agree that it is not only the number of facts one knows but the quality of one's knowledge that counts and perhaps one only needs the opportunity to secure knowledge beyond a certain point to fare well. Would a measure of educational attainment do? Perhaps not if the number of years of education do not really capture what students learn. Is appreciation distinct from pleasure? Perhaps aesthetic appreciation need not involve pleasure at all but could amount to an experience of the sublime. Maybe we care about many nonpleasurable experiences. If we have an account of the kinds of appreciation or experiences that matter, we should be sure not to double count pleasure (insofar as these experiences involve it) unless the theory tells us this is legitimate. And measuring the extent to which people engage, or have the chance to engage, in worthwhile activities is probably no easier. One needs to explain what constitutes an activity and what makes those activities worthwhile. This may even involve a whole account of the activities' moral and intellectual value unless one specifies that the only prudentially valuable activities are those that contribute to other aspects of one's well-being. In which case, it is not obvious that we must measure them at all. If worthwhile activities are independently valuable, and no reasonably good measures for capturing their value exist, one might propose creating a measure of these from a survey tool asking people how satisfied they are with their

achievements, etc., but there are serious reasons to doubt people are good judges in many cases. If so, one would either need to develop new measures or argue that the existing measures do a good-enough job of approximating well-being for one's purposes. Moreover, insofar as the account is supposed to be sensitive to differences between individuals and their values, the measure is, at best, a proxy for individuals' well-being—whatever policies, etc. one arrives at using the measure should allow for exceptions and include procedures for considering individuals' needs even if the measure suggests they have met the relevant threshold.

14 We cannot expect scientists to resolve all philosophical disputes (or perhaps any of them). They may wrongly think they are measuring well-being if they utilize the wrong theory. Moreover, most existing theories require significant development to be operationalizable. Still, it is important for scientists to have at least a good enough theory to arrive at a good measure for their purpose.

15 Some argue that traditional experimental philosophy does not benefit philosophy in general, but I believe this evidence can help build, criticize, and justify philosophical theories even if one does not believe researchers must appeal to broadly shared intuitions like those reported in most experimental philosophical work. This does not get to the objection that individuals' reports in traditional philosophical experiments do not constitute real intuitions or the worry that individuals' intuitions may have no real bearing on what views people should accept. I do not have the space to engage with the general worries here, so will simply refer interested readers to some of the discussion in collections cited in the references (Cruft 2015).

16 As Anthony Appiah put it, in figuring out what to identify as philosophy, "we will be guided, willy-nilly, by our sense not only of where we are but also of where we need to go" (Appiah 2008, 9). "The separation of philosophy from the empirical succeeded as an institutional project, but falter[s] … as an intellectual one" (Appiah 2008, 12).

References

Alexander, Joshua. 2012. *Experimental Philosophy: An Introduction*. Cambridge: Polity Press.

Alfano, Mark, and Don Loeb. 2014. "Experimental Moral Philosophy." In *The Stanford Encyclopedia of Philosophy*, edited by Edward N. Zalta. Stanford University: Metaphysics Research Lab.

Andow, James. 2016. "Qualitative Tools and Experimental Philosophy." *Philosophical Psychology* 29, no. 8: 1128–41.

Angner, Erik. 2011. "Are Subjective Measures of Well-Being 'Direct'?" *Australasian Journal of Philosophy* 89, no. 1: 115–30.

Anstey, Peter, and Alberto Vanzo. 2012. "The Origins of Early Modern Experimental Philosophy." *Intellectual History Review* 22, no. 4: 499–518.

Appiah, Anthony. 2008. *Experiments in Ethics*. Cambridge, MA: Harvard University Press.

Banerjee, Abhijit, Rukmini Banerji, James Berry, Esther Duflo, Harini Kannan, Shobhini Mukerji, Marc Shotland, and Michael Walton. 2017. "From Proof of Concept to Scalable Policies: Challenges and Solutions, with an Application." *Journal of Economic Perspectives* 31, no. 4: 73–102.

Basu, Kaushik. 2014. "Randomisation, Causality and the Role of Reasoned Intuition." *Oxford Development Studies* 42, no. 4: 455–72.

Bishop, Michael A. 2015. *The Good Life: Unifying the Philosophy and Psychology of Well-Being*. New York: Oxford University Press USA.

Braybrooke, David. 1987. *Meeting Needs*. Princeton: Princeton University Press.

Cohen, G. A. 1991. "The Tanner Lectures on Human Values." In *Incentives, Inequality, and Community*, 263–329. Salt Lake City, UT: Tanner Humanities Center.

Cohen, Joshua. 2002. "Taking People as They Are?" *Philosophy and Public Affairs* 30, no. 4: 363–386.

Copp, David. 2003. "'Ought' Implies 'Can', Blameworthiness, and the Principle of Alternate Possibilities." In *Moral Responsibility and Alternative Possibilities: Essays on the Importance of Alternative Possibilities,* edited by D. Widerker, and M. McKenna. Burlington, VT: Ashgate Publishing.

Cruft, Rowan. 2015. "From a Good Life to Human Rights: Some Complications." In *Philosophical Foundations of Human Rights*, edited by Rowan Cruft, Matthew S. Massimo Renzo Liao, 101–16. Oxford: Oxford University Press.

Cushman, Fiery, Joshua Knobe, and Walter Sinnott-Armstrong. 2008. "Moral Appraisals Affect Doing/Allowing Judgments." *Cognition* 108, no. 1: 281–89.

Deaton, Angus. 2009. "Instruments of Development: Randomization in the Tropics, and the Search for the Elusive Keys to Economic Development." *Proceedings of the British Academy* 162: 123–60.

Deaton, Angus, and Nancy Cartwright. 2017. "Understanding and Misunderstanding Randomized Controlled Trials." *Social Science & Medicine* 210: 2–21.

Estlund, David. 2019. *Utopophobia: On the Limits (If Any) of Political Philosophy*. Princeton: Princeton University Press.

Farrelly, Colin. 2007. "Justice in Ideal Theory: A Refutation." *Political Studies* 55, no. 4: 844–64.

Fischer, Eugen, and John Collins. 2015. *Experimental Philosophy, Rationalism, and Naturalism. Rethinking Philosophical Method*. Milton Park: Routledge.

Gerald A, Cohen. 2003. "Facts and Principles." *Philosophy and Public Affairs* 31, no. 3: 211–45.

Gerald A, Cohen. 2008. *Rescuing Justice and Equality*. Cambridge, MA: Harvard University Press.

Hammer, Jeffrey. 2017. *Randomized Control Trials for Development? Three Problems*. Washington, DC: Brookings.

Hassoun, Nicole. 2009. "Meeting Need." *Utilitas* 21, no. 3: 250–75.

Hassoun, Nicole. 2010. "Empirical Evidence and the Case for Foreign Aid." *Public Affairs Quarterly* 24, no. 1: 1–20.

Hassoun, Nicole. 2014. "Global Justice and Charity: A Brief for a New Approach to Empirical Philosophy." *Philosophy Compass* 9, no. 12: 884–93.

Hassoun, Nicole. 2015. "The Human Right to Health." *Philosophy Compass* 10: 275–83.

Hassoun, Nicole. 2016. "Experimental or Empirical Political Philosophy." In *A Companion to Experimental Philosophy*, edited by J. Sytsma, W. Buckwater. Chichester, UK: Blackwell.

Hassoun, Nicole. 2020. *Global Health Impact: Extending Access on Essential Medicines for The Poor*. Oxford: Oxford University Press.

Hassoun, Nicole, Nathan Lubchenco, and Emir Malikov. 2016. "How People Think About Distributing Aid." *Philosophical Psychology* 29, no. 7: 1029–044.

Haybron, Daniel, and Valerie Tiberius. 2015. "Well-Being Policy: What Standard of Well-Being?" *Journal of the American Philosophical Association* 4: 712–33.

Heathwood, Chris. 2006. "Desire Satisfaction and Hedonism." *Philosophical Studies* 128, no. 3: 539–63.

Hendrick, Susan. 1988. "A Generic Measure of Relationship Satisfaction." *Journal of Marriage and the Family* 50, no. 1: 93–8.

Hersch, Gil. 2019. "Well-Being Internalism." *The British Journal for the Philosophy of Science* 70.

Hersch, Gil. "No Theory-Free Lunches in Well-Being Policy." *The Philosophical Quarterly* 70, no. 278 (January 2020): 43–64. Doi: 10.1093/pq/pqz029.

Horvath, Joachim, and Thomas Grundmann. 2010. "Introduction: Experimental Philosophy and Its Critics, Parts 1 and 2." *Philosophical Psychology* 23, no. 3: 283–92.

Howard-Snyder, Frances. 2006. "'Cannot' Implies 'Not Ought.'" *Philosophical Studies* 130, no. 2: 233–246.

Hubbard, Tim, and James Love. 2004. "A New Trade Framework For Global Healthcare R&D." *PLoS Biology* 2, no. 52.

Karni, E, Tim Salmon, and Barry Sopher. 2008. "Individual Sense of Fairness: An Experimental Study." *Experimental Economics* 11: 174–89.

Katz, Leonard. (Winter 2016). "Pleasure." *Stanford Encyclopedia of Philosophy* Available from: https://plato.stanford.edu/archives/win2005/entries/pleasure/.

Kauppinen, Antti. 2007. "The Rise and Fall of Experimental Philosophy." *Philosophical Explorations* 10: 95–118.

Klosko, George. 1994. "Political Obligation and the Natural Duties of Justice." *Philosophy & Public Affairs* 23: 251–70.

Knobe, Joshua. 2007a. "Experimental Philosophy." *Philosophy Compass* 2, no. 1: 81–92.

Knobe, Joshua. 2007b. "Experimental Philosophy and Philosophical Significance." *Philosophical Explorations* 10, no. 2: 119–21.

Knobe, Joshua, and Shaun Nichols. 2008. *Experimental Philosophy*. Oxford: Oxford University Press.

Krosnick, Jon, and L. R. Fabrigar. 2006. *The Handbook of Questionnaire Design*. New York: Oxford University Press.

Lindauer, Matthew. 2020. "Experimental Philosophy and the Fruitfulness of Normative Concepts." *Philosophical Studies* 177, no. 8: 2129–52.

Lindauer, Matthew, and Christian Barry. 2017. "Moral Judgment and the Duties of Innocent Beneficiaries of Injustice." *Review of Philosophy and Psychology* 8, no. 3: 671–86.

London, Alex. 2006. "Reasonable Risks in Clinical Research: A Critique and a Proposal for the Integrative Approach." *Statistics in Medicine* 25: 2869–85.

Mallon, Ron. "Naturalistic Approaches to Social Construction." *Stanford Encyclopedia of Philosophy* (August 27, 2013).

Miller, David. 2001. "Distributing Responsibilities." *Journal of Political Philosophy* 9: 453–71.

Muralidharan, Karthik, and Paul Niehaus. 2017. "Experimentation at Scale." *Journal of Economic Perspectives* 31, no. 4: 103–24.

Nahmias, Eddy, Stephen Morris, Thomas Nadelhoffer, and Jason Turner. 2006. "Is Incompatibilism Intuitive?" *Philosophy and Phenomenological Research* 73, no. 1: 28–53.

Nahmias, Eddy, Stephen Morris, Thomas Nadelhoffer, and Jason Turner. 2008. "Surveying Freedom: Folk Intuitions About Free Will and Moral Responsibility." *Philosophical Psychology* 18: 561–84.

North, Richard. 2016. "Principles as Guides: The Action-Guiding Role of Justice in Politics." *Journal of Politics* 79, no. 1: 75–88.

Nwabueze, Remigius N. 2013. *Legal and Ethical Regulation of Biomedical Research in Developing Countries*. 1st edition. Milton Park: Routledge.

Paxton, Molly, Carrie Figdor, and Valarie Tiberius. 2012. "Quantifying the Gender Gap: An Empirical Study of the Underrepresentation of Women in Philosophy." *Hypatia* 27: 949–57.

Peters, Jörg, Jörg Langbein, and Gareth Roberts. 2017. "Generalization in the Tropics: Development Policy, Randomized Controlled Trials, and External Validity." *The World Bank Research Observer* 33, no. 1: 34–64.

Pogge, Thomas. 2008. "Access to Medicines." *Public Health Ethics* 1, no. 2: 73–82.

Pogge, Thomas. 2013. "Poverty and Violence." *Law, Ethics and Philosophy* 1: 87–111.

Pogge, Thomas, and Aidan Hollis. 2012. "The Health Impact Fund: Enhancing Justice and Efficiency in Global Health." *Journal of Human Development and Capabilities* 12, no. 4: 537–59.

Polonioli, Andrea. 2017. "New Issues for New Methods: Ethical and Editorial Challenges for an Experimental Philosophy." *Science and Engineering Ethics* 23, no. 4: 1009–34.

Puri, Jyotsna, Anastasia Aladysheva, Vegard Iversen, Yashodhan Ghorpade, and Tilman Brück. 2017. "Can Rigorous Impact Evaluations Improve Humanitarian Assistance?" *Journal of Development Effectiveness* 9, no. 4: 519–42.

Rawls, John. 1980. "Kantian Constructivism in Moral Theory." *Journal of Philosophy* 77, no. 9: 512–72.

Rawls, John. 1993. *Political Liberalism*. New York: Columbia University Press.

Rosen, Laura, Orly Manor, Dan Engelhard, and David Zucker. 2006. "In Defense of the Randomized Controlled Trial for Health Promotion Research." *American Public Health Association* 96, no. 7: 1181–6.

Scholl, Brian. 2008. *Two Kinds of Experimental Philosophy (and Their Methodological Dangers)*. Philadelphia: University of Pennsylvania.

Simmons A, John. 2010. "Ideal and Nonideal Theory." *Philosophy and Public Affairs* 38, no. 1: 5–36.

Sinnott-Armstrong, Walter. 1984. "'Ought' Conversationally Implies 'Can'." *Philosophical Review* 93, no. 2: 249–61.

Sinnott-Armstrong, Walter. 2019. "Consequentialism." In *The Stanford Encyclopedia of Philosophy*, edited by Edward N. Zalta. Stanford University: Metaphysics Research Lab.

Talbot, Marianne. 2015. "Critical Reasoning." *Philosophy Now* 106: 6–9.

Tollefson, Jeff. 2015. "Can Randomized Trials Eliminate Global Poverty?" *Nature* 527, no. 7564: 150–3. Accessed December 3, 2017. http://www.nature.com/news/can-randomized-trials-eliminate-global-poverty-1.18176.

Al-Ubaydli, Omar, John A. List, and Dana L. Suskind. 2017. "What Can We Learn from Experiments? Understanding the Threats to the Scalability of Experimental Results." *American Economic Review* 105, no. 5: 282–6.

Valentini, Laura. 2006. "On the Apparent Paradox of Ideal Theory." *The Journal of Political Philosophy* 17, no. 3: 332–55.

Vanderschraaf, Peter. 2006. "The Circumstances of Justice." *Politics, Philosophy & Economics* 5, no. 3: 321–51.

Vranas, Peter B. 2007. "I Ought, Therefore I Can." *Philosophical Studies* 136, no. 2: 167–216.

Weinberg, Justin. 2013. "The Practicality of Political Philosophy." *Social Philosophy and Policy* 30, no. 1: 330–51.

Wenar, Leif. 2007. "The Basic Structure as Object: Institutions and Humanitarian Concern." In *Global Justice, Global Institutions*, edited by Daniel Weinstock. Calgary, AT: University of Calgary Press.

Wendler, David. 2017. "A Pragmatic Analysis of Vulnerability in Clinical Research." *Bioethics* 31: 515–25.

Wilhelm, Isaac, Sherri Conklin, and Hassoun Nicole. 2018. "New Data on the Representation of Women in Philosophy Journals: 2004–2015." *Philosophical Studies* 175: 1–24.

World Health Organization. 1998. "The World Health Report: 1998." *World Health Organization*.

Woolfolk, Robert L. 2013. "Experimental Philosophy: A Methodological Critique." *Metaphilosophy* 44, no. 1: 79–87.

7

How Do People Balance Death against Lesser Burdens?

Veronika Luptakova and Alex Voorhoeve

1. Introduction

In health policy, governments often face difficult decisions about who to prioritize for care when resources do not suffice to help everyone in need. In this chapter, we focus on circumstances in which a decision-maker must choose whether to save a first group of people from a greater individual harm or a second, no less numerous group from a smaller individual harm. The membership of the two groups does not overlap, and in each case, saving group members from harm is assumed to fully eliminate the harm. Moreover, in our cases, the harms are such that if unaided, the members of the first group will be worse off than the members of the second group. An example is a case in which a decision-maker must choose whether to cure 100 young adults from a fatal illness or instead cure an equally sized or larger group of young adults of an illness which presents a moderate individual health burden. We confine ourselves to cases of certainty, thereby ruling out decisions to give people mere chances at aid, for example, by using a lottery to determine which group to assist. Rather, the decision-makers must simply decide which group to prioritize or instead indicate that they should have equal priority.

The principles of distributive justice most commonly employed to make such decisions in practice have two notable characteristics. First, when the two groups are equally large, these principles prioritize by severity. For example, they require saving a number of young people from early death rather than saving a same-sized group of young people from a lesser harm, such as paraplegia. Second, when both the number of people that can be saved from harm and the degree of harm they can be saved from vary, these commonly employed principles are fully aggregative: one death at a young age can be outweighed not merely by a large number of substantial burdens such as paraplegia but also by a sufficiently large number of very minor burdens, such as a case of toenail fungus (Fleurbaey, Tungodden, and Vallentyne 2009).

Prioritization by severity when the number of people one can save from harm is fixed does not occasion much controversy among leading thinkers; nor, to our knowledge, is it often challenged in practice. In contrast, unlimited aggregation has been challenged in both theory and practice. Many philosophers have proposed principles of distributive justice that embody a limited form of aggregation. According to such principles, preventing a large number of cases of substantial harm less bad than death, such as paraplegia, can take priority over preventing one early death. But no number of minor harms, such as cases of toenail fungus, can take priority over preventing one such death (see, e.g., Kamm 1993; Scanlon 1998; Otsuka 2006; Lefkowitz 2008; Temkin 2012; Kelleher 2014; Voorhoeve 2014; Voorhoeve 2017; Tadros 2019; Walen 2020; Brown 2020; Rueger 2020; Steuwer 2021; Mann 2021a, Mann 2021b).[1] Moreover, at least one country, the Netherlands, has adopted such limitedly aggregative priority-setting principles (RVZ 2006; ZiN 2017; 2018; 2020; Voorhoeve 2020).[2]

One reason often cited in favor of such limited aggregation is that in blocking the ability of comparatively minor harms to collectively outweigh a much greater individual harm, it aligns with common-sense moral case judgments (see, e.g., Otsuka 2004, 424–6; RVZ 2006, 82; Temkin 2012; ZiN 2017). In contrast, in permitting such outweighing of very grave individual harms by a multitude of very minor harms, unlimited aggregative views are purported to be at odds with common-sense judgment.

This conformity (or lack thereof) of distributive principles with people's case judgments is important for several reasons. First, on the method of reflective equilibrium in theorizing about justice, one seeks principles of distributive justice that offer a rationale for considered, confidently held case judgments and that cohere with other attractive normative principles and still deeper moral ideals (Rawls 1999; Daniels 2013). Any inconsistency between such case judgments and apparently attractive principles requires resolution, by revising the case judgments, or by reconsidering one's principles of distributive justice. On this method, the supposed nonconformity of fully aggregative principles of distributive justice with widely held, considered case judgments may weaken our confidence in these principles. Moreover, the supposed conformity of limitedly aggregative principles with common case judgments may bolster such principles.

Second, priority-setting institutions make decisions in the public's name, using its resources. The legitimacy of these institutions depends in part on the public's view that they are employing reasonable decision-making principles (Van de Wijngaard 2021). Moreover, when such institutions make decisions that offend the public's sense of justice, these institutions may find their decisions are unworkable.[3]

There is, however, a lack of evidence for the claims made about the public's attitudes toward unlimited aggregative principles. Neither the contributions to the philosophical literature nor the Dutch priority-setting authority cite evidence of the public's views on this topic. Moreover, a recent review finds only a small number of relevant surveys, many of which have significant shortcomings, including small, nonrepresentative samples and problematic framing (Voorhoeve 2018). In this chapter, we aim to fill this lacuna in our knowledge. We examine the responses of a representative sample of the UK population ($N = 389$) to priority-setting dilemmas that have been structured to alleviate the framing issues in previous work. These dilemmas allow us to establish the extent to which respondents' views align with both prioritization by severity when group sizes are equal and with unlimited aggregation when they are not. We found to our surprise that 44 percent respondents do not always adhere to prioritization by severity. We also found that philosophers' and Dutch priority-setters' conjecture that unlimited aggregation is unpopular is borne out. For among those who *do* prioritize by severity, only one-fifth give responses that align with unlimited aggregation, while more than half offer limited aggregative responses. Our results therefore challenge the idea that commonly used priority-setting principles can count on public support. They also suggest that principles embodying a limited form of aggregation may well garner more support.

We proceed as follows. In Section 2, we offer a brief overview of key priority setting principles. In Section 3, we summarize previous research and some of its limitations. In Section 4, we outline our survey and experiment. In Section 5, we report our findings. In Section 6, we discuss their significance and limitations.

2. Priority-Setting Principles

The leading theories of distributive justice that respect the Pareto principle (the rule that if one can improve a person's well-being without reducing anyone else's, then one should do so) can be arranged along a continuum by the degree of extra concern they show for the less well-off. At one end of the continuum is utilitarianism, which requires maximizing the sum total of well-being. Utilitarianism has no special concern for the less well-off, as it regards a fixed increment of well-being as just as valuable when it accrues to a worse-off person as when it accrues to a better-off person. At the other end of this continuum is leximin, which requires maximizing the well-being of the least well-off, and once this has been accomplished, of the second-least well-off, and so on. One prominent example of a view in between these two end points is pluralist, moderate egalitarianism, which aims to both reduce inequality and improve total well-being (Tungodden 2003). On this form of pluralist egalitarianism, a gain in well-being to someone who is worse off than others is more (but not infinitely more) valuable than an equally sized gain to a better-off person, as it both reduces inequality and improves well-being. Another example of a view on the spectrum is prioritarianism, which does not care about inequality itself, but simply regards a gain in well-being as somewhat more important (but not infinitely more important), the lower the level of well-being from which it arises, irrespective of whether there is anyone who is better off (or worse off) than the person being aided (Parfit 1995; Adler 2012).

If, as is common in health economics, we take quality-adjusted life years (or QALYs) as the relevant unit of health-related well-being, then utilitarianism is embodied in standard cost-effectiveness analysis which prioritizes interventions by their cost per QALY gained. An example is the approach championed by the World Health Organization's (WHO) CHOICE project, which stands for CHOosing Interventions that are Cost-Effective (Betram and Edejer 2021). Views in between utilitarianism and leximin are embodied by common forms of equity-weighted cost-effectiveness analysis that give noninfinite additional weight to QALY gains to the worse-off (Bognar and Hirose 2014). An example is the priority-setting principles proposed by the Norwegian Committee on Priority Setting in the Health Sector, on which a QALY gained by someone facing a large health burden is taken to be one and a half times more valuable than a QALY gained by someone facing a middling health burden, and three times more valuable than a QALY gained by someone facing a small health burden (Ottersen et al. 2016).

Insofar as practical policymaking in health is guided by explicit principles of distributive justice, the dominant principles in use are either utilitarianism in the form of standard cost-effectiveness or moderate pluralist egalitarianism/prioritarianism in the form of equity-weighted cost-effectiveness with noninfinite additional weights for improvements for the worse-off. In this chapter, we shall focus on two characteristics of such commonly applied principles. First, in the choices of the kind outlined in the Introduction, when the groups facing the greater harm and the lesser harm are equal in size, they prioritize by severity. For saving the group facing the greater individual burdens in such a case both maximizes total well-being and improves the lot of the worse off. Second, these common principles mandate saving a larger group from a lesser individual harm if the larger group is sufficiently numerous, even when the lesser harm is much less severe than the greater harm (Fleurbaey et al. 2009). The only difference is that for utilitarianism, fewer people are required for the balance to tip in favor of the people facing the lesser harm than for moderate egalitarianism or prioritarianism. To illustrate, consider a very mild chronic ailment that reduces health-related well-being in an otherwise healthy population by one-thousandth of a QALY for every year of its duration. Suppose that it starts at the age of twenty and lasts until the person dies suddenly (from other causes) at eighty. On the form of utilitarianism embodied in standard cost-effectiveness, it would take one thousand such cases to outweigh one death of a young person at twenty who, if saved, would otherwise live in good health until eighty. On the Norwegian proposal, the death of the young person would receive three times this weight, so it would take three thousand such cases.

As mentioned in the Introduction, from the 1990s onward, a growing number of philosophers have argued that unlimited aggregation is problematic, because no number of such small harms to people who would in any case lead good lives should together outweigh one young person's death. Leximin shares this judgment, because in such cases, it prioritizes the young person facing death no matter how many others one could save from the minor ailment. But leximin's degree of priority for the worst-off is extreme. For it demands that we eschew any amount of improvement in the second-least well-off position in a distribution of well-being for the sake of the tiniest improvement in the very worst position. It also prioritizes aiding a lone person in the worst position over saving any number of people from lesser, but still very substantial health burdens, such as paraplegia. These problematic implications mean that it has not, to our knowledge, been employed by policymakers as a guiding principle for priority setting. They have also led critics of unlimited aggregation to propose other principles, on which some number of substantial impairments, but no number of very minor ones, can together outweigh a young person's untimely death.

The proposed limited aggregative principles can be divided into two broad types. One type posits an absolute threshold level of well-being and holds that an increment in well-being below this threshold, no matter how minute and no matter how few people would obtain it, always outweighs an increment above this threshold, no matter how sizable the increment and no matter how numerous its recipients. When all gains accrue to people below the threshold, then the number of people benefited counts, as does the size of the gains and the level of well-being from which they take place (Crisp 2003; Brown 2005; Liao and Lim 2022). A proposed rationale for this type of view is that harms that present substantial obstacles to leading an unqualifiedly good life are normatively different in kind from those that do not do so, and that alleviating (in whole or in part) the former kind of harm should take lexical priority over alleviating the latter kind of harm.

A second type of view, in contrast, eschews an absolute threshold. Instead, it focuses on comparing the strength of the claim of a person who has most at stake in the decision with the strength of the competing claim of each person who has less at stake. It then holds that when the gap between the strength of the strongest claim and a weaker, competing claim is too large, no number of the weaker claims can together outweigh the strongest claim. On this type of view, whether weaker claims aggregate therefore depends on their strength *relative* to the strongest competing claim. One example of this approach is Aggregate Relevant Claims, or ARC (Voorhoeve 2014), which we focus on for illustrative purposes. In our cases, ARC holds the following:

1. Each person whose fate is at stake has a claim.
2. People's claims compete just in case they cannot be jointly satisfied.
3. A person's claim is stronger:

    3.1 the greater the gain in their health-related well-being generated by aiding them; and
    3.2 the less health-related well-being they would enjoy if they were not aided.

4. A claim is relevant if and only if it is strong enough when compared to the strongest competing claim.
5. The decision-maker should satisfy the greatest sum of strength-weighted, relevant claims.

(Voorhoeve 2014, 66)

ARC is inspired by the idea expressed in Nagel (1979, 118 and 126) that both an aggregative and a non-aggregative approach capture part of the demands of distributive justice. On the aggregative approach, the equal moral importance of each person's well-being requires that we assign the same and positive marginal moral importance to every person's claim of a given strength. It meets this demand by holding that fulfilling two claims of a given strength is twice as important as meeting one such claim, and so on for all claims. The upshot is a requirement to meet the greatest sum of strength-weighted claims.

The non-aggregative approach embodies a different conception of equal concern which takes extremely seriously the distinctness of each individual's life. To fully respect the distinction between persons, it holds that one must compare each person's claim, taken separately, with each competing claim, considered separately (Nagel 1979, 116f). In this confrontation, a stronger claim always wins out. On this view, one therefore always has strongest reason to meet the individually strongest claim.

Nagel (1979) suggests that a full theory of justice must incorporate elements of both approaches, while arbitrating between them in a reasonable way. ARC does so by maximizing the total fulfilment of strength-weighted claims under the restriction that the fulfilled claims are close enough in strength to be relevant to each other. It therefore follows the aggregative approach so long as one does not thereby depart too far from the demand of the non-aggregative approach.

Naturally, to offer guidance in particular cases as well as a fuller rationale for their views, proponents of ARC must explain how it determines which weaker claims are still relevant to competing, stronger claims, and which are not. A number of such proposals exist (Voorhoeve 2014; Voorhoeve 2017; Brown 2020). Proponents of threshold views must of course also try to meet the related challenge about where to locate the boundary between harms that substantially impair the ability to lead a good life and those that do not (Crisp 2003; Liao and Lim 2022). While there is also a lively debate about which of these types of limited aggregative views to favor, we set this debate aside in the remainder of this chapter. For our concern is to uncover the extent to which subjects favor this family of unorthodox, limited aggregative views over unlimited aggregation. Our survey therefore does not distinguish between the forms of limited aggregation, just as it does not distinguish between the utilitarian, prioritarian, or pluralist egalitarian views that make up the family of fully aggregative views.

Limited aggregative views require further specification to be applied to healthcare priority setting. An example is offered by the method used by the Netherlands' Institute for Healthcare (ZiN 2018, 4) for judging whether treatments are cost-effective. For individuals who suffer health burdens equal to or larger than 0.1 QALY per year, it employs a form of equity-weighted cost-effectiveness. Interventions that alleviate a burden of illness ranging from 0.1 to 0.4 QALY per year are judged cost-effective up to €20,000 per QALY gained, those that alleviate a burden of between 0.4 and 0.7 QALY per year are judged cost-effective up to €50,000 per QALY generated, and those that alleviate a burden of more than 0.7 QALY per year are judged cost-effective up to €80,000 per QALY gained. In line with a form of limited aggregation, it regards an annual individual burden of less than 0.1 QALY as not generating a call on public resources which could instead be used for life-saving interventions.[4]

3. Previous Research on the Public's Judgments

As mentioned in the Introduction, both the method of reflective equilibrium and considerations of legitimacy give us reason to consider people's moral preferences regarding resource allocation decisions, and to incorporate them into public decision-making if they are reasonable. To do so, we must be able to reliably elicit these preferences and establish whether they are based on rational judgments and morally acceptable views (Dolan et al. 2003, 549).

In this section, we review the existing empirical literature on people's preferences about distributive justice in health care. Specifically, we focus on evidence, or lack thereof, for the assertion that people tend to prioritize by severity (Section 3. 1) and that they fully aggregate existing claims on public resources (Section 3.2).

Decisions about the allocation of healthcare resources are about making trade-offs. However, when people are asked to make trade-offs, which are often difficult, many of them provide *nontrade* responses. These refusals to prioritize may be expressions of deeply held moral beliefs, but they may also represent "protest" responses when people are resistant to the idea of having to make difficult trade-offs (Damschroder et al. 2007). In order to properly interpret and account for people's preferences, it is important to understand what drives such nontrade responses. We now review two types of such responses that are pertinent to our investigation: so-called "equivalence refusals" and "off-scale refusals."

3.1 Refusals to Prioritize by Severity

A prominent way in which individuals refuse to prioritize between two programs that can fully cure the same number of people who have health conditions of different severity is to declare that these programs should have equal priority (Damschroder et al. 2007, 266). This form of denial of priority by severity in same-sized group cases is known as an "equivalence refusal" and contradicts all commonly employed priority-setting principles as well as the unorthodox, limited aggregative ones considered here. (Note that not every equivalence *response* to a priority-setting question is an equivalence *refusal*. The latter are, by definition, only those that cannot be explained through any of the theories of distributive justice outlined.)

Nord (1995) and Damschroder et al. (2007, 266) point out that it is unclear how to interpret such responses—whether to count them as considered moral judgments that express a strong preference for ensuring equal access to treatment for everyone in need (even when needs are substantially different), or whether to regard them as reflecting people's unwillingness to make difficult choices.

In this section, we review existing empirical evidence on the prevalence of such refusals. We will use this as a proxy for the share of the public who do not prioritize by severity in fixed-number cases.

We focus our review on empirical studies that involved elicitations using the Person Trade-Off (PTO) method. This method elicits moral preferences over interpersonal trade-offs by choosing between treatment programs for two distinct groups of people, which generally differ in their size and/or in the severity of illness that they can be cured of. The PTO approach requires decision-makers to choose between (i) providing a large health benefit for a few people and (ii) a smaller health benefit for many others (Schwarzinger et al. 2004, 172). Typically, respondents' preferences are elicited either directly or in two steps. In "direct" elicitations, respondents are presented with a description of two treatment programs that help two different groups of patients and are asked, "If one programme helps ten (or some other baseline number of) patients suffering from condition X, how many patients suffering from condition Y would the second programme have to help in order for you to be indifferent between the two programmes?" In "step-wise" elicitations, respondents are asked in step one to prioritize for treatment one of two same-sized groups that can be cured of ailments of differing severity. In step two, the characteristics of the group that was prioritized for treatment at step one are kept constant, but the number of people in the group that was deprioritized is varied to find the point of indifference, or "equal choiceworthiness" between the two programs. By way of illustration: in the first step, a respondent is asked to prioritize either program A, which cures 100 patients of a fatal illness, or program B, which cures 100 patients of paraplegia, or to indicate that these programs should have equal priority. If they choose program A, in the second step, this respondent is asked how many people would have to be cured of paraplegia to make them consider the two treatment programs equally choiceworthy. If, instead, the respondent indicates that the two programs are equally choiceworthy when they both save 100 people, even though they view early death as significantly more severe than paraplegia, then their response is counted as an equivalence refusal.

Only a limited number of PTO studies report the share of equivalence refusals among the public. In many studies, the condition that equivalence refusals must be at odds with all leading theories of distributive justice is not met or the share of the equivalence refusals is not reported.

For instance, some PTO studies do not directly compare treatment programs that help the same number of people with conditions of differing severity. Instead, the numbers of people helped are adjusted based on the severity that respondents assigned to the respective health conditions. For instance, respondents who, on a scale on which the well-being of time alive in perfect health is rated at one and death is rated at zero, had previously indicated that a debilitating knee condition has a well-being value of 0.5, while a case of acute appendicitis (which is terminal if untreated) has a well-being of zero, were then asked whether they would rather cure ten people acute appendicitis or twenty people of the knee condition or whether they were indifferent between the two (Ubel et al. 1996). Providing an equality response (indicating indifference) in such a case would not count as an equivalence *refusal* as one of the leading theories of justice—utilitarianism—would indicate such equality.

Reviewed studies with a suitable design that reported the share of equivalence refusals provide a rather broad range, between 0 percent and 43 percent (Nord et al. 1993; Nord 1995; Schwarzinger et al. 2003; Schwarzinger et al. 2004; Damschroder et al. 2005; Damschroder et al. 2007). Although all reviewed studies asked for trade-offs between health conditions that appeared to be clearly different in severity and asked respondents to assume the treatment programs could cure (or prevent the onset of ill health for) the same number of people, they differed on several dimensions, such as, sample size, representativeness, framing of the question, including a life-threatening condition, comparing health conditions of the same or of different kinds (e.g., mild vs. moderate vs. severe shortness of breath or moderate leg pain vs. severe shortness of breath), and giving participants an opportunity to discuss, reflect on, and change their responses.

The estimates that are probably most representative of the views of the public come from two studies in Damschroder et al. (2007). Both studies were conducted using relatively large samples ($N = 388$ and 878) recruited from an internet panel and were representative of the US population. They tested the impact of different contexts and framings on the share of equivalence refusals. They found that people were more likely to give equivalence refusals when making a decision from an *evaluator* perspective (i.e., being in a more detached role) than from a *decision-maker* perspective (i.e., being in a role directly responsible for the decision), with the share of equivalence refusals being 32 percent and 21 percent, respectively. Furthermore, their results showed that reminding people of the consequences of their choice (i.e., that people in the group which was not selected will be untreated, *a rationing perspective*) resulted in an even lower share of equivalence refusals (12 percent), while asking people to make the choice from a *benefits perspective* (asking them which group of people received a greater benefit rather than which group should be prioritized) led to a higher share of equivalence refusals (43 percent).

The results also show that people who felt outraged about the idea of rationing and those with lower numeracy were more likely to give equivalence refusals. Interestingly, those who reported finding the questions difficult to answer were *least* likely to give equivalence refusals (Damschroder et al. 2007, 270–1, 274), which might reflect their level of engagement.

One limitation of the reviewed studies is that the spectrum of harms was somewhat limited, as both very minor health complications and fatal conditions were omitted.[5] This can have an impact on the share of equivalence refusals, as respondents tend to be sensitive to the difference in severity between the compared conditions. They were most likely to give equivalence refusals when the difference in severity was small (e.g., moderate vs. mild shortness of breath) and the least likely when the difference was large (e.g., quadriplegia vs. foot numbness) (Nord et al. 1993; see also Schwarzinger et al. 2004; Damschroder et al. 2007). It must be noted, however, that in some cases, comparing fatal diseases with other severe but not life-threatening conditions might be problematic as some respondents consider conditions such as paraplegia or quadriplegia to be worse than death (Schwarzinger et al. 2003; Damschroder et al. 2005). In such cases, one cannot say whether respondents really gave equivalence refusals or whether, instead, they judged the compared conditions to be approximately equally severe.

Lastly, available empirical research provides relatively little qualitative analysis. Therefore, we lack a solid understanding of what drives equivalence refusals, and whether they are protest responses or considered moral judgments that apply principles different from those outlined in Section 2.

In sum, only a handful of studies identify genuine equivalence refusals, which we take to be a major source of a refusal to prioritize by severity. This leaves a lacuna in our knowledge that we aim to fill. As we detail in Section 4, in our study design, we aimed at overcoming several of the identified weaknesses to arrive at a more precise estimate of the prevalence of equivalence refusals among the general population. We used a large, representative sample of the UK population; we included a wide spectrum of harms to let people compare conditions with a very large as well as rather small difference in severity; and we tested for individual perceptions of the severity of compared health conditions (rather than assuming these or using average assessments).

3.2 Refusals to Fully Aggregate Claims

What are known as "off-scale refusals" arise when people indicate that the program curing the more severe ailment should always be prioritized, no matter how large the number of people treated under the alternative program which cures the less severe ailment. Such answers are inconsistent with fully aggregative views, but they are compatible with both leximin and limited aggregative approaches. The latter two differ, however, in the circumstances under which they generate off-scale refusals. Leximin requires prioritizing the more severe condition in all circumstances, even when the somewhat less severe condition is substantial. By contrast, limited aggregative approaches permit a large number of cases of the less severe condition to outweigh a small number of cases of the more severe condition when both conditions impose substantial harms. To find support for limited aggregation, one would therefore need to see the share of off-scale refusals increase when one moves from a choice between groups of people who each face substantial harm to a choice where the members of one group face very substantial harm and the members of the other group face only minor harm.

In this section, we review the three studies that come closest to providing evidence of the extent of such a pattern in off-scale refusals in healthcare priority setting. Ubel et al. (1996) surveyed a small sample of university students ($N = 42$), who were asked to evaluate a choice between curing ten individuals of an otherwise terminal case of appendicitis and curing a less burdensome health problem in a number of others. The lesser health burden in question was either very small (a ganglion cyst on a tendon which caused a bulge and occasional minor pain, but which did not limit activities) or substantial (a benign meningioma—a growth in the tissues around the brain—leading to regular, debilitating headaches though without an impact on life expectancy). Participants were asked which number of people cured of the illness causing the smaller burden would produce the same total benefit brought about by saving ten lives (Ubel et al. 1996, 111). In line with the pattern predicted by limited aggregation, off-scale responses of "no number" or "infinity" were more frequent in the lives versus cyst case, with 40.5 percent of responses being off-scale refusals, than in the lives versus meningioma case, with 4.8 percent of responses being off-scale refusals.

As noted in Voorhoeve (2018, 128–32), this study has two shortcomings. First, it involves a small convenience sample. Second, it uses a *benefit frame*, asking which number of lesser burdens one would need to alleviate to generate the same benefit as saving ten lives. But many defenses of limited aggregation are deontological, or nonconsequentialist (see, e.g., Kamm 1993; Scanlon 1998): they regard it as wrong to save a great many people from very minor harms rather than ten from death even if saving people from the very minor harms would produce a greater aggregate benefit. The survey fails to capture such deontologically motivated responses, which would be better reflected in a *choice frame*, which requires individuals to specify for which number of people (if any) facing the lesser harm we should prioritize saving them rather than saving the ten from death.

In the study reported in Pinto-Prades and Lopez-Nicolas (1998), participants (Spanish students, $N = 83$) were told they could either establish a neonatal care unit which would save the lives of ten newborns or implement a policy that would treat a "very large number (e.g., 100,000)" of others for an ailment that causes a smaller health loss. The latter loss varied; the smallest burden was living with moderate pain and discomfort which did not prevent the activities of daily life. They were then asked which program they would *prefer* to see implemented. The paper reports only the majority answers for various trade-offs: a majority chose to save ten newborns rather than treat the moderate chronic pain of a "very large number" of people and a majority was willing to alleviate the somewhat greater burdens (still short of death) of a multitude rather than save the lives of ten neonates (Pinto-Prades and Lopez-Nicolas 1998, 290). It follows that at least some respondents must have expressed preferences that align with limited aggregation, holding that saving a number of lives takes priority over saving a very large number from small harms, while also holding that saving a very large number of people from serious harms should take priority over saving a small number of lives.

This *preference framing* may be regarded as superior to the benefit framing in Ubel et al. (1996) since it involves a judgment about which program one would want to see prioritized. But it is still not ideal, since of course it is conceivable that someone would prefer (on other grounds, e.g., self-interest) to see a policy implemented that they regarded as morally impermissible.

There are several further weaknesses in the study design. For one, it again involved a small convenience sample. Moreover, to test for off-scale refusals, respondents should have been asked whether they preferred to save the ten lives for *any* (natural) number of people they could cure of the lesser ailment. The magnitude of the benefits of the possible interventions was underdescribed. It was left open what the quality of life of the neonates would be if they were saved and the extent to which the lesser conditions would be alleviated by treatment. The fact that it involves neonatal death also muddies the waters, since on some moral views, neonates lack the mental capacities of persons, and the death of a nonperson that lacks a conception of itself as a being that persists through time and that has, as yet, no desires and plans for the future is less bad than the death of a person (Millum 2015).

Study 1 in Damschroder et al. (2007) improved on these studies in two respects. First, it involved a larger sample ($N = 827$) chosen to represent the US population in various key respects. Second, it employed a choice frame and specified the magnitude of the benefits at stake for each person. Participants were asked to choose between saving a small number from a greater individual burden against saving a larger number from a lesser burden. The most substantial burden considered was quadriplegia and the least significant was paralysis in one foot. As in Ubel et al. (1996), the overall pattern of responses suggested that a substantial share of participants chose in line with limited aggregative views. In the choice involving the greatest gap in severity of condition—curing ten quadriplegics or instead up to 1 million people of foot paralysis—40 percent of respondents said that they would always cure the quadriplegics. By contrast, in the choice involving the smallest gap in severity—curing ten people of quadriplegia or up to 1 million of paraplegia—7 percent said that they would always prioritize the former. Of course, these responses do not, strictly speaking, register off-scale refusals, since they involve an upper bound. But there is evidence that these were primarily off-scale refusals. For participants who chose to aid the quadriplegics rather than up to a million people with a lesser health burden were also asked whether there was a number of people "in the world" for which they would prioritize a program alleviating the lesser burden over saving the ten quadriplegics. Most (59 percent) answered negatively (Damschroder et al. 2007, 270). The principal shortcoming of this study, however, is that the spectrum of harms is insufficiently wide. For permanent paralysis in one foot is still quite a substantial harm. The design therefore fails to catch some respondents who hold that a multitude of cases of foot paralysis can outweigh a case of quadriplegia, but that no number of very minor ailments could outweigh loss of a young person's life.

4. Our Survey and Experiment

4.1 Objective

The reviewed empirical studies suggest that there are two distinct ways that individuals may choose contrary to all commonly employed principles of distributive justice in health. (1) Some refuse to prioritize by severity between groups that are equally large, even when the difference in severity is substantial; and (2) others, in contrast, refuse to let a multitude of small benefits to the better-off, no matter how numerous this multitude, outweigh a fixed number of large benefits to the worse-off, that is, they fail or refuse to fully aggregate. We also outlined that (2) may be rationalized by the unorthodox, but still widely discussed, partially aggregative views outlined in Section 2.

The objective of our empirical research was to provide a better estimate of the prevalence of both types of departures among the general population through improvements in the research design, which would address some of the shortcomings identified in Section 3, namely: nonrepresentative samples, failing to check whether individuals ordered the severity of the conditions in question the way the survey designer intended, not clearly specifying the benefits at stake in the trade-off, using a benefit or preference frame rather than a choice frame, and unduly limiting the spectrum of harms under consideration.

We also aimed to test whether people's decisions are influenced by the assumed status quo, that is, by what people believe is currently covered through the healthcare system.[6] If people's views are disproportionately influenced by the status quo, it poses a problem for policymakers, especially if there is a need for a reform, as people might be inclined to preserve possibly inequitable allocations of healthcare resources (Dolan and Robinson 2001).[7]

There is persuasive evidence from experimental (lab and field) research that human decisions are disproportionately influenced by the status quo.[8] This has been tested and identified in a variety of decisions, including choosing investment portfolios, choosing between job offers, selecting a car color, choosing auto insurance, or choosing a cancer-testing program for oneself (Samuelson and Zeckhauser 1988; Fernandez and Rodrik 1991; Kahneman, Knetch, and Thaler 1991; Johnson, Hershey, Meszaros, and Kunreuther 1993; Salkeld, Ryan, and Short 2000). However, the vast majority of the empirical research to date focuses on *nonmoral* or purely prudential domains. It is unclear, however, whether the status quo also influences decisions involving *moral* judgments involving interpersonal trade-offs (Caviola et al. 2014). Although the presumption seems to be that matters that influence decisions in the nonmoral domain will also do so in the moral domain, the context-dependence of decision rules means this cannot be assumed. While moral philosophers have discussed and theoretically demonstrated the potential impact of the assumed status quo on moral judgments (e.g., Bostrom and Ord 2006; Wasserman 2015; Sparrow 2015), the proposition requires further experimental confirmation.

4.2 Method

We used an online questionnaire to capture participants' trade-offs between healthcare programs treating conditions of different severity. The least severe condition—Nail Disease—caused minor, but still appreciable, discomfort. The intermediate condition—Paraplegia—was serious but not life-threatening. The most severe condition—Fatal Autoimmune Disorder—was deadly within a short period if left untreated. We asked participants to make two trade-offs, one between the most severe and the least severe health conditions (Lives vs. Nails Scenario, large severity gap) and the other between the most severe condition and the serious but not life-threatening condition (Lives vs. Paraplegia Scenario, moderate-to-small severity gap).

We believed it would be easier for people to imagine concrete health conditions. Therefore, we did not use a generic health status instrument, such as EurQol, but instead we provided participants with a short description of three quite specific health conditions, including their typical symptoms and prevalence.[9]

To check whether respondents perceived the severity of the selected health conditions as intended, we asked them to perform an assessment of the severity for each condition at the beginning of the survey. Specifically, they were asked to indicate "how difficult it is for a person to live with a respective health condition" on a scale from 0 to 100 (where 0 was "Not difficult at all" and 100 was "Extremely difficult"). Answers of those who did not indicate that living with the fatal disorder is more difficult than living with the partial paralysis and that living the partial paralysis is more difficult than living with the nail disease (i.e., their severity was not ordered as intended) were excluded from the analysis.[10] Moreover, we believed that engaging in this assessment was likely to induce more careful consideration of the individual burden posed by these illnesses.

We used the PTO method to elicit people's preferences. We selected this method for three reasons. First, it is a matching type of elicitation which should encourage deliberation more than simple choosing (Skedgel 2013). Second, it prompts respondents to adopt a societal rather than a purely individual perspective and thus allows them to incorporate concerns for distributive justice (Dolan and Green 1998; Singh et al. 2012). Third, it explicitly requires people to make a trade-off between two options, rather than assessing each one of them in isolation. Making such trade-offs is typically at the heart of decisions on distributive justice, including in health care, and therefore using the PTO method is helpful (Payne et al. 1992; Schwarzinger et al. 2004; Singh et al. 2012).

Participants were instructed to assume for each decision that: (a) the treatment would be a full cure; (b) there was no alternative way to secure the treatment, and so patients suffering from the condition that is not chosen would go untreated; (c) the total cost of the programs treating the different health conditions would be the same; and (d) the budget had to be allocated to one condition or the other and could not be split.

Each participant was asked to answer two pairwise PTO questions. In Lives vs. Nails, they compared a program that would cure people of the nail disease with a program that would cure people of the fatal disorder. In Lives vs. Paraplegia, they compared a program that would cure people of paraplegia with a program that would cure people of the fatal disorder.

In each scenario, in the first stage, participants were asked which of the two programs they would choose to fund if each program would cure 100 people, or if instead they held that both programs should have the same priority (i.e., an equivalence refusal). If they chose the program that provided a cure for the fatal disorder, they were asked how many people would have to be cured under the other program (i.e., treating the nails disease or paraplegia) in order for them to be indifferent between the two programs (the matching task). Either they could choose a specific number from the range provided (from 101 people to the total number of people in the healthcare system) or they could indicate that there is *some* number, but they did not know what the number is, or they could select the option that there was *no* number large enough and that the program curing the fatal disorder should always be prioritized (i.e., an off-scale refusal). When participants selected a non-numerical response (an equivalence or off-scale refusal), they were asked to give a rationale for their response, if they could, before being directed to the next section of the survey.

The questions in both decisions were asked from the perspective of an "advisor." Participants were asked to imagine that a healthcare system director is deciding how to allocate budget for the upcoming period and were then asked which program the director *should* choose. This perspective aligns well with the role of the public in healthcare policy decisions—people can typically express their judgments about how the decision-makers should decide, rather than having to decide themselves.[11] The decision was presented as one that is still to be made rather than one that has already been made, as we assumed the former would be more engaging.

As one of the robustness checks, we tested for the impact of the status quo on people's allocation decisions. We used a between-subjects study design to avoid carryover effects that could affect a within-subjects design. Participants were randomly allocated into three groups, each presented with different information on current coverage from the healthcare budget, that is, the status quo. Participants in the Control group were informed that treatment for none of the health conditions under consideration is currently covered.[12] Participants in the Less Severe Currently Covered group were informed that milder conditions out of those under consideration are currently covered as these affect a large number of people but the most serious (fatal) health condition is not currently covered as it only affects very few patients. We conjectured that this version would incline participants toward an aggregative perspective ("aggregative nudge"), on which it is permissible to treat less serious diseases for a sufficiently large number of people instead of treating a serious health condition for very few. Participants in the Fatal Currently Covered group were informed that treatment for the most serious health condition under consideration is currently covered as it is fatal if untreated. We conjectured that this specification of the status quo would incline participants toward giving priority to those who have the most at stake ("anti-aggregative nudge"). As a result, we hypothesized that the number of off-scale refusals in the Less Severe Currently Covered group would be lower and that in the Fatal Currently Covered group it would be higher (compared to the Control group), which would have an impact on the prevalence of choices in line with limited aggregative views.

At the end of the section in which the information on the status quo was provided, we included a test of whether people really understood what was assumed to be currently covered in the healthcare system (we will refer to this as the "status quo comprehension check").

4.3 Sample

With an aim to secure a sample size that is more representative of the general UK population than a convenience sample of university students, we used a paid panel of participants through Prolific Academic. Participants were required to be at least eighteen years old and have UK citizenship. Respondents were paid a fixed fee for participating in the study, provided they completed the survey, which took them around six minutes on average.

We received 446 responses from participants who gave their consent to participate in the research study. These were equally split between males and females[13] and were randomly allocated to the Control, Less Severe Currently Covered, and Fatal Currently Covered groups. We excluded two responses that were duplicates and two responses where sex was not specified correctly.[14] We further excluded fifty-three respondents who did not judge the order of severity of selected health conditions as intended,[15] reducing the sample size from 446 to 389 (Control group: $N = 121$, Less Severe Currently Covered group: $N = 137$, Fatal Currently Covered group: $N = 131$). Also 321 of the remaining 389 subjects passed the status quo comprehension check.[16]

Overall, the sample was sufficiently representative of the UK population and well balanced across the treatment conditions. On average, the (remaining) subjects considered the difference in severity between the Nail disease and the Fatal disorder to be around eighty-two and between Paraplegia and the Fatal disorder around twenty-three, out of 100.

4.4 Analytical Approach

In our research set-up, participants who gave no equivalence refusals and no off-scale refusals align with an aggregative approach. Judgments of participants with no equivalence refusals and two off-scale refusals correspond to leximin. Participants who gave no equivalence refusals and gave an off-scale refusal in Lives vs. Nails but not in Lives vs. Paraplegia are considered to hold limited aggregative views.

When analyzing equivalence refusals, we can adopt two classifications. Under a broader classification, we consider an equivalence refusal any response from a participant who both ordered the health conditions as intended (i.e., judged the Nail disease to be less severe than Paraplegia and Paraplegia to be less severe than the Fatal Autoimmune Disorder) and indicated in a given scenario that both groups should have the same priority when curing the same number of people. Under a narrower classification, we do not count as equivalence refusals the responses of those who indicated that there was only a small difference in severity between the two health conditions that they judged to be of equal priority.[17]

To analyze the impact of the status quo on people's preferences, we calculated the average of the sum of off-scale refusals in each treatment group separately and compared it with the average for the control group.

5. Findings

Figure 7.1 summarizes the observed pattern of responses. It is noteworthy that relatively few respondents align with unlimited aggregation (10 percent of all included respondents on the broad classification of equivalence refusals; 12 percent on the narrow classification). At the same time, a small share (12 percent) conforms to leximin. The most common responses align with limited aggregative views (25 percent on the

Total n = 389 (100 percent)			Lives vs. Paraplegia			
			Paraplegia for equal numbers	Equal priority for equal numbers	Lives for equal numbers / Paraplegia for a number > 100	Always Lives
Lives vs. Nails		Nails for equal numbers	1%	0	0	0
		Equal priority for equal numbers	1%	4%	1%	0
	Lives for equal numbers	Nails for a number > 100	5%	6% / 2%	10%	1%
		Always Lives	6%	20% / 8%	25%	12%

Figure 7.1 Matrix of responses to prioritization decisions. © Veronika Luptakova and Alex Voorhoeve.

Notes: Fields in light gray (without any pattern) represent responses with no explanation in terms of the philosophical principles surveyed in Section 2. Fields highlighted with a dashed line represent equivalence refusals. The field with vertical stripes represents responses that correspond to the leximin principle. Fields with a grid pattern represent responses that correspond to fully aggregative views: utilitarianism, prioritarianism, or pluralist egalitarianism, using the broad classification of equivalence refusals (black background only) or the narrow one (both gray and black background). Checkerboard-pattern fields represent responses that correspond to limited aggregative views such as the threshold view or ARC on the broad (black background only) or narrow classification of equivalence refusals (both gray and black background). Percentages displayed are rounded; therefore they do not add up to 100 percent.

broad classification of equivalence refusals, 33 percent on the narrow classification). It is also striking that, even on the narrow classification of equivalence refusals, taken together, the responses that align with either aggregative views, leximin, or limited aggregative views make up only slightly more than half of all responses (56 percent). This means that just under half of respondents (44 percent) gave a combination of answers that cannot be rationalized by any of the philosophical principles surveyed in Section 2. The main cause of this departure from these philosophical principles was respondents' failure to prioritize by severity.[18] The most common instance of such failure were equivalence refusals, when respondents indicated an equal priority for programs curing the same number of people with conditions of different severity.

As described above, we used two classifications to identify equivalence refusals. Based on the broader classification, we identified about 6 percent of responses to the Lives vs. Nails Scenario and about 39 percent of responses to the Lives vs. Paraplegia Scenario as equivalence refusals. When we excluded responses of those who considered paraplegia and the fatal autoimmune disorder to be close in severity, the share of equivalence refusals for the second scenario dropped to 29 percent.[19] We consider this share to be a rather conservative estimate of genuine equivalence refusals, which we take to represent the most frequent case of a failure to prioritize by severity.

In line with the previous research reviewed in Section 3, we found that (i) equivalence refusals were much more likely when the severity difference was rather small (21 to 39 percent) than when it was large (6 percent) and (ii) off-scale refusals were much more likely when the severity difference was large (71 percent) than when it was small (13 percent).

We now turn to our embedded experiment, which tested for the influence of the status quo by providing participants with different information on what is currently covered under the healthcare system. The observed pattern of responses aligns to some extent with our hypothesis that the assumed status quo influences the rate of off-scale refusals. When considering a base model without any covariates and including

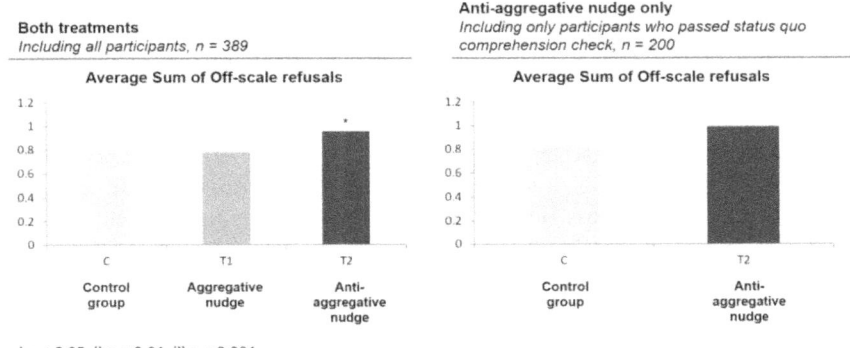

Figure 7.2 Experimental findings—the impact of status quo. © Veronika Luptakova and Alex Voorhoeve.

all respondents who properly ordered the health conditions, telling respondents that only the fatal condition was currently covered—the anti-aggregative nudge—had a statistically significant treatment effect in the predicted direction; that is, it made off-scale refusals more likely compared to the control ($p = 0.028$). Telling them that only the less severe conditions were current covered—the aggregative nudge—had no significant treatment effect. However, when we further analyzed the data for the anti-aggregative nudge[20] and controlled for all and selected sets of covariates, the treatment effect was no longer statistically significant. The model with the highest explanatory power was obtained when the following explanatory variables were included: age, financial situation, self-reported health assessment, and religiosity[21] ($N = 252$, $p = 0.056$, adj. $R^2 = 0.0288$). Also, when we excluded from the analysis those participants who failed the status quo comprehension check, the treatment effect of the anti-aggregative nudge was not statistically significant ($N = 200$, $p = 0.06$; see Figure 7.2 and Table 7.1 in Appendix). In sum, we find no robust evidence for a status quo effect.

6. Discussion and Conclusion

Our aim in this chapter was to provide empirical evidence on the public's degree of support for the most commonly used principles of distributive justice in health care. Our study design eliminated some of the shortcomings identified in existing research, such as small, unrepresentative samples, poor framing, and limited spectra of harms. We analyzed the responses of a representative sample of the UK population to priority-setting dilemmas about the provision of healthcare resources. The dilemmas were designed to check participants' conformity with two features of commonly employed principles: (i) prioritization by severity when groups of patients are of the same size and differ substantially in the severity of the harms they face, and (ii) unlimited aggregation when the groups differ both in size and in the severity of the harms they face.

In our survey, an overwhelming share of the public (88 percent) did not make choices in full conformity with these commonly used principles. These "nonconformists" fall into three camps: 44 percent of all subjects chose in ways that clearly depart from prioritization by severity; 33 percent of all subjects prioritized by severity but accepted only a limited form of aggregation, on which only substantial harms could together outweigh saving a life; and a further 12 percent accepted prioritization by severity but rejected unlimited aggregation by giving lexical priority to saving lives.

We found the widespread rejection of prioritization by severity to be particularly surprising, as the principle is, to our knowledge, not often disputed in healthcare priority-setting policy discussions and is also relatively uncontroversial in philosophical debates on distributive justice. There are, however, uncommon philosophical views which might motivate at least some such departures from prioritization by severity. For example, Taurek (1977) holds that when a bystander can save either a first group from a harm or a second, equally large group of a smaller harm, this bystander may, to guide their decision-making, adopt the permissible moral perspective of any of the people whose well-being is at stake. Taurek takes this permissible moral perspective to include a significant (though limited) degree of special concern for one's own well-being over the well-being of a stranger—for example, he holds that a person may permissibly prioritize saving themselves from a substantial harm over saving a stranger from an even larger harm such as imminent death. It follows that it is permissible, on a Taurekian view, for the bystander to save either group so long as the harm faced by the group facing the smaller harm is such that an individual facing that harm could permissibly save themselves from this harm rather than a stranger from the larger harm. If one assumes that it is permissible for a person to save themselves from paraplegia rather than a stranger from the fatal autoimmune disorder, but it is not permissible for a person to save themselves from the nail disease rather than a stranger from the fatal disorder, then the upshot of a Taurekian view would be that while a decision-maker is required to always prioritize the fatal disorder over the nail disease, they are permitted to give equal priority to saving 100 people from paraplegia over saving 100 from the fatal disorder. Such a Taurekian view may therefore account for the around 20 percent of subjects who give an answer of this kind while judging that the difference in severity between these conditions is substantial. Indeed, on this Taurekian view, it is also permissible to prioritize the paraplegics over those with a fatal disorder in this case (as a further 6 percent of respondents did); just as it is permissible to prioritize those with the fatal disorder (as many other respondents who conform to prioritization by severity did). Given the range of responses that such a Taurekian view permits, our survey is not well-suited to fully distinguish subjects motivated by this view from those motivated by other views; nonetheless, the fact that it can account for roughly a quarter of the responses that none of the other surveyed views can accommodate makes the question of the degree to which people support it worthy of future investigation.[22]

It is also important that 33 percent of respondents favored limited aggregation. This offers some support for the conjectures of philosophers that many people's morality incorporates a form of limited aggregation. And, to return to the policy in the Netherlands which does not permit small harms to outweigh life-saving treatments mentioned in the Introduction, if one assumes the UK and Dutch publics hold similar views on distributive justice in health, our findings can bolster the Dutch priority-setting authority's previously unsubstantiated claim that their policy has significant public support.

We emphasize, however, that we find substantial pluralism among the views expressed. Indeed, our findings suggest that this pluralism is more extensive than is commonly recognized. Discussions of moral pluralism in healthcare priority setting sometimes assume that we are operating within the confines of the continuum of views that runs from utilitarianism to leximin; the only dimension of moral pluralism that is then considered, and that public opinion is surveyed on, is the degree of priority to the worse-off (see, e.g., Adler 2012, 392–9; Dolan and Tsuchiya 2011; Norheim 2013; Robson et al. 2017). This narrow framing ignores the very large proportion of the public (76 percent)[23] who, in our survey, espouse views that do not align with this core assumption.

Given that the legitimacy of priority-setting arrangements depends in part on public acceptance of these arrangements, our findings raise the question whether the common practice of using unlimited aggregative distributive principles to set healthcare priorities has sufficient legitimacy. To us, our findings also suggest that limited aggregative views, such as those embodied in the Dutch priority-setting principles, are worthy of consideration, since they have an apparently reasonable philosophical rationale and may have broader public support.

In sum, we submit that empirical investigations like ours can have value in two principal ways. First, they may help us to better understand the public's views and the concomitant question of which policies can be said to be implemented with their support. Second, insofar as they reveal an apparent mismatch between orthodox views and the public's choices, they may encourage further scrutiny of unorthodox views by philosophers and psychologists, to see whether these views have previously unrecognized merits, or whether, instead, these unorthodox views flow from biased or otherwise unreasonable judgments. In this way, empirical studies of the public's views of distributive justice are an impetus to engage in an interdisciplinary and inclusive search for reflective equilibrium.

While our results offer novel insights into the public's views and may serve to stimulate debate about, it is important to highlight several limitations. First, using a fatal disease as the most severe condition, while common in the literature using the person-trade-off methodology, may have forced respondents to deal with complicated questions regarding comparing the harm of early death with the harms of life with a substantial impairment such as paraplegia. For this reason, it might be advisable in future research to make the most severe condition an enduring, nonfatal one.

Second, although we included several prompts for deliberation, such as the initial severity assessment, using a matching rather than simple choice task, as well as asking respondents to justify their choices, we did not include an element of discussion or qualitative research techniques to clarify people's judgments. Previous research has shown that such discussions or joint deliberations might have an impact on people's preferences (Nord 1995; Schwarzinger et al. 2003) and that qualitative exploration might uncover potential misinterpretations of people's true judgments (Thompson 2022).

Third, although our findings show that a large share of the public prefers limited aggregation to full aggregation, the design of our study did not allow us to generate insight into people's reasoning about how to draw the line between harms that do and those that do not aggregate against more severe harms.

Fourth, we only used two decisions and three specific conditions. This does not allow us to confidently extrapolate to other conditions or to other contexts of distributive justice.

Despite these limitations, our results indicate that a very large share of the public hold views about the application of distributive justice in health care that depart from the principles that are normally used. This invites further empirical investigation of the prevalence and stability of these views, and of people's reasons for holding them. We have outlined several suggestions for further research, including providing more space for deliberation and discussion, using multiple scenarios, and a study design that would distinguish between those who use an absolute threshold from those who make the permissibility of aggregation depends on the relative strength of competing claims. This research should go hand in hand with greater philosophical scrutiny of the merits and demerits of views of distributive justice that deny an obligation to help the more severely burdened (when numbers are equal) and that limit the extent to which premature death can be outweighed by lesser burdens.

Acknowledgments

This chapter was presented at Georgetown University, the LSE, Oxford University, Pompeu Fabra University, the Society for Experimental Philosophy Conference, the U.S. National Institutes of Health, the University of Konstanz, and the University of York. We are grateful to our audiences and to Matthew Adler, Kristoffer Berg, Matteo Galizzi, Dario Krpan, Matthew Lindauer, and Michael Otsuka for comments. Alex Voorhoeve's work on this article was supported through the Bergen Centre for Ethics and Priority Setting's project "Decision Support for Universal Health Coverage," funded by NORAD grant RAF-18/0009.

Appendix

Table 7.1 Results of Regression Analyses

Regression models: The Sum of Off-Scale Refusals, all models for Treatment 2, including all participants (models 1–4) and including only those participants who passed the comprehension check (models 5–7)

(1) Base model (2) Basic demographics (3) Best model (in terms of the highest adjusted R^2) (4) All covariates (5) Base model (6) Best model (7) All covariates

	(1)	(2)	(3)	(4)	(5)	(6)	(7)
Treatment	0.177*	0.161	0.150	0.147	0.174	0.134	0.109
	(0.0800)	(0.0835)	(0.0825)	(0.0854)	(0.0921)	(0.0982)	(0.103)
Sex		0		0			0
		(.)		(.)			(.)
2		−0.0125		−0.0517			−0.0966
		(0.0828)		(0.0861)			(0.0996)
Age		0		0		0	0
		(.)		(.)		(.)	(.)

	(1)	(2)	(3)	(4)	(5)
2	−0.0203	0.0318	−0.0363	−0.0460	−0.147
	(0.0993)	(0.0986)	(0.106)	(0.116)	(0.125)
3	0.230*	0.267*	0.233	0.186	0.141
	(0.115)	(0.117)	(0.123)	(0.137)	(0.143)
4	0.0465	0.0801	−0.0104	0.0147	−0.114
	(0.178)	(0.175)	(0.188)	(0.198)	(0.212)
5	0.138	0.195	0.104	0.100	−0.00639
	(0.462)	(0.457)	(0.470)	(0.471)	(0.481)
Ethnicity	0		0		0
	(.)		(.)		(.)
2	0.182		0.0963		0.159
	(0.328)		(0.341)		(0.473)

	(1)	(2)	(3)	(4)	(5)	(6)	(7)
3		−0.411		−0.342			−0.479
		(0.330)		(0.339)			(0.407)
4		0.0105		0.0793			0.140
		(0.223)		(0.246)			(0.275)
5		0.162		0.249			0.175
		(0.685)		(0.700)			(0.723)
Education							
		0		0			0
		(.)		(.)			(.)
2		0.131		0.0557			0.122
		(0.102)		(0.108)			(0.130)

3	0.101		0.00612	0.0514
	(0.138)		(0.147)	(0.168)
4	0.129		0.118	0.217
	(0.245)		(0.247)	(0.274)
5	0.158		0.0320	−0.0572
	(0.183)		(0.194)	(0.227)
Financial situation				
	0	0	0	0
	(.)	(.)	(.)	(.)
2	−0.285	−0.298	−0.282	−0.313
	(0.188)	(0.185)	(0.192)	(0.225)
3	−0.211	−0.224	−0.213	−0.237
	(0.170)	(0.171)	(0.176)	(0.206)

	(1)	(2)	(3)	(4)	(5)	(6)	(7)
4		-0.313	-0.311	-0.314		-0.346	-0.320
		(0.179)	(0.179)	(0.186)		(0.211)	(0.219)
5		0.00162	0.0882	0.0893		-0.139	-0.130
		(0.250)	(0.251)	(0.259)		(0.290)	(0.298)
6		-0.329	-0.305	-0.266		-0.399	-0.378
		(0.360)	(0.358)	(0.368)		(0.381)	(0.391)
7			0	0		0	0
			(.)	(.)		(.)	(.)
Religion			0.0793	0.0996		0.0610	0.111
			(0.264)	(0.275)		(0.312)	(0.321)

2	−0.123	−0.0819	−0.119	−0.128
	(0.250)	(0.263)	(0.296)	(0.306)
3	−0.0882	−0.111	−0.0461	−0.100
	(0.234)	(0.253)	(0.272)	(0.291)
4	−0.168	−0.193	−0.136	−0.177
	(0.208)	(0.229)	(0.240)	(0.262)
5	−0.877	−0.935	−0.933	−1.144*
	(0.497)	(0.531)	(0.522)	(0.570)
Health	0	0	0	0
	(.)	(.)	(.)	(.)
2	−0.284*	−0.248	−0.225	−0.189
	(0.137)	(0.145)	(0.158)	(0.166)

	(1)	(2)	(3)	(4)	(5)	(6)	(7)
3			−0.195	−0.161		−0.119	−0.0710
			(0.145)	(0.152)		(0.166)	(0.173)
4			−0.266	−0.222		−0.156	−0.0885
			(0.181)	(0.191)		(0.212)	(0.225)
5			−0.375	−0.311		−0.217	−0.170
			(0.198)	(0.209)		(0.239)	(0.252)
Political views							
				0			0
				(.)			(.)
2				−0.110			−0.113
				(0.133)			(0.164)

	(1)	(2)	(3)	(4)	(5)	(6)	(7)
3				0.0127			−0.0792
				(0.171)			(0.204)
4				−0.186			−0.330
				(0.154)			(0.188)
5				−0.0738			−0.00108
				(0.221)			(0.279)
_cons	0.777***	0.879**	1.323***	1.362***	0.817***	1.377***	1.423**
	(0.0577)	(0.276)	(0.275)	(0.382)	(0.0707)	(0.311)	(0.439)
N	252	252	252	252	200	200	200
Adj. R^2	0.015	0.006	0.029	−0.002	0.013	−0.007	−0.018

Note: Standard errors in parentheses.

* $p < 0.05$, ** $p < 0.01$, *** $p < 0.001$.

© Veronika Luptakova and Alex Voorhoeve.

Notes

1. Limited aggregative views have also faced substantial criticism. See, e.g., Tomlin (2017) and Horton (2018).
2. The Netherlands' Institute for Health Care, *Zorginstituut Nederland*, or ZiN, advises the government on what should be covered in the country's mandatory package of health insurance. This package is heavily subsidized for the less well-off. The limited aggregative criterion was first proposed by a previous instantiation of this institute, the Council for Public Health and Care, or *Raad voor Volksgezongheid en Zorg* (RVZ).
3. The well-known case of Oregon's 1990 Medicaid priority-setting exercise is an example. Officials there proposed to set priorities by simple cost-effectiveness. It emerged, however, that on this proposal, tooth capping should be prioritized over treatment for terminal appendicitis, because the former was estimated to be more cost-effective. This ordering of interventions led to outrage and the policy was subsequently withdrawn (Morell 1990; Ubel et al. 1996).
4. Voorhoeve (2020) defends a form of limited aggregation but argues that the threshold for relevance should be set in a different manner, and in many cases substantially lower, than it is in the Dutch context.
5. Participants were asked to compare three conditions involving paralysis, ranging from complete foot numbness to leg paralysis (paraplegia) to quadriplegia (the "paralysis triad") and three conditions involving shortness of breath, from mild to moderate to severe (the "shortness of breath triad").
6. For instance, if people say that *no* number of patients cured of a mild disease should compensate for not saving one person's life (an off-scale refusal), would they make the same judgment even if they learned that such trade-offs are currently being made (i.e., the status quo is that treatments for prevalent minor health conditions are funded but treatments for some rare and much more serious conditions are not covered)?
7. Dolan and Robinson (2001) make this point in relation to loss aversion, which is one of the potential drivers of status quo bias.
8. Samuelson and Zeckhauser (1988) coined the term "status quo bias" to describe people's tendency to *disproportionately* stick with the status quo. Decision-makers exhibit the bias to the extent to which they choose the status quo option "more frequently than would be predicted by a canonical model" (p. 8). This model assumes that people make choices solely based on their preferences. Therefore, irrelevant aspects of options under consideration, such as their order, framing, or being labelled as "status quo," should not have an impact on the actual decision (Samuelson and Zeckhauser 1988).
9. **Nail disease:** A fungal nails infection that causes yellow discoloration and thickening of toenails. People suffering from the disease complain about unpleasant looks and mild itching but usually it is not painful and does not cause further health complications. It is quite a common disease, affecting around 15,000 out of 100,000 adults.

    Partial body paralysis (Paraplegia): An impairment in motor or sensory function of lower part of the body. People with this condition cannot move their legs due to a spinal cord injury. Many patients suffering from this type of paralysis feel chronic pain that can be alleviated only partly. Although there are several health complications resulting from this condition (such as incontinence, depression, impotence, circulation disorders, etc.), it is typically not life-threatening. While it is a less common condition, it still affects significant number of people, about 40 out of 100,000 adults.

Fatal autoimmune disorder: A rare life-threatening autoimmune disorder that causes people to lose control over some of their muscles. It is characterized by painful involuntary muscle contractions in different parts of the body. Patients are gradually unable to perform normal activities such as walking, eating, or talking and in later stages have problems breathing. The disease progresses rather quickly, with average survival of about thirty months after the onset of symptoms. Currently its prevalence is very low, affecting only 2 out of 100,000 adults.

Note, that it has been shown that people care not only about the absolute number of lives saved but about how many lives were saved in relation to how many were at risk (Slovic and Västfjäll 2013). Therefore, information of prevalence of a disease could possibly lead respondents to prefer programs that cure people suffering from less prevalent conditions as the proportion of cured over affected was higher. However, we estimate the impact of this was minimal as we included the information on prevalence just to make the initial descriptions realistic and this information was not displayed at the point of making a decision. Furthermore, although in step 1, when the number of cured people was fixed to 100, they would cure a different proportion of all people affected by each condition, in step 2, respondents had an opportunity to indicate their own number of people that would have to be cured (in order for them to be indifferent between the programs) and that could reflect for instance the prevalence of conditions, if that was their concern.

10 We had pre-tested this spectrum of health conditions before launching the survey to the online panel. Still, as we point out in the Findings section, there were a significant number of participants that perceived the spectrum of health conditions differently than intended.

11 It has been hypothesized that using a more detached perspective, such as the one of an advisor, could make it easier for respondents to discriminate between the groups of people as it would not force them to make "tragic choices," which could result in a utility loss (Dolan et al. 2003, 550). However, empirical research conducted by Damschroder et al. (2007) has shown that while a detached perspective of an "evaluator" leads to lower number of off-scale refusals (compared to a decision-maker's perspective), it actually increases equivalence refusals.

12 Alternatively, the information about the status quo could have been omitted or both treatments could have been covered. However, the former alternative might prompt people to make their own assumptions about what the status quo is, and the latter could trigger loss aversion, either of which could confound the results.

13 To ensure that the sample was gender balanced, we recruited male and female participants separately.

14 The participant used his/her unique Prolific Academic number to fill out the survey twice, once as a male, once as a female, which is an indication of cheating.

15 About half of the excluded responses considered paralysis and fatal disorder to be equally difficult to live with.

16 We have not excluded these responses from our baseline analysis as their failure to pass the comprehension check could also be due to selecting the wrong answer by accident (and there was no option to go back). They could also think it was a "trick"

question (as it was a rather simple one). However, when analyzing the experimental data, we accounted for the potential impact of a failed status quo comprehension check on the treatment effect.
17 We considered the conditions to be perceived as close in severity when the difference in a respondent's severity ratings for the respective conditions was ten points or less on a 100-point scale. The ten-point threshold was chosen post hoc based on our intuitive assessment, to ensure our estimates of equivalence refusals are reasonably conservative; it could have been somewhat smaller or larger.
18 A very small share of respondents (1 percent) departed from these principles by prioritizing by severity but then holding that some number of cases of toenail fungus, but no number of cases of paraplegia, can outweigh saving 100 people from the fatal disease.
19 No responses were excluded from the Lives vs. Nails scenario as the perceived difference between the nail disease and the fatal autoimmune disorder was always greater than 10 points.
20 Comparing the results for Control group and Fatal Currently Covered group.
21 Note that our sample was not fully balanced on age and ethnicity. The inclusion of all covariates ($p = 0.086$) would have resulted in a sizable decrease of adj. R^2 (-0.002).
22 Refusals to prioritize by severity may, of course, have other motivations. For instance, a respondent who prioritized saving 100 people from paraplegia over saving 100 people from the fatal autoimmune disorder (while considering living with the later condition to be more difficult than living with the former) argued that "the people with the fatal disease will not suffer indefinitely … the partial paralysis is not fatal, so the suffering would be prolonged without a cure." The respondent chose saving lives over curing nails in Lives vs. Nails scenario (with an off-scale refusal) but chose curing paraplegia over saving lives in Lives vs. Paraplegia scenario (for equal numbers). The respondent passed the comprehension check and provided the following severity assessments: 9 – 62 – 81 for nail disease, paraplegia, and fatal disorder, respectively, which means there was a sufficient difference in perceived severity between paraplegia and fatal disorder and it is unlikely that paraplegia was judged to be worse than death.
23 Those who chose in line with full aggregation are 12 percent and a further 12 percent aligned with leximin. It follows that 76 percent cannot be placed on the continuum that runs from utilitarianism to leximin.

References

Adler, M. 2012. *Well-Being and Fair Distribution: Beyond Cost-Benefit Analysis*. Oxford, England: Oxford University Press.

Betram, M., and T. T. T. Edejer. 2021. "Introduction to the Special Issue on 'The World Health Organization Choosing Interventions That Are Cost-Effective (WHO-CHOICE) Update'". *International Journal of Health Policy and Management* 10: 670–2. Doi: 10.34172/IJHPM.2021.105

Bognar, G., and I. Hirose. 2014. *The Ethics of Health Care Rationing*. Abingdon, England: Routledge.

Bostrom, N., and T. Ord. 2006. "The Reversal Test: Eliminating Status Quo Bias in Applied Ethics." *Ethics* 116, no. 4: 656–79. Doi: 10.1086/505233

Brown, C. 2005. "Priority or Sufficiency ... or Both?" *Economics and Philosophy* 21, no. 2: 199–220. Doi: 10.1017/S0266267105000568

Brown, C. 2020. "Is Close Enough Good Enough?" *Economics and Philosophy* 36: 29–59. Doi: 10.1017/S0266267119000099

Caviola, L., A. Mannino, J. Savulescu, and N. Faulmüller. 2014. "Cognitive Biases Can Affect moral Intuitions About Cognitive Enhancement." *Frontiers in systems neuroscience* 8, no. 195: 1–5. Doi: 10.3389/fnsys.2014.00195

Crisp, R. 2003. "Equality, Priority, and Compassion." *Ethics* 113, no. 4: 745–63. Doi: 10.1086/373954

Damschroder, L. J., T. R. Roberts, C. C. Goldstein, M. E. Miklosovic, and P. A. Ubel. 2005. "Trading People Versus Trading Time: What Is the Difference?" *Population Health Metrics* 3, no. 1: 10. Doi: 10.1186/1478-7954-3-10

Damschroder, L. J., T. R. Roberts, B. J. Zikmund-Fisher, and P. A. Ubel. 2007. "Why People Refuse to Make Tradeoffs in Person Tradeoff Elicitations: A Matter of Perspective?" *Medical Decision Making* 27, no. 3: 266–80. Doi: 10.1177/0272989x07300601

Daniels, N. 2013. "Reflective Equilibrium." In *The Stanford Encyclopedia of Philosophy* (Winter 2013 edition), edited by Edward N. Zalta. http://plato.stanford.edu/archives/win2013/entries/reflective-equilibrium/.

Dolan, P., and C. Green. 1998. "Using the Person Trade-Off Approach to Examine Differences Between Individual and Social Values." *Health Economics* 7, no. 4: 307–12. Doi: 10.1002/(SICI)1099-1050(199806)7:4<307::AID-HEC345>3.0.CO;2-N

Dolan, P., and A. Tsuchiya. 2011. "Determining the Parameters in a Social Welfare Function using Stated Preference Data: An Application to Health." *Applied Economics* 43: 2241–50. Doi: 10.1080/00036840903166244

Dolan, P., J. A. Olsen, P. Menzel, and J. Richardson. 2003. "An Inquiry into the Different Perspectives that Can Be Used When Eliciting Preferences in Health." *Health Economics*, 12, no. 7: 545–51. Doi: 10.1002/hec.760

Dolan, P., and A. Robinson. 2001. "The Measurement of Preferences over the Distribution of Benefits: The Importance of the Reference Point." *European Economic Review* 45: 1697–709. Doi: 10.1016/s0014-2921(00)00052-0

Fernandez, R., and D. Rodrik. 1991. "Resistance to Reform: Status Quo Bias in the Presence of Individual-Specific Uncertainty." *The American Economic Review* 81, no. 5: 1146–55. Doi: 10.1257/0002828041464425

Fleurbaey, M., B. Tungodden, and P. Vallentyne. 2009. "On the Possibility of Nonaggregative Priority for the Worst Off." *Social Philosophy and Policy* 26: 258–85. Doi: 10.1017/s0265052509090116

Horton, J. 2018. "Always Aggregate." *Philosophy and Public Affairs* 46, no. 2: 160–74. Doi: 10.1111/papa.12116

Johnson, E., J. Hershey, J. Meszaros, and J. Kunreuther. 1993. "Framing, Probability Distortions, and Insurance Decisions." *Journal of Risk and Uncertainty* 7, no. 1: 35–51. Doi: 10.1007/978-94-011-2192-7_3

Kahneman, D., J. Knetsch, and R. Thaler. 1991. "Anomalies: The Endowment Effect, Loss Aversion, and Status Quo Bias." *Journal of Economic Perspectives* 5, no. 1: 193–206. Doi: 10.1017/cbo9780511803475.009

Kamm, F. M. 1993. *Morality, Mortality, Vol. I*. Oxford: Oxford University Press.

Kelleher, P. 2014. "Relevance and Non-Consequentialist Aggregation." *Utilitas* 26, no. 4: 385–408. Doi: 10.1017/S0953820814000144

Lefkowitz, D. 2008. "On the Concept of a Morally Relevant Harm." *Utilitas* 20, no. 4: 409–23. Doi: 10.1017/s0953820808003245

Liao, S. M. and J. E. Lim. 2022. "Lives, Limbs, and Liver Spots: The Threshold Approach to Limited Aggregation." Manuscript shared by author.

Mann, K. 2021a. "The Relevance View: Defended and Extended." *Utilitas* 33, no. 1: 101–10. Doi: 10.1017/s095382082000028x

Mann, K. 2021b. "Relevance and Nonbinary Choices." *Ethics* 132, no. 2: 382–413. Doi: 10.1086/716873

Millum, J. 2015. "Age and Death: A Defense of Gradualism." *Utilitas* 27, no. 3: 279–97. Doi: 10.1017/s0953820815000047

Morell, V. 1990. "Oregon Puts Bold Health Plan on Ice." *Science* 249: 468–71. Doi: 10.1126/science.2382125

Nagel, T. 1979. *Mortal Questions*. Cambridge, England: Cambridge University Press.

Nord, E. 1995. "The Person-Trade-Off Approach to Valuing Health Care Programmes." *Medical Decision Making* 15, no. 3: 201–8. Doi: 10.1177/0272989x9501500302

Nord, E., J. Richardson, and K. Macarounas-Kirchmann. 1993. "Social Evaluation of Health Care Versus Personal Evaluation of Health States: Evidence on the Validity of four Health-State Scaling Instruments Using Norwegian and Australian Surveys." *International Journal of Technology Assessment in Health Care* 9, no. 4: 463–78. Doi: 10.1017/s0266462300005390

Norheim, O. F. 2013. "Atkinson's Index Applied to Health. Can Measures of Economic Inequality Help Us Understand Tradeoffs in Health Care Priority Setting?" In *Inequalities in Health: Concepts, Measures, and Ethics*, edited by N. Eyal, S. A. Hurst, O. F. Norheim, and D. Wikler, 214–30. Oxford, England: Oxford University Press.

Otsuka, M. 2004. "Skepticism About Saving the Greater Number." *Philosophy and Public Affairs* 32, no. 4: 413–26. Doi: 10.1111/j.1088-4963.2004.00020.x

Otsuka, M. 2006. "Saving Lives, Moral Theory, and the Claims of Individuals." *Philosophy and Public Affairs* 34, no. 2: 109–35. Doi: 10.1111/j.1088-4963.2006.00058.x

Ottersen, T., R. Førde, M. Kakad, A. Kjellevold, H. O. Melberg, A. Moen, ... O. F. Norheim. 2016. "A New Proposal for Priority Setting in Norway: Open and Fair." *Health Policy* 120, no. 3: 246–51. Doi: 10.1016/j.healthpol.2016.01.012

Parfit, D. 1995. *Equality or Priority?* The Lindley Lecture. Kansas City, KA: The University of Kansas.

Payne, J., J. Bettman, and E. Johnson. 1992. "Behavioral Decision Research: A Constructive Processing Perspective." *Annual Review of Psychology* 43, no. 1: 87–131. Doi: 10.1146/annurev.ps.43.020192.000511

Pinto-Prades, J. L., and A. Lopez-Nicolas. 1998. "More Evidence of the Plateau Effect: A Social Perspective." *Medical Decision Making*, 18, no. 3: 287–94. Doi: 10.1177/0272989x9801800306

Rawls, J. 1999. *A Theory of Justice*. Revised, 2nd edition. Oxford: Oxford University Press.

Robson, M., M. Asaria, R. Cookson, A. Tsuchiya, and S. Ali. 2017. "Eliciting the Level of Health Inequality Aversion in England." *Health Economics* 26, no. 10: 1328–34. Doi: 10.1002/hec.3430

Rueger, K. 2020. "Aggregation with Constraints." *Utilitas* 32, no. 4: 454–71. Doi: 10.1017/s095382082000014x

RVZ. 2006. *Zinnige en Duurzame Zorg*. Zoetermeer, The Netherlands: RVZ.

Salkeld, G., M. Ryan, and L. Short. 2000. "The Veil of Experience: Do Consumers Prefer What They Know Best?" *Health Economics* 9, no. 3: 267–70. Doi:10.1002/(sici)1099-1050(200004)9:3<267::aid-hec511>3.0.co;2-h

Samuelson, W., and R. Zeckhauser. 1988. "Status Quo Bias in Decision Making." *Journal of Risk and Uncertainty* 1, no. 1: 7–59. Doi: 10.1007/bf00055564

Scanlon, T. M. 1998. *What We Owe to Each Other.* Cambridge, MA: Harvard University Press.
Schwarzinger, M., J. Lanoë, E. Nord, and I. Durand-Zaleski. 2004. "Lack of Multiplicative Transitivity in Person Trade-Off Responses." *Health Economics* 13, no. 2: 171–81. Doi: 10.1002/hec.808
Schwarzinger, M., M. E. A. Stouthard, K. Burström, and E. Nord. 2003. "Cross-National Agreement on Disability Weights: The European Disability Weights Project." *Population Health Metrics* 1, no. 1: 9. Doi: 10.1186/1478-7954-1-9
Singh, J., J. Lord, L. Longworth, S. Orr, T. McGarry, R. Sheldon, and M. Buxton. 2012. "Does Responsibility Affect the Public's Valuation of Health Care Interventions? A Relative Valuation Approach to Health Care Safety." *Value in Health* 15, no. 5: 690–8. Doi: 10.1016/j.jval.2012.02.005
Skedgel, C. D. 2013. *Estimating Societal Preferences for the Allocation of Healthcare Resources using Stated Preference Methods.* (Doctoral dissertation). University of Sheffield.
Slovic, P., and D. Västfjäll. 2013. "The More Who Die, the Less We Care: Psychic Numbing and Genocide." In *Behavioural Public Policy*, edited by A. Oliver, 94–114. Cambridge, England: Cambridge University Press. Doi: 10.1017/cbo9781107337190.005
Sparrow, R. 2015. "Imposing Genetic Diversity." *The American Journal of Bioethics* 15, no. 6: 2–10. Doi: 10.1080/15265161.2015.1028658
Steuwer, B. 2021. "Aggregation, Balancing and Respect for the Claims of Individuals." *Utilitas* 33, no. 1: 17–34. Doi: 10.1017/s0953820820000217
Tadros, V. 2019. "Localized Restricted Aggregation." In *Oxford Studies in Political Philosophy, Vol. 5*, edited by D. Sobel, P. Vallentyne, and S. Wall, 171–204. Oxford, England: Oxford University Press. Doi: 10.1093/oso/9780198841425.003.0007
Taurek, J. 1977. "Should the Numbers Count?" *Philosophy and Public Affairs* 6: 293–316.
Temkin, L. 2012. *Rethinking the Good.* Oxford, England: Oxford University Press.
Thompson, K. 2022. "Qualitative Methods Show that Surveys Misrepresent "Ought Implies Can" Judgments." *Philosophical Psychology*: 1–29. Doi: 10.1080/09515089.2022.2036714
Tomlin, P. 2017. "On Limited Aggregation." *Philosophy and Public Affairs* 45, no. 3: 232–60. Doi: 10.1111/papa.12097
Tungodden, B. 2003. "The Value of Equality." *Economics and Philosophy* 19, no. 1: 1–44.
Ubel, P. A., G. Loewenstein, D. Scanlon, and M. Kamlet. 1996. "Individual Utilities Are Inconsistent with Rationing Choices: A Partial Explanation of Why Oregon's Cost Effectiveness List Failed." *Medical Decision Making* 16, no. 2: 108–16. Doi: 10.1177/0272989x9601600202
Van de Wijngaard, Q. 2021. *Priority-Setting in the Netherlands: A Case for Public Participation and Against Proportional Shortfall.* (Master's thesis), Erasmus University Rotterdam.
Voorhoeve, A. 2014. "How Should We Aggregate Competing Claims?" *Ethics* 125, no. 1: 64–87. Doi: 10.1086/677022
Voorhoeve, A. 2017. "Why One Should Count Only Claims with Which One Can Sympathize." *Public Health Ethics* 10, no. 2: 148–56. Doi: 10.1093/phe/phw006
Voorhoeve, A. 2018. "Balancing Small Against Large Burdens." *Behavioural Public Policy* 2, no. 1: 125–42. Doi: 10.1017/bpp.2017.4
Voorhoeve, A. 2020. "Healthy Nails Versus Long Lives: An Analysis of a Dutch Priority Setting Proposal." In *Measuring the Global Burden of Disease: Philosophical Dimensions*,

edited by N. Eyal, S. Hurst, C. Murray, S. A. Schroeder, and D. Wikler, 273–92. Doi: 10.1093/med/9780190082543.003.0016

Walen, A. 2020. "Risks and Weak Aggregation: Why Different Models of Risk Suit Different Types of Cases." *Ethics* 131: 62–86. Doi: 10.1086/709985

Wasserman, D. 2015. "Disability, Diversity, and Preference for the Status Quo: Bias or Justifiable Preference?" *The American Journal of Bioethics* 15, no. 6: 11–12. Doi: 10.1080/15265161.2015.1028676

ZiN. [Zorginstituut Nederland] 2015a. Van goede zorg verzekerd: Hoe zorginstituut Nederland adviseert over de inhoud van het basispakket [Good care assured: How the Netherlands Healthcare Institute advises on the content of the basic package]. 1–25, Rep.). Diemen: Zorginstituut Nederland.

ZiN. 2015b. Kosteneffectiviteit in de praktijk [Cost-effectiveness in practice]. 1–19, Rep.). Diemen: Zorginstituut Nederland.

ZiN. 2017. Pakketadvies in de praktijk: Wikken en wegen voor een rechtvaardig pakket [Package advice in practice: Deliberation and weighing for a fair package]. 1–25, Rep.). Diemen: Zorginstituut Nederland.

ZiN. 2018. Ziektelast in de praktijk: De theorie en praktijk van het berekenen van ziektelast bij pakketbeoordelingen [Burden of disease in practice: Theory and practice of calculating the burden of disease in package assessments]. 1–25, Rep.). Diemen: Zorginstituut Nederland.

ZiN. 2020. *Beoordeling Van nieuwe zorg* [Review of new care]. https://www.zorginstituutnederland.nl/over-ons/werkwijzen-en-procedures/adviseren-over-en-verduidelijken-van-het-basispakket-aan-zorg/beoordeling-van-nieuwe-zorg

Part Two

New Directions

8

Automated Psycholinguistic Analysis of the Anglophone Manosphere

Mark Alfano, Joanne Byrne, and Joshua Roose

> Would anyone like to have a little look down into the secret of how *ideals are fabricated* on this earth? Who has enough pluck? … Come one! Here we have a clear glimpse into this dark workshop.
> —Friedrich Nietzsche, *On the Genealogy of Morality*, I:14

1. Introduction

The 2015 Charleston church mass shooting, which left nine people dead, was planned and executed by white supremacist Dylann Roof. According to prosecutors, Roof was radicalized online (Berman 2016, 1). As Alfano et al. (2018) document, the same is true of many other terrorists and white supremacists, some of whom have engaged in lone-wolf terrorism (Weimann 2012).

Scholars suggest that this form of terrorism is facilitated by the internet (Precht 2007; von Behr et al. 2013, §3). However, the specific mechanisms by which the internet facilitates self-radicalization are disputed. According to Bjelopera (2010), it does so by normalizing behaviors and attitudes which, in wider society, would typically be viewed as unacceptable and be met with disapprobation. By contrast, Silber et al. (2007) argue that the internet facilitates self-radicalization by generating an echo chamber: people interested in radical ideology tend to communicate directly or indirectly only with each other, reinforcing and exacerbating their preexisting predilections. The combination of these predilections and social media recommender systems—tailoring content to personal preferences, biases and interests—is commonly termed the "filter bubble" (Pariser 2011). In a recent conceptual analysis, Nguyen (2020) argues that it is worthwhile to distinguish bubbles, which are characterized by ignorance of dissenting views, from echo chambers, which are characterized by intensive ingroup trust and outgroup distrust. A related view is that the phenomenon of online group polarization in chat forums drives radicalization (Sunstein 2011; 2018).[1] Recent scholarship has associated filter bubbles and echo chambers with radicalization but, as Conway

(2017) cautions, more research is needed to establish a causal relationship. Moreover, experimental research involving randomization to conditions is impossible because it would clearly violate principles of research ethics.

The construct of masculinity seems to play a significant role in the recruitment or radicalization of many perpetrators. Here we understand masculinity in simple terms as the social construction of what it is to "be a man" (Kimmel 2013; Bridges 2014). Connell's body of scholarship is arguably the "central reference point for many, if not most, writers on men and masculinity" (Wetherell and Edley 1998, 156). Connell and Messerschmitt use two ideal types to explain the centrality of power to masculinity formation. "Hegemonic masculinity" is "normative," embodying "the most honoured way of being a man" and ideologically legitimating the subordination of women to men (Connell and Messerschmitt 2005, 832). Subordinated masculinities by contrast are those that fall outside the spectrum of this "normative" and socially acceptable masculinity. Subordinated masculinities intersect with race, class, sexuality and physical ability/disability among other categories. They may be variously represented as "threat" (Black male sexuality) or effeminate (gay masculinities) as a mechanism of coercion and forcible control or as in "deficit" (disabled men). Responses from these men range from demonstrations of hyper-masculinity, anger, and resentment through to active and self-empowering advocacy and activism.

The vast majority of lone-wolf shooters are men, as are the vast majority of participants (and groups such as the Proud Boys) in violence such as the Unite the Right rally in Charlottesville in 2017 and the US Capitol insurrection in 2021. As the present study shows, the definition, structure, and praxis of masculinity are particularly important to such men who populate what is sometimes called the "manosphere." The manosphere is an amorphous grouping of social movements, gender theories, and sociality hosted on various websites, message boards and digital social spaces.[2] This otherwise loose (and at times contradictory) association of people and ideas is united through a "common preoccupation with male hegemony as it relates to heterosexual [...] gender relations" (Ging 2019, 653). Through the concept of hegemonic masculinity, Connell and Messerschmitt (2005) provide an "overarching framework for understanding how gender inequalities are produced and reproduced" (Jeweks et al., 2015, cited in Theofanos et al. 2021). In this framework, the hegemonic structure of masculinity is relational, shaped by the domination of women and subordination of other men (Connell 2005). That is, masculinity is largely defined by the things that are avoided, dominated, or "cast out" for their association with femininity (Connell 2005; Connell and Messerschmitt 2005).

Some have argued that contemporary expressions of masculinity have become more fluid, dynamic, or egalitarian and thus look toward a future of "inclusive masculinities," rejecting the hegemonic structure proposed by Connell and Messerschmitt (Anderson 2009; Kimmel 2012). However, these works have been countered in subsequent scholarship (De Boise 2014; O'Neill 2014; Ging 2019) as they generally downplay the accommodations for fluidity and dynamism in the definition of hegemonic masculinity and overlook expressions of masculinity in digital spaces (Vitale 2019). The manifestos analyzed in this study reflect a complicated interplay between hegemonic masculinity and the affordances of digital spaces.

In digital spaces, manosphere-aligned men respond to the (perceived) threat of feminism with severe, sometimes violent, backlash, suggesting that they do not inhabit filter bubbles but rather echo chambers, as characterized above. The writings and manifestos analyzed here represent some of the most intense vitriol of the manosphere and reflect an unresolved irony that permeates manosphere writing and digital communities. Though not a cohesive or unified group, manosphere interpretations of gender relations assume men's dominance over women to be natural. However, at the same time, manosphere men are frustrated with the structure of men's dominance over other men predicated on men's sexual dominance over women. Massanari (2017) identifies this particular irony as a (nonexclusive) trait of "geek masculinity." Such men simultaneously reject and reify elements of hegemonic masculinity[3] (Connell and Messerschmidt 2005), recreating the hegemonic structures they rail against. Indeed, in the digital communities and manifestos analyzed herein—particularly in the Rodgers Manifesto and texts produced by self-described "braincels" and "spergs"—acute attention is paid to the perceived rules and "unmet promises" of masculinity.

As such, it is necessary to examine the interwoven tapestries of masculinity, violent extremism, and digital space. We do so via linguistic analysis of the corpora associated with and produced by a range of groups and individuals. In particular, we analyze two corpora from each of: manifestos of male domestic terrorists (Brenton Tarrant and Elliot Rodger), male supremacists (the Australian Lads Society and Men Going Their Own Way), and men's rights groups (the Men's Rights Agency and the Australian Men's Rights Agency).[4] We use semi-automated linguistic analysis of these corpora to profile and compare these groups and individuals. Our results indicate that there are four distinct strands of thinking, language, and behavior in these groups:

- *dominant masculinity*, grounded in the normative domination of women and other men perceived as; a threat, as somehow effeminate, or in deficit,
- *subsidiary masculinity*, which manifests in particular responses grounded in anger and resentment at perceived domination by other men,[5]
- *misogyny*, grounded in resentful or outright hateful attitudes and actions towards women (especially women who are perceived as withholding men's entitlements), and
- *xenophobia*, which manifests in fearful and vengeful reactions to (perceived) invasion by foreigners and other outsiders (especially people of color).

As we show below, each of these four strands may lead to violent extremism, but dominant masculinity seems to be especially associated with collective action, whereas subsidiary masculinity seems to be more associated with individual action.

If this is on the right track, we can connect the current analysis with the existing philosophical literature in at least two ways. First, we see a connection to work in the philosophy of (political) language on the link between hate speech and the violence it inspires and licenses (Tirrell 2012). Tirrell argues that hate speech that demonizes, invokes contempt and disgust, and employs coded metaphors is sometimes treated as granting permission to engage in acts of violence that would otherwise be seen as morally impermissible. Her main example concerns the Rwandan genocide, which was a form of collective action taken by some members of the Hutu tribe against Tutsi victims. Our work suggests that hate speech in masculinist movements may similarly inspire and grant permission to engage in collective violence against both women and other groups of men who are seen as competitors in mating markets.

Second, and more critically, we see a connection to work on the nature of political speech, especially the overly constrained Rawlsian notion that political speech must refer to public reasons (Rawls 1997). What we find in this discourse is speech, most of which is produced in the allegedly liberal democracies that concern Rawls (he explicitly mentions Western Europe, the United States, Israel, and India) that cannot be denied political import and yet which is stridently addressed only to a parochial ingroup in order to pit them against both compatriots and foreigners (especially immigrants). Whereas Rawls only countenances speech that is addressed universally to fellow citizens, the speech under consideration here is primarily aimed at movement-building, coalition-strengthening (sometimes with the aim of excluding noncitizens), and (perhaps most importantly) meaning-making. In fact, such speech seems functionally similar to speech from more palatable activist movements studied by those interested in hermeneutic injustice (e.g., Fricker 2007, but even more so Medina 2013). Medina describes at length the ways in which social imaginaries—which are interactively constructed by members of a community in conversation, trying to make sense of their world and their experience—can make some experiences, phenomena, and action potentials salient while making others less so or even unintelligible. When a social movement forges new words and new concepts through discursive interaction over time, he argues, what they are doing is to make possible a new way of understanding one's position in the social world, as well as to give one a sense of who one's allies and adversaries are. Fricker famously uses the example of the coinage "sexual harassment" by the women's movement in the second half of the twentieth century to illustrate this phenomenon. What we find in the current research is that members of a range of masculinist movements have been doing the same sort of thing, but with examples such as "incel" (a coinage that they appropriated from a bisexual Canadian woman) and "monkey-branching" (marrying up multiple times). Indeed, perhaps the most notorious appropriation by these groups and allied right-wing political movements is of the term "red pill," which in *The Matrix* movie trilogy refers to the epiphanic experience of seeing the social and political world in a new and different way—and which the creators of these films have revealed to have originally been a metaphor for realizing that one is trans.[6] To sum up: whereas Rawls sees political speech solely as the giving and taking of reasons in a universal public sphere, we find that much political speech functions to make meaning for parochial and sometimes violent social movements.

2. Methodology

We chose to examine digital corpora on websites for three main reasons. First, they are much more easily accessible than printed or spoken corpora. Second, they are already digitized, making their analysis with digital tools straightforward. And third, the internet increasingly seems to be a venue or pathway for radicalization, extremism, and conspiracy theories (Alfano et al. 2018, 2021).

We focused on examples of confirmed violent extremists/terrorists who had authored some form of manifesto prior to the act and progenitor groups. We then looked at progenitor groups. These may be considered progenitor political groups. These legal civil society groups are focused on developing and enacting ideas through political action and seek a fundamental reordering of society, though they have not graduated to violent extremism. They therefore offer broad insights into groups that do or may eventually engage in political violence.

In particular, we downloaded and analyzed corpora associated with the following groups and individuals:

Lone-Wolf Manifestos:

- **Elliot Rodger** (https://www.nytimes.com/interactive/2014/05/25/us/shooting-document.html): Entitled "My Twisted World: The Story of Elliot Rodger," this manifesto reads as an autobiographical account of the many real and perceived humiliations Rodger experienced during his youth, leading up to his resolution to go on a shooting spree in Isla Vista, California.
- **Brenton Tarrant** (https://www.ilfoglio.it/userUpload/The_Great_Replacementconvertito.pdf): Entitled "The Great Replacement," this manifesto reads as an eco-fascist call to arms directed in the first instance at white Australians and New Zealanders and more generally towards whites around the world.

Male Supremacy:

- **Men Going Their Own Way** (https://www.mgtow.com/): This is a loosely affiliated group of men who have decided to isolate themselves from women. Most seem to be heterosexual divorcés who have given up on the possibility of amicable inter-gender relations.
- **Lads Society** (https://www.ladssociety.com/): This is a masculinist and nationalist group that has engaged in harassment of African Australians, among other minorities. They portray themselves as champions of traditional values and have a strong emphasis on individual self-improvement and individual responsibility (though the responsibility is to a narrowly conceived "real" Australia).

Men's Rights:

- **Australia's Men's Rights Association** (http://australianmensrights.com/Mens_Rights_Agency-Australia.aspx): This is an advocacy group that promotes men's rights in Australia. They pay special attention to laws, regulations, and social norms that they perceive as unjust toward men (e.g., domestic violence, divorce, child support, etc.).
- **Men's Rights Agency** (https://mensrights.com.au/): This group is very similar to the previous one.

Corpora were collected from October 26, 2019, to December 19, 2019. These corpora are not perfectly comparable because they differ in the amount of editorial control exercised by their authors or owners. For example, the authors of the manifestos exercised complete editorial control over their wording and publication. By contrast, the Lads Society features several authors, and the website for Men Going Their Own Way enables comments from pseudonymous users. In addition, the timing of their production differs in important ways: the manifestos are meant to explain particular acts of violence, whereas the other four corpora are more general reflections on and discourse about society. Despite these differences, the size of the corpora makes it possible to draw some illuminating comparisons. Table 8.1 represents the word count of each corpus.

Table 8.1 Summary Word Counts for Six Corpora

Corpus	Word count
Elliot Rodger	105,946
Brenton Tarrant	17,045
Men Going Their Own Way	960,565
Lads Society	13,943
Australia's Men's Rights Agency	423,533
Men's Rights Agency	705,257
Total	**2,226,289**

© Mark Alfano, Joanne Byrne, and Joshua Roose.

Naturally, over 2 million words are too much to analyze via close reading, so we approached these corpora using both pre-built and custom dictionaries of Linguistic Inquiry and Word Count (LIWC, see Pennebaker (2011) and Pennebaker et al. (2015) for more details). LIWC works by counting the number of words belonging to various categories in a text. For instance, LIWC combs through a text to examine how many first-person singular pronouns (e.g., *I, me, my*), how many first-person plural pronouns (e.g., *we, us, our*), and how many articles (e.g., *a, an, the*) are used per 100 words. Beyond these so-called *function words*, LIWC has dictionaries for words that indicate complexity of thinking (e.g., *nevertheless, whereas, but*), asking questions (e.g., *who, what, why*), and a range of psychological processes that includes positive and negative emotions, discrete emotions such as anger and sadness, and drives for affiliation, achievement, power, reward, and risk.

Over the last few decades, Pennebaker and his collaborators have shown that this seemingly simple method can reveal quite a bit about individuals, their relationships, and the groups to which they belong. In the context of this study, it is highly relevant that Pennebaker and his colleagues have done consulting work for American police and Homeland Security to try to predict the likelihood that various groups will engage in violence to advance their causes. Independent researchers have also used LIWC to study the language used by Islamist terrorist groups (Smith 2013; Vergani and Bliuc 2018).[7]

One useful functionality of LIWC is the ability to create and share custom dictionaries for categories of interest. Recent work in social and political psychology suggests that, when groups engage in violence, they often believe that they are doing the morally right thing (Fiske and Rai 2014). A popular framework for understanding and comparing the moral values of individuals and groups is Moral Foundations Theory (Haidt 2013). Moral Foundations Theory posits that there are five moral domains to which people are sensitive and that different people (and groups) focus more on some domains than others. The domains include *care, fairness, loyalty, authority,* and *sanctity*. The first two domains (care and fairness) tend to be associated with left-wing and educated people and groups, and are sometimes called the *individualizing* domains. By contrast, the other three (loyalty, authority, and sanctity) tend to be associated with right-wing and uneducated people and groups, and are sometimes called the *binding* domains. Each domain is bipolar, with the positive pole indicating a range of virtues and the negative pole indicating a range of vices. For instance, virtues related to care include *kindness, compassion,* and *empathy,* whereas vices related to care include *cruelty* and a disposition to cause *harm.* Research suggests that groups with heightened emphasis on the binding domains display greater liability to violence—including both punishment of in-group deviants and attacks on outsiders viewed as threats (Leidner and Castano 2012). Frimer et al. (2019) have created a custom LIWC dictionary that contains words associated with both poles of all five dimensions (meaning it contains ten sub-dictionaries).

Additionally, we created four custom LIWC dictionaries that are keyed to specific aspects of masculinity. Based in tandem on research by philosopher and social critic Kate Manne (2017) and sociologist RW Connell (2005), we conceptualize masculinities in terms of dominance and subordination along three dimensions: intra-gender, inter-gender, and inter-group. More specifically, many men evince intense concern for (what they take to be) their position in male dominance hierarchies. Some are (or see themselves as) dominant with respect to other men, whereas others are (or see themselves as) subsidiary to other men. Likewise, many men are (or see themselves as) dominant or subsidiary with respect to women.[8] Finally, many men perceive their group as dominant or subsidiary with respect to other groups, especially racial, ethnic, and religious groups.

To study the language used to talk about such (perceived) dominance hierarchies, we developed custom LIWC dictionaries for the categories of *dominant masculinity, subsidiary masculinity, misogyny,* and *xenophobia*. The first two dictionaries include terms that are used to describe men: the dominant masculinity dictionary includes words that refer to men who are (perceived as) dominant in relation to other men, whereas the subsidiary masculinity dictionary includes words that refer to men who are (perceived as) dominated by other men or by women. Note that these words are not necessarily used reflexively: a man who feels subsidiary might, for instance, complain about the "Chads" (dominant men) in his community. The misogyny dictionary includes terms of abuse that are sometimes hurled at women in these corpora.[9] Finally, the xenophobia dictionary includes terms of abuse that are sometimes hurled out perceived outsiders in these corpora, along with words and phrases that refer to intergroup domination and subordination (e.g., "white genocide").

The dictionaries were developed via a two-step process. First, we brainstormed lists of words and n-grams that seemed, intuitively, to be distinctively associated with the four categories of interest. Second, one of the authors read through the corpora and noted words and n-grams that seemed to be associated with the same categories. The manifestos and Lads Society corpus were read in full. Approximately 10 percent of each of the other corpora was ready. The full dictionaries are available in the online supplementary materials associated with this chapter.

3. Results

The results section is subdivided into three parts. First, we present summaries of the corpora under study in the form of word clouds, topic models, and a dendrogram. Next, we use the built-in LIWC dictionaries to begin analyzing the corpora. Finally, we use custom dictionaries to explore the role of moral foundations and masculinity in the corpora.

3.1 Corpora Summaries

In this subsection we use the quanteda package for R (Benoit et al. 2018) to provide thumbnail summaries of each corpus in the form of word clouds (Figure 8.1), followed by a dendrogram that clusters the corpora based on similarity (Figure 8.2). In each word cloud, word size represents prevalence in the corpus, with larger words being more prevalent than smaller ones. To aid legibility, text color divides words into bands of roughly equivalent prevalence. The most prevalent words are also placed in the center of each cloud, with less prevalent words at the periphery.

Altogether, these corpora represent a range of topics and underlying interests and concerns. For example, the Tarrant manifesto is primarily about race, culture, and violent intergroup conflict. By contrast, the Rodger manifesto is much more focused on a small number of individuals (especially Rodger's parents and friends) and (potential) sexual relationships. The Men Going Their Own Way corpus evinces less emphasis on specific individuals and more on broad generalizations about men and (even more so) women. Next, the Lads Society corpus seems to resemble the Tarrant manifesto in its emphasis on intergroup conflict, paired with intense focus on hierarchy and social order. Finally, the men's rights corpora look very similar, with two primary focal points: family relations and the law.

These impressions are borne out by the dendrogram pictured in Figure 8.2, which clusters the corpora hierarchically based on their similarities and differences. The men's rights corpora are quite similar to one another and very different from the other four corpora. The Lads Society and Men Going Their Own Way corpora are most similar to each other and also quite similar to the Tarrant manifesto. The Rodger manifesto appears, at least in this context, to be one of a kind.

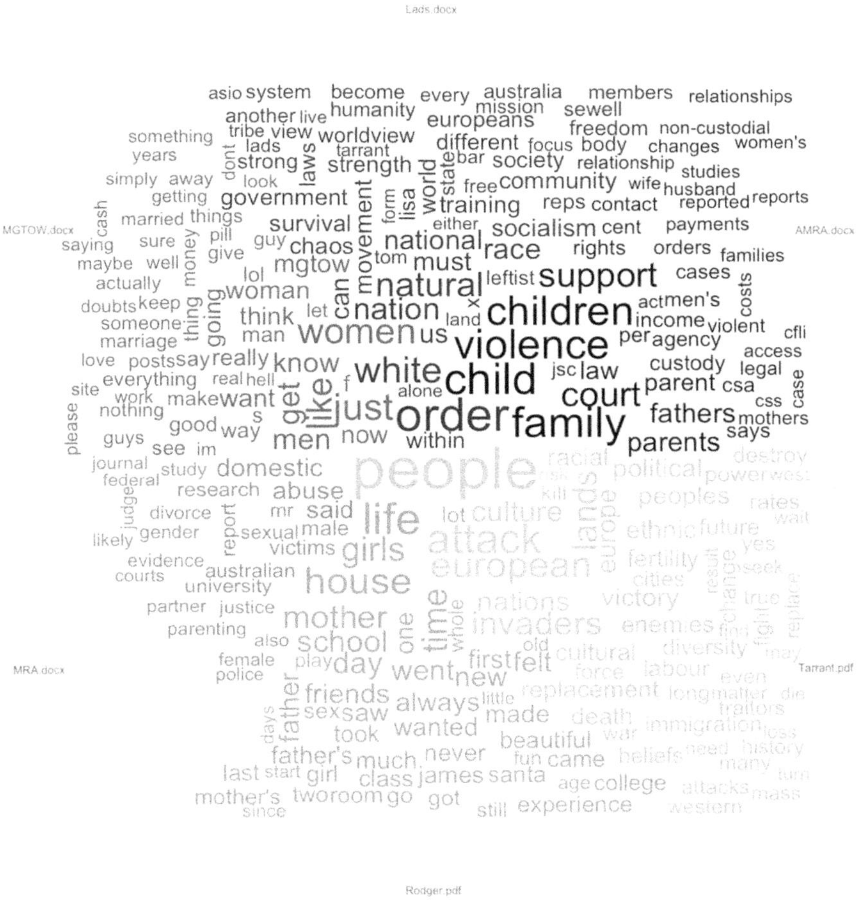

Figure 8.1 Word cloud representing the six corpora under study. Word size represents prevalence. Word color represents document. © Mark Alfano, Joanne Byrne, and Joshua Roose.

3.2 Analysis Using Built-in LIWC Dictionaries

We now turn to more fine-grained analyses of the corpora under study, beginning with four aggregate measures developed specifically for the most recent edition of LIWC: Analytic, Clout, Authentic, and Tone (Pennebaker et al. 2015). These categories are based on proprietary algorithms that draw inputs from multiple subcategories. The Analytic dimension is associated with formal, logical, and structured thinking and expression; higher scores represent more analytical thinking. The Authentic dimension is based on algorithms from a string of studies by Pennebaker and his colleagues that examined honesty and deception. Higher scores are associated specifically with honest self-disclosure (and not necessarily with other aspects of honesty). The Clout dimension

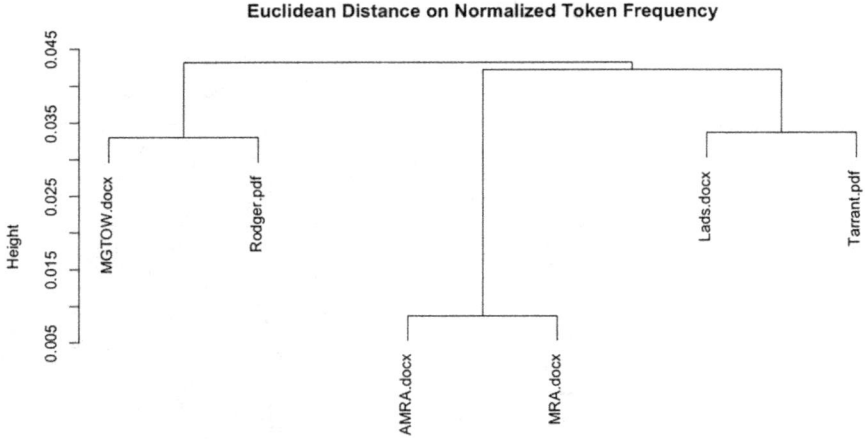

Figure 8.2 Dendrogram of the corpora under study. Greater vertical distance represents greater dissimilarity. © Mark Alfano, Joanne Byrne, and Joshua Roose.

Table 8.2 Normalized Scores (Ranging from 0 to 100) for the Categories of Analytic, Clout, Authentic, and Tone

Corpus	Analytic	Clout	Authentic	Tone
Brenton Tarrant	77.38	77.61	32.08	13.65
Elliot Rodger	62.62	35.58	83.96	38.20
Men Going Their Own Way	54.81	69.57	29.27	35.61
Lads Society	78.41	82.00	28.71	40.33
Australia's Men's Rights Agency	91.01	82.17	12.14	13.57
Men's Rights Agency	89.21	81.82	13.32	10.72

© Mark Alfano, Joanne Byrne, and Joshua Roose.

is associated with social status and leadership; higher scores represent greater clout. Finally, the Tone dimension represents the relative emotional and affective positivity versus negativity of a corpus, with higher scores representing a predominance of positivity and lower scores a predominance of negativity. All scores are normalized on a scale that ranges from 0 to 100. Table 8.2 represents these normalized scores for all four categories.

These numbers present broad-strokes sketches of each corpus. Most are highly analytic, with the exception of Men Going Their Own Way. Most speak with a good deal of clout, with the exception of Men Going Their Own Way and, even more so,

Elliot Rodger. By contrast, with the exception of Elliot Rodger, most score quite low on authenticity, suggesting a lack of honest self-disclosure. Finally, all have predominantly negative tone, with Brenton Tarrant and the men's rights groups scoring lowest in tone.

To shed further light on these corpora, we now turn to more specific categories that provide inputs to the aggregate measures. The first category we examine is use of first-person pronouns. Two indicators that LIWC tracks are the frequencies of first-person singular and first-person plural pronouns. One might intuitively think that use of the first-person singular would be associated with narcissism and high status. However, Pennebaker has consistently found across many studies that the first-person singular is used more by people who are self-conscious, low-status, depressed, or socially isolated.[10] In addition, frequent use of the first-person plural is associated in some cases with high status (e.g., the so-called *royal "we"*) or of strongly identifying with one's group. Unfortunately, LIWC is not able to distinguish these two uses of the first-person plural. Table 8.3 represents the frequency of both types of pronouns in each corpus under analysis, along with their ratio.

Table 8.3 Frequency and Ratio of First-Person Singular and First-Person Plural by Corpus

Corpus	1st-singular	1st-plural	Singular/plural ratio
Brenton Tarrant	1.34	1.43	.93
Elliot Rodger	8.55	.62	13.80
Men Going Their Own Way	2.80	.50	5.65
Lads Society	.65	2.97	.22
Australia's Men's Rights Agency	.63	.32	1.97
Men's Rights Agency	.76	.44	1.71

Note: Values for 1st-singular and 1st-plural represent the percent of total words; values for the ratio greater than 1 indicate greater individual self-focus, which is associated with self-consciousness, low status, and depression, whereas values less than 1 indicate greater identification with one's group, and potentially also greater confidence, status, and arrogance.

© Mark Alfano, Joanne Byrne, and Joshua Roose.

The corpora associated with Elliot Rodger and Men Going Their Own Way stand out as intensely individually self-focused. At the opposite extreme, these results suggest that members of the Lads Society are high-status, confident, and/or identified with their community. Whereas the Tarrant manifesto is heavily focused on the first-person plural, the Rodger manifesto is highly focused on the first-person singular. In this sense, the Tarrant manifesto resembles more the Lads Society corpus, while the Rodger manifesto resembles the Men Going Their Own Way corpus. To illustrate, contrast the following examples (relevant terms are highlighted in boldface):

Brenton Tarrant: "**We** must crush immigration and deport those invaders already living on **our** soil. It is not just a matter of **our** prosperity, but the very survival of **our** people."

Elliot Rodger: "As **I** made **my** way back from school one day during the first week, **I** stopped at a stoplight in Isla Vista when **I** saw two hot blonde girls waiting at the bus stop. **I** was dressed in one of **my** nice shirts, so **I** looked at them and smiled. They looked at **me**, but they didn't even deign to smile back. They just looked away as if **I** was a fool. As **I** drove away **I** became infuriated. It was such an insult. This was the way all girls treated **me**, and **I** was sick and tired of it. In a rage, **I** made a U-turn, pulled up to their bus stop and splashed **my** Starbucks latte all over them."

Lads Society: "National Socialism is the worldview of Truth. Another word for Truth is Nature. By Truth or Nature, **we** are referring to the Natural laws of the universe. **We** affirm that there are Natural laws that make up reality, an example being gravity. **We** have decided to obey these laws as **we** know that **we** will be punished if **we** do not; if you deny the Truth of gravity, and decide to jump off a cliff without a means of slowing your descent, then you will be punished with death."

Men Going Their Own Way: "**I'm** new to the site so **I'm** just now learning the ropes. **I** thought **I'd** tell you guys this site feels like it was made for **me**. **I** just wish **I** found it sooner. **I** recently went through a traumatizing experience with a woman. For so long **I've** been seeking the companionship and approval from these parasites, but no more. **I** must improve **myself** for **myself** from now on. **I** must go my own way."

Next, we address several indicators of mental health and illness. In his previous work using LIWC, Pennebaker has found that people who have the best mental health outcomes display a particular profile: they tend to use many positive emotion words, a middling number of negative emotion words, and many words associated with cognitive processes that help people to make sense of their lives and the world (e.g., words related to insight and understanding, as well as words that represent causal and inferential connections).[11] Table 8.4 represents the frequencies of each of these types of words.

By these measures, most groups look similar. The two male supremacist groups talk more than the others about cognitive processes. To illustrate, consider these examples from Men Going Their Own Way and the Tarrant and Rodger manifestos:

Men Going Their Own Way: "She may, of course, go on to obtain various degrees and diplomas. These increase her market value in the eyes of men, for men **believe** that a woman who can recite things by heart must also **know** and **understand** them."

Brenton Tarrant: "Whilst we may use edgy humour and memes in the vanguard stage, and to attract a young audience, eventually we will need to show the reality of our thoughts and our more serious intents and wishes for the future. For now we

Table 8.4 Frequency of Positive Emotion, Negative Emotion, and Cognitive Process Words

Corpus	Pos-emo	Neg-emo	Cogproc
Brenton Tarrant	2.64	3.30	9.74
Elliot Rodger	3.16	2.32	9.25
Men Going Their Own Way	2.97	2.14	10.49
Lads Society	2.49	1.66	10.04
Australia's Men's Rights Agency	2.14	2.78	8.40
Men's Rights Agency	2.07	2.94	8.54

Note: Values represent the percent of total words. The cogproc category includes the following sub-categories: insight, causation, discrepancy, tentativeness, certainty, and differentiation.

© Mark Alfano, Joanne Byrne, and Joshua Roose.

> appeal to the anger and black comedic nature of the present, but eventually we will need to show the **warmth** and genuine **love** we have for our people."
>
> Elliot Rodger: "My life turned into a living hell after I started desiring them when I hate puberty. I desire them intensely, but I could never have them. I could never have the experience of holding hands with a beautiful girl and walking on a moonlit beach, I could never **embrace** a girlfriend and feel her **warmth** and **love**, I could never have passionate sex with a girl and drift off to sleep with her sexy body beside me. Women deemed me unworthy of having them, and so they deprived me of an **enjoyable** youth, while giving their **love** and sex to other boys."

In addition, there seem to be differences in the use of positive and negative emotion words among these groups. However, negative emotions are quite diverse, including both high-arousal approach emotions such as anger and low-arousal withdrawal emotions such as sadness. To shed further light on the emotional states of these groups, we examine three distinct negative emotions in the corpora: anxiety, anger, and sadness. Anxiety is an anticipatory emotion. It prompts attentional narrowing on (potential) future risks and harms, as well as motivation to seek relief from perceived threats (Derryberry 2001). Anger, by contrast, is more focused on the present. It is also more active and typically involves an approach-orientation that leads the angry person to confront whomever they are angry with.[12] Finally, sadness is a more passive, past-oriented emotion. It responds to the loss of someone or something valuable.[13] Table 8.5 represents the frequencies of each of these three types of words.

These numbers help to shed more light on the emotional tone of each corpus. Whereas the Tarrant manifesto stands out for being overwhelmingly angry, the Rodger manifesto (while still angry) expresses a good deal more sadness. To illustrate, consider the following examples:

Table 8.5 Frequency of Anxiety, Anger, and Sadness

Corpus	Anxiety	Anger	Sadness
Brenton Tarrant	.39	1.92	.51
Elliot Rodger	.43	.87	.67
Men Going Their Own Way	.30	.79	.39
Lads Society	.25	.68	.29
Australia's Men's Rights Agency	.31	.93	.34
Men's Rights Agency	.33	1.03	.35

Values represent the percent of total words.

© Mark Alfano, Joanne Byrne, and Joshua Roose.

Brenton Tarrant: "The only Muslim I truly **hate** is the convert, those from our own people that turn their backs on their heritage, turn their backs on their cultures, turn their back on their traditions and become blood **traitors** to their own race. These I **hate**."

Elliot Rodger: "I felt so **heartbroken** that I left the two of them and **cried** to myself, ruining my whole experience at the museum. *How could girls check out Addison but not me?* I asked myself repeatedly as I tried to hide my **tears** from people who walked by me. I walked out to the edge of the grant terrace of the museum, looking out at the city lights of Los Angeles as well as the stars above. In that moment, I fell into a sort of **despair**-ridden trance."

Men Going Their Own Way: "One morning, a woman comes downstairs, to the kitchen, to find her husband **crying**, inconsolably, over his coffee. Worried, she tries everything to find the reason for his upset. Finally, the husbank takes a short break from his **grief**, and asks his wife 'Do you remember when your father caught us fooling around, with your panties around your ankles? ... and he told me that if I didn't marry you, he would have me arrested and sent to prison?' The wife smiled, and said 'Yes, I could never forget that !'. The husbank began **sobbing** again, even louder than before."[14]

Next, we examine words that represent social relations. In particular, LIWC has dictionaries for family (e.g., *daughter*, *uncle*), friends (e.g., *buddy*, *neighbor*), women (e.g., *girl*, *mom*), and men (e.g., *boy*, *dad*). Table 8.6 represents the frequencies of each of these four types of words.

Across the board, the men's rights groups have a lot to say about family and gender, as well as (to a lesser extent) friends. While they talk more than most of the other groups about women, they focus even more on men. Men Going Their

Table 8.6 Frequency of Family, Friend, Female, and Male References, along with Female:Male Ratio

Corpus	Family	Friend	Female	Male	F:m
Brenton Tarrant	.20	.04	.13	.32	.42
Elliot Rodger	1.02	.42	1.35	1.46	.92
Men Going Their Own Way	.59	.33	1.76	1.52	1.16
Lads Society	.21	.13	.43	.77	.56
Australia's Men's Rights Agency	2.35	.30	1.45	2.21	.66
Men's Rights Agency	2.02	.27	1.52	2.14	.71

Note: Values represent the percent of total words except for the ratio: when the ratio is greater than 1, there are more references to women than to men, whereas when the ratio is less than 1, there are more references to men than to women.

© Mark Alfano, Joanne Byrne, and Joshua Roose.

Own Way displays a slightly different pattern: they have relatively little to say about family but are intensely interested in friends and gender. In addition, and perhaps ironically they focus more on women than on men. To illustrate, consider the following examples:

> Australia's Men's Rights Agency: "Coercion into sexual intimacy under threat; whether it be to end the relationship or marriage, to withhold your rights during Property Settlement or to abuse the **children** including threats to seek intimacy with your **daughter** or **son**."
>
> Men Going Their Own Way: "In a span of about three years virtually all gone. **neighbor buddy** died, probably my best **friend**."

Next, we turn our attention to words related to various aspects of embodiment. LIWC has four separate dictionaries of such words that represent bodies generally, health, sexuality, and eating. Table 8.7 represents the frequencies of each of these four types of words.

Across the board, Men Going Their Own Way seems to be concerned with all aspects of embodiment. By contrast, the Lads Society seems to pay a lot of attention to all aspects of embodiment *except* sexuality. The high value of the men's rights groups on the health dimension seems to be driven by the fact that they frequently talk about the "red pill," and *pill* is one of the words in the health dictionary; this result should therefore be disregarded as an artifact of the methodology. To illustrate, consider the following examples:

Table 8.7 Frequency of Body, Health, Sexuality, and Eating Words

Corpus	Body	Health	Sexuality	Eating
Brenton Tarrant	.31	.48	.13	.07
Elliot Rodger	.33	.84	.28	.39
Men Going Their Own Way	.52	.70	.37	.37
Lads Society	.41	.74	.08	.25
Australia's Men's Rights Agency	.19	.57	.17	.08
Men's Rights Agency	.22	.62	.25	.11

© Mark Alfano, Joanne Byrne, and Joshua Roose.

Men Going Their Own Way: "I'm not **bald**, but thinning. I cut off my almost **waist** length **hair** earlier this year to go back to a crew cut that was easier to take care of. My **beard** is **chest** length."

Men's Rights Agency: "Within the men's rights movement, activists commonly refer to their '**red pill**' moment—the moment when they were exposed to the truth, discovering a reality which they never knew existed. Having spent an entire weekend engaging with the perspectives and ideas of the men's rights movement, I can now proudly say that I have had my own **red pill** moment. Will you take the **red pill?**"

Men Going Their Own Way: "If an average girl works hard enough, she will be able to have a **one-night stand** with a '**hot**' guy every now and then because he happened to be **horny** and wanted an **easy lay**. The girl then thinks that she actually can get such a man to commit to her for the long term, and so doesn't give the average guys a chance, holding out for the type of **stud** that she had a brief **sexual** encounter with in the past."

Men Going Their Own Way: "I wouldn't waste the money hiring a cleaning lady and I don't **eat** out every **meal** because **cooking** and cleaning are so easy ... why would I want an over priced wife to **cook** and clean for me?"

Next, we consider the drives that seem to motivate each group and individual. These include affiliation, achievement, power, reward, and risk. In her work for the US Department of Homeland Security, Allison Smith has found that those who display high focus on *both* affiliation and power are the most likely to engage in collective action in support of their goals (see also Pennebaker and Chung 2008; Pennebaker 2011, 281 endnote). Table 8.8 summarizes these results.

The results for the affiliation category are consistent with those found for the first-person plural category above, with the Lads Society showing the greatest sense of affiliation. The results in the final column of the table indicate that the groups most likely

Table 8.8 Frequency of Drives to Affiliation, Achievement, Power, Reward, and Risk, along with the Product of Affiliation and Power

Corpus	Affiliation	Achievement	Power	Reward	Risk	Aff*pow
Brenton Tarrant	2.31	1.84	4.24	.96	.57	9.79
Elliot Rodger	2.03	1.21	2.06	1.15	.33	4.18
Men Going Their Own Way	1.52	1.08	2.20	1.27	.62	3.35
Lads Society	4.34	1.97	3.66	.96	.50	15.91
Australia's Men's Rights Agency	2.83	1.11	4.20	.75	.68	11.88
Men's Rights Agency	2.72	1.09	4.08	.74	.71	11.12

Note: Values represent the percent of total words except for the final column, which represents the value of the affiliation column multiplied by the value of the power column.

© Mark Alfano, Joanne Byrne, and Joshua Roose.

to engage in collective action are the Lads Society and the men's rights organizations, as well as those inspired by Brenton Tarrant. By contrast, the Elliot Rodger manifesto most resembles the corpus of Men Going Their Own Way. To illustrate, consider the following examples:

> Brenton Tarrant: "There is no nation in the world that wasn't founded by, or maintained by, the use of **force**. **Force** is **power**. History is the history of **power**. Violence is **power** and violence is the reality of history."

> Elliot Rodger: "I continued to build up my faith that I am destined to win the Megamillions jackpot. It is the future that was meant for me; the perfect, **happy** conclusion to the tragic life I've had to experience in the past. I couldn't wait to rub my **status** as a **wealthy** man right in the faces of all the people who looked down on me, and all of the girls who thought of me as **unworthy**. I mused that once I became **wealthy**, I would finally be **worthy** enough to all of the beautiful girls."

> Lads Society: "[W]e are the rightful heirs to **our** civilisation. For if there was not **power** in **our** ideas, why would **we** need to be shut down? If there is **power** in **our** ideas then why?"

3.3 Analysis Using Custom LIWC Dictionaries

Next, we turn to our custom dictionaries. As mentioned above, groups that engage in violence tend to have a very positive view of their own moral standing. Moreover, groups that place greatest weight on the binding moral foundations of loyalty, authority,

Table 8.9 Moral Foundations Profiles of All Corpora

Corpus	Care	Fairness	Loyalty	Authority	Sanctity
Brenton Tarrant	1.73	.37	1.23	.88	.89
Elliot Rodger	.96	.21	.33	.41	.41
Men Going Their Own Way	.84	.32	.34	.36	.89
Lads Society	.84	.45	1.18	1.37	.81
Australia's Men's Rights Agency	2.62	.83	1.09	1.10	.44
Men's Rights Agency	2.45	.77	.95	.98	.48

Note: Numbers represent the percentage of words in the total corpus that refer to each foundation.

© Mark Alfano, Joanne Byrne, and Joshua Roose.

and sanctity display a greater propensity to violence than groups that emphasize the other two dimensions of care and fairness. To help differentiate the corpora under study, we used a custom LIWC dictionary of moral foundations to compare corpora. Table 8.9 represents the moral foundations profiles of each corpus.

The men's rights groups place much more emphasis on the care foundation than the other eight groups, which should be unsurprising given their focus on fatherhood and fatherly care of children (especially during and after divorce). They also focus more on fairness than the other groups, though not by as large a margin; this too makes a certain amount of sense because they often complain about what they perceive to be unjust and unfair laws and norms that favor women over men. The corpora most focused on the binding dimension of loyalty are associated with Brenton Tarrant, the Lads Society, and Australia's Men's Rights Agency. The corpus most focused on the binding dimension of authority is the Lads Society. In light of the findings discussed above, this suggests that the groups most likely to engage in what Fiske and Rai (2014) call "virtuous violence" are the Lads Society and anyone inspired by Tarrant's manifesto. To illustrate, consider these examples:

> Brenton Tarrant: "Unsurprisingly, **ethno-nationalists** and **nationalists** seek employment in areas that **serve** their **nations** and **community**. I would estimate the number of **soldiers** in European armed forces that also belong to **nationalist** groups to number in the hundreds of thousands, with just as many employed in **law enforcement** positions."

> Lads Society: "Our first **loyalty** is to our direct Family, then to our **tribe** or community, then to our greater **Nation** or Ethnic group (in the case of new world Europeans such as Australians or Americans this is a Pan-European heritage) and finally for all Europeans our **loyalty** is to the Race, that is to a European World."

> Men Going Their Own Way: "MGTOW is not a group. It's a population of individuals."

Table 8.10 Frequency of Dominant Masculinity, Subsidiary Masculinity, Misogyny, and Xenophobia

Corpus	Hegmasc	Submasc	Misogyny	Xeno
Brenton Tarrant	.22	.05	.01	.56
Elliot Rodger	.07	.27	.02	.00
Men Going Their Own Way	.15	.24	.17	.02
Lads Society	.46	.06	.04	.04
Australia's Men's Rights Agency	.08	.02	.02	.00
Men's Rights Agency	.09	.02	.02	.00

© Mark Alfano, Joanne Byrne, and Joshua Roose.

In order to further investigate the role of masculinity in these corpora, we now turn to analysis using our own custom dictionaries. Table 8.10 represents the frequencies of words and n-grams associated with each category.

In line with the analyses above, the Tarrant manifesto and—even more so—the Lads Society corpus demonstrate intense focus on dominant masculinity. By contrast, the Elliot Rodger manifesto demonstrates heightened focus on subsidiary masculinity. As measured by our new custom dictionary, the Men Going Their Own Way corpus is unique in showing a high focus on both dominant and subsidiary masculinity, as well as being by far the most misogynistic. Finally, the Tarrant manifesto is the most xenophobic. To illustrate, consider the following examples:

> Brenton Tarrant: "**Mass immigration** will disenfranchise us, subvert our nations, destroy our communities, destroy our **ethnic binds**, destroy our cultures, destroy our peoples. Long before **low fertility levels** ever could. Thus, before we deal with the **fertility rates**, we must deal with both the **invaders** within our lands and the **invaders** that seek to enter our lands. We must crush immigration and **deport** those **invaders** already living on our soil. It is not just a matter of our prosperity, but the very survival of our people."

> Elliot Rodger: "My father drove up to Santa Barbara to meet me a few days later. The two of us went to have lunch at a restaurant in the Camino Real Marketplace, an area that I often frequented. When we sat down at our table, I saw a young couple sitting a few tables down the row. The sight of them enraged me to no end, especially because it was a dark-skinned Mexican guy dating a hot blonde white girl. I regarded it as a great **insult** to my dignity. How could an **inferior** Mexican guy be able to date a white blonde girl, while I was still suffering as a **lonely virgin**? I was ashamed to be in such an **inferior** position in front my father. When I saw the two of them kissing, I could barely contain my rage. I stood up in anger, and I was about to walk up to them and pour my glass of soda all over their heads. I

probably would have, if father wasn't there. I was seething with **envious** rage, and my father was there to watch it all. It was so **humiliating**."

Men Going Their Own Way: "Being so closely affiliated with MGTOW on Youtube, people identifying as '**incel**' usually get exposed to MGTOW and end up on soft-mgtow channels like TFM or Sandman … if they're inquisitive enough, they get tired of the cheap content and search for the original content by Barbar and Stardusk. … they continue down the rabbit hole going through phases of MGTOW growth: exposure, **red-pill** acquisition, understanding **hypergamy** & evo-psych, then **red pill** rage, then internalization, **black pill** acceptance, self-actualization. The **incel** fad-trend is another symptom of how the MGTOW message is growing larger sociologically."[15]

Lads Society: "What we got wrong about the '**Chad/Sperg**' ratio' was that we believed we needed both **Chads** and **Spergs** in order to have a functioning movement. There was differences between States, and some managed to have a 'culling of the **Spergs**' while in others the **Spergs** outnumbered the **Chads** and eventually the **Chads** stopped bothering to attend **holocaust revision** society. What we must do differently this time is realise that we must embody the old ways. We must not be of **Chad** or **Sperg** alone, but that every man must take the best qualities of both and live the **14 words**, becoming the **Warrior** Poet, the Scholar **Athlete**, the **Freeman**, the **Übermensch**, the **Hyperborean** … the **Chad Sperg**."[16]

As these examples illustrate, gender and race are tightly intertwined strands in the language and attitudes of these individuals and groups. Even the Rodger manifesto, which does not register as highly xenophobic when using word counts, evinces an obsession with racial and ethnic hierarchies, with white blondes at the top and people with darker skin tones and hair color below. Likewise, the Tarrant manifesto, which does not register as highly misogynistic when using word counts, evinces an obsession with women as bearers of children. The Men Going Their Own Way corpus includes many terms and phrases related to subsidiary masculinity and misogyny, whereas the Lads Society corpus includes many terms and phrases related to dominant masculinity. This ties into broader international studies that assert the intersection of far-right and anti-women attitudes (DiBranco 2017; Roose 2020).

4. Concluding Remarks

In this chapter, we used automated psycholinguistic analysis to profile and compare six corpora. Two were manifestos authored by men who went on to commit terrorist violence. The other four were authored by men who have not, to our knowledge, committed any acts of violence. However, two of those four resemble the manifestos in disturbing ways: the Lads Society corpus is strikingly similar to the Tarrant manifesto, while the Men Going Their Own Way corpus resembles the Rodger manifesto. By contrast, the corpora associated with the men's rights agencies resemble each other but are notably different from both the manifestos and the corpora associated with the Lads Society and Men Going Their Own Way.

All six corpora engage with the topics of gender and race in interrelated ways. To better understand these strands of thought, we developed four custom dictionaries for the categories of dominant masculinity, subsidiary masculinity, misogyny, and xenophobia. We hope that these dictionaries will be of use in future research on masculinity and online radicalization. To that end, we have made them available via the Open Science Framework.

In closing, we want to suggest that philosophical reflections on political discourse need to move beyond analyses of the exchange of reasons and arguments in an idealized public sphere. A robust democracy is not only a state in which Rawlsian public reasons are offered by various parties but also a state that recognizes and responds to existential threats. In other words, even in an ideal Rawlsian democratic state, people need to be aware of and critically responsive to the use of *nonpublic* reasons such as those employed by the masculinist movements studied in this chapter. Simply ignoring people and movements who don't play by the utopian rules is not a viable option.

The corpora documented in this chapter are clearly not addressed to the full population with the aim of persuading via reasons. Elliott Rodger had no interest in persuading women to treat him differently. Brenton Tarrant had no interest in rationally persuading immigrants of color not to relocate to Australia or New Zealand. The only exceptions may be the men's rights agencies, which seem to be genuinely interested in changing laws and social norms via persuasion. The other corpora are better understood as recruitment tools for extremist ideologies and attempts to forge a hermeneutical framework that warrants such ideals—and perhaps even as hate speech and incitement to violence. If this is right, then the current study may help to expand the range of types of language considered by empirically oriented political philosophers.

Acknowledgments

We would like to thank Arash Ghassemi for helping to collect the corpora analyzed in this chapter. In addition, we are grateful to James Pennebaker, Marc Cheong, Holly Lawford-Smith, M. Dentith, J. Adam Carter, Serene Khader, and Matthew Lindauer for helpful feedback on and guidance in preparing this manuscript.

Grants:

This research was supported by the Australian Research Council (DP190101507), the Templeton Foundation (#61378), and the Victoria Government Department of Justice and Community Safety (R00027).

The findings of this research do not necessarily represent the views of the funders.

Corresponding author:

Mark Alfano
25 Wally's Walk, Macquarie University NSW 2109, Australia
mark.alfano@gmail.com

Content Warning:

Please be advised that the community of study frequently uses language that some readers may find shocking or offensive.

Notes

1. Other researchers question the underlying assumption that the internet is the sort of thing we should blame. Omotoyinbo (2014, 58), for example, argues that in these cases the "Netizen [user of the Internet] is the criminal and that the Net is a guiltless accomplice." Those inclined to turn an eye away from the medium itself have sought various alternative explanations for the phenomenon of self-radicalization, such as social alienation (Abrahams 2002; Torok 2011).
2. With no single "home," the manosphere populates various digital social spaces including: Reddit (r/TheRedPill, r/MGTOW, and (now defunct) r/incels & r/braincels), image—or message boards: 4chan's/b, (now defunct) PUAHate, (now defunct) SlutHate, conventional social media sites (Facebook, Twitter), "free speech" alternative social media sites (Voat, Parler) and a collection of others such as A Voice for Men, Return of Kings, and MensRights.
3. For example, men who do not embody hegemonic masculine traits (e.g., athleticism) may valorize a different subset of traits associated with masculinity (e.g., intellect). While they are themselves subordinated to lower rungs on the hierarchy, the performance of and hyperfocus on their subset of masculine traits enable subordinate men to uphold the hegemonic exclusion and domination of women and other men (see Massanari 2017; Vitale 2019).
4. It is noteworthy in this context that, in his manifesto, Tarrant writes, "**From where did you receive/research/develop your beliefs?** The internet, of course. You will not find the truth anywhere else." Likewise, Rodger writes in his manifesto, "Joining chatrooms through AOL temporarily filled in the social void for a few weeks. This will definitely not be the first time I would try to fill in that void with the internet."
5. This line of thinking is summed up in the Rodger manifesto, where he writes, "The boys who girls find attractive will live pleasure-filled lives while they dominate the boys who girls deem unworthy."
6. For a similar diagnosis of the so-called "Dark Enlightenment" advocated by the alt-right, see Aikin (2019).
7. In the interest of open science, we decided whenever possible to use the *R* package LIWCalike, which imitates and expands the functionality of LIWC. Doing so introduces slight discrepancies because of the way LIWC and LIWCalike tokenize and count words. However, the patterns remain the same regardless of which software is used. The LIWCalike package was created and is maintained by Kenneth Benoit at https://devhub.io/repos/kbenoit-LIWCalike.

8   For instance, in his manifesto, Rodger writes, "The world truly is a brutal place, where a man must fight a bitter struggle against all other men to reach the top." Later in the manifesto, he says, "I wanted to inflict pain on all young couples. It was around this point in my life that I realized I was capable of doing such things. I would happily do such things. I was capable of killing them, and I wanted to. I wanted to kill them slowly, to strip the skins off their flesh. They deserve it. The males deserve it for taking the females away from me, and the females deserve it for choosing those males instead of me."

9   In the interest of open science (including open data and open methods), corpora and code are available at the Open Science Framework page associated with this project: https://osf.io/4nyuz/?view_only=2cc86ad8b4564063ba3a092171add5f7.

10 See Pennebaker (2011, chapters 2 and 3) for a summary of these studies. See also Pennebaker and Chung (2011), Campbell and Pennebaker (2003), Seih et al. (2011), Stirman and Pennebaker (2001), and Rude et al. (2004).

11 See Pennebaker et al. (1997), Moore and Brody (2009), and Graham et al. (2009).

12 See, among others, Cherry and Flanagan (2018).

13 See, among others, Gotlib (2017).

14 The term "husbank" is a portmanteau of "husband" and "bank" that expresses the idea that the only reason a woman would marry a man is to gain access to his money. It is one of many terms included in the subsidiary masculinity dictionary.

15 The term "incel" is internet slang for a man who is involuntarily celibate, i.e., who would like to and believes he has a right to have a sexually-active relationship but is unable to find a willing partner. The term "hypergamy" refers to the act of "marrying up" in a social hierarchy; men in these groups seem to believe that women tend to try to marry up, whereas they themselves would be content to be with someone who is their status equivalent. Drawing an analogy with the movie *The Matrix*, men who participate in this discourse distinguish between the so-called red and blue pills. In the movie, Morpheus offers Neo a choice between taking a red pill or a blue pill. The red pill will reveal to him the true, horrifying nature of reality, whereas the blue pill will put him to sleep and erase his memory. In this context, a man who has taken the red pill has awoken to a dystopian vision of intra-masculine and inter-gender hierarchies, whereas a man who has taken the blue pill remains ignorant of them. The "black pill" is internet slang for an even more extreme, nihilistic version of the red pill phenomenon, in which the man realizes that he will always be too low on various hierarchies to have a sexually satisfying life.

16 The term "sperg" is internet slang for a person with Asperger's syndrome and seems to be stereotyped in this context as associating a person with single-minded obsessiveness about an *idée fixe*. The phrase "14 words" refers to the neo-nazi slogan "We must secure the existence of our people and a future for white children," which Tarrant also alludes to in his manifesto.

References

Abrahams, M. 2002. "What Terrorists Really Want: Terrorist Motives and Counterterrorism Strategy." *International Security* 32: 86–9.

Aikin, S. 2019. "Deep Disagreement, the Dark Enlightenment, and the Rhetoric of the Red Pill." *Journal of Applied Philosophy* 36, no. 3: 420–35.

Alfano, M., J. A. Carter, and M. Cheong. 2018. "Technological Seduction and Self-radicalization." *Journal of the American Philosophical Association* 4, no. 3: 298–322.

Alfano, M., J. A. Carter, A. Ebrahimi Fard, P. Clutton, and C. Klein. 2021. "Technologically Scaffolded Atypical Cognition: The Case of YouTube's Recommender System." *Synthese* 199: 835–858.

Anderson, E. 2009. *Inclusive Masculinity: The Changing Nature of Masculinities*. New York: Routledge.

Berman, M. 2016. "Prosecutors Say Dylann Roof 'Self-Radicalized' online, Wrote Another Manifesto in Jail." *Washington Post*, August 22.

Benoit, K., K. Watanabe, H. Wang, P. Nulty, A. Obeng, S. Müller, and A. Matsuo. 2018. "Quanteda: An R Package for the Quantitative Analysis of Textual Data." *Journal of Open Source Software* 3, no. 30: 774. doi: 10.21105/joss.00774, https://quanteda.io.

Bjelopera, J. P. 2010. "American Jihadist Terrorism: Combating a Complex Threat." DIANE Publishing. https://fas.org/sgp/crs/terror/R41416.pdf.

Bridges, T. 2014. "A Very 'Gay' Straight? Hybrid Masculinities, Sexual Aesthetics, and the Changing Relationship between Masculinity and Homophobia." *Gender & Society* 28, no. 1: 58–82.

Campbell, R., and J. Pennebaker. 2003. "The Secret Life of Pronouns: Flexibility in Writing Style and Physical Health." *Psychological Science* 14: 60–5.

Cherry, M., and O. Flanagan. 2018. *The Moral Psychology of Anger*. London: Rowman & Littlefield International Ltd.

Connell, R. W. 2005. *Masculinities*. Berkeley: University of California Press.

Connell, R. W., and J. W. Messerschmidt. 2005. "Hegemonic Masculinity: Rethinking the Concept." *Gender & Society* 19, no. 6: 829–59.

Conway, M. 2021. "Online Extremism and Terrorism Research Ethics: Researcher Safety, Informed Consent, and the Need for Tailored Guidelines." *Terrorism and Political Violence* 33, no. 2: 367–80.

De Boise, S. 2014. "'I'm Not Homophobic, 'I've Got Gay Friends': Evaluating the Validity of Inclusive Masculinity." *Men and Masculinities* 18: 318–39.

Derryberry, D. 2001. "Emotion and Conscious Experience: Perceptual and Attentional Influence of Anxiety." In *Finding Consciousness in the Brain: A Neurocognitive Approach*. *Advances in Consciousness Research*, edited by P. Grossenbacher. Amsterdam: John Benjamins.

DiBranco, A. 2017. "Mobilizing Misogyny." *Political Research Associates*. Accessed April 30, 2021. https://www.politicalresearch.org/2017/03/08/mobilizing-misogyny.

Feldman, B. 2018. "Posts Indicate Suspect in Toronto Attack Was Radicalized on 4chan." *New York Magazine*. Accessed June 23, 2018. http://nymag.com/selectall/2018/04/suspect-in-toronto-posts-about-incel-rebellion.html.

Fiske, A., and T. Rai. 2014. *Virtuous Violence: Hurting and Killing to Create, Sustain, End, and Honor Social Relationships*. Cambridge: Cambridge University Press.

Fricker, M. 2007. *Epistemic Injustice*. Oxford: Oxford University Press.

Frimer, J. A., R. Boghrati, J. Haidt, J. Graham, and M. Dehgani. 2019. *Moral Foundations Dictionary for Linguistic Analyses 2.0*. Unpublished manuscript.

Ging, D. 2019. "Alphas, Betas, and Incels: Theorizing the Masculinities of the Manosphere." *Men and Masculinities* 22, no. 4: 638–57.

Gotlib, A. 2017. *The Moral Psychology of Sadness*. London: Polity.

Graham, H., R. Glaser, T. Loving, W. Malarkey, J. Stowell, and J. Kiecolt-Glaser. 2009. "Cognitive Word Use During Marital Conflict and Increases in Proinflammatory Cytokines." *Health Psychology* 28: 621–30.

Haidt, J. 2013. *The Righteous Mind: Why Good People are Divided by Politics and Religion.* London: Vintage.
Jewkes, R., M. Flood, and J. Lang. 2015. "From Work with Men and Boys to Changes of Social Norms and Reduction of Inequities in Gender Relations: A Conceptual Shift in Prevention of Violence Against Women and Girls." *The Lancet* 385, no. 9977: 1580–89.
Jewkes, R., R. Morrell, J. Hearn, E. Lundqvist, D. Blackbeard, G. Lindegger, M. Quayle, Y. Sikweyiya, and L. Gottzén. 2015. "Hegemonic Masculinity: Combining Theory and Practice in Gender Interventions." *Culture, health & sexuality* 17, no. sup2: 112-27.
Kimmel, M. 2012. *Manhood in America: A Cultural History.* New York: Oxford University Press.
Kimmel, M. S. 2013. "Masculinity as Homophobia: Fear, Shame, and Silence in the Construction of Gender Identity." In *Toward a New Psychology of Gender*, 223–242. Routledge.
Leidner, B., and E. Castano. 2012. "Morality Shifting in the Context of Intergroup Violence." *European Journal of Social Psychology* 42, no. 1: 82–91.
Majeed, K. 2016. *Combating Violent Extremism and Radicalization in the Digital Era.* Hershey, PA: IGI Global.
Manne, K. 2017. *Down Girl: The Logic of Misogyny.* Oxford: Oxford University Press.
Massanari, A. L. 2017. "'Damseling for Dollars': Toxic Technocultures and Geek Masculinity." In *Race and Gender in Electronic Media: Content, Context, Culture*, edited by Rebecca Ann Lind, 1st edition, 312–27. Routledge.
Medina, J. 2013. *The Epistemology of Resistance.* Oxford: Oxford University Press.
Moore, S., and L. Broady. 2009. "Linguistic Predictors of Mindfulness in Written Self-disclosure Narratives." *Journal of Language and Social Psychology* 28: 281–96.
Nguyen, T. 2020. "Echo Chambers and Epistemic Bubbles." *Episteme* 17, no. 2: 141–61.
Omotoyinbo, F. 2014. "Online Radicalization: The Net or the Netizen?" *Socialnės Technologijos* 1: 51–61.
O'Neill, R. 2014. "Whither Critical Masculinity Studies? Notes on Inclusive Masculinity Theory, Postfeminism, and Sexual Politics." *Men and Masculinities* 18: 100–20.
Pariser, E. 2011. *The Filter Bubble: What the Internet Is Hiding from You.* London: Penguin UK.
Pennebaker, J. 2011. *The Secret Life of Pronouns: What Our Words Say About Us.* Bloomsbury Press.
Pennebaker, J., and C. Chung. 2008. "Computerized Text Analysis of Al-Qaeda Transcripts." In *A Content Analysis Reader*, edited by K. Krippendorf, and M. Bock, 453–65. Thousand Oaks: Sage.
Pennebaker, J., and C. Chung. 2011. "Expressive Writing and Its Links to Mental and Physical Health." In *Oxford Handbook of Health Psychology*, edited by H. Friedman. Oxford: Oxford University Press.
Pennebaker, J., T. Mayne, and M. Francis. 1997. "Linguistic Predictors of Adaptive Bereavement." *Journal of Personality and Social Psychology* 72: 863–71.
Pennebaker, J., R. Boyd, K. Jordan, and K. Blackburn. 2015. *The Development and Psychometric Properties of LIWC2015.* Austin, Texas.: University of Texas at Austin. DOI: 10.15781/T29G6Z.
Precht, T. 2007. "Home Grown Terrorism and Islamist Radicalisation in Europe." *From Conversion to Terrorism.* http://www.justitsministeriet.dk/sites/default/files/media/Arbejdsomraader/Forskning/Forskningspuljen/2011/2007/Home_grown_terrorism_and_Islamist_radicalisation_in_Europe_-_an_assessment_of_influencing_factors__2_.pdf.

Rawls, J. 1997. "The Idea of Public Reason Revisited." *University of Chicago Law Review* 64, no. 3: 765–807.
Roose, J. M. 2020. *The New Demagogues: Religion, Masculinity and the Populist Epoch*. London: Routledge.
Rude, S., E. Gortner, and J. Pennebaker. 2004. "Language Use of Depressed and Depression-Vulnerable College Students." *Cognition and Emotion* 18: 1121–33.
Seih, Y., C. Chung, and J. Pennebaker. 2011. "Experimental Manipulations of Perspective Taking and Perspective Switching in Expressive Writing." *Cognition and Emotion* 25, no. 5: 926–38.
Silber, M. D., A. Bhatt, and Senior Intelligence Analysts. 2007. "Radicalization in the West: The Homegrown Threat." http://moonbattery.com/graphics/NYPD_Report-Radicalization_in_the_West.pdf.
Smith, A. 2013. *The Relationship Between Rhetoric and Terrorist Violence*. Milton Park, Abingdon, Oxon: Routledge.
Stirman, S., and J. Pennebaker. 2001. "Word Use in the Poetry of Suicidal and Non-suicidal Poets." *Psychosomatic Medicine* 63: 517–22.
Sunstein, C. 2011. *Going to Extremes: How Like Minds Unite and Divide*. Oxford: Oxford University Press.
Sunstein, C. 2018. *#Republic: Divided Democracy in the Age of Social Media*. Princeton University Press.
Theofanos, M. F., S. S. Prettyman, J. Evans, and S. Furman. 2021. Voices of NIST: A Study of Gender and Inclusivity.
Tirrell, L. 2012. "Genocidal Language Games." In *Speech and Harm: Controversies over Free Speech*, edited by I. Maitra, and M. K. McGowan. Oxford: Oxford University Press.
Torok, R. 2011. "Facebook Jihad: A Case Study of Recruitment Discourses and Strategies Targeting a Western Female." http://ro.ecu.edu.au/icr/26/.
Vergani, M., and A. M. Bliuc. 2018. "The Language of New Terrorism: Differences in Psychological Dimensions of Communication." *Dabiq* and *Inspire. Journal of Language and Social Psychology* 37, no. 5: 523–40.
Vitale, S. 2019. "Men Who Love Bukowski: Hegemonic Masculinity, Online Dating, and the Aversion toward the Feminine." *Peitho* 22, no. 1. Available at: https://cfshrc.org/article/men-who-love-bukowski/.
Von Behr, I., A. Reding, C. Edwards, L. Gribbon, Rand Europe, and United Kingdom. 2013. "Radicalisation in the Digital Era: The Use of the Internet in 15 Cases of Terrorism and Extremism." https://www.ncjrs.gov/App/Publications/abstract.aspx?ID=266610.
Weimann, G. 2012. "Lone Wolves in Cyberspace." *Journal of Terrorism Research* 3. doi:10.15664/jtr.405.
Wetherell, M., and N. Edley. 1998. "Gender Practices: Steps in the Analysis of Men and Masculinities." In *Gender and psychology. Standpoints and differences: Essays in the practice of feminist psychology*, edited by K. Henwood, C. Griffin, and A. Phoenix, 156-73. London: Sage Publications.

9
Experimental Immigration Ethics

Mollie Gerver, Patrick Lown, and Dominik Duell

1. Introduction

At age eleven, Agnesa Murselaj fled war in Kosovo, arrived in the UK, and went to school in Glasgow. At age fifteen she was woken at dawn by a border official wearing a bullet-proof vest, accompanied by ten other officials who brought her to a detention center in England. Years later she recalled how she felt: "A stranger coming into your room when you're asleep ... it just takes me back to Kosovo and what happened there." She was ultimately freed from detention after her friends organized a national campaign in her aid, which additionally aimed to end dawn raids against all immigrants. The campaign did not succeed in ending dawn raids against all migrants, but it sparked media focus on immigration enforcement, and in particular on the detention of refugees (BBC 2019).

The idea that it is wrong to detain refugees is fairly uncontroversial among political philosophers (Gibney 2004; Miller 2005; Silverman 2014; Mendoza 2015; Hidalgo 2018; Hosein 2019; Brock 2020; Lister 2020). In contrast, this idea is controversial among voters in a range of countries (Betts 2001; Bruneau, Kteily, and Laustsen 2018; Koos and Seibel 2019). In this chapter, we argue that the opinions of the latter should concern the former. More specifically, experiments aiming to understand the opinions of the public are important for establishing what voters and policymakers morally ought to do.

In Sections 1 and 2, we present two reasons why experiments matter for ethics in general. First, experiments can provide evidence of what is popular, and so evidence of what policymakers are able to do. A policymaker attempting to pass unpopular legislation concerning immigration—such as legislation to stop detention of refugees—may be unable to do so if voted out of office before the legislative process is complete. If she cannot pass such legislation due to popular opposition, and ought implies can, she has no duty to pass such legislation.

Second, experiments can establish what individual voters ought to try to do. Sometimes voters trying to follow a given principle hold implicit biases that they struggle to counteract. For example, imagine voters try to apply a principle of liability to immigration policies, and hold that it is wrong to harm migrants not liable to harm, including refugees like Agnesa, who do not pose any threat. Imagine, also, that voters trying to follow this principle end up applying implicit biases, viewing migrants from certain regions as liable to more harm. Given the effects of trying to follow the principle, these voters have one reason to not try and follow this principle, and activists have one reason to not encourage voters to try and follow this principle. While this reason needn't be decisive, it is one consideration, and experiments can provide evidence of when this consideration arises.

In Sections 3 and 4, we present a factorial vignette-based experiment we conducted which fulfilled the above two functions. The experiment, conducted in the US and UK, sought to establish evidence for whether voters support policies consistent with a principle of liability in immigration ethics, and whether they demonstrate implicit bias in following this principle. We found that subjects supported policies in a way that was generally consistent with a principle of liability, and that subjects generally (with one potential exception) did not demonstrate bias when sensitive to liability. Based on this suggestive pattern of results, we argue in Section 5 that there is evidence that (a) from the standpoint of public opinion, policies sensitive to liability are possible for policymakers to implement, and (b) encouraging voters to be sensitive to a principle of liability would not necessarily result in voters holding a biased application of this principle. If so, activist organizations need not refrain from appealing to liability out of fear that this will create bias amongst voters.

2. What Policymakers Can Do

We presume an elected policymaker has no duty to pass a given piece of legislation if she cannot do so. An elected policymaker cannot pass legislation if she will lose an election before the legislative process is complete. Such is the case when a policymaker starts the legislative process, causing them to be voted out of office before the process is complete, resulting in the next elected policymaker not completing the legislative process. For example, passing a law to grant permanent residency to all unauthorized migrants might take several years of persuading co-parliamentarians to vote for this law, or simply take several years for the bill to navigate parliamentary procedures. If a policymaker begins the process, and beginning the process results in her being voted out of office before the process is complete, she cannot have an obligation to complete the process.

Though a policymaker has no duty to pass a law if she cannot do so, sometimes a policymaker can pass a law by persuading voters to support the law, ensuring that she can complete the legislative process. Experiments can examine how malleable public opinion is on a particular issue, and whether policymakers will likely be able to sway public attitudes. For example, imagine a policymaker seeks to establish if she has public support to pass legislation which prevents the deportation of those who would face risks in their home countries. An experiment can establish if she is likely to obtain public support if she successfully communicates key information to the public. The experimenter might ask voters to assess whether they think a given migrant should be deported, and then randomly assign some participants to be told about the risks the migrant will face if deported (i.e., treatment group) and others to receive no information (i.e., control group). If those in the treatment group are more likely to oppose the deportation, this provides evidence that policymakers can increase public support for legislation banning certain deportations by communicating risks certain migrants face. If the information is persuasive enough, policymakers cannot claim that passing such a policy is not possible, and so cannot claim they lack a duty to do so based on such an impossibility.

It is worth noting that the above claims about the value of experiments are consistent with a broad range of theories of the relationship between public opinion and philosophical truths. In particular, our claims are consistent with moral realism, the claim that at least some moral facts are real whether people think they are or not (Enoch 2011; Parfit 2011). For example, we presume the moral fact "ought implies can" is real whether people think it is or not; it is just that, if ought implies can, experiments can help establish what legislation policymakers may have no duty to pass, on account of being unable to pass such legislation. And they can establish whether policymakers may indeed be able to pass legislation, if they present voters with certain information.

Of course, if it turned out that voters do not support a given piece of legislation even with certain information, and this indicates that policymakers cannot (and therefore have no duty to) pass legislation, the state as a whole may still be committing a wrong. If states have certain obligations, and states are constitutive of both voters and policymakers, then states act wrongly in instituting policies which violate obligations regardless of whether policymakers themselves are responsible. However, the above experiments have implications for what individual policymakers ought to do, and so implications for the ethics of individual actions.

3. Bias

To understand the second value of experiments we describe, it is necessary to first defend a more basic claim: sometimes trying to follow a rule is wrong, even if the rule is not. This claim has been most famously defended in the context of consequentialism; if we ought to maximize good consequences, trying to maximize good consequences can be wrong when this will not maximize good consequences (Sidgwick 1907; Parfit 2011). There is debate over whether this undermines certain types of consequentialism, and whether a principle is self-defeating when holding that individuals ought to bring about outcomes which can only be brought about if they do not try to bring about these outcomes. We needn't resolve this debate to accept a more basic claim: if we take it as a brute fact that there are a certain wrongful actions we ought to not engage in, then we have a pro tanto reason to not try to follow a principle when doing so will make it very difficult or impossible to avoid engaging in these wrongful actions. This is true even if the principle does not itself imply that we ought to engage in these wrongful actions, and merely trying to follow the principle has this effect.

For a concrete example, consider the principle of liability. There is debate over what this principle entails, but one prominent view holds that it is wrong to harm those not liable to harm, and one is not liable to harm if either posing no threat or not responsible for this threat (McMahan 2011). In the context of immigration, some claim migrants can pose various threats: they can threaten the democratic functioning of a state when entering (Miller 2016), or threaten citizens' freedom of association (Wellman 2008), or even threaten citizens' ability to refrain from taking on duties, as when migrants enter and must be provided health care (Blake 2019). Less controversially, migrants pose a threat if carrying a contagious disease, as during a global pandemic. When migrants pose a threat via migration, they are not liable to harm from enforcement if not responsible for their migration. They are not responsible if forced to enter a country because they are trafficked or fleeing life-threatening conditions.

Now, imagine a border official tried to follow a principle of liability—only targeting those posing a threat and responsible for this threat—but she overwhelmingly targeted migrants from the Middle East based stereotypes that they were more likely to be voluntarily migrating to pose a threat to citizens. Similarly, imagine voters trying to follow a principle of liability ended up endorsing candidates who targeted migrants from the Middle East, exaggerating the odds that such migrants posed a responsible threat, or targeting Middle Eastern migrants liable to harm more than non-Middle Eastern migrants liable to harm. Assuming that those trying to follow the principle of liability ended up drawing upon biases they had little control or awareness of, and this lead them to engage in wrongful actions—targeting migrants or voting in a wrongful manner—they would have moral reason to not try to follow this principle. This reason might not be decisive—trying to follow the principle might be worth it if yielding some morally valuable result—but the effects of trying to follow the principle matter in the overall assessments of what they ought to try to do.

To be clear: we are not claiming that one has reason to avoid following a principle if this will lead to wrongful actions; one could often just follow the principle and not engage in the wrongful actions. For example, one could often exclude migrants posing a responsible threat without using their ethnicity as a criterion for whether they are excluded. Our claim is more specific: when trying to follow a principle will make it nearly impossible to avoid acting based on implicit biases one has little awareness or control over, such that one cannot simply try following the principle and avoid the biases, this creates one reason to not try to follow the principle.[1] Of course, if all plausible principles one attempts to follow lead to the application of biases, it may be that one ought to just pick the principle which is better in other regards, but assuming that trying to follow other plausible principles do not have this effect, one might have decisive reason to try following one or more of these other principles instead.

A close variant of this claim has been made by Matthew Lindauer. Lindauer defends the claim that, when a principle has the effect of increasing bias, it is less "fruitful" in one way compared to a principle which does not increase bias or reduces bias. A principle which reduces bias is "fighting back" against injustice (Lindauer 2019). Our claim is inspired by his, but more explicitly highlights the distinction between cases where the letter of the principle contributes to biases and cases where trying to follow the principle contributes to bias. Even if faithfully following a principle does not lead to bias, because the letter of the principle clearly stipulates that bias is prohibited, it remains the case that establishing what principle someone should try to follow requires establishing whether trying to follow that principle will lead to bias. The principle of liability might not itself lead to bias, in that it specifies individuals' liability based on whether they pose a responsible threat rather than whether they are of a given ethnicity or country, but trying to follow the principle may still lead to bias. When it does, one has reason to not try to follow the principle, at least when one has no control or awareness of this bias arising.

If the above is true, third parties also have reason to avoid persuading individuals to try to follow a principle that leads these individuals to hold or apply biases. For example, human rights organizations have reason to avoid persuading individuals to try to follow a principle of liability in immigration if this increases unjust biases against certain migrants.

If the above claims stand, experiments can serve the valuable function of providing evidence of what individuals and organizations have reason to try to do, and reason to not try to do. This is because experiments can provide evidence of whether bias arises when individuals try to follow a given principle.

To see how, it is worth noting that there is more than one way a person might try to follow a principle. One way is by being presented a principle, and instructed to try to follow this principle. An experiment can establish if individuals really are trying to follow the principle, and whether they demonstrate bias in doing so. For example, an experiment could present a treatment group with a principle of liability, and a control group with no such principle, and then present both groups with vignettes of fictional migrants who are attempting to cross the border. The vignettes would vary in the degree that migrants are responsible for their migration choices, with some forced to migrate due to war, and others making a purely voluntary choice. The vignettes would further vary in the degree that migrants pose threats, with some being on a terrorist watch list, others carrying a contagious disease, and still others posing no specified threat. Importantly, migrants would vary in their ethnicity and/or region of origin. Subjects would then be asked whether they support deporting different migrants in the vignettes presented. If subjects instructed to follow the principle of liability were less likely compared to the control group to support deporting migrants posing no threat or forcibly migrating, this would suggest that subjects were following the principle of liability set out. If subjects who followed this principle were also more likely to discriminate against migrants from a given ethnicity or region as compared to subjects in the control group—more likely to think deporting these migrants justified even when no more likely to be liable—this would provide evidence that trying to follow the principle contributes to bias.

There is another way a person might try to follow a principle. A person might be trying to follow a principle without quite being aware they are. They might be responding to certain attributes when presented with specific cases, aware that these attributes are important, but never spelling out the precise principle explaining why these attributes are important. We take such a phenomenon to be common. For example, border officials and voters may avoid harming those who seem to pose no threat, or who seem forced to migrate, roughly following a principle of liability without being aware they are. An experiment can establish both if this is the case and if bias arises in their application of the principle. This is because an experiment can assess how principles might be applied "organically" in the absence of any explicit instruction on the application of principles by the experimenter(s). The experiment would be designed in a similar manner as that above, using vignettes that vary descriptions of migrants, but without a treatment group providing instructions regarding a principle of liability.[2] We now describe in more detail one such experiment we conducted.

4. Immigration and Liability: An Experiment

In this section, we first present the principle of liability as applied to immigration in more detail. We then outline our precise hypotheses about whether UK and US citizens are sensitive to this principle and biased in its application, followed by our experimental methods to test these hypotheses, and our results. In the penultimate section, we present implications of these findings for what various agents ought to do.

4.1 Liability: Some Further Details

For the purposes of this chapter, we adopt the principle of liability articulated in the last section: an individual is liable if she (a) poses a threat and (b) is responsible for their threat (McMahan 2011). In some cases, this view provides a fairly straightforward evaluation of whether a migrant is liable to harm: if a migrant is forced at gunpoint to enter a country, and poses a threat because she is potentially carrying a contagious disease, she is not liable to harm. It might still be all-things-considered permissible to require that she remain in quarantine for an extended period of time if necessary, but this would be permissible for reasons unrelated to liability.

Some cases are more complex, because they involve an individual who was responsible for one action, and they pose a risk in virtue of both this action and another action they are not responsible for. Consider a migrant who committed a crime, or joined a terrorist organization, and then is forced by war to migrate to the United States. These sorts of cases are difficult, because the choice to join the terrorist organization or commit the crime may be voluntary, and the individual is therefore responsible for this choice, but not the choice to migrate.

We lack the room to completely address whether such migrants are liable to the harms of immigration enforcement, including deportation and detention. However, we will presume at least this: the fact that a migrant is forced to migrate is relevant for determining the harm she is liable to experience, assuming that her intention in migrating is to avoid life-threatening conditions, and the risks she poses are below a given threshold. While a person who will definitely commit a terrorist act may be liable to detention and deportation even if she was forced to leave her home country, a person who previously joined a terrorist organization, but shows no indication of still being a member of the organization, is not liable to life-threatening or injurious deportation if she was forced to migrate.

4.2 Hypotheses

We hypothesize that citizens will care about these considerations, and while they won't perfectly align their opinions with the demands of justice—people rarely do (Hidalgo

2018; Vries et al. 2019)—they will care about whether a migrant poses a threat as well as whether they migrated because they had little other choice. More specifically, we hypothesize the following:

Hypothesis 1 *The less a threat a migrant appears to pose, the more unreasonable citizens find the use of immigration enforcement.*

Given that liability also concerns justified harm against those who do pose a threat but are not responsible for this threat, we hypothesize that respondents will be less supportive of enforcement against migrants who pose a threat in migrating but are not responsible for migrating. In particular, they are less supportive of enforcement against those who pose a threat but are forced to migrate due to conditions in their home countries:

Hypothesis 2 *There is less acceptance among citizens for the use of immigration enforcement against migrants posing a threat who are migrating to avoid harm in home countries, as compared to those who are posing a threat and not migrating to avoid harm in home countries.*

Though we hypothesize that the principle of liability is at least loosely followed, it is likely applied in a biased manner. Earlier experiments on immigration attitudes have found bias in general, with subjects often more supportive of migrants not from the Middle East (Dustmann and Preston 2007; Lee 2008; Aalberg, Iyengar, and Messing 2012; Hainmueller and Hopkins 2015a). We therefore hypothesize:

Hypothesis 3 *Citizens are more likely to support immigration control against migrants from the Middle East as compared to other migrants.*

4.3 Methodology

Sample Characteristics. To test these hypotheses, we conducted an online survey with national samples in both the UK and the US. The British sample was collected via Prolific Academic ($N = 1,745$) and was 67.0 percent female, 57.1 percent under the age of thirty-five, and 52.4 percent of respondents had university degrees. The American sample was collected via Qualtrics ($N = 1,804$) and was 52.5 percent female, 32.6 percent under the age of thirty-five, and 44.6 percent had university degrees. In terms of political ideology, the British sample identified as more leftist ($M = 5.9$, $SD = 2.1$) on a 10pt self-reported ideology scale while the American sample leaned right of center ($M = 4.1$, $SD = 2.6$).

Factorial vignette design. Our design used experimental vignettes (Atzmuller and Steiner 2010; Hainmueller and Hopkins 2015b; Turper 2017) to evaluate the extent that respondents support a given instance of enforcement. The advantage of such designs is that it allows researchers to evaluate the impact of many elements in a complex scenario in parallel. Respondents were presented with five vignettes involving an unnamed fictional migrant who seeks to enter or remain in the UK or US, depending on the sample, with varying types of enforcement utilized to compel them to leave or prevent their entrance. We additionally varied the harm arising from enforcement, migrants' reasons for migrating, the threats migrants pose, and their region of origin. Respondents were asked to decide the extent that denying this migrant the ability to enter or remain in the US/UK was unreasonable on a scale of 1 to 7 (extremely reasonable to extremely unreasonable).

We randomly vary attributes of the immigration case in a single-profile factorial vignette.

Below are more details of these varying attributes:[3]

- **The migrant's country of origin:** collapsed by region, for the UK: Africa, Eastern Europe, the Middle East, or Southeast Asia and for the US: Africa, the Middle East, Eastern Europe, Central and South America, East Asia;[4]
- **The migrant's reasons for attempting to enter the UK/US, indicating whether the migrant was forced to migrate:** voluntary migrants are entering/wishing to remain in the UK/US to seek non-necessitous *Economic Opportunity*. Forced migrants are entering/wishing to remain in the UK/US because they are fleeing *Extreme Poverty, Ethnic Persecution*, or to receive *Medical Treatment*;
- **The reasons for being denied a visa to live in the UK/US, indicating whether the migrant poses a threat:** we presume that individuals pose a threat if they are denied a visa because they have a *Criminal Record*, their name is on a *Terror Watchlist*, or they obtained a *COVID-19 Positive* test result. We presume that an individual does not clearly pose a threat if they are denied a visa because they are *Unemployed* or *Immigration quotas* do not permit the provision of further visas.
- **The potential consequences of removing the migrant:** migrants could face nonlethal bodily *Harm* due to *Persecution* in their home countries, due to *Malnutrition* in their home countries, due to *Illness* in their home countries, due to being in *Custody* during enforcement, or due to *Deportation* itself. They could, alternatively, face *Death* due to *Persecution* in their home countries, due to *Malnutrition* in their home countries, due to *Illness* in their home countries, due to being in *Custody* during enforcement, or due to *Deportation* itself.[5]

The attributes presented above are the ones relevant for the analyses in this chapter. However, in the full design, we also varied the gender of the migrant and whether the migrant had already crossed the border. The data presented here is part of an ongoing project and the full analyses are included in other forthcoming work.[6]

Beyond the factorial vignette described above, we also implemented a between-respondent information treatment, which only serves as robustness check of the results presented here and is described in the Appendix.

4.4 Results

Throughout the discussion of our empirical results, we present marginal means, which are the means of our outcome measure for the group of respondents that saw a vignette including a specific attribute level (e.g., a female migrant) averaging over all other attributes (Leeper, Hobolt, and Tilley 2020). In the survey, participants were asked the degree to which "Denying migrant entry is unreasonable" in response to each vignette. To ease interpretation when presenting responses on this outcome measure, we reversed the survey coding throughout so that the high end is finding exclusion to be reasonable, which we interpret as support for excluding the migrant in question.[7] We obtained the following key findings:

The less a threat a migrant appears to pose, the less reasonable respondents found the use of any enforcement. As noted above, we considered a migrant to pose a threat if, in the vignette, they were denied a visa because they were on a terrorist watch list, had a criminal history, or had contracted Covid-19. Migrants who did not pose these threats were depicted as being denied a visa because they had not secured employment or would exceed immigration quotas. Respondents were significantly less supportive of all enforcement for those posing no threat as compared to those who did.[8] Figure 9.1 illustrates this pattern for both the US and the UK, though it is stronger in the latter.

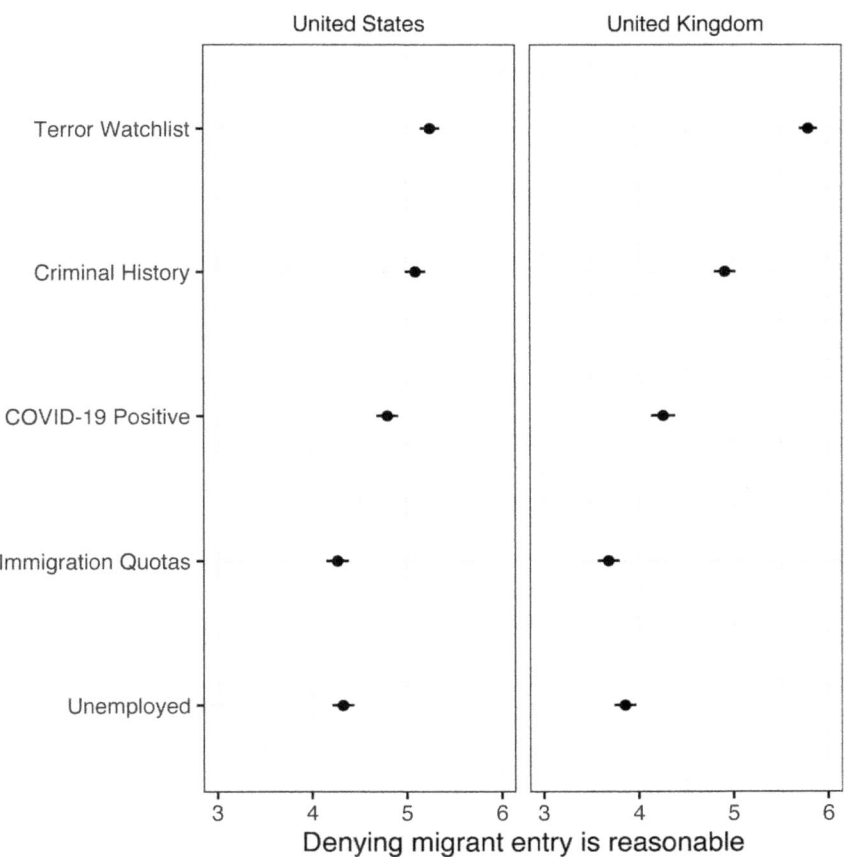

Figure 9.1 Marginal mean of how reasonable it is to deny a given migrant entry to the country by the reason for which entry was denied. We show 95 percent confidence bounds computed from standard errors clustered at the respondent-level. © Mollie Gerver, Dominik Duell, and Patrick Lown.

UK respondents found enforcement against migrants posing a threat as less reasonable if migrants were forced to leave their home countries. No such findings arose in the United States. As noted, we presumed that a migrant who engaged in a voluntary act which poses a threat (i.e., voluntarily committed a crime) is liable to less harm if they were forced to migrate. This claim is perhaps controversial, but we argued that subjects would generally view enforcement as less reasonable if migrants posing a threat were forced to migrate. This hypothesis was confirmed in the UK, but not in the US. In the UK, the marginal mean of reasonableness of exclusion of a voluntary migrant is 5.23 (*SE* = 0.046), while the one of the forced migrant is only 4.75 (*SE* = 0.052). The quantities in the United States are 5.02 (*SE* = 0.049) and 5.08 (*SE* = 0.046), respectively. The former difference is significant, while the latter is not.[9]

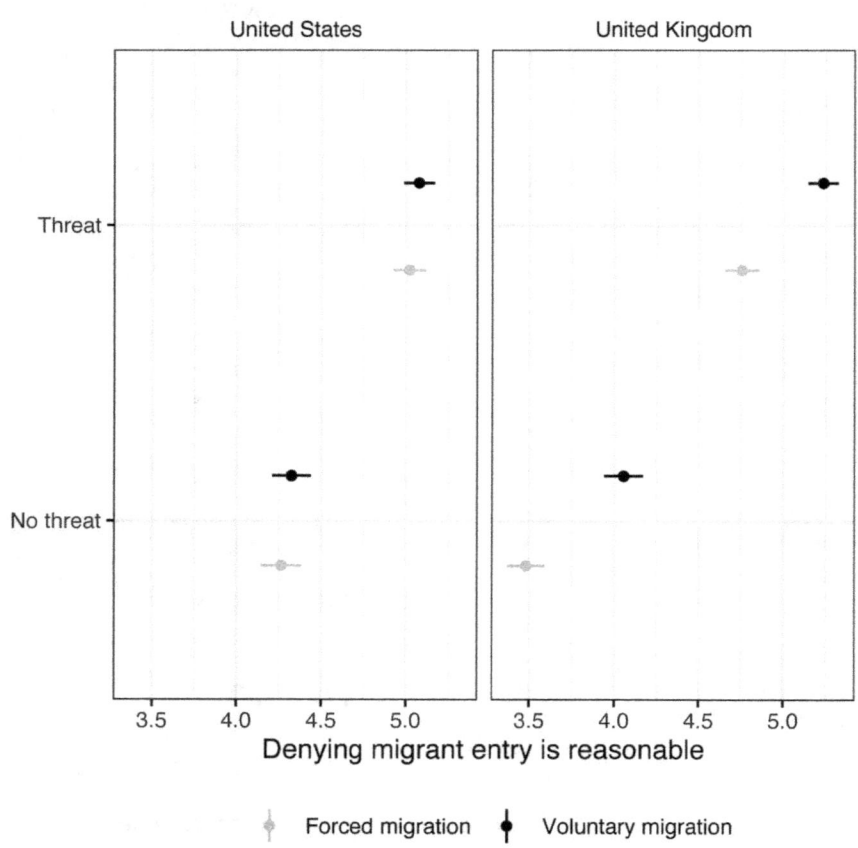

Figure 9.2 Marginal mean of how reasonable it is to deny a given migrant entry based on whether they are a threat and whether they were forced to migrate. We show 95 percent confidence bounds computed from standard errors clustered at the respondent-level. © Mollie Gerver, Dominik Duell, and Patrick Lown.

Figure 9.2 shows that British respondents gave responses consistent with the second hypothesis, in that they indicated enforcement against a threatening forced migrant (i.e., terror watch-list, criminal history, or Covid-19 positive) was less reasonable than enforcement against a threatening voluntary migrant. No such distinction was found among US respondents, who treat voluntary and forced migrants identically when both pose a threat.

Enforcement against Middle Eastern migrants is not seen as more reasonable than enforcement against non-Middle Eastern migrants. However, in the UK there was bias against Middle Eastern migrants who are posing a threat and facing no harm of injury or death from enforcement. Figure 9.3 shows that in both the US and

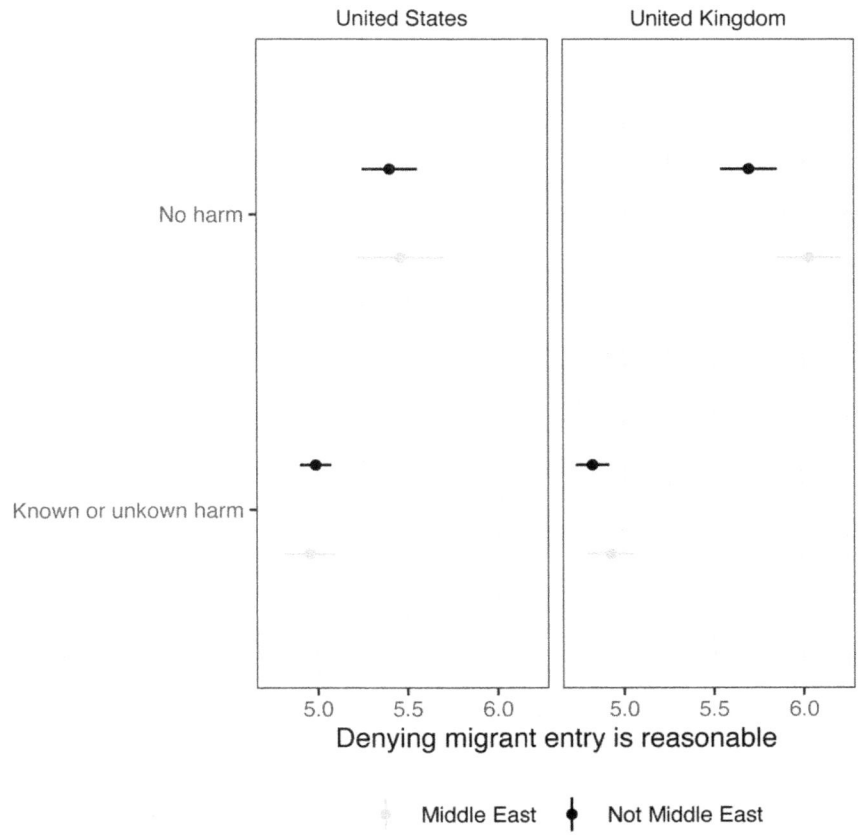

Figure 9.3 Marginal mean of how reasonable it is to deny a given migrant entry to the country by whether they would not be harmed as a consequence of returning home or whether harm they could be exposed to is known or unknown. We show estimates for threatening migrants only. We show 95 percent confidence bounds computed from standard errors clustered at the respondent-level. © Mollie Gerver, Dominik Duell, and Patrick Lown.

UK, on the aggregate, there was no significant difference between subjects' views of whether enforcement against Middle Eastern migrants was reasonable, as compared to enforcement against non-Middle Eastern migrants.

However, there was one type of bias. As noted in the overview of our methods, the vignettes varied in the degree that migrants would face harm from both enforcement itself and conditions in home countries. Some vignettes included migrants dying or becoming injured in immigration detention, during deportation, and after returning to their home countries. Some vignettes included migrants who faced no such harms at all. When it came to vignettes where harm against migrants took place (either during enforcement or in home countries), there was no region-based bias in either the US or UK, but where no harm took place, British respondents viewed it as more reasonable to deny entry or remove Middle Eastern migrants posing a threat as compared to other migrants posing a threat.

In the UK, for migrants posing a threat who would not be harmed upon being denied entry, the marginal mean is 6.03 ($SE = 0.09$) for Middle Eastern migrants but only 5.69 ($SE = 0.08$) for migrants from other regions. The difference between those two marginal means is significant, while the difference between those quantities in the United States is not; further, the difference of the marginal means for Middle Eastern and other migrants when being harmed is also not significant.[10]

5. Implications

Before addressing potential implications of findings for what various agents ought to do, it is worth spelling out some limitations.

First, we only asked individuals to state their judgments about individual migrants. It may be that voters would not be sensitive to whether migrants posed a threat or were forced to migrate—that is, would not be sensitive to attributes important for liability—if they were asked to judge cases involving far more migrants. This could be because of the "psychic-numbing" effect, where individuals are less likely to feel the need to stop harms against large numbers of individuals as compared to specific individuals (Slovic et al. 2013). Because there are a large number of nonliable migrants, a policymaker attempting to reduce harm for all such migrants may be voted out of office before able to do so. Or, alternatively, a policymaker may need to focus on presenting voters with cases of individual nonliable migrants to persuade them to support policies which avoid deporting all nonliable migrants; in other words, perhaps the psychic-numbing effect can be counteracted precisely by presenting all voters with the sorts of individual cases that appear in our experiment. Further experiments could assess if this is the case, and to more thoroughly understand what messaging persuades voters to support enforcement consistent with a principle of liability.

Second, this is but one experiment; further experiments are necessary to establish if the results are replicable, and so our findings here are not decisive. Relatedly, there is a possibility that subjects were sensitive to liability-related attributes in the vignettes, despite secretly or subconsciously thinking such attributes irrelevant. We therefore cannot fully establish how people will act at the polls based on the result of this experiment.

Finally, it is important not to draw strong conclusions from differences between the British and American findings, given the different ways in which the samples were gathered. In particular, the Prolific sample in the UK seems to be more politically sophisticated (based in part on their open-ended responses not discussed here), which may account for some of the discrepancies in the results.[11] Moreover, in both the UK and US subjects did not express a perfect commitment to a principle of liability. They simply were sensitive to this principle, in that they viewed harm inflicted on individuals not liable to harm as far less reasonable than those liable to harm.

With the above caveats in mind, below are some tentative implications from our findings for how three groups of actors ought to act.

5.1 Elected Policymakers

If citizens are sensitive to liability in some regards—they distinguish between those who do and do not pose a threat via their migration, and those who are and are not forced to migrate—this suggests policymakers are not limited by lack of popular support to pass legislation sensitive to liability. Of course, not being constrained by popular support does not mean passing legislation is possible. Vocal minorities—such as far right voters not sensitive to liability—could sway the majority, and party heads might prevent party members from attempting to pass legislation (Hampshire 2013). Nonetheless, our findings weaken the claim that policymakers are unable to pass liability-sensitive legislation specifically because of general opposition.

This claim—that there is general support for liability, even if other barriers persist—is important. It suggests that at least some liability-based changes do not face a barrier faced by other principles endorsed by philosophers. For example, many philosophers claim states have a duty to accept far more refugees (Gibney 2004; Carens 2013; Miller 2016; Hidalgo 2018), but the majority of citizens in a range of countries oppose a major increase in refugees accepted (Ferwerda, Flynn, and Horiuchi 2017; Horiuchi and Ono 2018; Kalogeraki 2019; Cope and Crabtree 2020). Even in the United States, where a majority support accepting at least 95,000 refugees for resettlement each year (Da Silva 2021), the majority do not support accepting the millions that the United States has a duty to accept according to a range of plausible theories of global justice. Many philosophers additionally support increases in immigration more generally (Gibney 2004; Carens 2013; Brock 2020), despite opposition among the general public (Hidalgo 2018). Were a policymaker to attempt to begin the legislative process of significantly increasing the number of refugees or migrants provided visas, she might be quickly voted out of office before the process was complete. In contrast, reducing the harm instigated against nonliable migrants during enforcement may be popular enough to render legislation politically feasible. If so, this could have implications for a range of policies. Consider a UK policy where those who have a criminal history can be subject to deportation, even if arriving in the UK to avoid life-threatening conditions, and even if they will face a high risk of death upon return. The only exception to this policy is if an individual is returning to a country where they will face specific human rights violations, including torture. Those who would face a life-threatening famine or lack of medical care can still be deported (AS and DD v Secretary of State for the Home Department 2008; BB, PP, W.U, Y and Z v Secretary of State for the Home Department 2016; Anderson 2017).

Respondents in our experiment, in contrast to the above policies, seem sensitive to the reasons an individual who committed a crime arrived in the UK, viewing enforcement against those forced to arrive as less reasonable than against those voluntarily arriving. Were policymakers to attempt to pass legislation which would provide additional protections to those forced to arrive in the UK, including those with a criminal history, they may be able to pass such legislation without being voted out of office.

This assumes, however, that such legislation could be passed and applied in a nonbiased manner. As noted in our findings, there is some evidence of bias among UK subjects, who were more likely to support enforcement against Middle Eastern migrants posing a threat, so long as no injury or death arose in enforcement. When such bias arises, policymakers could face a dilemma: either they could support legislation more in line with liability, but only for some migrants, and thus resulting in discrimination, or they could attempt to pass such legislation without bias against Middle Eastern migrants, but likely unable to actually pass such legislation. We do not resolve this dilemma here, and it may not actually arise when it comes to liability itself. Liability concerns justified harm; bias did not arise in the UK when it came to migrants facing harm, in that subjects made no distinction between Middle Eastern and non-Middle Eastern migrants facing harm. It was simply that UK subjects were biased between groups experiencing no harm. If so, then legislatures may be able to change policies specifically concerning migrants who would face harm from enforcement, without instituting any bias. For example, the UK could refrain from deporting those fleeing violence back to life-threatening conditions, even if they have committed a crime in the past.

The above analysis mostly assumes that the public is the only barrier to reforming policies. Even when there are other barriers—such as political parties and a vocal far-right minority—the public's general attitude may be a good proxy for deciding which other barriers to try to overcome. For example, if there is especially strong opposition to deporting refugees to life-threatening violence after they commit a crime, but a political party head insists on such deportations in light of far-right protests, individual policymakers may have strong reason to try and persuade the political party head and/or vocal minority to change their minds, or refuse to acquiesce to the far-right demands. In contrast, when all oppose a change—when the general public, a vocal minority, and political party heads all insist that current policy is reasonable—overcoming such opposition may be beyond an individual policymaker's capabilities.

5.2 Voters

As noted, we found that US respondents were both sensitive to one aspect of liability—they were less supportive of enforcement against those not posing a threat—and did not demonstrate bias against migrants from the Middle East. If one ought to generally follow a principle of liability, but one has reason to avoid doing so when this contributes to bias against Middle Easterners, this particular reason does not seem to apply in the United States. If so, US voters should not avoid trying to follow a principle of liability based on fear that this will contribute to bias against Middle Easterners. This is true regardless of one's general views of immigration.

For example, imagine a given US voter thinks it is justified to limit the number of migrants arriving or remaining, because she thinks a major increase in immigration can have negative economic repercussions for disadvantaged members of society in the short term, and because a major increase in immigration can strain the state's ability to prevent crime. She doesn't think migrants are more likely to commit crimes, only that some limits in inward migration can prevent the straining of law enforcement in the short term. Put aside whether she is right about these facts; she thinks these facts are true, but is also against using harm against migrants not liable to harm. In other words, she thinks it is justified to deport or detain individuals to limit immigration, because of the effects of immigration on law enforcement, but still thinks that immigrants should not be deported or detained if they would face harm they are not liable to face. Scrolling on her newsfeed, she learns about a migrant who faces deportation after committing a serious crime, and she is uncertain whether she thinks it is wrong to deport this migrant. She thinks the migrant is liable to the harm of imprisonment, but not the harm of deportation, because the migrant will return to life-threatening conditions if deported. If she is choosing between a candidate who supports the deportation of this migrant or migrants like him and one who does not, she should account for these candidates' positions in her overall assessment of how she should vote. She should not avoid appealing to considerations of liability out of fear that accounting for this consideration will cause her to hold biased beliefs. She should not think, "in forming my opinion about whether migrants should be deported, and how I should vote, I should ignore whether they are liable to harm, because this will cause me to have implicit biases (which I have no awareness or control over) against migrants from the Middle East. I will end up judging them as more liable than migrants who are not from the Middle East." There is no evidence that accounting for liability has this effect.

In the UK, findings were more ambiguous. As noted, while there was no clear bias in general, there was a statistically significant difference between attitudes about nonharmful enforcement against Middle Eastern migrants posing a threat and nonharmful enforcement against non-Middle Eastern migrants posing a threat. As a reminder, "non-harmful" refers to enforcement causing no death or injury, or no known death or injury.

It is not clear why respondents were biased when migrants posing a threat faced no risk of death or injury from enforcement, but they may have thought that such bias (if they were aware of it at all) was not wrong. We presume it is, because we presume that bias can be wrong even if there is no obvious harm (Slavny and Parr 2015). Moreover, enforcement against individuals from the Middle East likely always involves at least some harm (even if not death or injury), such as the harm of being denied the legal right to remain in a country in virtue of one's region of origin (Mendoza 2014; Reed-Sandoval 2019).

If so, this raises the question of whether UK voters should try being sensitive to principles of liability. One good reason to be sensitive to liability is that such sensitivity might not itself contribute to bias; it may be that individuals are already biased against Middle Eastern migrants who would face no death or injury from immigration enforcement, and put aside such bias when exposed to cases of migrants who would face such harms. If this is the case, voters choosing to be sensitive to liability at least avoid bias for migrants who would face such harms. Put another way: ignoring liability may lead to bias against both Middle Eastern migrants who face harms of death or injury and those who would not face such harms, but being sensitive to liability at least avoids bias against Middle Eastern migrants who would face harms of death or injury. Alternatively, perhaps voters' choosing to be sensitive to liability does lead to greater bias. For example, perhaps subjects exposed to cases with injury or death show no bias against Middle Eastern migrants in such cases, but as a result of being exposed to such cases show greater bias against Middle Eastern migrants who face no death or injury. This could serve as evidence that making these liability-related features salient, and being sensitive to these features, contributes to bias against Middle Eastern migrants who would face no harm, as compared to non-Middle Eastern migrants who would face no harm. Further experiments can establish if this is the case.

5.3 Organizations and Activists

The above analysis has related implications for organizations. Imagine a refugee rights organization emphasizes that refugees who committed crimes are being deported to life-threatening conditions, and voters agree that such refugees should not be deported, but this causes voters to begin supporting the deportation of Middle Eastern nonrefugee migrants who commit crimes and would face no risks in home countries, as compared to non-Middle Eastern migrants who commit crimes and would face no risks in home countries. Given that refugee rights organizations have a responsibility to not contribute to injustice, and given that discrimination is unjust even if not resulting in injury or death, such organizations would have reason to not emphasize life-threatening conditions refugees would face if deported. While this reason might not be decisive—the benefits of preventing the deportation of refugees may outweigh the harms of discrimination—this reason is one of many in organization's overall assessment of how to act.

Our findings suggest that the above is not relevant for US organizations. US subjects showed no bias in evaluating whether migrants who would face no injury or death from enforcement were wronged. If so, organizations engaging with US citizens act responsibly—in the sense of not contributing to bias—when emphasizing facts relevant for liability.

For a concrete example, consider a 2015 Human Rights Watch campaign aimed at stopping the deportation of individuals with a criminal history but who did not seem liable to the harm of deportation. The campaign included profiles of these two migrants:

> Abdulhakim Haji-Eda, a refugee from Ethiopia who came to the US at the age of 13, was ordered removed as a drug trafficker for a single conviction for

selling a small quantity of cocaine at the age of 18. Now 26 years old, he has no other convictions and is married to a US citizen and has two US citizen children.

"Mr. V.," a refugee and permanent resident from Vietnam, was ordered deported in 2008 for a 1999 conviction for possession of crack cocaine. Although he has since been granted a full and unconditional pardon from the state of South Carolina, Mr. V. remains under a deportation order and remains in the US only because of restrictions on the repatriation of certain Vietnamese nationals.

(Human Rights Watch 2015)

Some might fear that, by emphasizing that the above migrants are not liable to harm because they are refugees, the campaigners risked increasing support for the deportation of African and Southeast Asians who had a criminal history and were not refugees, as compared to non-African and non-Southeast Asian migrants who had a criminal history and were not refugees. Our findings found no such bias in the United States. This suggests that the above campaigns were not objectionable for reasons relating to bias.

Because of potential bias against Middle Eastern migrants arising in the UK, the implications there are less clear. Moreover, in both the US and UK we did not include migrants from every possible region, and bias may indeed arise against migrants from regions not included. For example, consider a particularly effective UK campaign to halt the deportation of fifty migrants back to Jamaica in 2020. The campaign did not shy away from discussing the crimes some individuals had committed, but emphasized that many left Jamaica because of risks, and would face risks if deported, including risks of death. This campaign, including fundraising from the campaign to cover legal costs, meant only thirteen of the original fifty immigrants were deported (Sky News 2021). It may be that such campaigns—emphasizing harm from deportation—contribute to bias against migrants from Jamaica who both committed crimes and would not face risks of injury or death from deportation, as compared to non-Jamaican migrants who committed crimes and would not face risks of death or injury from deportation. While our experiment could not establish if being sensitive liability *contributes* to bias, and we did not include migrants from Jamaica, establishing broader biases and effects would be valuable for future research, and for helping organizations determine future campaign messaging.

6. Conclusion

We set out to describe two ways that experiments are relevant for moral and political philosophy. First, they provide evidence of whether a policymaker has public support to pass a given piece of legislation without being voted out of office before the legislative process is complete; if she cannot pass the legislation, and ought implies can, she cannot have a duty to pass the legislation. Second, experiments can establish whether individuals trying to follow a given principle end up applying this principle in a biased manner. When the bias is difficult to counter, this can create one reason to avoid trying to follow the principle, and/or avoid encouraging others to do so.

We presented an example of an experiment aiming to fulfil the above functions. The experiment sought to understand whether applying a principle of liability to immigration has public support, and whether those sensitive to this principle demonstrate implicit bias in its application. We demonstrated that the general public is sensitive to considerations of liability. In both the US and UK, subjects viewed harm against migrants not posing a threat as less reasonable than harm against other groups of migrants, and in the UK they viewed harm against migrants posing a threat but forced to migrate as less reasonable than harm against migrants posing a threat but voluntarily migrating. Moreover, subjects in the both the US and UK did not generally demonstrate any bias against migrants from a given region, though we found evidence of specific bias in the UK against Middle Eastern migrants posing a threat who would face no injury or death from enforcement.

These findings indicate that policymakers may be able to pass legislation which, at least in some ways, is sensitive to whether migrants are liable to harm. Moreover, US activists aiming to implement more ethical immigration policies needn't worry that appeals to liability will increase bias. At least, there is no evidence from the experiment to indicate that they need fear this effect, though this is less clear in the UK.

The experiment we presented was limited: it only pertained to attitudes about individual migrants and may not indicate how US and UK citizens will actually vote in the polls. However, the experiment provides one example of how empirical findings can impact what individuals ought to do, and what they ought to persuade others to do.

Online Appendix

Between Subjects Treatment: Certainty of Information Because a principle of liability relates to harm, we also sought to establish if respondents thought a given level of harm justified based on the threat and responsibility of a given migrant (the latter defined as whether they were forced to migrate). We have three experimental conditions relating to harm in a between-subject design. In Condition 1, respondents are provided with certain information about the harm arising from enforcement (*Certain*). In Condition 2, respondents are provided with information that is probabilistic (*Small chance, High chance, Near certain*). Finally, in Condition 3, respondents are provided with no information about what happens to the migrant in the vignette (*No outcome information*). For the purpose of the results presented here, the between-respondent information treatment serves as robustness check; we present results below pooling observations across treatments (see Figure A.3).

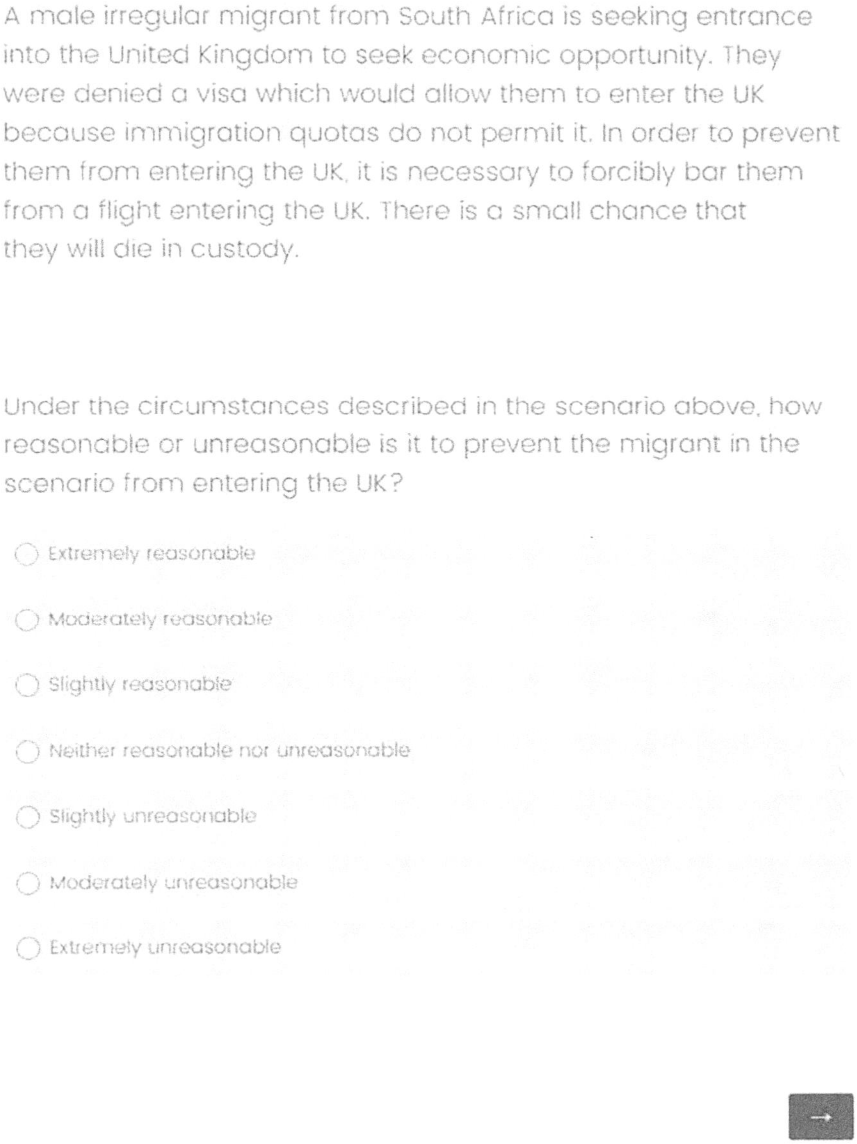

A male irregular migrant from South Africa is seeking entrance into the United Kingdom to seek economic opportunity. They were denied a visa which would allow them to enter the UK because immigration quotas do not permit it. In order to prevent them from entering the UK, it is necessary to forcibly bar them from a flight entering the UK. There is a small chance that they will die in custody.

Under the circumstances described in the scenario above, how reasonable or unreasonable is it to prevent the migrant in the scenario from entering the UK?

○ Extremely reasonable

○ Moderately reasonable

○ Slightly reasonable

○ Neither reasonable nor unreasonable

○ Slightly unreasonable

○ Moderately unreasonable

○ Extremely unreasonable

Figure A.1 Screenshot of one realization of the factorial vignette as shown to respondents in the UK sample. © Mollie Gerver, Dominik Duell, and Patrick Lown.

A female irregular migrant from Syria is seeking to remain in the United States to seek economic opportunity. They were denied a visa which would allow them to remain in the U.S. because their name is on a terrorism watch-list. In order to prevent them from remaining in the U.S., it is necessary to detain them in the U.S. until they agree to return home. The consequences of their returning home are unknown.

Under the circumstances described in the scenario above, how reasonable or unreasonable is it to remove the migrant in the scenario from the U.S.?

○ Extremely reasonable

○ Moderately reasonable

○ Slightly reasonable

○ Neither reasonable nor unreasonable

○ Slightly unreasonable

○ Moderately unreasonable

○ Extremely unreasonable

Figure A.2 Screenshot of one realization of the factorial vignette as shown to respondents in the US sample. © Mollie Gerver, Dominik Duell, and Patrick Lown.

Experimental Immigration Ethics

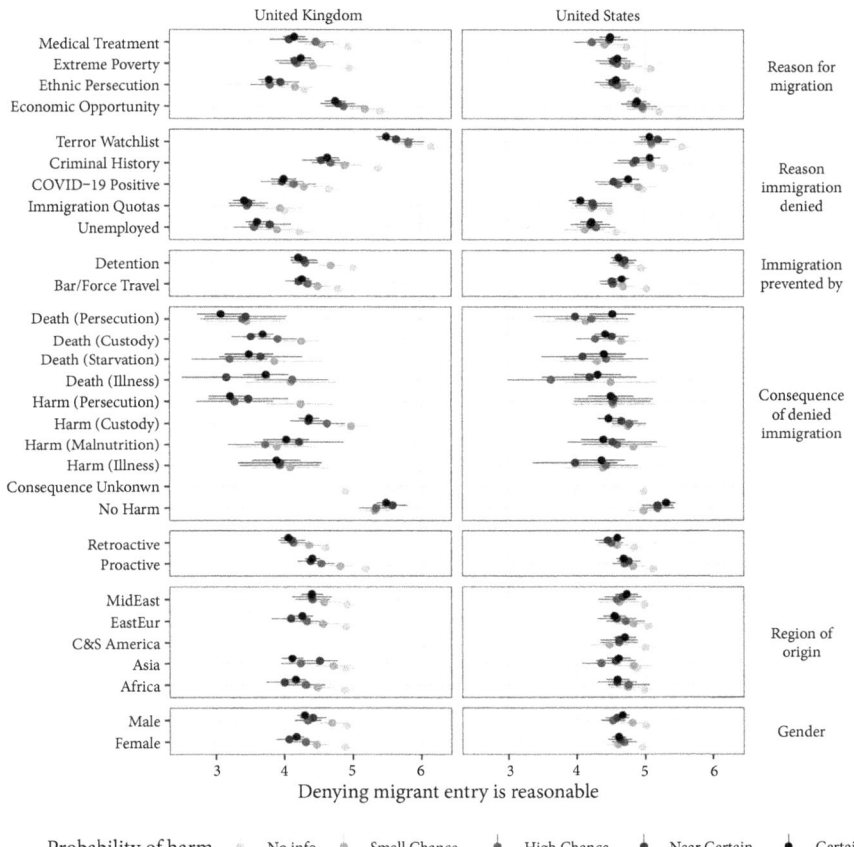

Figure A.3 Marginal mean of how reasonable it is to deny a given migrant entry to the country by immigration case attribute and the between-respondent probability of harm treatment. We show 95 percent confidence bounds computed from standard errors clustered at the respondent-level. The figure omits the country of origin attribute for ease of display but categorizes the country of origin into a region of origin indicator. © Mollie Gerver, Dominik Duell, and Patrick Lown.

Table A.1 OLS Regression of the Outcome Measure on the Fully Factorized Attribute Reason for Which Entry Was Denied (Taking Either Unemployed or Immigration Quotas as Reference Category)

Reference category	Unemployed		Immigration quotas	
Sample	United States	United Kingdom	United States	United Kingdom
(Intercept)	4.325***	3.855***	4.267***	3.682***
	(0.059)	(0.059)	(0.060)	(0.058)
Immigration Quotas	−0.058	−0.173*		
	(0.069)	(0.072)		
Unemployed			0.058	0.173*
			(0.069)	(0.072)
COVID-19 Positive	0.473***	0.406***	0.530***	0.580***
	(0.073)	(0.080)	(0.073)	(0.079)
Criminal History	0.769***	1.058***	0.826***	1.232***
	(0.070)	(0.072)	(0.070)	(0.073)
Terror Watchlist	0.923***	1.939***	0.981***	2.113***
	(0.071)	(0.069)	(0.071)	(0.070)
R^2	0.038	0.132	0.038	0.132
Adj. R^2	0.037	0.132	0.037	0.132
Num. obs.	9,019	8,627	9,019	8,627
RMSE	2.009	1.988	2.009	1.988
N Clusters	1,839	1,728	1,839	1,728

Note: ***$p < 0.001$; **$p < 0.01$; *$p < 0.05$.

Standard errors are clustered at the respondent level.

© Mollie Gerver, Dominik Duell, and Patrick Lown.

Table A.2 OLS Regression of the Outcome Measure on the Variable *Forced* Run on Observations of Migrants Who are Posing a Threat (Those on a Terrorist Watch List, with a Criminal Record, or Who had Contracted Covid-19)

Sample	United States	United Kingdom
(Intercept)	5.077***	5.234***
	(0.046)	(0.046)
Forced	−0.056	−0.481***
	(0.054)	(0.057)
R^2	0.000	0.014
Adj. R^2	0.000	0.013
Num. obs.	5,428	5,178
RMSE	1.962	2.041
N Clusters	1,805	1,704

Note: ***$p < 0.001$; **$p < 0.01$; *$p < 0.05$.

The variable *forced* takes on value *forced* for the attribute levels fleeing extreme poverty and fleeing ethnic persecution and *voluntary* otherwise; standard errors are clustered at the respondent level.

© Mollie Gerver, Dominik Duell, and Patrick Lown.

Table A.3 OLS Regression of the Outcome Measure on the Variable *Forced* Run on Observations of Migrants Who are Posing a Threat (Those on a Terrorist Watch List, with a Criminal Record, or Who had Contracted Covid-19)

Sample	United States		United Kingdom	
Consequence	Known or unknown harm	No harm	Known or unknown harm	No harm
(Intercept)	4.988***	5.403***	4.825***	5.697***
	(0.044)	(0.079)	(0.047)	(0.080)
Middle East	−0.032	0.062	0.103	0.335**
	(0.073)	(0.141)	(0.071)	(0.115)
R^2	0.000	0.000	0.000	0.008
Adj. R^2	−0.000	−0.001	0.000	0.007
Num. obs.	4,581	847	4,374	804
RMSE	1.988	1.776	2.083	1.681
N Clusters	1,753	635	1,656	607

Note: ***$p < 0.001$; **$p < 0.01$; *$p < 0.05$.

The variable *forced* takes on value *forced* for the attribute levels fleeing extreme poverty and fleeing ethnic persecution and *voluntary* otherwise; standard errors are clustered at the respondent level.

© Mollie Gerver, Dominik Duell, and Patrick Lown.

Notes

1. There is a rich debate over whether individuals are responsible and/or blameworthy for their implicit biases and the discriminatory actions resulting from these biases (Saul 2013; Washington and Kelly 2016; Holroyd, Scaife, and Stafford 2017). Our general claim is not dependent on the outcome of this debate: regardless of whether one is responsible and blameworthy for implicit biases and actions arises from these biases, one has moral reason to avoid trying to follow principles that result in biases that are truly difficult or impossible to resist.

2. The distinction made in the previous two paragraphs between experiments that do and do not explicitly describe a principle is similar to what Lindauer refers to as "intervention-based" versus "non-intervention based" methods. These are apt phrases to describe the distinction we have in mind, but we avoid using them here, as an experiment could include an intervention other than that of a philosophical principle. For example, some subjects may be presented with cases of migrants who are forced to migrate while others are not. This is a type of intervention, but would be categorized under Lindauer's "non-intervention-based" method because there is no presentation of a principle. We therefore thought it may be confusing to refer to such experiments as using a non-intervention-based method. For more on this topic, see Lindauer (2020 ibid at 2134–5).

3. Figures A.1 and A.2 in the appendix show one example permutation of the factorial vignettes as shown to respondents in the UK and US, respectively.

4. Africa: Nigeria, Ethiopia, South Africa, Kenya; Eastern Europe: Poland, Romania, Russia, Ukraine; the Middle East: Iran, Syria, UAE, Israel; Southeast Asia: India, Bangladesh, Pakistan, Myanmar; South and Central America: Venezuela, Nicaragua, Brazil, Mexico; East Asia: China, the Philippines, Vietnam, Myanmar.

5. These are broadly divided into harm due to the actions of border agents and harms due to the migrant returning to their country of origin. In the latter case, it is therefore necessary that these covary with the migrant's initial reason for migrating, rather than being fully randomized. For example, a migrant who left their home country due to persecution and faced harm after being deported would face harm from persecution, rather than illness.

6. Replication data are available from the project Dataverse: \\ https://dataverse.harvard.edu/dataset.xhtml?persistentId=doi:10.7910/DVN/ZFOTRO. For further analysis, see Gerver et al. (forthcoming).

7. Figure A.3 in the appendix shows the marginal mean of the outcome measure on all attribute levels included in the factorial vignette excluding separating the country attribute in all its levels but including a regional indicator for ease of display.

8. We find a positive and significant coefficient at $a = .05$ on the attribute levels terrorist watch list, criminal history, and had contracted Covid-19 in an OLS regression of the outcome measure on the fully factorized attribute reason for which entry was denied (taking either unemployed or immigration quotas as reference category); standard errors are clustered at the respondent level (see Table A.1 in the appendix).

9. In the UK, we find a positive and significant coefficient at $a = .05$ on the variable *forced* in an OLS regression of the outcome measure on the variable *forced* run on observations of migrants who are posing a threat (those on a terrorist watch list, with a criminal record, or who had contracted Covid-19). The variable *forced* takes on value *forced* for the attribute levels fleeing extreme poverty and fleeing ethnic

persecution and *voluntary* otherwise; standard errors are clustered at the respondent level. The coefficient on *forced* is not significant in the US (see Table A.2 in the appendix).

10 In the UK, we find a positive and significant coefficient at a =.05 on the variable *Middle Eastern* in an OLS regression of the outcome measure on the variable *region* run on observations of migrants who are posing a threat (those on a terrorist watch list, with a criminal record, or who had contracted Covid-19) separably for observations where the migrant was not harmed vs when the migrant was harmed upon being denied entry; standard errors are clustered at the respondent level (see Table A.3 in the appendix).

11 For example, in both surveys we included post-experimental questions asking respondents their opinions about whether they supported granting medical care to unauthorized migrants, and permanent residency to migrants who had served as frontline workers during the Covid-19 pandemic. Both surveys included closed-ended questions concerning these policies, and open-ended questions which respondents could answer, asking them why they gave the answers they gave. As compared to the US Qualtrics sample, the UK prolific sample was far more likely to answer these open-ended questions, and far more likely to give long, multi-sentence responses.

References

Aalberg, Toril, Shanto Iyengar, and Solomon Messing. 2012. "Who Is a 'Deserving' Immigrant? An Experimental Study of Norwegian Attitudes." *Scandinavian Political Studies* 35, no. 2: 97–116.

Anderson, David. 2017. *Deportation with Assurances*.

AS and DD v Secretary of State for the Home Department. 2008. EWCA Civ 289, [2008] HRLR 28.

Atzmuller, Christiane, and Peter M. Steiner. 2010. "Experimental Vignette Studies in Survey Research." *Methodology* 6, no. 2: 128–38.

BB, PP, W.U, Y and Z v Secretary of State for the Home Department. 2016. Appeal Nos. SC/39/2005 &c.

Betts, Katharine. 2001. "Boat People and Public Opinion in Australia." *People and Place* 9, no. 4: 34–48.

Blake, Michael. 2019. *Justice, Migration, and Mercy*. Oxford: Oxford University Press.

Brock, Gillian. 2020. *Justice for People on the Move: Migration in Challenging Times*. Cambridge: Cambridge University Press.

Bruneau, Emile, Nour Kteily, and Lasse Laustsen. 2018. "The Unique Effects of Blatant de-Humanization on Attitudes and Behavior Towards Muslim Refugees During the European 'Refugee Crisis' Across Four Countries." *European Journal of Social Psychology* 48, no. 5: 645–62.

Carens, Joseph. 2013. *The Ethics of Immigration*. Oxford: Oxford University Press.

Chantal, Da Silva. 2021. "Majority of Americans Think the US Should Resettle at Least 95,000 Refugees." Forbes. 14 June. Accessed on 27 March 2023 at https://www.forbes.com/sites/chantaldasilva/2021/06/14/majority-of-americans-think-us-should-resettle-at-least-95000-refugees-per-year-poll-finds/.

Cope, Kevin L, and Charles Crabtree. 2020. "A Nationalist Backlash to International Refugee Law: Evidence from a Survey Experiment in Turkey." *Journal of Empirical Legal Studies* 17, no. 4: 752–88.

Dustmann, Christian, and Ian P Preston. 2007. "Racial and Economic Factors in Attitudes to Immigration." *The BE Journal of Economic Analysis & Policy* 7, no. 1: 1–39.

Enoch, David. 2011. *Taking Morality Seriously: A Defense of Robust Realism*. Oxford: Oxford University Press.

Ferwerda, Jeremy, D. J. Flynn, and Yusaku Horiuchi. 2017. "Explaining Opposition to Refugee Re-settlement: The Role of NIMBYism and Perceived Threats." *Science Advances* 3, no. 9: e1700812.

Gerver, Mollie, Patrick Lown, and Dominik Duell. Forthcoming. "Proportional Immigration Enforcement," *Journal of Politics*

Gibney, Matthew J. 2004. *The Ethics and Politics of Asylum: Liberal Democracy and the Response to Refugees*. Cambridge: Cambridge University Press.

Hainmueller, Jens, and Daniel J Hopkins. 2015a. "The Hidden American Immigration Consensus: A Conjoint Analysis of Attitudes Toward Immigrants." *American Journal of Political Science* 59, no. 3: 529–48.

Hampshire, James. 2013. *The Politics of Immigration: Contradictions of the Liberal State*. Cambridge, UK and Malden, MA: Polity.

Hidalgo, Javier S. 2018. *Unjust Borders: Individuals and the Ethics of Immigration*. Abingdon: Routledge.

Holroyd, Jules, Robin Scaife, and Tom Stafford. 2017. "Responsibility for Implicit Bias." *Philosophy Compass* 12, no. 3: e12410.

Horiuchi, Yusaku, and Yoshikuni Ono. 2018. *Public Opposition to Refugee Resettlement: The Case of Japan*. Tokyo: RIETI.

Hosein, Adam. 2019. *The Ethics of Migration: An Introduction*. Abingdon: Routledge.

Human Rights Watch. 2015. *A Price Too High: Detention and Deportation of Immigrants in the US for Minor Drug Offenses*. Accessed on 6 July 2021 at https://www.hrw.org/report/2015/06/16/price-too-high/us-families-torn-apart-deportations-drug-offenses.

Kalogeraki, Stefania. 2019. "Opposition to Syrian Refugees and Immigrants During the Refugee Crisis in Greece." *Journal of Modern Greek Studies* 37, no. 2: 361–95.

Koos, Sebastian, and Verena Seibel. 2019. "Solidarity with Refugees Across Europe. A Comparative Analysis of Public Support for Helping Forced Migrants." *European Societies* 21, no. 5: 704–28.

Lee, Taeku. 2008. "Race, Immigration, and the Identity-to-Politics Link." *Annu. Rev. Polit. Sci.* 11: 457–78.

Leeper, Thomas J, Sara B Hobolt, and James Tilley. 2020. "Measuring Subgroup Preferences in Conjoint Experiments." *Political Analysis* 28, no. 2: 207–21.

Lindauer, Matthew. 2019. "Experimental Philosophy and the Fruitfulness of Normative Concepts." *Philosophical Studies*: 1–24.

Lister, Matthew. 2020. "Enforcing Immigration Law." *Philosophy Compass* 15, no. 3: e12653.

McMahan, Jeff. 2011. "Who Is Morally Liable to be Killed in War." *Analysis* 71, no. 3: 544–59.

Mendoza, José Jorge. 2014. "Discrimination and the Presumptive Rights of Immigrants." *Critical Philosophy of Race* 2, no. 1: 68–83.

Mendoza, José Jorge. 2015. "Enforcement Matters: Reframing the Philosophical Debate over Immigration." *The Journal of Speculative Philosophy* 29, no. 1: 73–90.

Miller, David. 2005. "Immigration: The Case for Its Limits." In *Contemporary Debates in Applied Ethics*, edited by A. Cohen and C. Wellman. Malden, MA: Blackwell Publishing.

Miller, David. 2016. *Strangers in Our Midst: The Political Philosophy of Immigration*. Cambridge: Harvard University Press.

Parfit, Derek. 2011. *On What Matters*. Vol. 2. Oxford: Oxford University Press.

Reed-Sandoval, Amy. 2019. *Socially Undocumented: Identity and Immigration Justice*. Oxford: Oxford University Press.

Saul, Jennifer. 2013. "Unconscious Influences and Women in Philosophy." In *Women in Philosophy: What Needs to Change*, 39–60. Oxford: Oxford University Press.

Sidgwick, Henry. 1981. *The Methods of Ethics* (7th Hackett reprint), Indianapolis: Hackett Publishing Co.

Silverman, Stephanie J. 2014. "Detaining Immigrants and Asylum Seekers: A Normative Introduction." *Critical Review of International Social and Political Philosophy* 17, no. 5: 600–17.

Slavny, Adam, and Tom Parr. 2015. "Harmless Discrimination." *Legal Theory* 21, no. 2: 100–14.

Slovic, Paul, et al. 2013. "Psychic Numbing and Mass Atrocity." In *The Behavioral Foundations of Public Policy*, 126–42. Princeton: Princeton University Press.

Sky News. 2021. "Deportation Flight to Jamaica Halts as 37 of the 50 Passengers Due to Fly," 2 December. Accessed on 27 March 2023 at https://news.sky.com/story/deportation-flight-to-jamaica-departs-without-37-of-the-50-passengers-due-to-fly-12148834.

Turper, Sedef. 2017. "Fearing What? Vignette Experiments on Anti-Immigrant Sentiments." *Journal of Ethnic and Migration Studies* 43, no. 11: 1792–812.

Vries, Ieke de, et al. 2019. "Anti-Immigration Sentiment and Public Opinion on Human Trafficking." *Crime, Law and Social Change* 72, no. 1: 125–43.

Washington, Natalia, and Daniel Kelly. 2016. "Who's Responsible for This? Implicit Bias and the Knowledge Condition." *Implicit Bias and Philosophy: Moral Responsibility, Structural Injustice, and Ethics* 2: 11–36.

Wellman, Christopher. 2008. "Immigration and Freedom of Association." *Ethics* 119: 109–41.

10

Love vs. Money: Understanding Unique Challenges in Care Workers' Labor Organizing

Grace Flores-Robles and Ana P. Gantman

In every society, children need to be raised (e.g., by parents), taught to read and do math (e.g., by teachers), and be taken care of when they are sick (e.g., by healthcare professionals). Indeed, every society relies on care workers to meet their basic needs. Care workers, like those described above, are responsible for meeting the emotional, psychological, developmental, and/or physical needs of others (England, Budig, and Folbre 2002). Throughout history, women have attended to many of these dependencies, not just for children but for any family or community members who are unable to be fully independent themselves (Kittay 1995). The labor involved in raising children, teaching children, or caring for children has been seen as part of their familial and community obligations. Women who were wealthy enough to avoid performing care labor themselves often outsource some or all of the work to other women, usually from lower-class backgrounds and from racial minority groups (ILO 2018). In the United States, as in many other societies, a gendered division of labor has ensured that many women perform care labor for little or no pay (Duffy 2011). These low wages have contributed, in part, to the care shortage in the United States.

1. Current Care Shortage in the United States

Many struggle to find assistance caring for elderly relatives or their children. Increased demands for care, high turnover rates, and an inability to fill vacancies in care work have contributed to this growing shortage. For example, as the baby boom cohort reached retirement, the need for necessary health and personal care services for the elderly increased (Smith and Baughman 2007). The need for nurses has also increased, particularly in the Covid-19 pandemic. Many healthcare facilities that were already understaffed, had high patient-to-nurse ratios, and required their nurses to work long shifts worsened at the start of the pandemic (Romero ad Bhatt 2021). Recent data from the Association of American Medical Colleges (2021) also projects an estimated shortage between 37,800 and 124,000 physicians by 2034, including shortfalls in both primary and specialty care. Many more examples demonstrate a growing shortage of care workers, though we only highlighted a few (e.g., Haspel 2021; Famakinwa 2021). Low wages, adverse working conditions, and high turnover rates are responsible for the shortage in most care professions (Espinoza 2017; García and Weiss 2019; Haddad, Annamaraju, and Toney-Butler 2021). However, the largest driving force behind turnover rates in care work is low pay.

1.1 Low Wages in Care Work

Although care work is socially valued, its workers often experience low levels of pay for their expertise. For example, an examination of US Census data found that workers in occupations involving care were paid 6 percent less than people in other types of occupations, even when accounting for job characteristics, including education and skill (England et al. 2002). Evidence of this wage penalty (also referred to as a "care penalty") has been replicated within the private and public sectors, among men and women, and across several countries. For example, care work carries a wage penalty for men in the private sector in Finland, France, Canada, the United States, and Mexico, among other countries (Budig and Misra 2010).[1] Women also experience a care penalty in the private sector, but most commonly experience wage penalties in the public sector. Finally, although men experience more care penalties than their female counterparts, the wage penalties experienced by female care workers are more severe (Budig and Misra 2010). Additional research has replicated wage penalties for nurturant and reproductive occupations (Duffy 2007; Barron and West 2013) and among occupations with higher levels of emotional labor demands, such as those in care work (Glomb, Kammeyer-Mueller, and Rotundo 2004). Taken together, this research suggests that working in occupations involving care reduces earnings for both women and men.

1.2 Importance of Care Workers During Covid-19

The Covid-19 pandemic highlighted something that many care theorists already know: care work is essential to a functioning society. Yet, even as care workers were praised for their commitment to their patients and students during the Covid-19 pandemic, many continued to experience low wages, despite their increased workload and hazard. For example, Folbre, Gautham, and Smith (2021) found that essential workers in care services (health, education, and social service industries) were paid less than other essential workers with comparable personal and work characteristics (those in law enforcement, support and waste services, transportation, agriculture, retail, and financial industries). Relatedly, op-eds with headlines like "America Never Valued Care Workers. Then a Pandemic Hit" (Covert 2020) and "Essential but Undervalued: Millions of Health Care Workers Aren't Getting the Pay or Respect they Deserve in the COVID-19 Pandemic" (Kinder 2020) highlight the economic impact of the Covid-19 pandemic on care workers already experiencing challenges in their workplace.

The care shortage and worsening conditions make it all the more urgent to understand *why* low wages persist in care work. Several sociological and economic theories have been used to explain these low wages, including the *fears of commodification argument*, and the *devaluation hypothesis*, which we will review below. One way we might imagine that care workers could increase their wages would be through labor organizing. But, as we posit in this chapter, care workers face unique opposition when they organize for better working conditions and higher pay. We argue that this unique opposition is moral outrage, and we will outline why we think that care workers might elicit outrage (from some) when they organize. Finally, we will provide evidence that paying care workers is critical to preventing their exploitation (Walker 2007). We will present some preliminary data to suggest that this is the case.

2. Why Do Low Wages Persist in Care Work?

At the core of the issue that care workers face is a perception that there is a trade-off between love and money in their work. First, we outline *the commodification argument* and *the devaluation hypothesis*, which each seek to explain low wages in care work through this broad lens. Then, we turn to our main question about care workers and labor organizing and find that perceptions of this same trade-off contribute to the outrage care workers face.

2.1 The Commodification Argument

One way that people have tried to understand why low wages persist in care work is by exploring the market value of care. Many of the views surrounding paid care emerge from dualistic views about gender; because males and females are opposite, beliefs about "women, family, love, and altruism" are distinct from beliefs about "men, rationality, and market-exchange" (Nelson and England 2002). This dichotomy suggests that it is not possible for love and money to exist in the same place (just as men and women cannot exist in the same place) or that waged labor can only erode or contaminate the value of love (Zelizer 2002). What these views are essentially debating is the boundaries that exist between objects that can be commodified and those that cannot.

Proponents of economic imperialism (Boulding 1969) favor the idea that everything can be explained in terms of a market transaction. Commodification is the process by which objects (activities, skills, etc.) are represented in terms of market transactions, particularly through an exchange of money (Carvalho and Rodrigues 2008). Two major arguments dominate the debate surrounding what, and when, objects should be commodified: the separate spheres thesis, which proposes that separate spheres exist for the market and nonmarket, and an opposing view that suggests there is room for complex relationships between market and nonmarket values (they are not dichotomous). We focus on the former in thinking about the commodification of care.

The separate spheres thesis argues that boundaries exist between objects that can be commodified and those that cannot. Sandel (1998) makes this point clear through discussions surrounding the moral limitations of commodification, as justified by concerns regarding coercion and corruption. First, Sandel (1998) argues that market exchanges are not always voluntary. Consider an individual who chooses to sell their organs. Although the individual may consent to selling their organs, they may be constrained by economic inequality (e.g., the need to buy food for one's family). That is, even where there appears to be consent in a market transaction, coercion may still exist in the background due to unfair conditions. Second, Sandel (1998) argues that moral and civic goods can be corrupted if they are given market values. Here, selling organs would be degrading for both the rich and the poor, because it violates the sanctity of human life. Taken together, these claims suggest that there are certain goods that cannot be given market values.

Some scholars suggest that certain types of labor (e.g., reproductive labor) should also exist outside of current labor markets. According to this view, extending the market to include the personal and private spheres, as in surrogacy or sex work, is improper because it fails to respect the intrinsic nature of reproductive or sexual labor (Satz 2010). Instead, many argue that reproductive labor should exist outside of other forms of human labor because it is fundamentally different, either because of biological features involved in the work (Satz 2010) or because it is more central to a woman's identity than productive labor (Pateman 1988). These views have been coined the essentialist thesis, because it holds that reproductive labor is *essentially* something that should not be bought and sold.

In short, arguments against the commodification of care rest on two key points: that certain goods would lose their intrinsic values if they were commodified, and that care labor is intrinsically different than other forms of productive labor because it represents essentialist differences between women and men. It is within this space that most discussions surrounding care reside.

2.1.1 Commodification and Quality of Care

Care is often thought to exist outside of the market. However, market values are already given to care, as individuals are already paid to provide love and affection to others in paid care professions (e.g., in nursing). Reminding others that care is commodified shifts the discussion from whether market values *should* be given to care (and how much) to whether higher pay in care work corrupts the moral value of care. In other words, the discussion shifts toward fears that commodification (i.e., via higher pay) will reduce the interpersonal elements that give care work meaning (we hereafter refer to this as the "fear of commodification").

Some evidence shows that these fears ring true for many Americans. For example, while acknowledging that some care workers do provide genuine care, feminist economist Himmelweit (1999) claimed that paying for care reduces its quality and authenticity; genuine care remains only if it resists complete commodification (Himmelweit 1999). Similarly, Held (2002) argues that the value of care only remains if it exists outside of the private sector, where market norms prevail. Finally, McCloskey (1996) wrote that if childcare "were paid labor, the love would disappear. Love in this regard is the *opposite of market exchange*." Representative of these fears is evidence that including gifts in market institutions makes them devoid of their intrinsic value (Anderson 1995) and that extrinsic motivators can diminish intrinsic motivation (Frey 1997; Deci, Koestner, and Ryan 1999).

To date, no quantitative work has directly examined the fear of commodification in care work. In this chapter, we propose one measure that captures fears surrounding the commodification of care and attempt to distinguish those fears from beliefs about gender.

2.2 The Devaluation Hypothesis and the Gender Pay Gap

As mentioned in our previous section, beliefs about care work are grounded in one's beliefs about women and family, and men and work. This dichotomy has inadvertently led to occupational segregation (i.e., women's increasing participation in paid care work), has contributed to a widening gender pay gap, and has led to the devaluation of care.

Women's labor force participation has been at a steady increase over the last few decades (56.8 percent in 2016 compared to 20 percent in 1900). Yet, while the gap between women and men's labor force participation is decreasing, there continue to be differences in women and men's wages, in large part due to occupational segregation (Blau and Winkler 2017). Women are concentrated in office and support occupations (e.g., secretaries), service occupations (e.g., childcare workers), and professional care occupations (e.g., teachers, registered nurses). In other words, women are concentrated in occupations with low pay. Some research has shown that predominantly female occupations pay less than predominantly male occupations after adjusting for skill requirements and working conditions (e.g., Barron and West 2013; Budig and Misra 2010; England, Budig, and Folbre 2002). These penalties are faced by both women and men in predominantly female occupations. Unsurprisingly, care work demonstrates this same pattern. Women and men in occupations involving care face a wage penalty. Analyses of interactive service work (a broader category that subsumes care work, such as waitressing) find that both men and women earn less in occupations in this broad category of work. Similarly, jobs associated with nurturance (measured by skillset and independently rated by undergraduates) carry a net wage penalty, even after controlling for skill and educational requirements, cognitive demands, and type of occupation (England et al. 1994). Others have reproduced the wage penalties for nurturant and reproductive occupations (England, Budig, and Folbre 2002; Budig and Misra 2010; Duffy 2011; Barron and West 2013), as well as occupations high in emotional labor demands (Glomb, Kammeyer-Mueller, and Rotundo 2004).

Women's lower wages can also be explained by traditional gender roles, particularly women's larger role in household labor. Given that women perform the majority of household responsibilities, including caregiving, they often put in less hours or less effort in their work, contributing to their lower wages. Indeed, Hersch (2009) found that, holding all else equal, increased hours spent on housework were associated with lower wages. To this end, care work faces a wage penalty because it is reflective of work that women are expected to do at home for free.

2.2.1 Association of Care with Women and Mothering

Given that care work is highly feminized and associated with work that women should do for free, it may come as no surprise that care work is viewed as lower in status than other careers. This is reflected in pay gaps between care and noncare occupations (e.g.,

Allegretto and Mishel 2016; ILOSTAT 2015), lower interest in health and education careers compared to science careers, particularly among men (Block, Croft, and Schmader 2018), and lower perceived worth to society (Block, Croft, and Schmader 2018). Some suggest that the lower perceived worth of care work stems from its association with women and motherhood. That is, because women are associated with care, and women are devalued in most societies, care work is also devalued (England 2005). Indeed, most feminist discussions surrounding care suggest that gender is the key explanatory factor for persisting low wages in care work; care is devalued in economic, political, and ethical terms because it is an activity undertaken by women (Fine 2015). To this end, many women undertake the role of caregiver because dependency is central to care, and dependents (i.e., children, the elderly) would be unable to survive or thrive without assistance in meeting their basic needs (Kittay 2013). Unfortunately, naturalizing women's social roles as caregivers can make it seem like they don't need to be compensated for performing care labor (Walker 2007). In taking on the role of caregivers, many women face the consequences associated with care work, namely, low pay.

3. What's a Care Worker to Do?

For those who wish to stay in the care profession or have no choice, what can they do to improve their conditions? One option, when faced with low wages and poor working conditions, is for the workforce to band together and advocate for higher pay (i.e., to participate in labor organizing). Labor organizing occurs when a group of workers collectively bargain with their employers, usually in unions, to improve their working conditions and wages. Although labor organizing is generally associated with strikes—the withholding of work to disrupt the workplace—it can consist of a variety of actions, including petition signing, phone banking, and demonstrations, much like other social movements (Carriere 2020). Organizing has brought workers the five-day work week (Sopher 2018), parental leave (Scholar 2016), higher wages (Robin 2021), and policy changes in the workplace (e.g., child labor and anti-discrimination laws; Schuman 2017; Arnesen 2021).

One component critical to the success of labor organizing is a strong ingroup identity among its workers (Carriere 2020). This poses a challenge for care workers who are employed by private agencies or individual clients because they have no obvious workplace or workplace culture (Stacey 2011). Homecare aides and childcare workers, in particular, are employed by several clients and often have very little contact with other caregivers. Unionizing is also difficult for care workers because they may have little time to participate in union activities or may be unwilling to pay union dues, in part due to their low wages. Care workers may also face structural obstacles to labor organizing resulting from their social positionality as a group with intersecting forms of marginalization (e.g., race, gender, and class; Anderson 2010; Gonalons-Pons 2021). Finally, persisting cynicism about unions remains a challenge for unionization among homecare workers. Promises of higher wages and greater benefits are not enough to convince aides to pursue unionization (Stacey 2011).

State and federal regulations also influence the likelihood that workers may go on strike. Some legislations, including the Public Employees' Fair Employment Act (i.e., the Taylor Law) in New York (New York Public Employment Relations Board 2021), prohibit teachers and other public employees from going on strike.[2] Other regulations that aim to protect workers often exclude care workers. The Fair Labor Standards Act (FLSA), for example, eliminates conditions detrimental to the standard of living necessary for workers, but did not extend coverage to domestic employees until 1974 (Biklen 2003) and direct care workers until 2015 (U.S. Department of Labor 2013). Questions over whether the FLSA protects other care workers remain, particularly under the companionship exemption, which states that workers who provide "fellowship and protection" do not qualify for overtime pay when workers are employed by an individual, family, or household (U.S. Department of Labor 2013). Whether at the state or federal level, legislation today reflects persisting tensions within care work: that there should be a boundary between paid labor and intimate care. In addition to these logistical and legal hurdles, there is a perceived moral hurdle as well.

4. Care Work and Moral Emotions

In addition to these logistical hurdles, care workers sometimes feel guilt when they organize. Specifically, Huget (2020) found that care workers often experience complex moral emotions (e.g., of guilt) when choosing between withstanding intolerable working conditions or abandoning those in their care. For example, in contemplating the possibility of their own strike, one nurse mentioned that she would feel "very uncomfortable being on strike ... [it's] a humiliating experience." Similarly, in response to a strike in California, another nurse claimed that "Nurses do not come into this profession to strike ... We're here because we want to provide safe patient care, but our employer leaves us no choice" (Colliver and Bulwa 2011). Nurses, like other care workers, feel conflicting emotions when contemplating a strike.[3] Third-party observers notice the moral conflict too. In talking about teachers on strike in West Virginia, for instance, one student noted that "a lot of them felt down during the strike, like they were failing us by not being in class." As made clear by both the nurses and students, care workers feel a moral conflict when they make a decision between providing care to their patients (love) or going on strike for higher wages (money).

We also see evidence of moral emotions from some observers of care workers who go on strike. But, rather than guilt, we sometimes see moral outrage: harsh character attributions to those believed to have violated ethical values, often expressed as a combination of anger and disgust (Giner-Sorolla and Chapman 2017). For instance, in response to striking teachers in California, former US Secretary of Education Betsy DeVos condemned teachers by suggesting that they were putting their own interests above those of their students (Balingit 2018). Others condemn healthcare workers who go on strike because it violates an informal agreement: when healthcare workers accept a job offer, they are voluntarily accepting their obligations, which prohibit them from striking in order to protect their patients (Clark 1979; Brecher 1985). Finally, countless examples of op-eds highlight moral outrage against care workers' labor organizing, including "Teachers Unions Bully Cities into Submission" (Washington Examiner 2020) and "Strike Today to Complicate Daycare for Poor" (Kaufman 2004), which highlight outrage against teachers and childcare workers, respectively. The outrage seems specific to the moment when care workers organize, few express outrage over the mere existence of nurses or teachers. It may be that the act of a strike or other demonstration highlights the trade-off between love and money inherent in care work that is usually invisible or ignored in everyday life.

4.1 Understanding Moral Outrage

4.1.1 Sacred Values and Taboo Trade-offs

Every culture has a set of values they hold to be sacred. The sanctity of human life, the need to protect children, and the need to preserve love and care are just some examples of sacred values. Trading those values against secular values (like money) is considered taboo (Tetlock et al. 2000). For instance, sanctioning an economic market for human organs, selling unwanted children to the highest bidder, and selling love, care, and sex are all seen as taboo trade-offs because they put a finite value on things that have moral importance (Schoemaker and Tetlock 2012). Sacred values differ from material values in that they incorporate moral beliefs and are thought to be absolute, inviolable, and are thus protected from trade-offs with other values (Atran and Axelrod 2008).

According to the Sacred Values Protection Model, when observers believe a decision-maker has entertained proscribed thoughts, like a taboo trade-off, they respond with moral outrage (e.g., contempt, anger, and disgust; Tetlock et al. 2000). It is possible that for some, care work can be perceived as a taboo trade-off because it straddles the divide between activities performed out of love and those performed for pay. We suspect that many do not consider the potential taboo trade-off in familiar care professions, like nursing and teaching, but that advocating for increased pay and better working conditions can make this possibility salient—and provide justification for opposing strikes, not meeting care workers' demands, or pressuring care workers not to organize at all.

A second component of the Sacred Values Protection Model predicts that decision makers will feel tainted by contemplating a taboo trade-off and will engage in symbolic acts of moral cleansing. In one study, Tetlock et al. (2000) found that participants judged a hospital administrator worse, and rated him as socially tarnished, after he contemplated a taboo trade-off between life and money. Even when the hospital administrator ultimately chose life over money, participants who read about the taboo trade-off sought moral cleansing by volunteering in a campaign to increase organ donations. In line with this notion, organizers have found that a majority of childcare workers mobilize only if they could advocate on behalf of the children and preserve their sense of being good care providers (MacDonald and Merril 2002). That is, care workers organize when they can maintain their moral selves. In line with the Sacred Values Protection Model, when trade-offs are unavoidable, workers may resort to reframing taboo trade-offs as tragic trade-offs (a trade-off between two sacred values), by suggesting that labor organizing is necessary in order to protect patient care. In doing so, workers are affirming their commitment to care as a sacred value. Accordingly, it is possible then that third parties will also expect care workers who organize either to frame their efforts in terms of better care for patients or to subsequently engage in acts of moral cleansing or both.

4.1.2 Care Is a Sacred Value

Care is central to all that we do. It is no surprise, then, that care has been established as one of the most dominant concerns in moral decision-making. Within moral psychology, care is framed as the inverse of harm (Haidt and Graham 2007). As discussed by Haidt and colleagues, the harm/care foundation evolved from mothers' needs to protect and care for their children. As such, harm/care is triggered by signs of suffering and is characterized by kindness, compassion, and nurturance toward victims of harm (Haidt and Graham 2007). Some researchers argue that harm is the most basic moral concern, and that all other concerns essentially reduce to concerns of harm (Gray, Young, and Waytz 2021; Schein and Gray 2015). In other domains of research, care has been given specific attention. Feminist scholars have emphasized an *ethic of care*, which takes responsibilities, relationships, and dependencies into account in moral reasoning (Gilligan and Attanucci 1988; Noddings 2012). Unsurprisingly, the ethics of care shape care work. Nurses, for example, apply the ethics of care into practice by establishing their moral commitment to make intentional connections with their patients as part of their profession (Lachman 2012).

5. Present Research

In sum, we are expanding the Sacred Values Protection Model to help us understand the dilemma faced by care workers who want to advocate for better working conditions (Huget 2020), and specifically, the outrage that care workers face when they do. While the Sacred Values Protection Mode has been previously used to understand opposition to some forms of care labor (e.g., sex work; Schoemaker and Tetlock 2012), this is the first time that it has been used to understand moral opposition to labor organizing. Accordingly, the primary goals of this research were to examine whether perceptions of love and money in care work were associated with support for teachers' labor organizing and the desire to see teachers "morally cleanse" after contemplating a strike. To do this, we created novel measures of support for labor organizing, fear of commodification, and taboo trade-offs. We predicted that increased perceptions of love and money in care work would be negatively associated with support for care workers' labor organizing. In this study, we focused on teachers' labor organizing because they are historically met with the most (visible) moral outrage when they organize, as indicated by popular media headlines showcasing opposition (e.g., Domanico 2020). Importantly, at the time of data collection, teachers were also preparing to return to in-person teaching during the pandemic and were ramping up their organizing.

6. Methods

To test this, we collected data from forty consenting participants, recruited through Prolific, an online survey platform. Participants ranged in age from 18 to 58 (M_{age} = 29.15, SD_{age} = 10.25, 53 percent Female, 45 percent Male, 63 percent White). All respondents were paid $1.10 for their participation and were debriefed at the end of the study. Post-hoc sensitivity analyses using G*Power confirmed that our sample provided us 92 percent power to detect a significant relationship between fears of commodification and support for labor organizing ($r = -.50$), and 99 percent power to detect a relationship between taboo trade-offs and support for labor organizing ($r = -.70$). All survey materials and code are available on the Open Science Framework.[4]

6.1 Materials

6.1.1 Strike Scenario

Participants read through a strike scenario adapted from a decade-long battle between the United Federation of Teachers and New York City (Brody 2020). In the scenario, as in real-life, teachers were demanding money that they were owed from the city. The strike scenario read,

> In 2014, New York City and its teachers' union struck a deal to secure a $900 million back pay (i.e., payment for work done in the past that was withheld) for its teachers. Now, NYC officials say they can't afford to pay the lump sum owed to its teachers because of the COVID-19 pandemic. The officials claim that the delayed payment will help the city save money during a time of fiscal crisis. The teachers' union says they are owed the money, especially as they are also facing hazardous conditions in the classroom during the pandemic.
>
> The teachers' union **will consider going on strike** in protest over the city's decision to delay the final payment the teachers are owed. The teachers are demanding that the city pay them the lump sum owed before they return to teaching.

6.1.2 Support for Teacher's Organizing

6.1.2.1 Strike Attitudes

We generated three items to measure attitudes toward the teachers' strike: "Is it appropriate for the teachers to consider a strike?"; "Is it reasonable for the teachers to consider a strike?"; "Is it justifiable for the teachers to consider a strike?" (1α = *Not at all* to 7 = *Extremely*). The combined items obtained high reliability, Cronbach's =.85, and were used to create a composite measure of strike attitudes.

6.1.2.2 Support for Labor Organizing

We generated nine items to assess support for teachers' labor organizing. Sample items included, "It's okay for teachers to go on strike in order to get the money they are owed)" and "Teachers should be happy with the wages they currently have" (reverse-scored). Items were rated on a Likert scale (1 = *Strongly disagree* to 7 = *Strongly agree*) and obtained high reliability, Cronbach's $\alpha = 0.87$.

6.1.2.3 Moral Cleansing

We generated five items to measure the desire to see workers morally cleanse (i.e., affirm their commitment to their students) by engaging in more acts of unpaid labor: Whether the teachers go through with the strike or not, they should "volunteer for overtime"; "Work extra shifts, even if it is unpaid"; "Stay late helping students manage stress"; "Put in extra hours taking care of their students, even if it is unpaid"; and "Show they are in their profession for more than just money" (1 = *Strongly disagree* to 7 = *Strongly agree*), $\alpha = 0.81$.[5]

6.1.3 Perceptions of Love and Money

6.1.3.1 Fears of Commodification

We generated three items to measure fears of commodification in care work: "Teachers' wages must stay as they are to make sure that only the most passionate people are teachers"; "Higher pay in teaching could lower the interpersonal elements that make students feel cared for"; and "If teachers' wages go up, there would be an influx of workers who gravitate toward teaching just for the money" (1 = *strongly disagree* to 7 = *strongly agree*), Cronbach's $\alpha = .63$.

6.1.3.2 Taboo Trade-offs

We generated eight items to measure how offensive or permissible participants perceived care work to be, for example, "Paying someone else to raise your child"; "Paying someone else to wash and clothe your sick relative" (1 = *Not at all offensive* to 7 = *Highly offensive*), Cronbach's $\alpha = .58$.[6] The full scale is listed in the Supplementary Material.

6.1.4 Gender Theories

Given the *devaluation hypothesis*, we were also interested in examining whether endorsement of gender norms and their associated roles in society moderated support for labor organizing. We used two measures of beliefs about gender: sex role essentialism and beliefs in social roles. We chose these theories because they capture beliefs that men and women have separate and natural skills because of their sex, which determine how they should act in society.

6.1.4.1 Sex Role Essentialism

Six items from the Modified Sex Role Egalitarianism Scale (Gordon 2016) were used to measure essentialist beliefs because they captured feelings about women as caregivers and beliefs about the types of jobs that women should work in. Sample items include, "Women are naturally inclined to be more caring and nurturing" and "Women are naturally inclined to excel in jobs such as secretary, nurse, and teacher" (1 = Strongly disagree to 7 = Strongly agree), $\alpha = 0.92$.

6.1.4.2 Social Roles

Four items from the Social Roles Questionnaire (Baber and Tucker 2006) were used to measure attitudes about women as workers. Sample items include, "Some types of work are just not appropriate for women" and "Mothers should only work if necessary" (1 = Strongly disagree to 7 = Strongly agree), $\alpha = 0.79$.

6.1.5 Demographics

Finally, participants indicated their gender identity, age, race, political identity, and occupation status (i.e., whether they were care workers).

6.2 Procedure

After informed consent, participants were told that they would be reading about workplace experiences during the Covid-19 pandemic. Participants were then given a scenario regarding a teacher union's threat to strike for back pay (i.e., teachers wanting the money they are owed). Next, participants responded to questions about how appropriate they thought it was for the teachers to consider a strike, how much they supported teachers' organizing, and their desire for teachers' moral cleansing (questions presented in random order). Finally, participants answered questions regarding tensions of mixing love and money in care work (i.e., fears of commodification, taboo trade-offs), beliefs about gender norms, and the demographic questions. Participants were debriefed at the end of the survey.

7. Results

Overall, participants were strong supporters of teachers' labor organizing ($M = 5.54$, $SD = 0.99$) and had positive attitudes toward the teachers' strike ($M = 5.31$, $SD = 1.37$). Below, we examine unique predictors of support for and attitudes toward the teachers' strike.

In line with our hypotheses, fears of commodification, $r = -.48$, 95% CI [−.69, −.20], $t(38) = -3.40$, $p = .002$, and taboo trade-offs, $r = -.61$, 95% CI [−.77, −.36], $t(38) = -4.71$, $p < .001$, were negatively associated with strike attitudes. Similarly, fears of commodification, $r = -.50$, 95% CI [−.70, −.22], $t(38) = -3.55$, $p = .001$, and taboo trade-offs, $r = -.70$, 95% CI [−.83, −.50], $t(38) = -6.06$, $p < .001$, were negatively associated with support for labor organizing. As fears of commodification and perceived taboo trade-offs in care work increased, attitudes toward the teachers' strike and support for labor organizing decreased (see Figure 10.1).

Finally, consistent with the Sacred Values Protection Model, fears of commodification, $r = .35$, 95% CI [.04,.59], $t(38) = 2.29$, $p = .03$, and taboo trade-offs, $r = .46$, 95% CI [.18,.68], $t(38) = 3.23$, $p = .003$, were positively associated with the desire to see teachers morally cleanse (see Figure 10.2). These results were unaffected by participant gender, p's $> .05$, indicating that both men and women are less supportive of teachers' labor organizing when they perceive teaching as trading love for money.

In an exploratory fashion, we were interested in examining whether endorsement of gender norms moderated any of the previous relationships. We did not find that sex role essentialism and beliefs in social roles moderated the relationships between perceptions of love and money and strike attitudes, support for labor organizing, or desire for moral cleansing (all p's $>.05$). When looking at endorsement of gender norms as individual predictors, we found that sex role essentialism, $r = -.58$, 95% CI [−.75, −.32], $t(38) = -4.36$, $p < .001$, and beliefs in social roles, $r = -.53$, 95% CI [−.72, −.26], $t(38) = -3.82$, $p < .001$, were negatively associated with strike attitudes. Similarly, sex role essentialism, $r = -.44$, 95% CI [−.66, −.15], $t(38) = -3.04$, $p = .004$, and beliefs in social roles, $r = -.58$, 95% CI [−.75, −.33], $t(38) = -4.37$, $p < .001$, were negatively associated with support for labor organizing. Beliefs about gender norms did not influence the desire to see teachers morally cleanse, (all p's $>.05$). In sum,

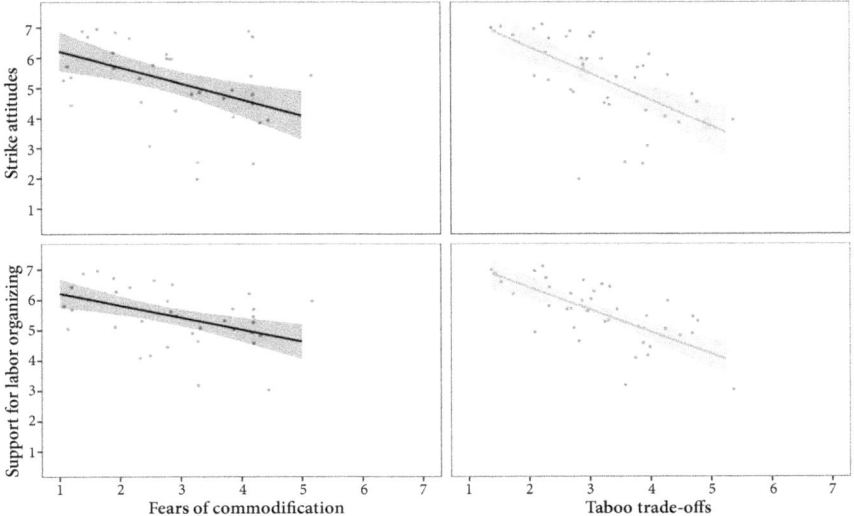

Figure 10.1 Scatter plot and fitted regression lines depicting increases in fears of commodification and taboo trade-offs are negatively associated with strike attitudes (top panel) and support for labor organizing (bottom panel). © Grace Flores-Robles and Ana P. Gantman.

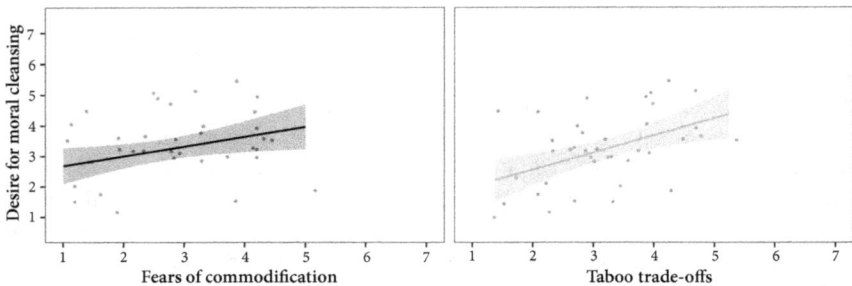

Figure 10.2 Scatter plot and fitted regression lines depicting increases in fears of commodification and taboo trade-offs are positively associated with desire for moral cleansing. © Grace Flores-Robles and Ana P. Gantman.

both attitudes about tensions between love and money in care work and attitudes and gendered roles in society, each separately explain variation in support for teachers' labor organizing, providing some support for all three theories to reviewed above, *fears of commodification, the devaluation hypothesis,* and the *Sacred Values Protection Model*.

8. Discussion

In the present research, we found evidence that perceptions of a trade-off between love and money in care work were negatively associated with attitudes toward teachers merely contemplating a strike and support for teachers' labor organizing—and the desire to see teachers who contemplate a strike engage in moral cleansing. These results remained even when we accounted for beliefs about women as caregivers (i.e., sex role essentialism, beliefs in social roles) and participant gender. Altogether, our research provides preliminary evidence that perceptions of love and money in care work are associated with opposition to care workers' labor organizing and are distinct from beliefs about women as caregivers.

We also found that sex role essentialism and beliefs in social roles negatively predict support for teachers' organizing. Importantly, both of these theories are used to enforce women's roles as mothers and caregivers. And, as we know from the *devaluation hypothesis*, the association of care work with mothering reinforces the idea that care labor should be performed without pay. Organizing for higher wages violates this belief. Critically, organizing for better working conditions is also *agentic*, which women are stereotyped not to be (Heilman and Caleo 2018). For those who strongly endorse essentialist beliefs about sex and the roles that people of different sexes are meant to take on in society, the agentic act of organizing may go against the roles that females are meant to inhabit, and may therefore penalize women who advocate for higher pay, including care workers. It could be the case that care workers who negotiate for higher compensation face social consequences because negotiations are associated with the masculine stereotype of the breadwinning man and contradicts the normative expectation of women as caregivers (e.g., Eagly 1987; Bowles, Riley, and Lai 2007).

8.1 Implications

These novel findings contribute to a growing literature in sociology, philosophy, and feminist economics by bringing together theories on care from different fields (e.g., Gilligan 1993; Kittay 1995). To this end, this research is the first to relate the belief that care cannot be commodified with opposition to labor organizing. Importantly, this research does not argue that care *shouldn't* be commodified. Rather, we propose, like many feminists before us, that thinking about the commodification of care—either as a payment for services with a price set by market mechanisms or as a subsidy that makes care work possible (Kittay 2013)—is important for preventing exploitation.

We have also generated measures for different perceptions regarding support for care workers' labor organizing and connected this to beliefs about gender essentialism. Historically, conversations about gender essentialism and labor organizing have not intersected, especially within philosophy. But, as we show, there is a relationship between the two spheres. In order to improve the working conditions of care workers (and other workers whose professions are tied to essentialized identities), we must consider how features of identity that are seen as defining of the person, immutable, and nonoptional for holding that identity, can make advocating for change uniquely difficult.

Although we provide evidence for this relationship, many feminists have already noted this in their writing about care. For instance, one feminist scholar claimed that there is a fine line between naturalizing women's social identities as caregivers and exploiting them (Walker 2007). To prevent exploitation, public policies must therefore recognize that many people have social identities that make care and work interconnected and focus on balancing the responsibilities of the two (Robinson 2006). Scholars can also work to distinguish between natural and ethical caring, because the former suggests that people do not need to be paid to provide care.

Finally, this research is the first to apply the *Sacred Values Protection Model* to labor organizing by proposing that care workers face moral outrage when they organize because they highlight the trade-off between love and money inherent in their work. This trade-off poses a non-negotiable conflict for care workers, in that it becomes impossible to satisfy their desire to maintain care as a sacred value while also successfully seeking higher wages (Tessman 2014).

In summary, our research has implications for the way that scholars talk about care work. Commodification, though it is seemingly in conflict with ideas about essentialism and the sacred value of care, is actually one mechanism through which care workers can be protected.

8.2 Limitations and Future Directions

Our research had several limitations. First, the study does not include a representative sample, from which we can accurately generalize our conclusions. Most of the participants in our study were White (63 percent) and from middle to upper-middle class backgrounds (65 percent). It is likely that our participants did not reflect the attitudes that most Americans feel toward care workers because care work tends to be lower in status. Future research should explore opposition to care workers' labor organizing among a sample that is racially and economically diverse. Relatedly, care occupations are also segregated by race and may lead participants to reference the racial stereotypes of caregivers. For example, immigrants, Latinas, and Black women are overrepresented as childcare workers and homecare aides (relative to their proportion of the US population), while most nurses (73 percent) and teachers (79 percent) are White women (U.S. Department of Health and Human Services 2019; U.S. Department of Education 2020). Future research can explore the role of race in support for care workers labor organizing.

Second, our distribution of support for labor organizing was negatively skewed. Although there was some variability in support among our participants, most were in favor of teachers' labor organizing, despite evidence that opposition exists in the real world (Balingit 2018; Darby 2018). One reason we may not be getting the full range of opposition is because it may be driven, in part, by political ideology. Moral outrage against teachers' labor organizing tends to come from conservative voices, as evidenced by popular media outlets (e.g., Markowicz 2021). Indeed, exploratory analyses show that conservatism is negatively associated with strike attitudes, $r = -0.58, p < .001, 95\%$ CI $[-0.76, -0.33]$, support for labor organizing, $r = -0.74, p < .001, 95\%$ CI $[-0.85, -0.56]$, and positively associated with the desire to see teachers morally cleanse, $r = 0.38, p = .02, 95\%$ CI $[0.08, 0.62]$. This suggests that political ideology may drive opposition. Much more research is needed in order to understand the factors that drive support for labor organizing. Further research should expand to other more indirect measures of support for labor-organizing efforts to minimize potential confounds with political ideology.

Third, our taboo trade-offs scale had low reliability among its items. One reason this may have occurred is because this is the first time the Sacred Values Protection Model (Tetlock et al. 2000) has been applied to labor organizing, and adapting the scale into another domain can reduce its reliability. Taboo trade-offs in care work also have large variability. For example, some might find it offensive to pay another person to *breastfeed* their child but not offensive to *take care* of their child. Future research should expand the number of items and increase the ways taboo trade-offs are measured within care work. Further research should hone this measure.

Finally, our work is limited by a lack of discriminant validity. Although we were able to establish that tensions between love and money predict opposition to care workers' labor organizing, we were unable to establish that the phenomenon exists in care work alone, because we did not compare support for teachers' labor organizing to organizing in other occupations. It is possible that fears of commodification and perceived taboo trade-offs are associated with opposition to labor organizing in *any* occupation. Future research should compare support for labor organizing between care workers and those in other occupations, including truckers and auto workers, which have a deep history of collective action in the United States (International Brotherhood of Teamsters, n.d.; United Auto Workers, n.d.).

8.3 Making Care Count

As demonstrated in sociology and feminist economics, there is a care shortage in the United States (Espinoza 2017; García and Weiss 2019; Haddad, Annamaraju, and Toney-Butler 2021). Nurses, teachers, and homecare aides face high turnover rates and an inability to fill their vacancies due to low wages and difficult working conditions, especially during the pandemic. One of the primary reasons for the undervaluation of care work, as we have established throughout this chapter, is the struggle to give a monetary value to care. So, how can we make care count?

Perhaps the most important way that scholars can increase public recognition of care work, including support for labor organizing, is by building a vocabulary that adequately captures the whole of care work—the interpersonal relationships, skilled interventions, and technical expertise involved in the work. Essentially, this involves shifting the conversation from thinking about care work as pitting love *versus* money to thinking about care work as being at the intersection of love *and* money. Scholars can do this in two ways. First, and in line with some of the strategies care workers use to advocate for higher wages, care workers can frame their work using a vocabulary of skill (i.e., highlighting technical skills) and virtue (i.e., highlighting the relational components of care work) to highlight the complexity of care work (MacDonald and Merrill 2002). Second, in line with the Sacred Values Protection Model, care workers can reframe labor organizing as necessary in order to protect patient care. By reframing the taboo trade-off in care work as unavoidable (e.g., a tragic trade-off), care workers may reduce moral outrage toward their organizing. Regardless of the strategy chosen to increase support for care workers' labor organizing, changing the vocabulary used to talk about the skills involved in care work can help increase the efficacy of care workers' labor organizing.

9. Conclusion

In this chapter, we demonstrate that opposition to care workers' labor organizing can be partly explained by how much people view engaging in care work as trading love for money. Specifically, we found evidence that care work may be perceived as a taboo trade-off because it blurs the divide between activities performed out of love and those performed for pay, and this tension becomes salient during strikes. Understanding the unique challenges that care workers face when organizing is a critical first step in increasing public support for care workers' labor organizing.

Notes

1 Some countries are exceptions. For example, both men and women in Sweden earn bonuses for engaging in care work, and women earn bonuses for engaging in care work in Germany and the Netherlands (Budig and Misra 2010).

2   The Taylor Law allows for unionization in the workplace and collective bargaining with employers but prohibits strike action. Similar laws prohibit teacher strikes in other states. In fact, teacher strikes are only legal in thirteen states as of 2019 (Nittler 2019). This, of course, does not mean that teachers will always adhere to those laws.
3   This is sometimes referred to as the prisoner of love argument, because care workers' attachment to their recipients makes it difficult to withhold services for higher pay (England and Folbre 2003).
4   Link to supplemental materials and code: https://osf.io/gzcfa/?view_only=48629aea1 3244b1687b17735e9b47981.
5   For similar reasoning about the relationship between passion in work and exploitation, see Kim et al. (2020).
6   Deleting one item did not drastically improve the reliability of the scale (=.58 compared to a =.61 with item removed), so we included the full range of items.

References

Anderson, Bridget. 2010. "Mobilizing Migrants, Making Citizens: Migrant Domestic Workers as Political Agents." *Ethnic and Racial Studies* 33, no. 1: 60–74.

Anderson, Elizabeth. 1995. *Value in Ethics and Economics*. Cambridge: Harvard University Press.

Allegretto, Sylvia A., and Lawrence Mishel. 2016. "The Teacher Pay Gap Is Wider than Ever: Teachers' Pay Continues to Fall Further Behind Pay of Comparable Workers." *Economic Policy Institute*.

Arnesen, Eric. 2021. "Civil Rights and the Labor Movement: A Historical Overview." February 24, 2021. https://teamster.org/2021/02/civil-rights-and-the-labor-movement-a-historical-overview/.

Association of American Medical Colleges. 2021. "The Complexities of Physician Supply and Demand: Projections From 2019 to 2034." https://www.aamc.org/media/54681/download.

Atran, Scott, and Robert Axelrod. 2008. "Reframing Sacred Values." *Negotiation Journal* 24, no. 3: 221–46.

Baber, Kristine M., and Corinna Jenkins Tucker. 2006. "The Social Roles Questionnaire: A New Approach to Measuring Attitudes Toward Gender." *Sex Roles* 54, no. 7: 459–67.

Balingit, Moriah. 2018. "Betsy DeVos to Oklahoma Teachers: 'Serve the Students.'" *Washington Post*. https://www.washingtonpost.com/news/education/wp/2018/04/09/betsy-devos-to-oklahoma-teachers-serve-the-students/.

Barron, David N., and Elizabeth West. 2013. "The Financial Costs of Caring in the British Labour Market: Is There a Wage Penalty for Workers in Caring Occupations?" *British Journal of Industrial Relations* 51, no. 1: 104–23.

Biklen, Molly. 2003. "Healthcare in the Home: Reexamining the Companionship Services Exemption to the Fair Labor Standards Act." *Colum. Hum. Rts. L. Rev.* 35: 113.

Blau, Francine D., and Anne E. Winkler. 2017. *Women, Work, and Family*. No. w23644. National Bureau of Economic Research.

Block, Katharina, Alyssa Croft, and Toni Schmader. 2018. "Worth Less?: Why Men (and Women) Devalue Care-oriented Careers." *Frontiers in Psychology*, 1353.

Boulding, Kenneth E. 1969. "Economics as a Moral Science." *The American Economic Review* 59, no. 1: 1–12.

Bowles, Hannah Riley, Linda Babcock, and Lei Lai. 2007. "Social Incentives for Gender Differences in the Propensity to Initiate Negotiations: Sometimes It Does Hurt to Ask." *Organizational Behavior and human decision Processes* 103, no. 1: 84–103.

Brecher, Robert. 1985. "Striking Responsibilities." *Journal of Medical Ethics* 11, no. 2: 66–9.

Brody, Leslie. 2020. "New York City Teachers Union Sets Plan for Strike-Authorization Vote." *Wall Street Journal (Eastern Ed.)* 31 August 2020. https://www.wsj.com/articles/new-york-city-teachers-union-head-pushes-coronavirus-testing-to-avert-strike-11598907300.

Budig, Michelle J., and Joya Misra. 2010. "How Care-Work Employment Shapes Earnings in Cross-National Perspective." *International Labour Review* 149, no. 4: 441–60.

Carriere, Kevin R. 2020. "Workers' Rights are Human Rights: Organizing the Psychology of Labor Movements." *Current Opinion in Psychology* 35: 60–4.

Carvalho, Luis Francisco, and Joao Rodrigues. 2008. "Are Markets Everywhere? Understanding Contemporary Processes of Commodification." In *The Elgar Companion to Social Economics, Second Edition*, edited by JB Davies and W. Dolfsma, 267–86. Northampton: Edward Elgar Publishing.

Clark, J. 1979. "The Right to Strike." *Nursing mirror* 149, no. 8: 20–1.

Claassen, Rutger. 2011. "The Commodification of Care." *Hypatia* 26, no. 1: 43–64.

Colliver, Victoria, and Demian Bulwa. 2011. "Striking Nurses Due to Return After Patient Death." *SF Gate*. Last modified September 27, 2011. https://www.sfgate.com/news/article/Striking-nurses-due-to-return-after-patient-death-2308060.php.

Covert, Bryce. 2020. "America Never Valued Care Workers. Then a Pandemic Hit." *The Nation*. Last modified June 1, 2020. https://www.thenation.com/article/society/coronavirus-child-care-nurses-essential/.

Darby, Luke. 2018. "Betsy DeVos, Matt Bevin, and the Smarmy Attack on Teachers." *GQ*, April 17, 2018. https://www.gq.com/story/betsy-devos-matt-bevin-teacher-strikes.

Deci, Edward L., Richard Koestner, and Richard M. Ryan. 1999. "A Meta-analytic Review of Experiments Examining the Effects of Extrinsic Rewards on Intrinsic Motivation." *Psychological Bulletin* 125, no. 6: 627.

Degarmo, Charges. 1892. "Annals of the American Academy of Political and Social Science. March, 1892. Ethical Training in the Public Schools." *The ANNALS of the American Academy of Political and Social Science* 2, no. 5: 1–23.

Domanico, Ray. 2020. "By Bending to Teachers Union, de Blasio Repeatedly Fails NY Schoolchildren." *New York Post*, December 8, 2020. https://nypost.com/2020/12/07/by-bending-to-teachers-union-de-blasio-repeatedly-fails-ny-schoolchildren/.

Duffy, Mignon. 2007. "Doing the Dirty Work: Gender, Race, and Reproductive Labor in Historical Perspective." *Gender & Society* 21, no. 3: 313–36.

Duffy, Mignon. 2011. *Making Care Count*. New Brunswick: Rutgers University Press.

Eagly, Alice H., and Mary E. Kite. 1987. "Are Stereotypes of Nationalities Applied to Both Women and Men?" *Journal of Personality and Social Psychology* 53, no. 3: 451.

England, Paula. 2005. "Emerging Theories of Care Work." *Annu. Rev. Sociol.* 31: 381–99.

England, Paula, Michelle Budig, and Nancy Folbre. 2002. "Wages of Virtue: The Relative Pay of Care Work." *Social Problems* 49, no. 4: 455–73.

England, Paula, and Nancy Folbre. 2003. "Contracting for Care." *Feminist Economics Today: Beyond Economic Man*, 61–79.

England, Paula, Melissa S. Herbert, Barbara Stanek Kilbourne, Lori L. Reid, and Lori McCreary Megdal. 1994. "The Gendered Valuation of Occupations and Skills: Earnings in 1980 Census Occupations." *Social Forces* 73, no. 1: 65–100.

Espinoza, Robert. 2017. "The Changing Policy Landscape of the Direct Care Workforce." *Public Policy & Aging Report* 27, no. 3: 101–5.

Famakinwa, Joyce. 2021. "Report Sheds New Light on Looming Caregiving Crisis." *Home Health Care News*, July 7, 2021. https://homehealthcarenews.com/2021/07/report-sheds-new-light-on-looming-caregiving-crisis/.

Fine, Michael. 2015. "Eva Feder Kittay: Dependency Work and the Social Division of Care." *The Palgrave Handbook of Social Theory in Health, Illness and Medicine*, 628–43.

Frey, Bruno S. 1997. "Not Just for the Money."

García, Emma, and Elaine Weiss. 2019. "The Teacher Shortage Is Real, Large and Growing, and Worse than We Thought. The First Report in 'The Perfect Storm in the Teacher Labor Market' Series." *Economic Policy Institute*.

Gilligan, Carol. 1993. *In a Different Voice: Psychological Theory and Women's Development*. Cambridge: Harvard University Press.

Gilligan, Carol, and Jane Attanucci. 1988. "Two Moral Orientations: Gender Differences and Similarities." *Merrill-Palmer Quarterly (1982-)*: 223–237.

Giner-Sorolla, Roger, and Hanah A. Chapman. 2017. "Beyond Purity: Moral Disgust Toward BadCharacter." *Psychological Science* 28, no. 1: 80–91.

Glomb, Theresa M., John D. Kammeyer-Mueller, and Maria Rotundo. 2004. "Emotional Labor Demands and Compensating Wage Differentials." *Journal of Applied Psychology* 89, no. 4: 700.

Gonalons-Pons, Pilar. 2021. "Servants of Production: The Politics of Domestic Workers' Labor Rights." *Social Politics: International Studies in Gender, State & Society*.

Gordon, Alynn Elizabeth. 2016. "Egalitarian Essentialism: Practical, Theoretical, and Measurement Issues." PhD diss., Kent State University.

Gray, Kurt, Adam Waytz, and Liane Young. 2021. "The Moral Dyad: A Fundamental Template Unifying Moral Judgment." *Psychological Inquiry* 23, no. 2: 206–15.

Haddad, Lisa M., Pavan Annamaraju, and Tammy J. Toney-Butler. 2021. "Nursing Shortage." *StatPearls [Internet]*. Last modified December 15, 2021. https://www.ncbi.nlm.nih.gov/books/NBK493175/#_NBK493175_pubdet_.

Haidt, Jonathan, and Jesse Graham. 2007. "When Morality Opposes Justice: Conservatives have Moral Intuitions that Liberals May Not Recognize." *Social Justice Research* 20, no. 1: 98–116.

Haspel, Elliot. 2021. "There's a Massive Child-Care Worker Shortage and the Market Can't Fix It." *The Washington Post*. May 27, 2021. https://www.childrensmovementflorida.org/theres-a-massive-child-care-worker-shortage-and-the-market-cant-fix-it/.

Heilman, Madeline E., and Suzette Caleo. 2018. "Gender Discrimination in the Workplace." *The Oxford Handbook of Workplace Discrimination*. https://doi.org/10.1093/oxfordhb/9780199363643.013.7.

Held, Virginia. 2002. "Care and the Extension of Markets." *Hypatia* 17, no. 2: 19–33.

Hersch, Joni. 2009. "Home Production and Wages: Evidence from the American Time Use Survey." *Review of Economics of the Household* 7, no. 2: 159–78.

Himmelweit, Susan. 1999. "Caring Labor." *The Annals of the American Academy of Political and Social Science* 561, no. 1: 27–38.

Huget, Hailey. 2020. "Care Workers on Strike." *Feminist Philosophy Quarterly* 6, no. 1: 1–28.

International Brotherhood of Teamsters. 2020. "Teamster History". International Brotherhood of Teamsters, January 14, 2020. https://teamster.org/about/teamster-history/.

ILO. 2018. *Care Work and Care Jobs for the Future of Decent Work*. Geneva: ILO.

ILOSTAT. 2015. *Key Indicators of the Labor Market*. http://www.ilo.org/ilostat/.
Kaufman, L. 2004. "Strike Today to Complicate Day Care for Poor." *New York Times*. https://www.nytimes.com/2004/06/09/nyregion/strike-today-to-complicate-day-care-for-poor.html.
Kim, Jae Yun, Troy H. Campbell, Steven Shepherd, and Aaron C. Kay. 2020. "Understanding Contemporary Forms of Exploitation: Attributions of Passion Serve to Legitimize the Poor Treatment of Workers." *Journal of Personality and Social Psychology* 118, no. 1: 121.
Kinder, Molly. 2020. "Essential but Undervalued: Millions of Health Care Workers Aren't Getting the Pay or Respect They Deserve in the COVID-19 Pandemic." Brookings, May 28, 2020. https://www.brookings.edu/research/essential-but-undervalued-millions-of-health-care-workers-arent-getting-the-pay-or-respect-they-deserve-in-the-covid-19-pandemic/.
Kittay, Eva Feder. 1995. "Taking Dependency Seriously: The Family and Medical Leave Act Considered in Light of the Social Organization of Dependency Work and Gender Equality." *Hypatia* 10, no. 1: 8–29.
Kittay, Eva Feder. 2012. *Love's Labor: Essays on Women, Equality and Dependency*. Abingdon: Routledge.
Kittay, Eva Feder. 2013. *Love's Labor: Essays on Women, Equality and Dependency*. Abingdon: Routledge.
Lachman, Vicki D. 2012."Applying the Ethics of Care to Your Nursing Practice." *Medsurg Nursing* 21, no. 2: 112–6.
Macdonald, Cameron Lynne, and David A. Merrill. 2002. "'It Shouldn't Have to Be a Trade': Recognition and Redistribution in Care Work Advocacy." *Hypatia* 17, no. 2: 67–83.
Markowicz, Karol. 2021. "Masking Kids and Closing Schools Is Irrational, Unscientific Child Abuse." *New York Post*. August 2, 2021. https://nypost.com/2021/08/01/masking-kids-and-closing-schools-is-irrational-child-abuse/.
McCloskey, Deirdre. 1996. "Love and Money: A Comment on the Markets Debate." *Feminist Economics* 2, no. 2: 137–40.
Nelson, Julie A., and Paula England. 2002. "Feminist Philosophies of Love and Work." *Hypatia* 17, no. 2: 1–18.
NYS Public Employment Relations Board (PERB). 2021. "The Taylor Law." June 21, 2021. https://perb.ny.gov/taylor-law/.
Nittler, Kency. 2019. "Collective Bargaining and Teacher Strikes." National Council on Teacher Quality (NCTQ). March 28, 2019. https://www.nctq.org/blog/Collective-bargaining-and-teacher-strikes.
Noddings, Nel. 2012. "The Language of Care Ethics." *Knowledge Quest* 40, no. 5: 52.
Pateman, Carole. 1988. "The Patriarchal Welfare State." *The Welfare State Reader* 2: 134–50.
Robin, Josh. 2021. "How We Got Here: A History of Minimum Wage Laws in America." *Spectrum News*. April 15, 2021. https://spectrumlocalnews.com/nc/charlotte/national-politics/2021/04/14/how-we-got-here--a-history-of-minimum-wage-laws-in-america-.
Robinson, Fiona. 2006. "Beyond Labour Rights: The Ethics of Care and Women's Work in the Global Economy." *International Feminist Journal of Politics* 8, no. 3: 321–42.
Romero, Laura, and Jay Bhatt. 2021. "Pandemic has Made Shortage of Health Care Workers Even Worse, Say Experts." *ABC News*. May 21, 2021. https://abcnews.go.com/US/pandemic-made-shortage-health-care-workers-worse-experts/story?id=77811713.
Sandel, Michael. 1998. "What Money Can't Buy: The Moral Limits of Markets." Delivered at Brasenose College, Oxford, May 11–12, 1998.

Satz, Debra. 2010. *Why Some Things Should Not Be for Sale: The Moral Limits of Markets.* Oxford: Oxford University Press.

Schein, Chelsea, and Kurt Gray. 2015. "The Unifying Moral Dyad: Liberals and Conservatives Share the Same Harm-Based Moral Template." *Personality and Social Psychology Bulletin* 41, no. 8: 1147–63.

Schoemaker, Paul J. H., and Philip E. Tetlock. 2012. "Taboo Scenarios: How to Think About the Unthinkable." *California management review* 54, no. 2: 5–24.

Scholar, Megan. 2016. *Getting Paid While Taking Time: The Women's Movement and the Development of Paid Family Leave Policies in the United States.* Philadelphia: Temple University Press.

Schuman, Michael. 2017. "History of Child Labor in the United States—Part 2: The Reform Movement." *Monthly Labor Review.* https://www.bls.gov/opub/mlr/2017/article/history-of-child-labor-in-the-united-states-part-2-the-reform-movement.htm.

Sholar, Megan. 2016. *Getting Paid While Taking Time: The Women's Movement and the Development of Paid Family Leave Policies in the United States.* Philadelphia: Temple University Press.

Smith, Kristin, and Reagan A. Baughman. 2007. "Low Wages Prevalent in Direct Care and Child Care Workforce."

Sopher, Philip. 2018. "Where the Five-Day Workweek Came From." *The Atlantic.* April 30, 2018. https://www.theatlantic.com/business/archive/2014/08/where-the-five-day-workweek-came-from/378870/.

Stacey, Clare L. 2011. *The Caring Self.* Ithaca: Cornell University Press.

Tessman, Lisa. 2014. *Moral Failure: On the Impossible Demands of Morality.* Oxford: Oxford University Press.

Tetlock, Philip E., Orie V. Kristel, S. Beth Elson, Melanie C. Green, and Jennifer S. Lerner. 2000. "The Psychology of the Unthinkable: Taboo Trade-offs, Forbidden Base Rates, and Heretical Counterfactuals." *Journal of Personality and Social Psychology* 78, no. 5: 853.

United Auto Workers. n.d. *UAW Through the Decades.* https://uaw.org/members/uaw-through-the-decades/.

U. S. Department of Education, Institute of Education Sciences, National Center for Education Statistics. 2020. *Race and Ethnicity of Public School Teachers and Their Students.* https://nces.ed.gov/pubs2020/2020103.pdf.

U.S. Department of Health and Human Services, Health Resources and Services Administration, National Center for Health Workforce Analysis. 2019. *Brief Summary Results from the 2018 National Sample Survey of Registered Nurses.* https://bhw.hrsa.gov/sites/default/files/bureau-health-workforce/data-research/nssrn-summary-report.pdf.

U.S. Department of Labor, Wage and Hour Division. 2013. *Fact Sheet: Application of the Fair Labor Standards Act to Domestic Service, Final Rule.* September 2013. https://www.dol.gov/sites/dolgov/files/WHD/legacy/files/whdfsFinalRule.pdf.

Walker, Margaret Urban. 2007. *Moral Understandings: A Feminist Study in Ethics.* Oxford: Oxford University Press.

Washington Examiner. 2020. "Teachers Unions Bully Cities into Submission." *The Washington Examiner.* September 7, 2020. https://www.washingtonexaminer.com/opinion/teachers-unions-bully-cities-into-submission.

Zelizer, Viviana. 2002. "Kids and Commerce." *Childhood* 9, no. 4: 375–96.

11

Experimental Political Philosophy: A Manifesto

John Thrasher

Ye shall know them by their fruits.

—Matthew 7:16

Superfluous branches
We lop away, that bearing boughs may live.

—Shakespeare, *Richard II* Act III, Scene 4

The adoption of formal and empirical tools has become commonplace in mainstream philosophy. The analytic revolution at the beginning of the last century was born largely out of advances in formal logic, which exposed and clarified a new set of philosophical problems. As philosophical questions increasingly overlapped with questions in cognitive science and linguistics, tools from those disciplines also became more common in philosophy. Many of the early innovators in decision theory and game theory were also philosophers (e.g., John Harsanyi, Richard Jeffrey, David Lewis) and those tools were quickly seen as important in philosophical investigation. Perhaps surprisingly, though, the empirical methods of the social and natural sciences, especially their most powerful method—randomized experiments—were slow to be adopted, only becoming widespread in the early part of the twenty-first century. It is too soon to say that experimental philosophy has transitioned from a topic to a commonly accepted tool, but it is certainly more common deployed and accepted as legitimate than it was twenty years ago.[1]

The use of formal methods from economics and political science (e.g., game theory and social choice theory) in political philosophy is now common, as are the core concepts of modern economic theory. Political philosophers, however, have been slow to embrace the core empirical methods of these disciplines, specifically experiments. Experimental philosophers have tended to ignore core questions in political philosophy as well. In the rest of this chapter, I will argue that there are good reasons for political philosophers to use experiments and to integrate experimental and empirical methods into their core training. My argument rests on two controversial claims that I aim to defend. First, that political philosophy is and ought to be a concerned with real political and social issues and, hence, will be thoroughly embedded with empirical claims. This means that neither can political philosophers be ignorant of the empirical methods and tools used to adjudicate these claims nor can they merely outsource their use to specialists. Second, because of this, political philosophers should embrace an integrative PPE (Philosophy, Politics, and Economics)-based approach to political philosophy generally and to the use of empirical methods specifically.

1. Empirical Political Philosophy

Experimental philosophy arose when philosophers started adopting tools and techniques from social psychology and cognitive science for use in their philosophical work. Initially, questions in epistemology and the philosophy of mind were at the center of the experimental philosophy. It was not long until moral theory and ethics also received the experimental treatment. In one sense, the application of experimental methods to ethics was merely a continuation of a case-based method already common in the literature. The most obvious example here is the ubiquitous "trolley problem," initially developed by Phillipa Foot (1967) and extended by Judith Jarvis Thomson (1976; 1985) and Frances Kamm (2006). Philosophers used this case and its variations as a "thought-experiment" to isolate elements of the case and test whether those or some other features were decisive in generating moral judgments. It was only natural that philosophically inclined cognitive scientists and moral psychologists such as Josh Greene (2004; 2008), Jonathan Haidt (2001), Fiery Cushman (2008; 2009), Josh Knobe (2008), Shaun Nichols (2002a; 2002b; 2004), and many others would find rich soil to work at the intersection of cognitive science and moral theory.

Experimental philosophy now has a foothold in most areas of philosophy, but there is still some dispute as to what the experimental program in philosophy amounts to. In the most general sense, experimental philosophy is just the use of experimental methods as a tool to answer philosophical questions. This raises the question, though, of what the "experimental method" is. After all, Hume (1739) claimed in the eighteenth century that his *Treatise* was "an attempt to introduce the experimental method of reasoning into moral subjects." He extends this point in the first *Enquiry*:

> When we run over libraries, persuaded of these principles, what havoc must we make? If we take in our hand any volume; of divinity or school metaphysics, for instance; let us ask, *Does it contain any abstract reasoning concerning quantity or number?* No. *Does it contain any experimental reasoning concerning matter of fact and existence?* No. Commit it then to the flames: For it can contain nothing but sophistry and illusion.
>
> (Hume 1748, sec. 12.34, SBN 165)

By "experimental reasoning," Hume seems to have meant something like empirical hypothesis testing in the context of philosophical problems. Philosophical questions, at root, make claims that either bear on or draw on matters of facts and existence or questions of relation and structure. On this view, there is no distinctive philosophical method or domain of inquiry. Rather, philosophy is characterized by the abstraction and generality of the questions it asks, as well as by the rigorous standards of justification that it employs. In philosophy, all claims must meet the bar of public, rational justification. As Wilfrid Sellars famously put this point:

> The aim of philosophy, abstractly formulated, is to understand how things in the broadest possible sense of the term hang together in the broadest possible sense of the term. Under "things in the broadest possible sense" I include such radically different items as not only "cabbages and kings", but numbers and duties, possibilities and finger snaps, aesthetic experience and death. To achieve success in philosophy would be, to use a contemporary turn of phrase, to "know one's way around" with respect to all these things, not in that unreflective way in which the centipede of the story knew its way around before it faced the question, "how do I walk?", but in that reflective way which means that no intellectual holds are barred.
> (Sellars 1963, 1)

In philosophy, "no intellectual holds are barred" in the sense that philosophy does not restrict the types of questions or calls for justification that can be levied against any claim.

Political philosophy, understood in this way, is the inquiry into fundamental normative and explanatory questions related to political and social life. This can include investigations into political concepts like "justice" or "freedom" as well as questions about the nature of a good or just society. Plato's *Republic* is, at least on its most obvious reading, a prolonged investigation into the nature of justice and how a just society related to justice as an individual virtue. Isiah Berlin's "Two Concepts of Liberty" and the literature it spawned are examples of a political conceptual investigation into freedom.[2] Few political philosophical questions are purely conceptual, though, and those that are concerned with concepts that are deeply embedded in practical, empirical contexts. It wouldn't be possible, and no serious political philosopher has tried, to think about what justice or freedom amounts to without thinking carefully about real political institutions and facts about social life.

It should be no surprise that all major political philosophers pursued their philosophical questions while taking empirical enquiry very seriously. This is most obvious in the early modern social contract theorists, but also stands out in the classical utilitarians and in the work of contemporary theorists, such as John Rawls, David Gauthier, Brian Barry, Robert Goodin, Philip Pettit, Gerald Gaus, Amartya Sen, David Schmidtz, and so on. All these thinkers are/were deeply concerned with understanding actual human nature, sociality, and reasoning. They all rely on empirical claims as both evidence and starting points for their normative and theoretical enquiry.

Not all political philosophers see their work as relating directly to or being grounded in empirical claims, though. The most striking case is probably Gerald Cohen (2003), who argued that many, if not most, principles related to political philosophy are independent of the facts. His argument is somewhat convoluted and it is hard to assess exactly what the implication of his view is (especially given the distinction he introduces between "principles" and "rules of regulation"), but this argument combined with his similar arguments against constructivism (2008) amount to a rejection of the claim that political philosophy is inherently practically focused and embedded in the empirical. David Estlund (2008, 264) has gone further, endorsing "hopeless" political theory that may have "no practical value." His approach is also distinctive in that it, in a rejection of one of the core traditions in political philosophy, rejects the importance of understanding human nature, psychology, and rationality for political theory (Estlund 2011; 2019). David Enoch (2011; 2013), along similar lines, has argued that political philosophy is downstream from moral philosophy, which is itself factual, but in some sort of nonempirical way (Enoch 2011, 102). This argument relies on a curious version of an indispensability argument in favor of moral facts, which combined with some creative claims about metaphysics, results in a defense of moral facts as non-natural but still, in some otherwise mysterious sense, real and objective. These moral facts serve as the basis of normative political principles (Enoch 2013).

Regardless of the specifics, the main objection to empirical political philosophy relies on seeing political philosophy as a branch of what amounts to applied moral philosophy. Moral philosophy, on this view, is independent of empirical concerns, making its application similarly independent. There is much to say in response to this general approach to political philosophy and much has been said recently in the context of what is often called the "ideal theory" debate (Stemplowska 2008; Sen 2009; Simmons 2010; Schmidtz 2011; Valentini 2012; Wiens 2012; Gaus 2016), so it is not my intention to address this question directly here. In any case, the mainstream of political philosophers from Plato and Aristotle to Hobbes and Rawls have all concerned themselves with empirical reality in their theories to a greater or lesser degree. In that sense, political philosophy is more obviously at home in a thoroughly empirical worldview than some other parts of philosophy. If this is right, then political philosophers should make sure they are familiar with the main empirical tools useful for investigating the social and political realm.

In the next two sections, I argue that there are two general approaches to experimental political philosophy, what I will call the "experimental philosophy of politics" approach and the "integrated approach." In practice, these approaches may often overlap, but it is worth looking at them separately to highlight the key features of each. The integrative approach is, as I argue, preferable since it is both more clearly integrated into the mainstream of economics and political science and more likely to be fruitful in the sense of making progress on political questions.

2. Experimental Philosophy of Politics

In experimental philosophy, it is common to distinguish between the "negative" and "positive" program. Both rely on the background assumption, common in most analytic philosophy, that intuitions are evidence in favor or against philosophical claims. The positive program uses experimental results to understand folk theories in philosophy and to establish basic philosophical claims (Alexander, Mallon, and Weinberg 2010). The negative program uses experimental data to show that the intuitions used as evidence by other philosophers are not trustworthy because they are not stable over different contexts and in different demographic groups. Thomas Nadelhoffer and Eddy Nahmias (2007) further subdivide this into three experimental projects: experimental analysis, experimental descriptivism, and experimental restrictionism. The first two roughly correspond to the positive project and third with the negative.

What they call "experimental analysis" is the project of using experimental data rather than common sense intuitions as evidence for or against philosophical views. In addition, many experimental philosophers are also concerned with the source of those views and the cognitive processes that generate one judgment rather than another. They believe it is "not only important to investigate what folk intuitions actually are, but it is also important to try to determine how these intuitions are generated" (Nadelhoffer and Nahmias 2007, 127). They do this in order to "use the evidence to show that certain philosophical theories do not comport with what we are learning about how the mind works" (2007, 127). The example they give of this kind of project is Josh Greene's work using neuro-imaging (fMRI) to examine the way the brain works when subjects make moral judgments in classic dilemma cases from moral philosophy to develop a dual-process model of moral judgment (J. Greene and Haidt 2002; J. Greene et al. 2004; J. Greene 2008). Another example would be Jonathan Haidt's work on social intuitionism (Haidt 2001). In both cases, experiments help motivate a model of moral decision-making, while also helping to test aspects of that model.

We can see this approach as being traditional philosophy waged by other means. The radical change involved is not so much in philosophical method as in a change of what counts as good or acceptable evidence for philosophical claims and theories. Within the context of experimental analysis, we can follow Alexander, Mallon, and Weinberg (2010) in distinguishing between *mentalism* and *extra-mentalism*. The distinction here relates to the target of analysis. If experimental data about what people think about free will is used as direct evidence in favor of this or that theory of free will, it is a form of extra-mentalism. The experimental data is evidence in favor of or against a claim about the world, not about people's views about the world.[3]

The negative program, or experimental restrictionism, uses experimental data to undermine or restrict the use of intuitions as philosophical evidence. This approach has proven to be extremely powerful in undermining many preciously held philosophical beliefs, but this power raises important philosophical questions. The negative program not only undermines traditional, intuition-based philosophy, it also potentially undermines many of the claims and strategies of the positive program of experimental philosophy. As Alexander, Mallon, and Weinberg (2010) argue, this means that we need to be clear about a number of meta-philosophical questions before we can know whether the experimental revolution will effectively eat its own.

The question for us is how political philosophy fits into this framework. I think there is a clear disanalogy between political philosophy and many other areas of philosophy that makes the positive/negative and mental/extra-mental division less important. Political philosophy, especially but not only in the context of democratic politics, cannot typically ignore what people think about political matters or how they come to their political judgments. Because of this, the positive and negative program may often go together in experimental political philosophy.

Matthew Lindauer (2020) argues that the positive program in experimental moral and political philosophy should focus on what he calls the "fruitfulness" of moral and political concepts. By "fruitfulness," Lindauer (2020, 2132) means "how well they help

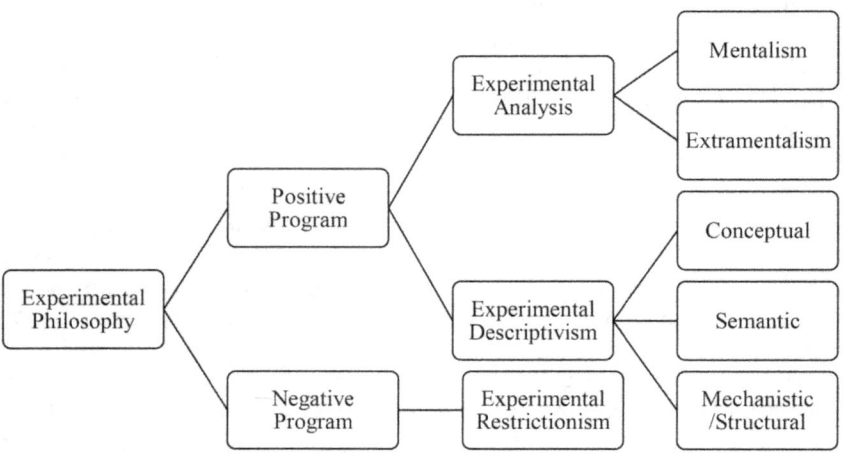

Figure 11.1 Taxonomy of Traditional Experimental Philosophy. © John Thrasher.

us to solve practical problems, problems that we inevitably face as human beings." Political and moral philosophies, on this view, have an irreducibly practical role, or at least that most political and moral philosophers are implicitly or explicitly committed to their practicality.[4] Lindauer argues that there are five ways of thinking about the general idea of fruitfulness for normative concepts: motivation, prevention, resilience, consensus, and guidance. There is some overlap here; questions of motivational potential or the plausibility of consensus will certainly bear on the question of how a concept provides normative guidance, for instance. Crucial to this approach is the idea that philosophers not only draw on experimental results in their research but also participate in designing and running experiments:

> On my view, evaluating the fruitfulness of normative concepts is part of the enterprise of doing moral and political philosophy. But conducting empirical research to determine the fruitfulness of these concepts and assessing the relevance of this research to philosophical debates are activities that involve attention to distinctions and subtleties that generally requires philosophical training. An important upshot of my view is that moral and political philosophers must be actively involved in conducting empirical research that will help us to ascertain whether particular normative concepts are fruitful ones.
>
> (Lindauer 2020, 2,148)

This is an important point, and I think an absolutely correct one. As I will argue below, I think this point is true not only of lab experiments but also of empirical research relevant to political philosophy more generally. After all, what can they know of political philosophy who only political philosophy know?

Some have argued that experimental philosophy should be used in a larger process of conceptual engineering understood as Carnapian explication (Shepherd and Justus

2015; Wakil 2021). Both the project of conceptual engineering generally and the project of Carnapian explication more specifically aim at developing a potentially revisionary conceptual framework for science. Conceptual engineering, or "prescriptive conceptual analysis" (Machery 2017, 213–14), takes ordinary language concepts and attempts to transform them into more precise and fruitful concepts. As Carnap (1962, 1) describes the process:

> By an explication we understand the transformation of an inexact, prescientific concept, the explicandum, into an exact concept, the explicatum. The explicatum must fulfill the requirements of similarity to the explicandum, exactness, fruitfulness, and simplicity.

Prescriptive conceptual analysis may also be explicitly revisionary, aiming to construct a concept based on other evaluative categories. Sally Haslanger's (2000) normative conceptual revisionism is an example. Machery (2017, 217) calls this second form of prescriptive conceptual analysis "Gramscian" after the Italian Marxist who believed that redefining the core concepts of social life was essential in undermining bourgeois cultural hegemony.

Whatever its form, prescriptive conceptual analysis attempts to engineer a conceptual scheme as kind of ideal language. Experimental philosophy, on this view, is useful either as a way of developing the material for explication or for testing the fruitfulness of revisionary concepts. As Jonah Schupbach (2017) argues, formal model building and specification can use experimental results to test different formal explications against one another. This method may have particular salience for political philosophers who typically use the formal tools of economics to generate models of, for instance, impartial choice. These models can then be deployed in experimental conditions to see which better align with the choices of real individuals.

Early and influential experiments in political philosophy adopt something like this method by asking subjects in a lab setting to choose, as if they are choosing in John Rawls' (1971) original position (Yaari and Bar-Hillel 1984; Frohlich, Oppenheimer, and Eavey 1987). Frohlich et al. (1987; 1990; 1993) discovered that Rawls was correct that significant convergence, even unanimity over a particular conception of justice, would emerge in the original position, just not over justice as fairness. The option most like justice as fairness, "Maximize the Floor" is the least popular option among subjects, while "Maximizing the Average with a Floor" a constrained utilitarian principle is by far the most popular. Many have thought that this finding undermines the plausibility of Rawls' theory (Miller 1992; 2001; Schmidtz 2006).

This work has spawned a massive literature. Some have refined this basic approach in terms of choice in the original position (Michelbach et al. 2003; Mitchell et al. 2003; Bruner and Lindauer 2018; Bruner 2018; Inoue, Zenkyo, and Sakamoto 2021), while others have looked at distributive justice, fair division, and impartial choice more generally (Scott et al. 2001; Schneider and Krämer 2004; Konow 2000; 2001; 2009). There is also a considerable literature on fair division and bargaining that goes beyond the Rawlsian model of the original position, often relying ultimatum games or public good games (for a good review, see Roth 2020).

Behavioral testing of Rawls' claim that representatives in the original position would choose his unique conception of justice—justice as fairness—is possible and potentially fruitful since Rawls claims that the principles of justice are not only the unique rational choice in the original position but also more compatible with actual human moral psychology than alternatives like utilitarianism. If rational choosers, in a similar set up, choose different principles, this suggests that either Rawls is wrong about the rationality of the principles or that experimental subjects are somehow disanalogous from the representatives in the original position, either because their rationality is different or because the choice situation is different. Since, as Rawls (1971, 15–16) argues,

> [O]ne conception of justice is more reasonable than another, or justifiable with respect to it, if rational persons in the initial situation would choose its principles over those of the other for the role of justice. Conceptions of justice are to be ranked by their acceptability to persons so circumstanced. Understood in this way the question of justification is settled by working out a problem of deliberation: we have to ascertain which principles it would be rational to adopt given the contractual situation. This connects the theory of justice with the theory of rational choice.

This last sentence expresses the core idea of both Rawls' contractualism and contractarian theories generally (Gaus and Thrasher 2015).

A different approach uses experimental results as the basic data for descriptive rather than prescriptive conceptual analysis. Rather than engineering concepts for use in an ideal language, this approach uses ordinary platitudes as the starting point of conceptual analysis. Instead of generating these platitudes from the intuitions of philosophers, however, this approach uses experimental data. This data can then act as the first stage in a "Canberra Plan" (Jackson 2000) style or "ecological" (Ulatowski 2017) approach to descriptive conceptual analysis. The "Canberra" account of norms developed by Geoffrey Brennan, Lina Eriksson, Robert Goodin, and Nicholas Southwood (Brennan et al. 2013) is a sophisticated example of the conceptual analysis of norms. One could imagine work being done in this territory on political concepts like coercion, rights, harm, and so on.

3. Integrative Experimental Political Philosophy

While experimental results can be useful in developing concepts for prescriptive analysis or conceptual engineering, this is not the only or even perhaps the most valuable reason for submitting political concepts to the experimental treatment. Cristina Bicchieri's (2006; 2016) work on social norms is a good example of what I will call the "integrative" approach to experimental political philosophy that is not primarily concerned with doing conceptual analysis by other means. While it can be seen as a form of experimental prescriptive analysis, doing so ignores many of the important features of the work. Instead, we should see her work and much other work in experimental political philosophy as diverging from the traditional methods of conceptual analysis and experimental philosophy and instead as embracing the general method of social scientific explanation. This is what I call the *integrative* approach to experimental political philosophy. It is integrative in that it draws on all the tools of social science and philosophy in order to answer philosophical problems.

Using Bicchieri's work as an example, we can see that her goal is not primarily to give an analysis of the concept of a norm or social norms. Rather, she is using ideas drawn from philosophy and economics to construct a model of norms that she can then test with experiments. The importance of norms, for her, arose as a solution to a puzzle relating to equilibrium selection in cooperative games (Bicchieri 1997, chap. 6). Most coordination and cooperative games do not have a unique solution. David Lewis (1969) offered his theory of convention as a way of explaining equilibrium selection in pure coordination games, though the exact mechanism for generating conventions was largely left open. In mixed-motive problems of coordination and cooperation, the problem is even harder, however. Given that we see largely stable solutions to these mixed-motive coordination problems, we need an explanation for stable equilibrium selection.

To solve this problem, Bicchieri develops the idea of norms as equilibria that have specific stability and existence properties. Namely, that they are Nash equilibria that rely on common expectations with expectations for punishment of non-compliance. In subsequent work, she used experiments to show how these social norms could be used to transform social dilemmas into mixed-motive games (Bicchieri 2002; 2006, chap. 4), explain the stability (and instability) of fairness in bargaining and distributional settings (Bicchieri 1999; 2008; Bicchieri and Chavez 2010), how unpopular norms can remain stable over time (Bicchieri and Fukui 1999; Bicchieri 2006, chap. 5; 2016), and how trust and trustworthiness relate to norms (Bicchieri, Xiao, and Muldoon 2011).

In this work she and her collaborators not only refine the idea of a norm but have also discovered contextual and substantive differences between types of norms and their functions. This goes beyond what is possible in traditional conceptual analysis, and the fruitfulness of this approach suggests that this kind of approach is generally better than alternative approaches (e.g., the "Canberra" theory of norms). Which is not to say that there is no value to other approaches to norms, even if they are less fruitful. For instance, the "Canberra" theory foregrounds some important aspects of norms that are not as prominent in Bicchieri's approach, as I have argued elsewhere (Gaus and Thrasher 2021, chap. 7). Nevertheless, the power of using operationalizable concepts in conjunction with empirical hypothesis testing is undeniable.

The work of Oliver Curry and his collaborators is also instructive here. Though not "political" in a narrow sense, Curry, et al. are concerned with understanding morality understood as interpersonal rules that govern social life. In this sense, they are engaged in investigating what Gerald Gaus called "social morality," the structure of norms and rules that serve as a foundation for social cooperation and political life. In a series of papers (Curry, Mullins, and Whitehouse 2019; Curry, Jones Chesters, and Van Lissa 2019), Curry and his collaborators used existing experimental data and moral theories to develop a model of "Morality-as-Cooperation" and test it in several different societies. They draw on the work of the moral and political philosopher David Gauthier as well as the moral psychologist Jonathan Haidt. The interesting feature of this approach, and its antecedents like Haidt's Moral Foundations Theory, is that it is not really testing the validity of moral concepts in the traditional way. Rather, it is using philosophical theory as a starting point for developing a model of morality and then using experiments to test the hypotheses that the model generates.

One of the distinctive aspects of this integrative approach and a feature that joins it methodologically to the main approach in the natural and social sciences is its use of "models." Traditional conceptual analysis, be it experimental or not, is not seeking a model of some social phenomenon such as "justice" or "morality." Rather, it is seeking a definition in the sense of trying to find necessary and sufficient conditions for a thing. To explain something through analysis of this sort is to identify the meaning of a thing in some fundamental sense. A model, in the sciences, is not an attempt to completely describe a phenomena or thing; rather a model is representation of the target phenomena of interest that the model constructs as part of a larger strategy of explanation or justification. Michael Weisberg (2006, 624) explains:

> Model building or modeling is the indirect representation and analysis of a real-world phenomenon using a model. It takes place in three stages: In the first, a theorist constructs a model, typically by writing down a mathematical description of this model. In the second, she analyzes the model, looking for characteristic behaviors such as equilibria, oscillations, regions of stability, etc. Finally, if warranted by the problem of interest the modeler assess the relationship between the model and real-world phenomena.

Crucially, all models are in a fundamental sense false: at best they represent reality indirectly but always with some important falsification and idealization. Models are useful because they allow us to isolate elements of the target phenomenon and to focus on crucial elements of the target that are important to the questions that concern the modeler. Modeling is a practical enterprise and good models may not always exhibit the same features. They should, however, allow us to generate better hypotheses about the target as well as better ways to test those claims. Models, then, are judged by their fruitfulness, not by their accuracy.

We can see now why "fruitfulness" as a standard of concepts in experimental philosophy can lead us directly to modeling and away from conceptual analysis. Political philosophical theories generate testable hypothesis, either on their own or because of the models that they rely on. The goal here is to understand the political world through hypothesis testing, with the secondary project being one of model building and taxonomy for the purpose of hypothesis testing. There are powerful tools and experimental paradigms to be found in experimental and behavioral economics for political philosophers to mine and to work within; an excellent overview of how experimental and behavioral economics can be used by philosophers can be found in Rubin, O'Connor, and Bruner (2019).

Again, this makes the experimental political philosophical project no different, in principle, from various other projects in the natural and social sciences. The only difference is the substance of the questions at issue and the hypotheses that are tested. As such, this makes experimental political philosophy of this sort especially apt for use in the interdisciplinary pursuit of what has become known as Philosophy, Politics, and Economics (PPE). One generally unappreciated reason is that this approach opens up not only the scope of experimentation but also the methods available, meaning that "natural experiments" or non-lab experiments may also be useful. This possibility will be explored in the next section.

4. Non-Experimental Empirical Tools

The most powerful way to test a hypothesis is a randomized lab experiment, but for many of the questions that concern political philosophers, this isn't a possible, ethical, or affordable option. In addition to lab experiments, though, political philosophers can use the evidence of history and economic and institutional data in conjunction with abstract models to test their claims. History and existing data do not, in themselves, help us to isolate the most important causal factors that may concern us, however. Communism has generally led to misery and repression in most places it has been tried, but we cannot infer from this alone that communism causes misery and repression. After all, the societies that tended to adopt communism were already poor and often had dysfunctional and/or colonial, extractive institutions, maybe things were so bad to begin with that communism didn't uniquely make them worse. Selection bias may be the best explanation. To establish causal links rigorously in a way that can help us adjudicate basic political questions will require us to find ways to distinguish true causal connections from spurious correlation and selection bias.

We obviously can't run lab experiments on what the effects of communism or capitalism will be on whole societies. Using historical data and econometric analysis to make causal identification is a way of doing experimental political philosophy by using "natural" experiments rather than controlled experiments. The main problem is that historical data is not randomly assigned into different treatments the way it would be in a controlled experiment. But sometimes we can investigate the data and use events as natural experiments that can function "as good as random" assignment. This can allow us to make causal inferences from what may initially look like merely descriptive or correlation data. This is possible because of the tools developed by economists for causal identification that emerged out of the so-called "credibility revolution" of the last several decades (Angrist and Pischke 2010). The main strategy here is a causal identification strategy that makes use of the tools of OLS regressions, instrumental variables, regression discontinuity design, difference in difference, and synthetic controls to find and measure the causal influence of some set of experimental variables on an outcome variable.[5] Increasingly causal identification strategies are developed with the use of causal maps in the form of directed acyclic graphs (DAGs) like the one below.[6]

Instrumental variables approaches and related techniques like regression discontinuity and difference in difference analysis all rely on isolating strategies to reduce or eliminate unobserved variables responsible for selection bias or endogeneity. In effect, the point is to try to reverse engineer an experiment from data that already exists by creating "as good as random" assignment in the analysis. For example, an

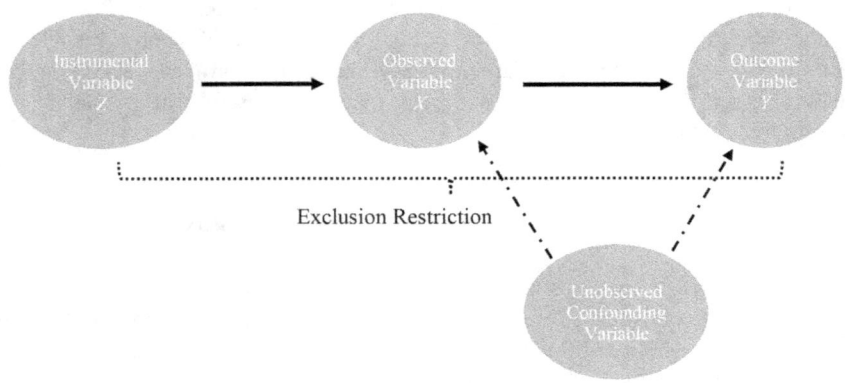

Figure 11.2 Directed Acyclical Graph (DAG) of a Simple Instrumental Variable. © John Thrasher.

instrumental variable is something that causes the observation variable, but not the outcome variable. If there is an unobserved confounding variable or selection effect related to the observation variable, the IV can isolate this effect and by using a two-stage least squares analysis, the true effect of the observation variable on the outcome variable can be evaluated. A classic, though perhaps overused, example in the political science literature is the effect of rain on electoral outcomes. Whether or not it is raining should have no effect on who is elected in an election, but it will likely influence who decides to vote, which will in turn have an effect on who is elected.[7]

A dramatic use of an instrumental variable occurs in Christopher Achen and Larry Bartels' influential *Democracy for Realists* (2016). Drawing on earlier research, they show that shark attacks occurring in 1916 on the New Jersey coast—the same attacks that inspired the novel and movie *Jaws*—had a crucial influence on electing Woodrow Wilson to the presidency. The conclusion that Achen and Bartels draw from this (and similar evidence) is that voters are irrational and cannot be relied upon to either prospectively or retrospectively discipline political behavior. This serves as a major pillar in the "realist" theory of democracy that they champion. This theory is, at root, a philosophical account of the normative status of democracy and how to evaluate democratic results. So, even though it is developed by political scientists, it stakes out important territory in the understanding of democracy in political philosophy. Its justification, however, relies on a series of empirical claims, and if those claims are called into question, the larger "realist" theory of democracy loses much of its support.

As with all IV studies, the crucial question is whether there is a violation of the "exclusion restriction" by the IV, that is, whether the IV is somehow directly causally related to the outcome variable. If so, using the IV doesn't solve the initial problem and may in fact replicate it at another level. Anthony Fowler and Andrew Hall (2018) argue that this is exactly what is going on in the shark attack example. There are reasons shark attacks and the perceived lack of response to them might affect how one views one's political representatives. Further, the effect doesn't replicate over the entire timeline of shark attacks in the area, raising additional puzzles about the case. Achen and Bartels (2018), perhaps unsurprisingly, disagree with this assessment of their work. Whoever is right here, Achen and Bartels are surely correct when they argue at the end of their response piece that:

> As the wisest statisticians have always recognized, persuasive empirical science does not come from applying abstract statistical considerations to poorly grasped research problems. Rather, it emerges from deep substantive knowledge in dialogue with relevant statistical theory ... In our view, that kind of thinking, imperfect and provisional as always, represents the way forward for empirical political science.
> (Achen and Bartels 2018, 1452)

An excellent example of work that integrates good statistics with a well-founded research problem can be found in the work of Daron Acemoglu and James Robinson on the long-term effects of different forms of colonialism. In their original paper, with Simon Johnson, they show that Europeans established extractive colonies in places where they did not themselves settle (Acemoglu, Johnson, and Robinson 2001). This work relies on a clever identification strategy using instrumental variables. In later work they showed that well-functioning societies have inclusive rather than extractive institutions. Inclusive or open institutions tend to allow for creative destruction and dynamism which encourages economic growth, while societies with extractive institutions do not (Acemoglu and Robinson 2012). Douglass North, John Wallis, and Barry Weingast (2009) come to a similar conclusion, though with a different explanation. Both research programs rely on analyzing historical data with econometric techniques and both are highly relevant to political philosophy.

This category of empirical politics is underutilized by philosophers and is largely left to economists and political scientists, but it need not be. Perhaps it is too much to expect political philosophers to become experts in econometric methods and causal identification, but it is also a mistake for philosophers to be ignorant of these powerful tools for hypothesis testing. As Lindauer (2020, 2148) argued in the context of lab experiments, philosophers should be active participants in hypothesis testing involving natural experiments. Only if philosophers are involved will we be able to draw attention to the specifically philosophical questions and models that generate the hypotheses that we care about. Interdisciplinary collaboration is crucial to making progress, and one way this can proceed is under the aegis of the Philosophy, Politics, and Economics movement. As with experimental methods, it will be important to educate the philosophical community on the importance and viability of empirical tools so that work relying on these techniques can be accepted within the philosophical mainstream. Philosophers need to take the time and effort to familiarize themselves with experimental and empirical methods from the social sciences in order to understand the key developments in adjacent fields as well as to contribute meaningfully and to even direct important research programs that can fruitfully address core questions in political philosophy.

5. Conclusion

Experimental philosophy has both a methodological and substantive component. As a methodology, it aims to bring empirical methods to bear on traditional philosophical questions. As such, it seems to be a radical departure from traditional philosophical methods that typically make use of a priori reasoning in the form of logical or conceptual arguments.

This methodological approach is not substantively neutral, though. Despite the differences in the views of experimental philosophers, all think that, as Josh Knobe and Shaun Nichols put it, they are "concerned with questions about how human beings actually happen to be" and that the "deepest questions of philosophy can only be properly addressed by immersing oneself in the messy, contingent, highly variable truths about how human beings actually are" (Knobe and Nichols 2008). Experimental philosophy relies on a kind of methodological naturalism that makes assumptions about how we learn about the world through experimentation and measurement.

Initially, this philosophical approach was developed and deployed by philosophers who by training or inclination were adjacent to psychology and cognitive science. They adopted methods drawn from psychology and cognitive science and argued both that we needed to understand what people believed as well as how the mind really works to get traction on many traditional philosophical questions in epistemology, philosophy of mind, and even ethics.[8]

It is a puzzling feature of the rise of experimental philosophy over the last several decades that political philosophy has never been integrated into the mainstream of experimental philosophical interest. Political philosophy, after all, seems to require knowledge about actual human nature and psychology. It is similarly puzzling that political philosophers have generally been slow to adopt experimental and other "naturalistic" methods. This is especially puzzling when one considers the general methodology of the great political philosophers of the past. Consider Hobbes' claim at the end of the Introduction to *Leviathan*:

> But let one man read another by his actions never so perfectly, it serves him onely with his acquaintance, which are but few. He that is to govern a whole Nation, must read in himselfe, not this, or that particular man; but Man-kind; which though it be hard to do, harder than to learn any Language, or Science; yet, when I shall have set down my own reading orderly, and perspicuously, the pains left another, will be onely to consider, if he also find not the same in himselfe. For this kind of Doctrine, admitteth no other Demonstration.
>
> (Hobbes 1651)

According to Hobbes, general knowledge of human nature as well as rationality is a pre-requisite for political philosophy. Rousseau states his problem, at the outset of *Du Contrat Social*, as "with men as they are and with laws as they could be, can there be in the civil order any sure and legitimate rule of administration?" (Rousseau 1762). But to know what "men as they are" are like and to know what laws could be, we surely need to know a considerable amount about actual human psychology, rationality, and motivation as well as the possible workings of political institutions.

It is likely that the experimental political philosophy revolution has not yet truly begun. It is relatively easy to, for instance, test claims of impartial choice in the original position in the lab and this probably explains why this approach has remained fruitful. Most questions that interest political philosophers, however, are more complex than this and it is harder to see how to isolate key elements of a question or claim in such a way that it can benefit from empirical or experimental testing. We can't simply take a question like "what makes a society dynamic" or "what institutions best promote the right kind of freedom" and apply an off-the-shelf experimental framework.[9] Instead, political philosophers will need to become more sophisticated in how to break their larger questions down into constituent parts so that the causal mechanism can be isolated and tested and so that models can be developed for key parts of the theory or question. Then empirical and experimental methods can be applied, where possible, to make progress. To do this well, political philosophers will need to spend a little more time with their cousins in political science and economics departments.

If I am right that the integrative approach to political philosophy is likely to be more fruitful than the traditional conceptual approach, then we should expect there to be low-hanging fruit just waiting to be picked by those who adopt this approach. Just as the adoption of new formal methods at the turn of the twentieth century created the soil for the flowering of analytic philosophy, we should expect the integration of formal and empirical methods from the social sciences into political philosophy to lead to similar flowering.

Acknowledgments

Thanks to Toby Handfield, Matt Lindauer, Ryan Muldoon, and Shaun Nichols for helpful comments and discussion on this chapter. Special thanks to Matt for his encouragement and patience.

Notes

1 Nevertheless, many of the top philosophy journals do not publish papers with experimental results. *Philosophical Review* is the most notable here and has not, as far as I can tell, ever published an experimental paper. Perhaps the top journal in ethics and social philosophy, *Ethics*, also explicitly states that it will not publish papers with novel experimental results. From their Instructions for Authors (on the website, but not in the print edition), "*Ethics* does not publish empirical studies or new statistical findings as such, but analytical essays that draw on such work and provide significant theoretical reflection are welcome." Despite this, *Ethics* did recently publish a paper that looked at data on gender representation in philosophy journals (Hassoun et al. 2022). It is not clear whether this represents a change in policy or whether the editors think the paper doesn't constitute "empirical study" or "new statistical findings."

2 For a good overview of political concepts, see Gaus (2000).
3 Justin Sytsma and Jonathan Livengood (2015).
4 As Lindauer notes, some political and moral philosophers reject the central practical nature of moral and political concepts, most notably Gerald Cohen (2003; 2008), David Enoch (2011; 2013), and David Estlund (2011; 2019), but they are in the extreme minority.
5 For a good introduction to the use of these techniques, see Angrist and Pischke (2009); Cunningham (2020).
6 On DAGS, see Pearl, Glymour, and Jewell (2016); Pearl and Mackenzie (2018).
7 For a close look at 127 IV studies using rain as the IV, see Mellon (2021).
8 Josh Knobe (2016) even argued that "experimental philosophy is cognitive science."
9 Thanks to Ryan Muldoon for making this point clear to me.

References

Acemoglu, Daron, and James Robinson. 2012. *Why Nations Fail: The Origins of Power, Prosperity, and Poverty*. New York: Crown Business.

Acemoglu, Daron, Simon Johnson, and James A. Robinson. 2001. "The Colonial Origins of Comparative Development: An Empirical Investigation." *American Economic Review* 91, no. 5: 1369–401. https://doi.org/10.1257/aer.91.5.1369.

Achen, Christopher H., and Larry M. Bartels. 2016. *Democracy for Realists: Why Elections Do Not Produce Responsive Government*. Princeton: Princeton University Press.

Achen, Christopher H., and Larry M. Bartels. 2018. "Statistics as If Politics Mattered: A Reply to Fowler and Hall." *The Journal of Politics* 80, no. 4: 1438–53. https://doi.org/10.1086/699245.

Alexander, Joshua, Ronald Mallon, and Jonathan M. Weinberg. 2010. "Accentuate the Negative." *Review of Philosophy and Psychology* 1, no. 2: 297–314. https://doi.org/10.1007/s13164-009-0015-2.

Angrist, Joshua D., and Jörn-Steffen Pischke. 2009. *Mostly Harmless Econometrics: An Empiricist's Companion*. Princeton: Princeton University Press.

Angrist, Joshua D., and Jörn-Steffen Pischke. 2010. "The Credibility Revolution in Empirical Economics: How Better Research Design Is Taking the Con out of Econometrics." *Journal of Economic Perspectives* 24, no. 2: 3–30. https://doi.org/10.1257/jep.24.2.3.

Bicchieri, Cristina. 1997. *Rationality and Coordination*. 1st edition. Cambridge: Cambridge University Press.

Bicchieri, Cristina. 1999. "Local Fairness." *Philosophy and Phenomenological Research* 59, no. 1: 229–36.

Bicchieri, Cristina. 2002. "Covenants Without Swords: Group Identity, Norms and Communication in Social Dilemmas." *Rationality and Society* 14, no. 2: 192–228.

Bicchieri, Cristina. 2006. *The Grammar of Society: The Nature and Dynamics of Social Norms*. New York: Cambridge University Press.

Bicchieri, Cristina. 2008. "The Fragility of Fairness: An Experimental Investigation on the Conditional Status of Pro-social Norms." *Philosophical Issues* 18, no. 1: 229–48.

Bicchieri, Cristina. 2016. *Norms in the Wild*. New York: Oxford University Press.

Bicchieri, Cristina, and Alex Chavez. 2010. "Behaving as Expected: Public Information and Fairness Norms." *Journal of Behavioral Decision Making* 23, no. 2: 161–78.

Bicchieri, Cristina, and Yoshitaka Fukui. 1999. "The Great Illusion: Ignorance, Informational Cascades, and the Persistence of Unpopular Norms." *Business Ethics Quarterly* 9, no. 1: 127–55.

Bicchieri, Cristina, Erte Xiao, and Ryan Muldoon. 2011. "Trustworthiness Is a Social Norm, but Trusting Is Not." *Politics, Philosophy & Economics* 10, no. 2: 170–87.

Brennan, Geoffrey, Lina Eriksson, Robert E. Goodin, and Nicholas Southwood. 2013. *Explaining Norms*. New York: Oxford University Press.

Bruner, Justin P. 2018. "Decisions Behind the Veil: An Experimental Approach." In *Oxford Studies in Experimental* Philosophy, *Volume 2*, edited by Tania Lombrozo, Joshua Knobe and Shaun Nichols, 167–180. Oxford: Oxford University Press. https://doi.org/10.1093/oso/9780198815259.003.0008.

Bruner, Justin P., and Matthew Lindauer. 2018. "The Varieties of Impartiality, or, Would an Egalitarian Endorse the Veil?" *Philosophical Studies*, October. https://doi.org/10.1007/s11098-018-1190-8.

Carnap, Rudolf. 1962. *Logical Foundations of Probability*. 2nd edition. Chicago: University Of Chicago Press.

Cohen, G. A. 2003. "Facts and Principles." *Philosophy and Public Affairs* 31, no. 3: 211–45.

Cohen, G. A. 2008. *Rescuing Justice and Equality*. Cambridge, MA: Harvard University Press.

Cunningham, Scott. 2020. "Causal Inference: The Mixtape." https://www.scunning.com/causalinference_norap.pdf.

Curry, Oliver Scott, Matthew Jones Chesters, and Caspar J. Van Lissa. 2019. "Mapping Morality with a Compass: Testing the Theory of 'Morality-as-Cooperation' with a New Questionnaire." *Journal of Research in Personality* 78 (February): 106–24. https://doi.org/10.1016/j.jrp.2018.10.008.

Curry, Oliver Scott, Daniel Austin Mullins, and Harvey Whitehouse. 2019. "Is It Good to Cooperate? Testing the Theory of Morality-as-Cooperation in 60 Societies." *Current Anthropology* 60, no. 1: 47–69. https://doi.org/10.1086/701478.

Cushman, Fiery. 2008. "Crime and Punishment: Distinguishing the Roles of Causal and Intentional Analyses in Moral Judgment." *Cognition* 108, no. 2: 353–80. https://doi.org/10.1016/j.cognition.2008.03.006.

Enoch, David. 2011. *Taking Morality Seriously: A Defense of Robust Realism*. Oxford: Oxford University Press.

Enoch, David. 2013. "The Disorder of Public Reason: A Critical Study of Gerald Gaus's the Order of Public Reason." *Ethics* 124, no. 1: 141–76.

Estlund, David. 2008. *Democratic Authority: A Philosophical Framework*. Princeton, NJ: Princeton University Press.

Estlund, David. 2011. "Human Nature and the Limits (If Any) of Political Philosophy." *Philosophy & Public Affairs* 39, no. 3: 207–37.

Estlund, David. 2019. *Utopophobia*. Princeton: Princeton University Press.

Foot, Philippa. 1967. "The Problem of Abortion and the Doctrine of the Double Effect." *Oxford Review* 5: 5–15.

Fowler, Anthony, and Andrew B. Hall. 2018. "Do Shark Attacks Influence Presidential Elections? Reassessing a Prominent Finding on Voter Competence." *The Journal of Politics* 80, no. 4: 1423–37. https://doi.org/10.1086/699244.

Frohlich, Norman, and Joe A. Oppenheimer. 1990. "Choosing Justice in Experimental Democracies with Production." *American Political Science Review* 84, no. 2: 461–77. https://doi.org/10.2307/1963529.

Frohlich, Norman, and Joe A. Oppenheimer. 1993. *Choosing Justice: An Experimental Approach to Ethical Theory*. Berkeley: University of California Press.
Frohlich, Norman, Joe A. Oppenheimer, and Cheryl L. Eavey. 1987. "Laboratory Results on Rawls's Distributive Justice." *British Journal of Political Science* 17, no. 1: 1–21. https://doi.org/10.1017/S0007123400004580.
Gaus, Gerald. 2000. *Political Concepts and Political Theories*. Boulder, CO: Westview Press.
Gaus, Gerald. 2016. *The Tyranny of the Ideal: Justice in a Diverse Society*. New York: Princeton University Press.
Gaus, Gerald, and John Thrasher. 2015. "Rational Choice in the Original Position: The (Many) Models of Rawls and Harsanyi." In *The Cambridge Companion to The Original Position*, edited by Timothy Hinton, 39–58. Cambridge: Cambridge University Press.
Gaus, Gerald, and John Thrasher. 2021. *Philosophy, Politics, and Economics: An Introduction*. Princeton: Princeton University Press.
Greene, Joshua. 2008. "The Secret Joke of Kant's Soul." In *Moral Psychology*, edited by Walter Sinnott-Armstrong, 3 The Neuroscience of Morality: Emotion, Brain Disorders, and Development, 35–80. Cambridge, MA: MIT.
Greene, Joshua, and Jonathan Haidt. 2002. "How (and Where) Does Moral Judgment Work?" *Trends in Cognitive Sciences* 6, no. 12: 517–23.
Greene, Joshua D., Fiery A. Cushman, Lisa E. Stewart, Kelly Lowenberg, Leigh E. Nystrom, and Jonathan D. Cohen. 2009. "Pushing Moral Buttons: The Interaction Between Personal Force and Intention in Moral Judgment." *Cognition* 111, no. 3: 364–71. https://doi.org/10.1016/j.cognition.2009.02.001.
Greene, Joshua, Leigh Nystrom, Andrew Oldenquist, John Darley, and Jonathan Cohen. 2004. "The Neural Bases of Cognitive Conflict and Control in Moral Judgment." *Neuron* 44, no. 2: 389–400.
Haidt, Jonathan. 2001. "The Emotional Dog and Its Rational Tail: A Social Intuitionist Approach to Moral Judgment." *Psychological Review* 108, no. 4: 814–34.
Haslanger, Sally. 2000. "Gender and Race: (What) Are They? (What) Do We Want Them to Be?" *Nous* 34, no. 1: 31–55.
Hassoun, Nicole, Sherri Conklin, Michael Nekrasov, and Jevin West. 2022. "The Past 110 Years: Historical Data on the Underrepresentation of Women in Philosophy Journals." *Ethics* 132, no. 3: 680–729. https://doi.org/10.1086/718075.
Hitchcock, Christopher, and Joshua Knobe. 2009. "Cause and Norm." *The Journal of Philosophy* 106, no. 11: 587–612.
Hobbes, Thomas. 1651. *Leviathan*. Edited by Noel Malcolm. Clarendon Edition of the Works of Thomas Hobbes. Oxford: Oxford University Press.
Hume, David. 1739. *A Treatise of Human Nature*. Edited by David Fate Norton, and Mary J. Norton. Oxford Philosophical Texts. New York: Oxford University Press.
Hume, David. 1748. *An Enquiry Concerning Human Understanding*. Edited by Tom Beauchamp. Oxford: Oxford University Press.
Inoue, Akira, Masahiro Zenkyo, and Haruya Sakamoto. 2021. "Making the Veil of Ignorance Work: Evidence from Survey Experiments." In *Oxford Studies in Experimental Philosophy Volume 4*, edited by Tania Lombrozo, Joshua Knobe, and Shaun Nichols, 4: 53–80. Oxford: Oxford University Press.
Jackson, Frank. 2000. *From Metaphysics to Ethics: A Defence of Conceptual Analysis*. Oxford: Clarendon Press.
Kamm, F. M. 2006. *Intricate Ethics: Rights, Responsibilities, and Permissible Harm*. 1st edition. Oxford; New York: Oxford University Press.

Knobe, Joshua. 2016. "Experimental Philosophy Is Cognitive Science." In *A Companion to Experimental Philosophy*, edited by Justin Sytsma and Wesley Buckwalter, 37–52. Oxford: John Wiley & Sons.

Knobe, Joshua, and Ben Fraser. 2008. "Causal Judgment and Moral Judgment: Two Experiments." In *Moral Psychology*, edited by Walter Sinnott-Armstrong, 2: 441–48. Cambridge, MA: MIT Press.

Knobe, Joshua, and Shaun Nichols. 2008. "An Experimental Philosophy Manifesto." In *Experimental Philosophy*, edited by Joshua Knobe, and Shaun Nichols, 3–16. New York: Oxford University Press.

Konow, James. 2000. "Fair Shares: Accountability and Cognitive Dissonance in Allocation Decisions." *American Economic Review* 90, no. 4: 1072–92. https://doi.org/10.1257/aer.90.4.1072.

Konow, James. 2001. "Fair and Square: The Four Sides of Distributive Justice." *Journal of Economic Behavior & Organization* 46, no. 2: 137–64. https://doi.org/10.1016/S0167-2681(01)00194-9.

Konow, James. 2009. "Is Fairness in the Eye of the Beholder? An Impartial Spectator Analysis of Justice." *Social Choice and Welfare* 33, no. 1: 101–27. https://doi.org/10.1007/s00355-008-0348-2.

Lewis, David. 1969. *Convention: A Philosophical Study*. Cambridge, MA: Harvard University Press.

Lindauer, Matthew. 2020. "Experimental Philosophy and the Fruitfulness of Normative Concepts." *Philosophical Studies* 177, no. 8: 2129–52. https://doi.org/10.1007/s11098-019-01302-3.

Machery Edouard. 2017. *Philosophy Within Its Proper Bounds*. Oxford: Oxford University Press.

Mellon, Jonathan. 2021. "Rain, Rain, Go Away: 176 Potential Exclusion-Restriction Violations for Studies Using Weather as an Instrumental Variable." SSRN Scholarly Paper 3715610. Rochester, NY: Social Science Research Network. https://doi.org/10.2139/ssrn.3715610.

MichelbachPhilip A., John T. Scott, Richard E. Matland, and Brian H. Bornstein. 2003. "Doing Rawls Justice: An Experimental Study of Income Distribution Norms." *American Journal of Political Science* 47, no. 3: 523–39. https://doi.org/10.1111/1540-5907.00037.

Miller, David. 1992. "Distributive Justice: What the People Think." *Ethics* 102, no. 3: 555–93.

Miller, David. 2001. *Principles of Social Justice*. Cambridge: Harvard University Press.

Mitchell, Gregory, Philip E. Tetlock, Daniel G. Newman, and Jennifer S. Lerner. 2003. "Experiments Behind the Veil: Structural Influences on Judgments of Social Justice." *Political Psychology* 24, no. 3: 519–47. https://doi.org/10.1111/0162-895X.00339.

Nadelhoffer, Thomas, and Eddy Nahmias. 2007. "The Past and Future of Experimental Philosophy." *Philosophical Explorations* 10, no. 2: 123–49. https://doi.org/10.1080/13869790701305921.

Nichols, Shaun. 2002a. "How Psychopaths Threaten Moral Rationalism: Is It Irrational to Be Amoral?" *The Monist* 85, no. 2: 285–303.

Nichols, Shaun. 2002b. "Norms with Feeling: Towards a Psychological Account of Moral Judgment." *Cognition* 84, no. 2: 221–36. https://doi.org/10.1016/S0010-0277(02)00048-3.

Nichols, Shaun. 2004. *Sentimental Rules: On the Natural Foundations of Moral Judgment*. Oxford: Oxford University Press.

North, Douglass C., John Joseph Wallis, and Barry R. Weingast. 2009. *Violence and Social Orders: A Conceptual Framework for Interpreting Recorded Human History*. New York: Cambridge University Press.

Pearl, Judea, and Dana Mackenzie. 2018. *The Book of Why: The New Science of Cause and Effect*. New York: Basic Books.

Pearl, Judea, Madelyn Glymour, and Nicholas P. Jewell. 2016. *Causal Inference in Statistics—A Primer*. 1st edition. Chichester, West Sussex: Wiley.

Rawls, John. 1971. *A Theory of Justice*. Revised. Cambridge, MA: Belknap Press.

Roth, Alvin E. 2020. "Bargaining Experiments." In *The Handbook of Experimental Economics*, edited by John Kagel and Alvin Roth, 253–348. Princeton: Princeton University Press. https://doi.org/10.1515/9780691213255-006.

Rousseau, Jean-Jacques. 1762. "On the Social Contract." In *The Basic Political Writings*, edited and translated by Donald A. Cress, 140–227. Indianapolis: Hackett Publishing.

Rubin, Hannah, Cailin O'Connor, and Justin Bruner. 2019. "Experimental Economics for Philosophers." In *Methodological Advances in Experimental Philosophy*, edited by Eugen Fischer, Mark Curtis, and James Beebe, 175–208. London: Bloomsbury Publishing.

Schmidtz, David. 2006. *The Elements of Justice*. Cambridge: Cambridge University Press.

Schmidtz, David. 2011. "Nonideal Theory: What It Is and What It Needs to Be." *Ethics* 121, no. 4: 772–96.

Schneider, Gerald, and Ulrike Sabrina Krämer. 2004. "The Limitations of Fair Division: An Experimental Evaluation of Three Procedures." *Journal of Conflict Resolution* 48, no. 4: 506–24. https://doi.org/10.1177/0022002704266148.

Schupbach, Jonah N. 2017. "Experimental Explication." *Philosophy and Phenomenological Research* 94, no. 3: 672–710. https://doi.org/10.1111/phpr.12207.

Scott, John T., Richard E. Matland, Philip A. Michelbach, and Brian H. Bornstein. 2001. "Just Deserts: An Experimental Study of Distributive Justice Norms." *American Journal of Political Science* 45, no. 4: 749–67. https://doi.org/10.2307/2669322.

Sellars, Wilfrid. 1963. "Philosophy and the Scientific Image of Man." In *Science, Perception and Reality*, 7–43. Atascadero, CA: Ridgeview Pub Co.

Sen, Amartya. 2009. *The Idea of Justice*. Cambridge, MA: Harvard University Press.

Shepherd, Joshua, and James Justus. 2015. "X-Phi and Carnapian Explication." *Erkenntnis* 80, no. 2: 381–402. https://doi.org/10.1007/s10670-014-9648-3.

Simmons, A. John. 2010. "Ideal and Nonideal Theory." *Philosophy & Public Affairs* 38, no. 1: 5–36.

Stemplowska, Zofia. 2008. "What's Ideal About Ideal Theory?" *Social Theory and Practice* 34, no. 3: 319–40.

Sytsma, Justin, and Jonathan Livengood. 2015. *The Theory and Practice of Experimental Philosophy*. Peterborough, Ontario: Broadview Press.

Thomson, Judith. 1985. "The Trolley Problem." *The Yale Law Journal* 94, no. 6: 1395–415.

Thomson, Judith Jarvis. 1976. "Killing, Letting Die, and the Trolley Problem." *The Monist* 59, no. 2: 204–17. https://doi.org/10.5840/monist197659224.

Ulatowski, Joseph. 2017. "An Ecological Approach in Experimental Philosophy." In *Commonsense Pluralism About Truth: An Empirical Defence*, edited by Joseph Ulatowski, 57–84. Cham: Springer International Publishing. https://doi.org/10.1007/978-3-319-69465-8_3.

Valentini, Laura. 2012. "Ideal vs. Non-Ideal Theory: A Conceptual Map." *Philosophy Compass* 7, no. 9: 654–64.

Wakil, Samantha. 2021. "Experimental Explications for Conceptual Engineering." *Erkenntnis*, June. https://doi.org/10.1007/s10670-021-00413-w.

Weisberg, Michael. 2006. "Forty Years of 'The Strategy': Levins on Model Building and Idealization." *Biology and Philosophy* 21, no. 5: 623–45. https://doi.org/10.1007/s10539-006-9051-9.

Wiens, David. 2012. "Prescribing Institutions Without Ideal Theory." *Journal of Political Philosophy* 20, no. 1: 45–70.

Yaari, M. E., and M. Bar-Hillel. 1984. "On Dividing Justly." *Social Choice and Welfare* 1, no. 1: 1–24.

Notes on Contributors

Mark Alfano works in philosophy (epistemology, moral psychology, philosophy of science), social science (personality psychology, social psychology), and computer science (ethics and epistemology of algorithms). He also brings digital humanities methods to bear on both contemporary problems and the history of philosophy (especially Nietzsche).

Cristina Bicchieri is S. J. Patterson Harvie Chair of Social Thought and Comparative Ethics, and Professor of Philosophy and Psychology at the University of Pennsylvania. She founded and directs the Center for Social Norms and Behavioral Dynamics. Bicchieri is a member of the American Academy of Arts and Science and the Germany Academy of Science, Leopoldina. She is Honorary Fellow of Wolfson College, Cambridge University.

Justin Bruner is Associate Professor in the Department of Political Economy and Moral Science at the University of Arizona. He's interested in political philosophy, social epistemology, and the ways formal and experimental methods can inform philosophical inquiry.

Joanne Byrne is a digital anthropologist interested in the complex interplay between technology and culture. Her research interests include gender, identity, and digital social spaces as well as identifying intersections between quantitative "Big Data" projects and qualitative social research. Her work is situated in digital ethnography, cross-disciplinary social media analysis, and investigations into the use, construction, and meaning of digital spaces.

Dominik Duell is Assistant Professor at the University of Innsbruck. He researches political and economic behavior in representative democracies with a special focus on how social identity influences citizens' choices.

Grace Flores-Robles is a doctoral candidate in Basic and Applied Social Psychology at the CUNY Graduate Center. Her research investigates the role of morality in labor and organizations. She is currently a junior scholar at the Stone Center on Socio-Economic Inequality.

Christopher Freiman is Associate Professor of Philosophy at William & Mary. He is the author of two books, *Unequivocal Justice* and *Why It's OK to Ignore Politics*. Chris has also published many articles and chapters on topics, including democratic theory, distributive justice, and immigration.

Ana P. Gantman is Assistant Professor of Psychology at Brooklyn College and CUNY Graduate Center. Her research investigates how moral psychology affects how we see, think, act, and interact in institutions.

Mollie Gerver is Assistant Professor of International Ethics in the Department of Political Economy at King's College London. She specializes in the ethics of immigration policies.

Nicole Hassoun is Professor of Philosophy at Binghamton University. She has held visiting positions at Cornell and Stanford Universities, the United Nations' World Institute for Development Economics Research in Helsinki, the Center for Poverty Research in Salzburg, the Franco-Swedish Program in Philosophy and Economics in Paris, and the Center for Advanced Studies in Frankfurt. She has published about a hundred papers in journals like the *American Philosophical Quarterly, Journal of Development Economics, Tropical Medicine and International Health, Australasian Journal of Philosophy, The European Journal of Philosophy, and Philosophy and Economics*. Her first book *Globalization and Global Justice: Shrinking Distance, Expanding Obligations* was published in 2012 and her second book *Global Health Impact: Extending Access on Essential Medicines for the Poor* appeared in 2020.

Leena Koni Hoffmann is an Africa Programme associate fellow at Chatham House and the research lead for its Social Norms and Accountable Governance Project (SNAG)—SNAG's biggest and longest-running project. She also leads a research program on Citizen Security Relations in West Africa. She was formerly a technical advisor to the Permanent Inter-State Committee for Drought Control in the Sahel (CILSS) in Ouagadougou (2016–20). Her research focuses on social change and the informal institutions which drive governance and democratic challenges, politics and food security, regional trade and cross-border cooperation in West Africa. She has worked as an investigator for Nigeria's Anti-Corruption Commission and a Marie Curie Research fellow at the Luxembourg Institute of Socio-Economic Research (LISER). Dr. Hoffmann received her PhD in African Studies from the University of Birmingham, MA in International Relations from the University of Lancaster, and BSc in Sociology from the University of Jos, Nigeria.

Adam Lerner is currently Post-doctoral Associate in the Center for Population-Level Bioethics at Rutgers University. Previously. He was Lecturer in the Philosophy Department at Princeton University and Assistant Professor/Faculty Fellow in the Center for Bioethics at New York University. He earned his PhD in the Philosophy Department at Princeton University in 2018. He is currently working on topics at the intersection of moral psychology and population ethics, animal ethics, environmental ethics, and metaethics. His work has appeared in venues such as *The Journal of Moral Philosophy, Oxford Studies in Metaethics, Philosophical Studies*, and *Philosophical Perspectives*.

Matthew Lindauer is Assistant Professor of Philosophy at Brooklyn College and CUNY Graduate Center. He works primarily in moral and political philosophy, moral psychology, and experimental philosophy. His recent research examines the role that normative concepts play in solving practical problems that we inevitably face in our interactions with one another.

Patrick Lown is a research fellow in the Department of Government at the University of Essex. His primary research interests include the public opinion of inequality and social welfare and the expression of empathy in politics.

Veronika Luptakova is a behavioral scientist and a doctoral candidate at the LSE's Department of Psychological and Behavioural Science. Veronika's PhD research lies at the intersection of experimental moral philosophy and cognitive psychology, aiming to inform public policy. Specifically, she explores how people deal with incoherence in their moral judgments. In addition to her PhD research, Veronika brings learnings from behavioral science to her consulting work for organizations seeking to build stronger ethical culture. Veronika holds MSc in Behavioural Science from LSE, Postgraduate Diploma in Theology (Christian Moral Reasoning) from the University of Oxford, a master's degree in law from Charles University in Prague, and a master's degree in economics from the University of Economics in Prague.

Ryan Muldoon is Associate Professor of Philosophy and Director of the Philosophy, Politics and Economics program at the University at Buffalo. His work focuses on diversity and dynamism in liberal societies. He is the author of *Social Contract Theory for a Diverse World: Beyond Tolerance*, and coedits the *Philosophy, Politics, and Economics* book series.

Shaun Nichols is Professor of Philosophy at Cornell University. His research concerns the psychological underpinnings of philosophical thought. He is the author of *Sentimental Rules*, *Bound: Essays on Free Will and Moral Responsibility*, and *Rational Rules*, as well as numerous articles in academic journals in philosophy and psychology.

Raj Patel is the co-lead researcher on the Chatham House Africa Programme's Social Norms and Accountability Project (SNAG), core member of Penn Social Norms and Behavioral Dynamics (PSNBD), and a postdoctoral fellow at the University of Pennsylvania's Department of Philosophy, Politics and Economics. His research interests revolve around the political economy of corruption and the provision of public goods in the Global South.

Joshua Roose is a political sociologist whose work focuses on violence, with a particular emphasis on the intersection of masculinities and violent extremism. Josh has published three monographs examining the relationship between masculinities and violence and articles in leading journals. He holds two Australian Research Council Discovery grants examining masculinity and the far-right and anti-women online movements. Josh has served on the Victorian Department of Premier and Cabinets Expert Reference Group on Social Cohesion and the Department of Home Affairs Ministers Academic Roundtable. He has given evidence to Federal and State

Parliamentary Inquires into violent extremism and is an expert witness for the New South Wales Crown Solicitors Office. Josh has been a visiting scholar at NYU, Harvard Law School, and received an ICLRS-Oxford Fellowship. His research has been covered in the global and national press including the BBC, *France 24*, *Al Jazeera*, *the Washington Post*, *The Economist*, *Time Magazine*, and 60 Minutes (Australia).

John Thrasher is Associate Professor of Philosophy at Chapman University in the Department of Philosophy and the Smith Institute for Political Economy and Philosophy. He is the author of *The Ethics of Capitalism* (2020) with Dan Halliday and *Philosophy, Politics, and Economics: An Introduction* (2021) with Jerry Gaus.

Alex Voorhoeve is Professor in the Department of Philosophy, Logic and Scientific Method at the London School of Economics and Political Science (LSE). He studied economics and philosophy at Erasmus University Rotterdam, Cambridge University, and UCL. He joined the LSE in 2004 and has worked here ever since, though he has held visiting positions at Harvard (2008–09), Princeton (2012–13), and the National Institutes of Health, USA (2016–17). His research covers decision theory, moral psychology, and the theory and practice of fair distribution, with particular application to the allocation of resources for health. He has served on the WHO Consultative Committee on Equity and Universal Health Coverage.

Index

Acemoglu, Daron 249
Achen, Christopher H. 248–9
action-guidance 3, 7–8, 13, 15–16, 105–8, 115, 116 n.3, 116 n.5
act-utilitarianism 8
additivity 58 n.4
Aggregate Relevant Claims (ARC) 127–8
aggregative principles 124, 126
Agner, Eric 110
Alexander, Joshua 241
Alfano, Mark 15–16, 161
Amazon's Mechanical Turk 71 n.7
Anglophone political theory 3, 16
anti-corruption policy 25–6, 28–9, 31, 42
Appiah, Kwame Anthony 118 n.16
    Cosmopolitanism 92–3
Aristotle 105, 240
    Politics 1
Association of American Medical Colleges 215
association of care with women/mothering 219–20, 228
Australia's Men's Rights Association 163, 165, 175, 178
axiomatic bargaining theory 52

Balanced Alternation (BA) 52
bargaining theory 52, 58 n.5
Bar-Hillel, Maya 58 n.7
Barry, Christian 10
Bartels, Larry M. 248–9
Berlin, Isaiah 239
Bicchieri, Cristina 13, 26–7, 244–5
Bjelopera, Jerome P. 161
black pill 180, 183 n.15
Brams, Steven 52–3
Brennan, Geoffrey 244
Brighouse, Harry 64
Brock, Gillian 4
Bruner, Justin 5–6, 13–14
Buchak, Lara 56, 59 n.16

Buchanan, James 51
Buckland, Luke 10–11
Byrne, Joanne 15–16

Canberra theory 244–5
care 4, 6–7, 13, 16, 43, 87, 89, 92–3, 109, 117 n.13, 123, 153 n.9, 167, 178, 192–3, 215, 223, 231, 249
    childcare workers 220, 222, 230
    commodification and quality of 217–19, 229
    shortage in the United States 215–17
caregivers 220, 226, 228–30
care labor 215, 218, 220, 223, 228
care work 16, 215, 225, 231 n.1
    beliefs 219
    love and money in 226, 228, 231
    low wages in 216–20
    and moral emotions 221–3
    public recognition of 231
    taboo trade-offs 226–7, 230–1
care workers 16, 215–17, 220–1, 228
    during Covid-19 216–17
    female 216, 219
    implications 229
    limitations and future directions 229–30
    making care count 231
    methods 224–6
    nurses 215, 221–3, 231
    present research 223
    results 226–8
    teachers 222, 226, 230–1
    unionizing 220, 232 n.2
    unique opposition 217
Carlyle, Thomas 13
Carnap, Rudolf 11
    Carnapian explication 242–3
Chatham House Africa Programme 26
    Local Understandings, Expectations and Experiences survey 36–7

civic equality 88, 99–100, 102
Cohen, Gerald Allan 64, 71 n.2, 239, 252 n.4
   folk morality 64–5
   intuitions 64
commodification argument (low wages in care work) 216–20, 224–30
communism 247
conceptual engineering 3, 11, 242–3
   and justice 11
   and political goals 12
   prescriptive conceptual analysis 243
Connell, Raewyn W. 162, 167
contested pile (CP) 53
contractarian approach 14, 49, 51, 58, 59 n.14, 244
Conway, Maura 161
corpora 164
   built-in LIWC dictionaries 169–77
   custom LIWC dictionaries 177–80
   dendrogram 168, 170
   gender and race 180–1
   Lone-Wolf Manifestos 165
   male supremacy 165
   men's rights 165, 174, 178
   semi-automated linguistic analysis 163
   summaries 168
   word counts 166
corruption 13, 25
   coercion and 217
   condemnation 34
   control 25
   diversity of 26
   empirical expectations 29–30
   and policy implications 42–4
   principal-agent problem 29
   social expectations 26
   social norms methodology (*see* social norms methodology)
   as social phenomenon 25
Covid-19 pandemic 194–5, 210 n.8, 211 n.11, 215, 224
   care workers during 216–17
   workplace experiences 226
credibility revolution 247
Curry, Oliver Scott 245
Cushman, Fiery 238

Damschroder, Laura J. 129–30, 133, 153 n.11
Dark Enlightenment 182 n.6
decision-makers 123, 127, 129, 131, 136, 141, 152 n.8, 222
   PTO approach 129, 136
decision theory 59, 237, 261
de Clippel, Geoffroy 52
descending demand rule 52, 54, 56–7
descriptive norms 27–8, 34, 44
DeVos, Betsy 221
directed acyclic graphs (DAGs) 247, 248
Dolan, Paul 152 n.7
dominant masculinity 163, 167, 179–81
dual-process model 241
Duell, Dominik 16

Eavey, Cheryl L. 4
Effective Altruism movement 9, 17 n.5
egalitarian intuitions 64–6, 72 n.11
   causal determinism 67
   equal distributions 70–1
   predictions 68–9
   results 69–70
egalitarian principles 5, 14, 16, 58 n.7, 63, 70–1, 125–6
Elbers, Benjamin 100
empirical evidence 105–6, 116 n.4, 117 n.10, 129, 140
   need for mid-level theory 111–15
   reasons to engage with 107–11
empirical expectations 26–7, 29–35, 39, 41, 43–4
empirical inquiry 105–6, 108
empirical political philosophy 238–40
empirical research 2–3, 7–8, 11, 17, 65, 84, 111, 115, 117 n.11, 129, 131, 134–5, 142, 153 n.11, 242, 251 n.1
   healthcare justice 15
   political philosophy and 12–13, 15
Enoch, David 240
epiphenomenalism 67
equality 3, 14, 63–6, 69–71, 87–8, 99–100, 102, 130
equivalence refusals 129–31, 138–9, 153 n.11, 154 n.17
Eriksson, Lina 244
Estlund, David 240

EurQol 135
expected utility theory (EU) 53–6, 59 n.17
experimental analysis 241
experimental political philosophy 1–12, 16–17, 71 n.4, 105–6, 237–8, 250, 252 n.8
  integrative 240, 244–7, 251
  natural experiments 247
  negative and positive program 240–1
  of politics 240–4
  role of 66–7
  taxonomy of traditional 242
experimental restrictionism 241
expertise defense 12, 65
Eyal, Nir 71 n.5

fact-sensitive principles 108, 116 n.4, 117 n.9
The Fair Labor Standards Act (FLSA) 221
fairness rules 14, 33, 49, 59 n.17
  Balanced Alternation (BA) 52
  correlation 55–6
  descending demand rule 52, 54
  expected utility and 54–5
  fair division and agreement 49–51, 59 n.14
  Kendall coefficient 55–6, 59 n.15
  maximum Nash welfare rule 49, 52
  normative criteria 49
  results 54–5
  risk-aversion and rules 56–7, 59 n.16
  and simulation set-up 51–3
  Strict Alternation (SA) 52
  undercut method 53
fatal autoimmune disorder 135, 139, 141, 153 n.9, 154 n.19, 154 n.22
filter bubble 161
first possession theory 76, 84
Fiske, Alan Page 178
Flores-Robles, Grace 16
Folbre, Nancy 216
folk intuitions 105, 107, 241
Foot, Phillippa 238
Fowler, Anthony 248
freedom 6–8, 190, 239, 251
Freiman, Christopher 14, 71 n.4
French Revolution 13
Fricker, Miranda 164

Frimer, Jeremy A. 167
Frohlich, Norman 4–5, 243
fruitfulness 101, 108, 112, 190, 240–6, 251
fundamentally nonrelational principle 70–1

game theory 237
Gantman, Ana 16
Gaus, Gerald 6
  social morality 245
Gautham, Leila 216
Gauthier, David 51, 245
geek masculinity 163
gender 109, 174, 217, 219, 228, 251 n.1
  essentialism 229
  inequalities 162
  norms 225–7
  pay gap 219–20
  and race 5, 11, 180–1
  and racial egalitarianism 16
gender theories (labor organizing) 225
  devaluation hypothesis 217, 219–20, 225, 228
  sex role essentialism 226–8
  social roles 226
Gerver, Mollie 16
Gini social welfare function (SWF) 56–7, 59 n.18
Goodin, Robert 244
Greene, Joshua 238, 241

Haidt, Jonathan 223, 238, 241, 245–6
  social intuitionism 241
Hall, Andrew 248
Harsanyi, John 6, 51, 56
Haslanger, Sally 11, 243
Hassoun, Nicole 3–4, 11, 15
Hawthorne/John Henry effect 111–12
health burdens 15, 123, 133
  findings 138–40
  paraplegia/quadriplegia 123–4, 130–1, 133–4, 137–8, 141, 154 n.18, 154 n.22
  prioritization by severity 123–6
  survey and experiment 134–6
healthcare 15, 129, 137, 139, 190
  distributive justice in 128, 134–5, 140, 142–3

moral pluralism in 141
policy decisions 136
trade-offs 135, 152 n.6
workers 221
Health Impact Fund (HIF) 108–9
hegemonic masculinity 162
affordances of digital spaces 162–3
traits 182 n.3
Held, Virginia 218
Hendy, Caroline 12
hermeneutical injustice 16, 164
Herreiner, Dorothea 58 n.8
Hersch, Joni 219
high corruption 29–30, 33–5, 45 n.1
Himmelweit, Susan 218
Hobbes, Thomas 8, 240
Leviathan 250
Hoffmann, Leena Koni 13
Hollis, Aidan 108–9
Hood, Bruce 77–8
Horvath, Joachim 65
Huget, Hailey 221
Human Rights Watch campaign 202–3
Hume, David 5
Enquiry 238
Treatise 238
husbank 174, 183 n.14
hypergamy 180, 183 n.15

ideal *vs.* nonideal theory 7, 88, 240
immigration 16, 187
bias 189–92, 210 n.1
consequentialism 189
control against migrants 193
experimental vignettes 193–4
factorial vignettes 205, 206
implications 198–203
elected policymakers 199–200
organizations and activists 202–3
voters 200–2
policymakers 188–9, 204
and principle of liability 188–90, 192–8, 204
immigration enforcement 16, 187, 192–3, 195–8, 201–2
impartiality 5–6
incel 164, 180, 183 n.15
inclusive masculinities 162

inequality 4, 8, 63–4, 75, 125, 162, 218
Inoue, Akira 6
interdependent behaviors 28–9

Jaws 248
justice 1, 3–5, 8–9, 12, 64–5, 71, 87–8, 91–2, 95, 99, 107–8, 128, 130, 192, 199, 239, 246
conceptual engineering and 11
as decision-making procedure 116 n.3
distributive 6–7, 14, 70, 123–8, 134–5, 140–3
as fairness 243–4
healthcare 15, 134
immigration 16
reflective equilibrium 124

Kamm, Frances 238
Kanngiesser, Patricia 77–8
Kant, Immanuel 4, 105
Khanna, Neha 117 n.6
Kilgour, D. Marc 53
Kilov, Daniel 12
Kiva 11, 109, 117 n.6
Klamler, Christian 53
Knobe, Joshua 238, 250, 252 n.8
Kohlberg, Lawrence 2

labor 14, 16, 75–7, 79–82, 84, 110, 115, 215, 218–21, 223, 228
labor mixing theory 14, 75–6, 84
first possession theory 76
intuitions 77
original acquisition 84
ownership and 76–7, 81, 84
rightful possession 84
studies 77–83
theory of property 14, 75, 77, 84
labor organizing 16, 217, 220–3, 227–31
gender essentialism and 229
gender theories (*see* gender theories (labor organizing))
support for teachers 224–5
Lads Society 165–6, 168, 171–2, 175–81
Laërtius, Diogenes 1
Lang, Jérôme 58 n.2
Lawford-Smith, Holly 9
Lerner, Adam 14
leveling-down objection 14, 63–4, 71 n.5

Index

egalitarian intuitions (*see* egalitarian intuitions)
   methods 67–8
   and pluralist reply 64–5, 67
   predictions 68–9
Levene, Merrick 76
Lewis, David 245
leximin 125–6, 132, 137–8, 141, 154 n.23
liability 16, 167, 187–204
Lichtenberg, Judith 9–10
limited aggregation 15, 124–6, 128–9, 132–3, 137–8, 141–2, 152 n.1, 152 n.4
Lindauer, Matthew 5–6, 10–11, 17 n.2, 71 n.10, 72 n.15, 190, 210 n.2, 241–2, 249, 252 n.4
   intervention- *vs.* non-intervention based methods 210 n.2
Linguistic Inquiry and Word Count (LIWC) 166–8
   Analytic, Clout, Authentic, and Tone 169, 170
   built-in 169–77
   custom 177–80
   and LIWCalike 182 n.7
   positive and negative emotion 172–3
Locke, John 4, 14, 76–7, 84
   Lockean proviso 75
   2nd Treatise on Government 75
Loewenstein, George 10
Lopez-Nicolas, Angel 132
Lown, Patrick 16
Lubchenco, Nathan 11
Luptakova, Veronika 15

Machery, Edouard 243
Malikov, Emir 11
Mallon, Ronald 241
Manne, Kate 167
manosphere 15, 162–3, 182 n.2
Marx, Karl 8
masculinity 162, 167, 179, 182 n.3
   dominant 163, 167, 179–81
   hegemonic 162–3
   moral foundations and 168
   and online radicalization 181
   subsidiary 163, 167, 179–81, 183 n.14
   unmet promises 163
Massanari, Adrienne L. 163

The Matrix 164, 183 n.15
maximum Nash welfare rule (MNW) 14, 49, 52–4, 56–7, 58 n.9
McCloskey, Deirdre 218
mediational analysis 67, 69
Medicaid priority-setting exercise (Oregon) 152 n.3
Medina, José 16, 164
Men Going Their Own Way 165–6, 168, 170–2, 174–81
Men's Rights Agency 16, 163, 165, 168, 171, 174–8, 181
mentalism and extra-mentalism 241
Messerschmidt, James W. 162
metaphysics 240
methodology 28, 36–7, 111–12, 164–8, 193–4, 250
Michelbach, Philip A. 5
mid-level philosophical theory 111–15
Miller, David 4–5, 107
   science and philosophical inquiry 107
   theory of justice 64–5
misogyny 15, 163, 167, 179–81
modern economic theory 237
Moehler, Michael 6
Moral Foundations Theory 167, 178, 246
morality 245–6
Morality-as-Cooperation model 245
moral norms 28
moral philosophy 1, 203, 240–2
moral psychology 2, 9–10, 223, 244
motivation 3, 8–12, 100, 154 n.22, 242
   egalitarianism 14
   intrinsic/extrinsic 218
Muldoon, Ryan 14, 89
Murray, Dylan 67
Murselaj, Agnesa 187–8

Nadelhoffer, Thomas 240
Nagel, Thomas 127–8
Nahmias, Eddy 67, 240
nail disease 135–7, 141, 152 n.9, 154 n.19, 154 n.22
Nash equilibria 245
National Integrated Survey of Households (NISH) 36–7
National Population Commission (NPC) 36
Netherlands' Institute for Healthcare 128
   Zorginstituut Nederland 152 n.2

Netizen 182 n.1
Nguyen, Thi 161
Nichols, Shaun 14, 71 n.4, 238, 250
Nigeria 13, 45 n.4
  and Federal Capital Territory (FCT) of Abuja 36
  Local Understandings, Expectations and Experiences survey 36–7
  social norms surveys 26
Nisbett, Richard 66
non-aggregative approach 127–9
non-experimental empirical tools 247–9
nonharmful enforcement (migrants) 201
Nord, Erik 129
normative conceptual revisionism 243
normative expectations 26–8, 33–6, 39–44
norms 26, 178, 181, 218, 225–7, 244–5.
  See also social norms
North, Douglass 249
Nozick, Robert 77, 80, 84
  Anarchy, State, and Utopia 14

off-scale refusals 129, 132–4, 137–40, 153 n.11
Omotoyinbo, Femi Richard 182 n.1
Open Science Framework 181, 183 n.9, 224
"Opinions about Medical Conditions" survey 71 n.7
Oppenheimer, Joe A. 4–5
original position 4–7, 243–4, 251
Øverland, Gerhard 10

pantyhose 66
Pareto principle 125
Pareto-superior condition 63–5, 67–8
Parfit, Derek 63, 70
partial body paralysis (Paraplegia) 152–3 n.9
pass-mark bribery 13, 27
  as Assurance Game 30–2, 44, 45 n.7
  conditionality measures 40–2
  deliberation 43
  moral questions 45 n.8
  payoff-dominant strategy 30–1
  personal normative beliefs and social expectations 37–40, 44
  and policy implications 42–4
  as Prisoner's Dilemma 31–2

Patel, Raj 13
Penn Center for Social Norms and Behavioral Dynamics (PCSNBD) 26
Pennebaker, James 166, 169, 171–2
Person Trade-Off (PTO) method 129–30, 135–6, 142
Pettit, Philip 7
philosophical inquiry 106–7, 110, 112–13, 115, 117 n.11
philosophical survey methods 116 n.1
philosophy of (political) language 163
Philosophy, Politics, and Economics (PPE) 238, 247, 249
Pinto-Prades, Jose-Luis 132
Plato 1, 240
  Republic 239
pluralist egalitarianism 68, 125–6, 128
pluralistic ignorance 13, 36, 40, 42–4, 45 n.7
pluralist reply 64–5, 67
Pogge, Thomas 9, 108–9
political philosophy 1–2, 7–9, 12–13, 16, 64–5, 76–7, 84, 87, 101, 203, 237, 239–43, 249–51
  democracy in 248
portfolio theory of identity 14–15, 90, 93, 95, 99–101
positive and negative duties 9–11, 17 n.4
post hoc rationalization 66
prescriptive conceptual analysis 243–4
prioritization by severity 123–6, 139–41
  case of failure 139
  fully aggregate claims, refusals to 132–4
  refusals to 129–31, 154 n.22
priority-setting principles 125–8, 132, 140–2
property rights 14, 75–6, 84
psychic-numbing effect 198
Public Employees' Fair Employment Act 221
publicity 1, 3–6, 13, 15
  immigration justice 16
  requirement 3–4, 14, 17 n.2
  results 4–5
Puppe, Clemens 58 n.8

quality relationship 114, 133

Rachmilevitch, Shiran 52
racial diversity 99
racial inequality 8
racial segregation 88-9, 95-6, 100
racism 5, 11, 15, 89-91, 96, 99-100, 162, 168, 174, 180-1, 230
Rai, Tage Shakti 178
randomized controlled trials 111-13
rank-dependent expected utility theory (REU) 56-7, 59 n.18
Rawls, John 1-2, 4, 7, 51, 59 n.16, 65, 70, 164, 181, 240, 243-4
    burdens of judgment 90-2, 94
    contractualism and contractarian theories 244
    impartiality (original position) 5-6
    Justice as Fairness: A Restatement 4, 243-4
    plausibility 243
    political speech 164
    restricted utilitarianism 4-5
    A Theory of Justice 2, 8-9, 65
realist theory of democracy 248
Reddit 182 n.2
residential segregation (United States) 87-8, 100-1, 102 n.5
restricted utilitarianism 4-8
Robinson, Angela 152 n.7
Robinson, James 249
Rochat, Philippe 76
Roose, Joshua 15-16
Rothe, Jörg 58 n.2
Rousseau, Jean-Jacques 1, 4, 13, 75
    Du Contrat Social 250
R package (LIWCalike) 182 n.7
rules 7, 13-14, 49, 163, 245. *See also* fairness rules
    risk and beliefs 14
Rwandan genocide 163

sacred values and taboo trade-offs (care work) 222-4
Sacred Values Protection Model 16, 222-3, 227-31
Sakamoto, Haruya 6
Samuelson, William 152 n.8
Sandel, Michael 217-18
Scanlon, Thomas Michael 5, 64

Schelling, Thomas 14, 88-92, 94-5, 97, 99-102. *See also* segregation/segregation model
Schupbach, Jonah 243
segregation/segregation model 14-15, 87, 90-1
    entropy index 95-6
    macro-level phenomenon 89, 99
    Manhattan model 93-5, 97-8
    match model 92-3, 97-8
    occupational 219
    priority model 91-2, 96-7
    radius-defined neighborhood 89
    residential (United States) 87-8, 100, 102 n.5
    results 95-9
    social identities 89-90, 96, 100-2
    spatial arrangement of citizens 87
self-radicalization 161, 182 n.1
Sellars, Wilfrid 239
Sen, Amartya 64
sexual harassment 164
shallow pond 9-10
Silber, Mitchell D. 161
Singer, Peter 9-10
Slovic, Paul 10
Small, Deborah A. 10
Smith, Adam 5
Smith, Allison 176
Smith, Kristin 216
social choice theory 58 n.5
social contract theory 4-7, 49-51, 53, 58, 237
social customs 28
social distance (Manhattan model) 93-5, 97, 99
social life 239, 243, 245
social norms 13, 27-8, 33, 35, 45, 181, 244-5
social norms methodology 26-7, 37
    definition of social norms 27-9
    social dilemmas/expectations 29-36
Southwood, Nicholas 7, 244
Sripada, Chandra 67
stability 1, 3, 6-7, 14, 142, 245
status quo bias 134-40, 152 n.8, 153 n.12
Strict Alternation (SA) 52

subordinated masculinities 162, 167, 182 n.3
subsidiary masculinity 163, 167, 179–81, 183 n.14
substantial pluralism 141
Swift, Adam 64
systemic corruption 13, 25–6, 29, 31, 34, 42, 44, 45 n.1. *See also* corruption

Taurek, John 140–1
Taylor Law 232 n.2
telic egalitarianism 14, 63, 69, 71 n.10
Temkin, Larry 63–4
Tetlock, Philip E. 222
Thomson, Judith Jarvis 238
Thrasher, John 14, 16–17
Tirrell, Lynne 163
Transparency International's Corruption Perception Index 37
Tullock, Gordon 51

Ubel, Peter A. 132–3
undercut method 53–4
United Federation of Teachers and New York City 224–5
   demographics 226
   fears of commodification 225, 227–8
   gender theories (*see* gender theories (labor organizing))
   moral cleansing 225
   procedure 226
   results 226–8
   strike attitudes 224
   strike scenario 224
   support for labor organizing 225
   taboo tradeoffs 225, 227–8, 230
the United States
   care shortage in 215–17, 231

   enforcement against migrants 196, 199
   labor 215, 230
   positive and negative duty 10
   residential segregation 87–8, 100–1, 102 n.5
Unite the Right rally in Charlottesville (2017) 162
US Capitol insurrection (2021) 162
utilitarianism 4–8, 51, 58 n.7, 70, 108, 125–6, 130, 141, 154 n.23, 243–4

veil of ignorance 4–5, 51, 56
veil of uncertainty 51, 57, 58 n.6
virtuous violence 178
Voorhoeve, Alex 15, 132, 152 n.4

Wallis, John 249
Weinberg, Jonathan M. 241
Weingast, Barry 249
Weisberg, Michael 246
well-being 113–15, 117–18 n.13, 118 n.14, 125, 127, 130, 140–1
   and global health justice 15
   quality-adjusted life years (QALYs) 125–6, 128
   Relationship Assessment Scale 114
well-justified theory 113, 115, 117 n.11
Wiegmann, Alex 65
Wilson, Timothy 66
World Health Organization's (WHO) CHOICE project 125
World Trade Organization 9

xenophobia 163, 167, 179–81

Yaari, Menahem 58 n.7

Zeckhauser, Richard 152 n.8
Zenkyo, Masahiro 6

www.ingramcontent.com/pod-product-compliance
Lightning Source LLC
Chambersburg PA
CBHW071812300426
44116CB00009B/1288